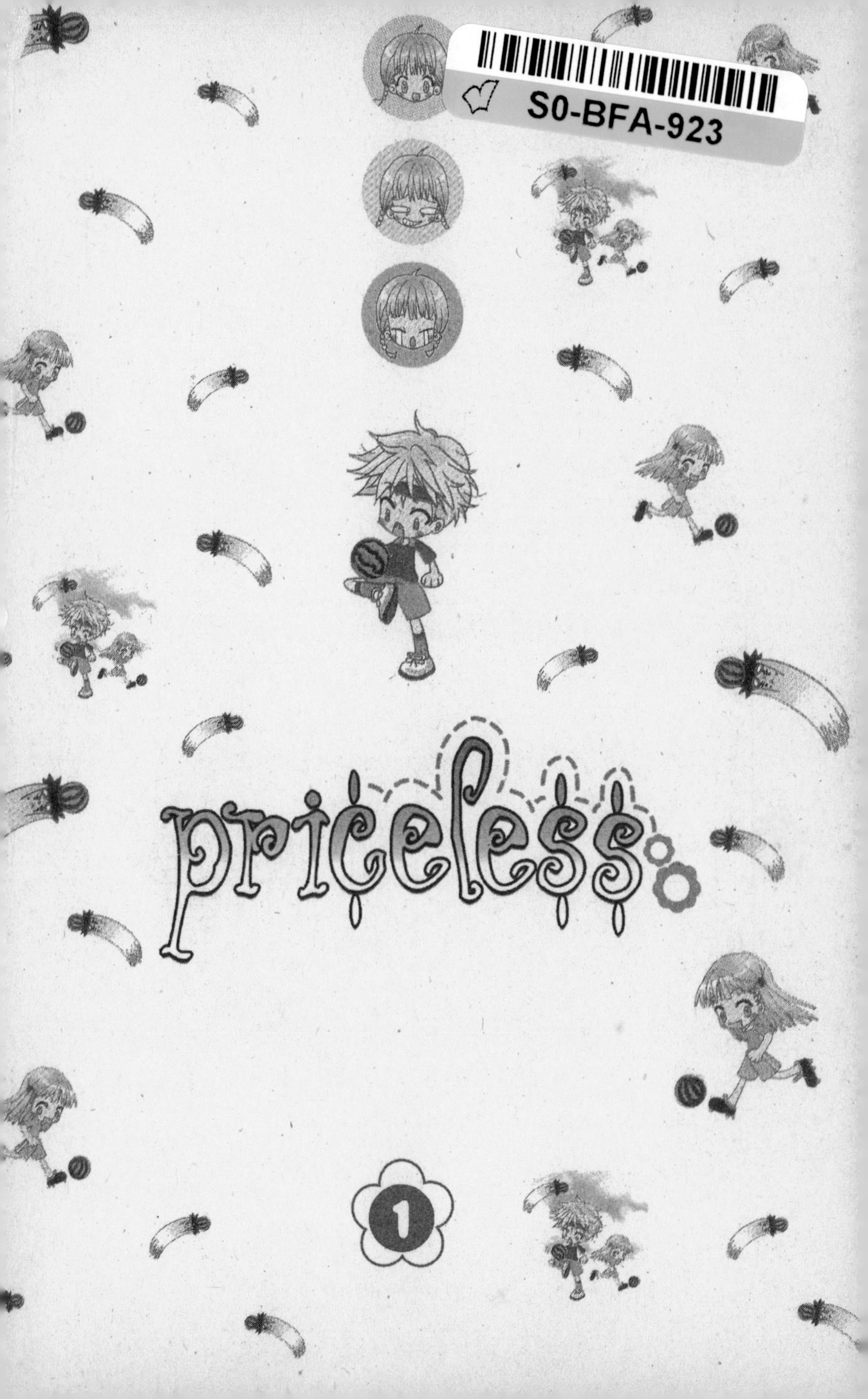
priceless
1

Priceless Volume 1
Created by Young-You Lee

Translation - Grace Min
English Adaptation - Hope Donovan
Copy Editor - Peter Ahlstrom
Retouch and Lettering - Fawn Lau
Production Artist - Jennifer Carbajal
Cover Design - Christian Lownds

Editor - Bryce P. Coleman
Digital Imaging Manager - Chris Buford
Production Manager - Jennifer Miller
Managing Editor - Lindsey Johnston
VP of Production - Ron Klamert
Publisher and E.I.C - Mike Kiley
President and C.O.O. - John Parker
C.E.O and Chief Creative Officer - Stuart Levy

A  Manga

TOKYOPOP Inc.
5900 Wilshire Blvd. Suite 2000
Los Angeles, CA 90036

E-mail: info@TOKYOPOP.com
Come visit us online at www.TOKYOPOP.com

ISBN: 1-59816-309-4

First TOKYOPOP printing: April 2006
10 9 8 7 6 5 4 3 2 1
Printed in the USA

Volume 1

Young-You Lee

HAMBURG // LONDON // LOS ANGELES // TOKYO

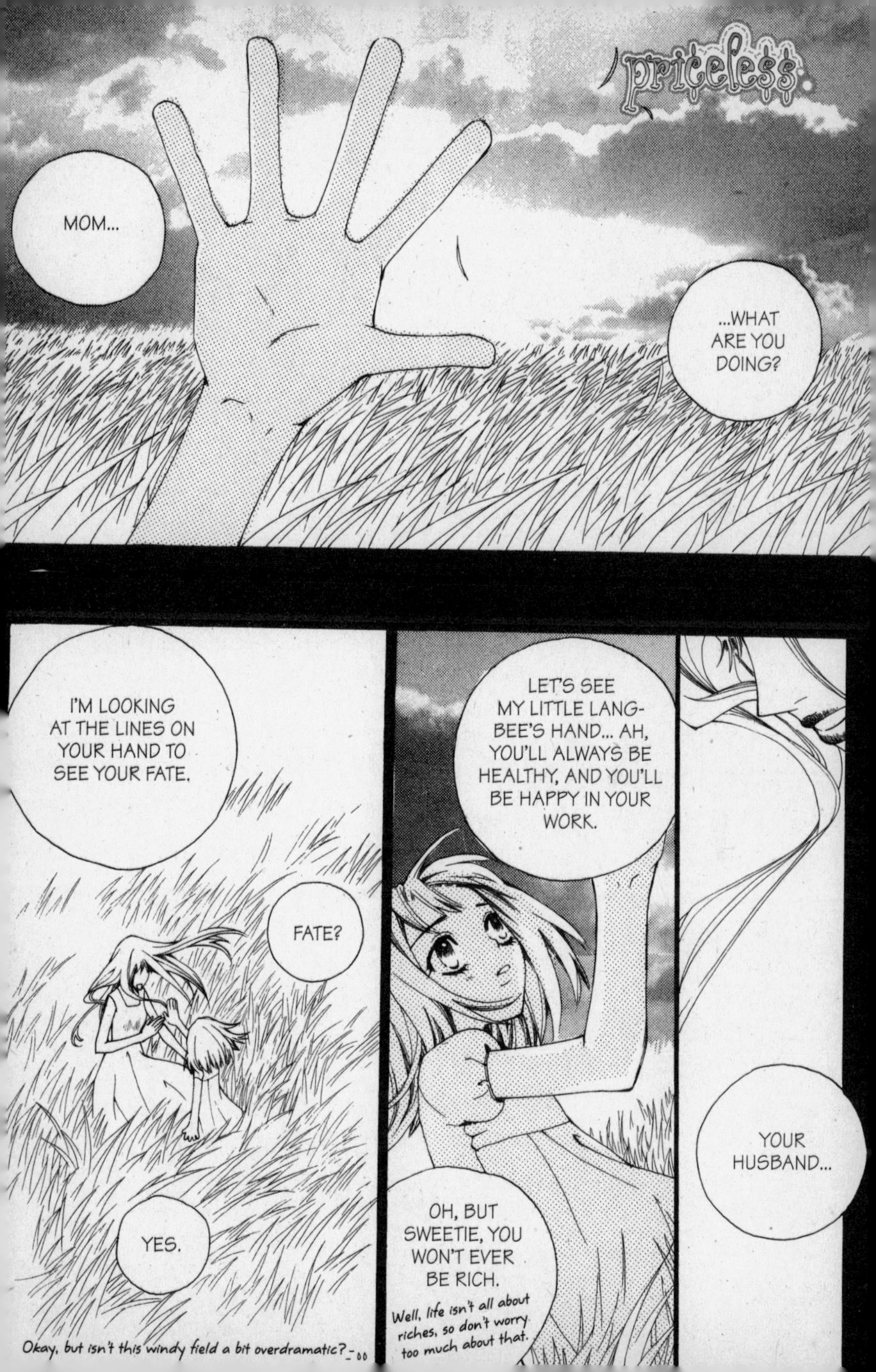
priceless
MOM...
...WHAT ARE YOU DOING?
I'M LOOKING AT THE LINES ON YOUR HAND TO SEE YOUR FATE.
FATE?
YES.
Okay, but isn't this windy field a bit overdramatic? -_oo
LET'S SEE MY LITTLE LANG-BEE'S HAND... AH, YOU'LL ALWAYS BE HEALTHY, AND YOU'LL BE HAPPY IN YOUR WORK.
OH, BUT SWEETIE, YOU WON'T EVER BE RICH.
Well, life isn't all about riches, so don't worry too much about that.
YOUR HUSBAND...

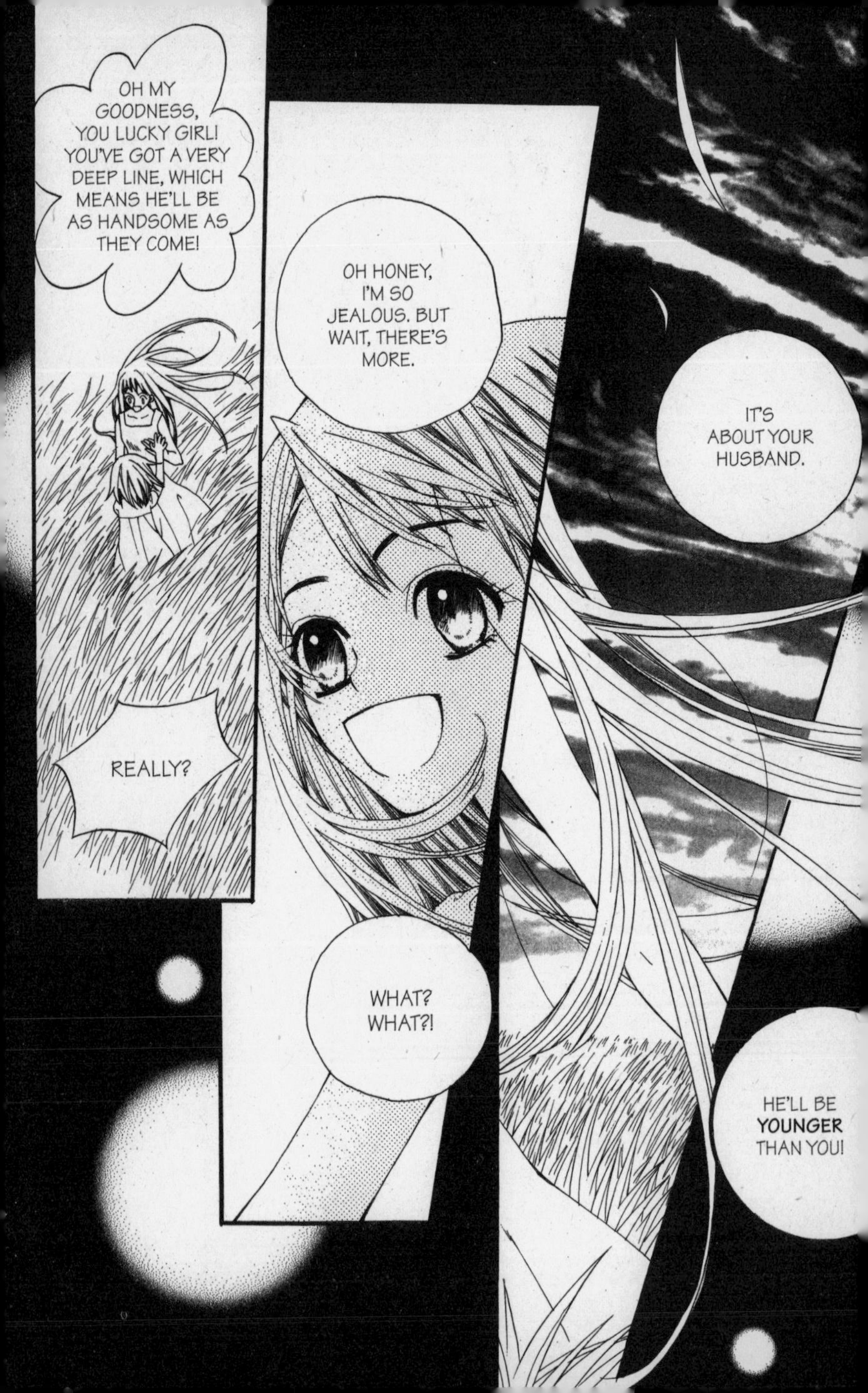
OH MY GOODNESS, YOU LUCKY GIRL! YOU'VE GOT A VERY DEEP LINE, WHICH MEANS HE'LL BE AS HANDSOME AS THEY COME!
REALLY?
OH HONEY, I'M SO JEALOUS. BUT WAIT, THERE'S MORE.
WHAT? WHAT?!
IT'S ABOUT YOUR HUSBAND.
HE'LL BE **YOUNGER** THAN YOU!

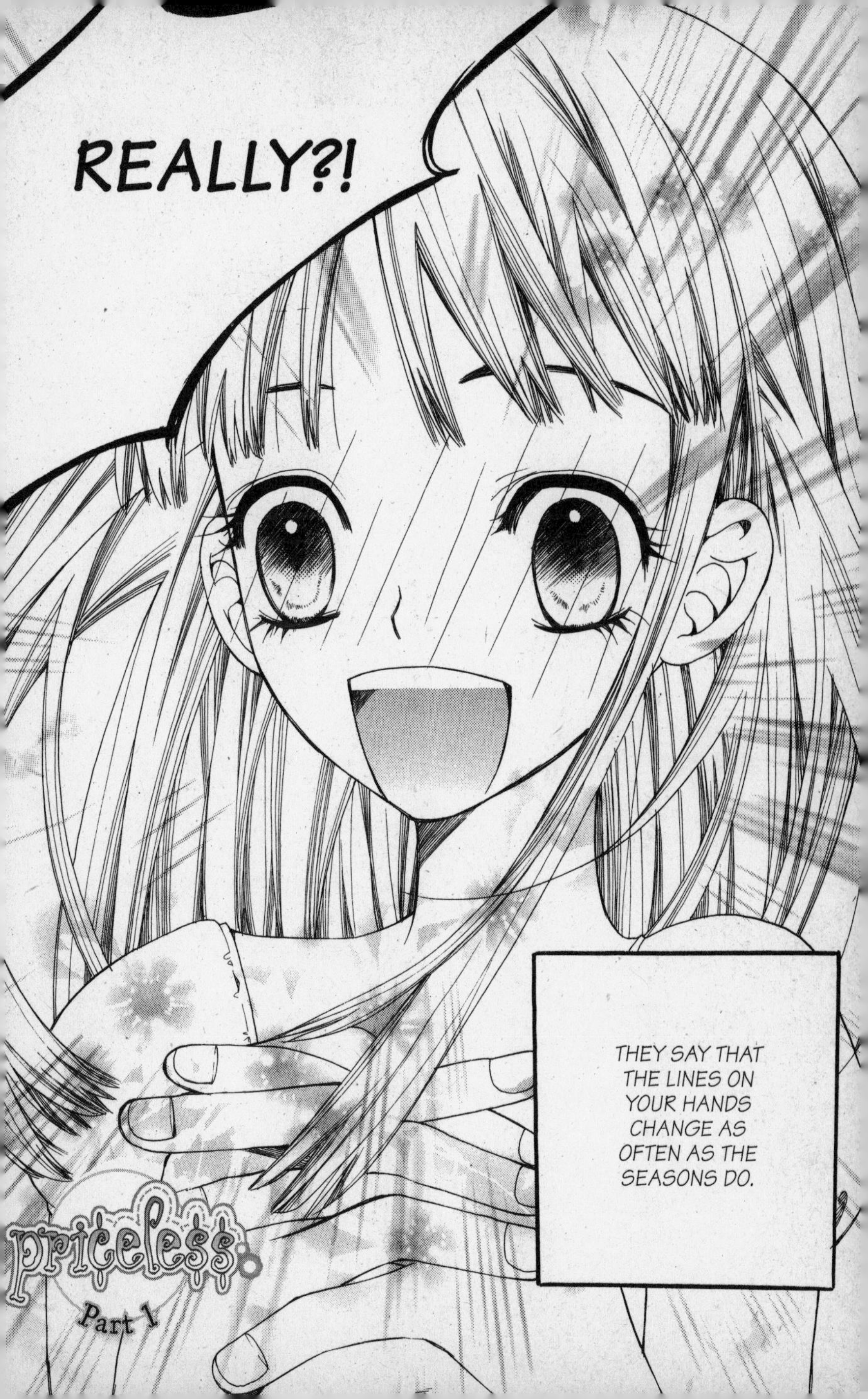
REALLY?!
THEY SAY THAT THE LINES ON YOUR HANDS CHANGE AS OFTEN AS THE SEASONS DO.
priceless
Part 1

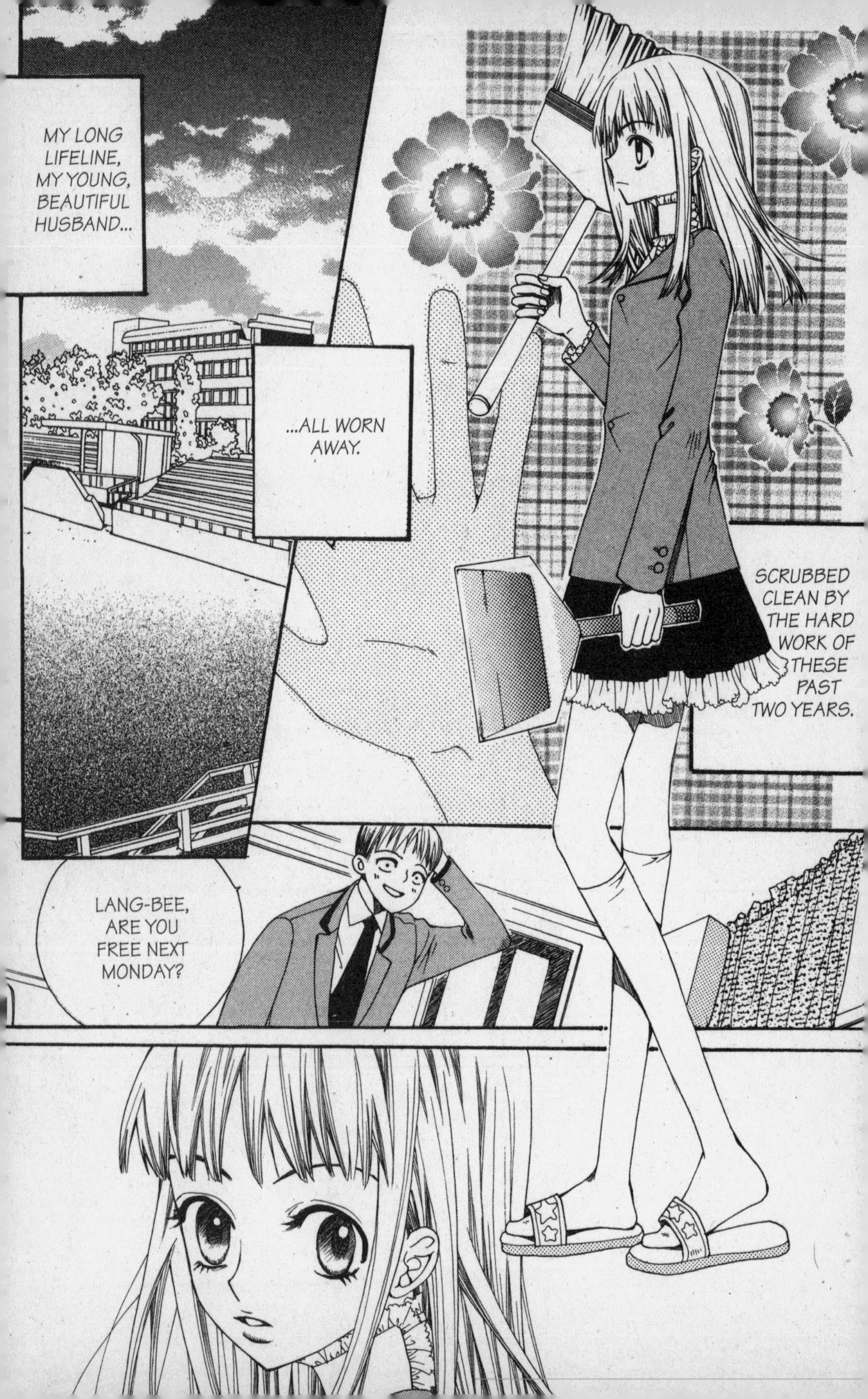
MY LONG LIFELINE, MY YOUNG, BEAUTIFUL HUSBAND...
...ALL WORN AWAY.
SCRUBBED CLEAN BY THE HARD WORK OF THESE PAST TWO YEARS.
LANG-BEE, ARE YOU FREE NEXT MONDAY?

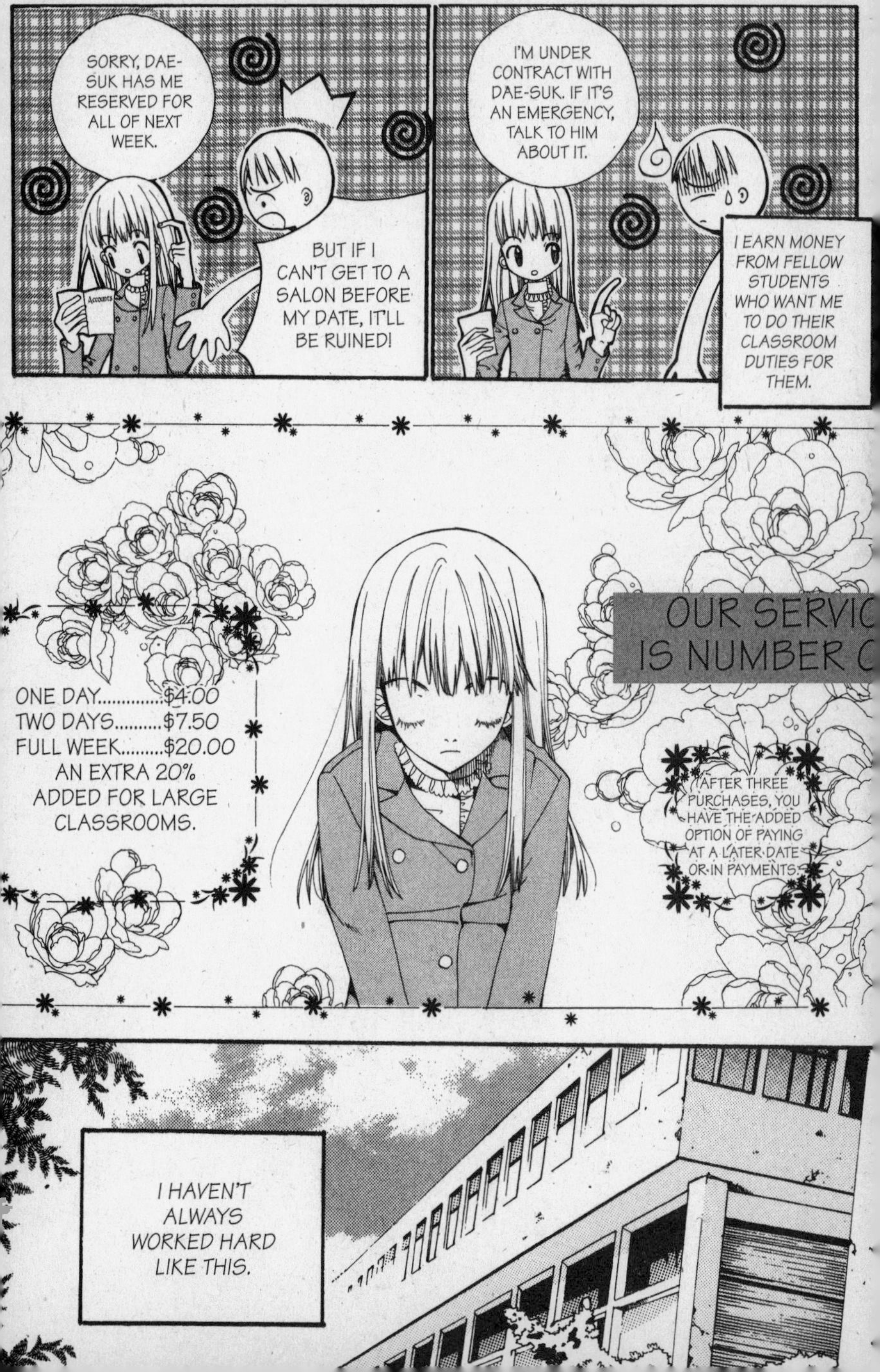
SORRY, DAE-SUK HAS ME RESERVED FOR ALL OF NEXT WEEK.
BUT IF I CAN'T GET TO A SALON BEFORE MY DATE, IT'LL BE RUINED!
Accounts
I'M UNDER CONTRACT WITH DAE-SUK. IF IT'S AN EMERGENCY, TALK TO HIM ABOUT IT.
I EARN MONEY FROM FELLOW STUDENTS WHO WANT ME TO DO THEIR CLASSROOM DUTIES FOR THEM.
ONE DAY..............$4.00
TWO DAYS..........$7.50
FULL WEEK.........$20.00
AN EXTRA 20% ADDED FOR LARGE CLASSROOMS.
OUR SERVIC
IS NUMBER O
AFTER THREE PURCHASES, YOU HAVE THE ADDED OPTION OF PAYING AT A LATER DATE OR IN PAYMENTS.
I HAVEN'T ALWAYS WORKED HARD LIKE THIS.

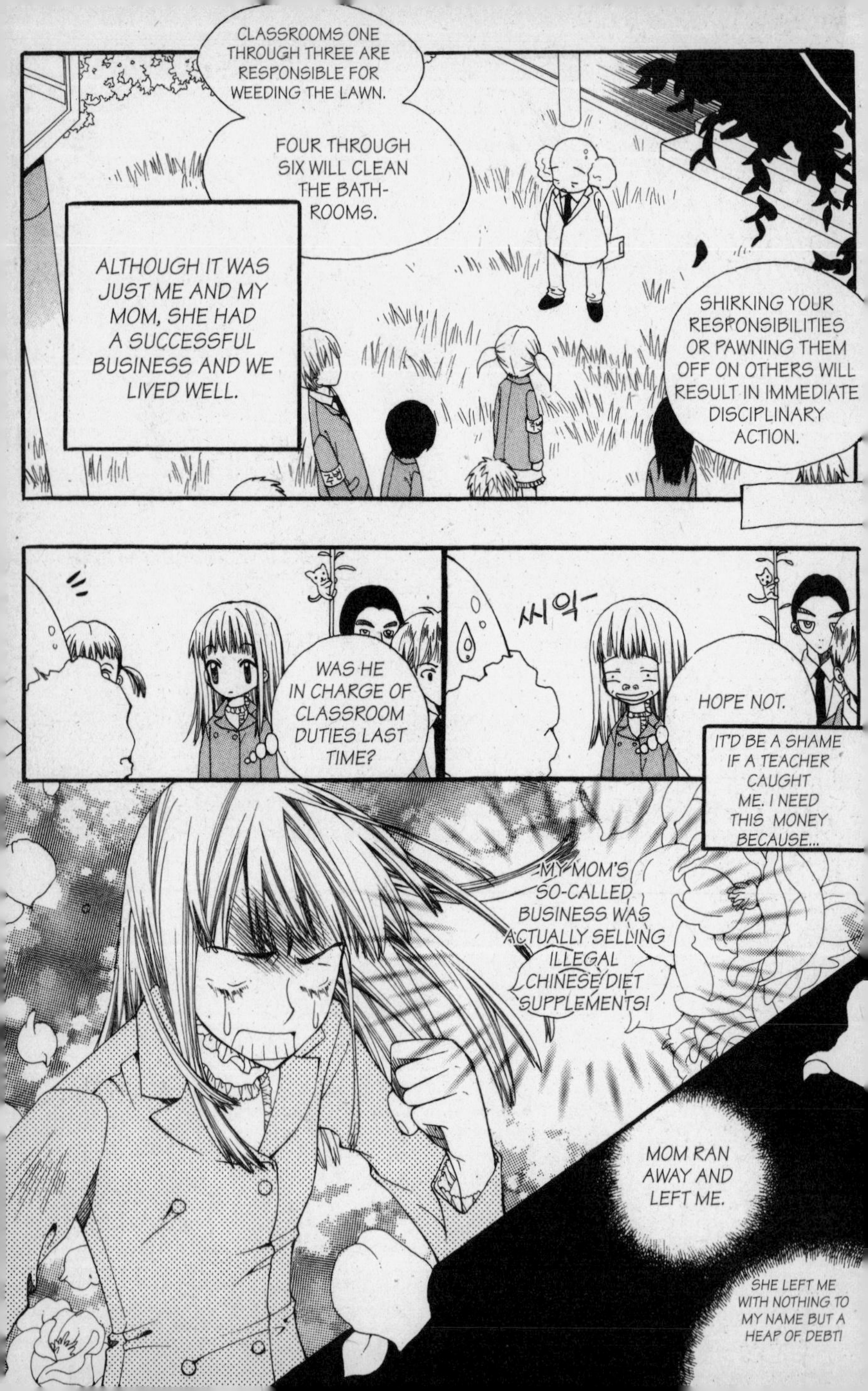
CLASSROOMS ONE THROUGH THREE ARE RESPONSIBLE FOR WEEDING THE LAWN.
FOUR THROUGH SIX WILL CLEAN THE BATH-ROOMS.
ALTHOUGH IT WAS JUST ME AND MY MOM, SHE HAD A SUCCESSFUL BUSINESS AND WE LIVED WELL.
SHIRKING YOUR RESPONSIBILITIES OR PAWNING THEM OFF ON OTHERS WILL RESULT IN IMMEDIATE DISCIPLINARY ACTION.
WAS HE IN CHARGE OF CLASSROOM DUTIES LAST TIME?
씨익-
HOPE NOT.
IT'D BE A SHAME IF A TEACHER CAUGHT ME. I NEED THIS MONEY BECAUSE...
MY MOM'S SO-CALLED BUSINESS WAS ACTUALLY SELLING ILLEGAL CHINESE DIET SUPPLEMENTS!
MOM RAN AWAY AND LEFT ME.
SHE LEFT ME WITH NOTHING TO MY NAME BUT A HEAP OF DEBT!

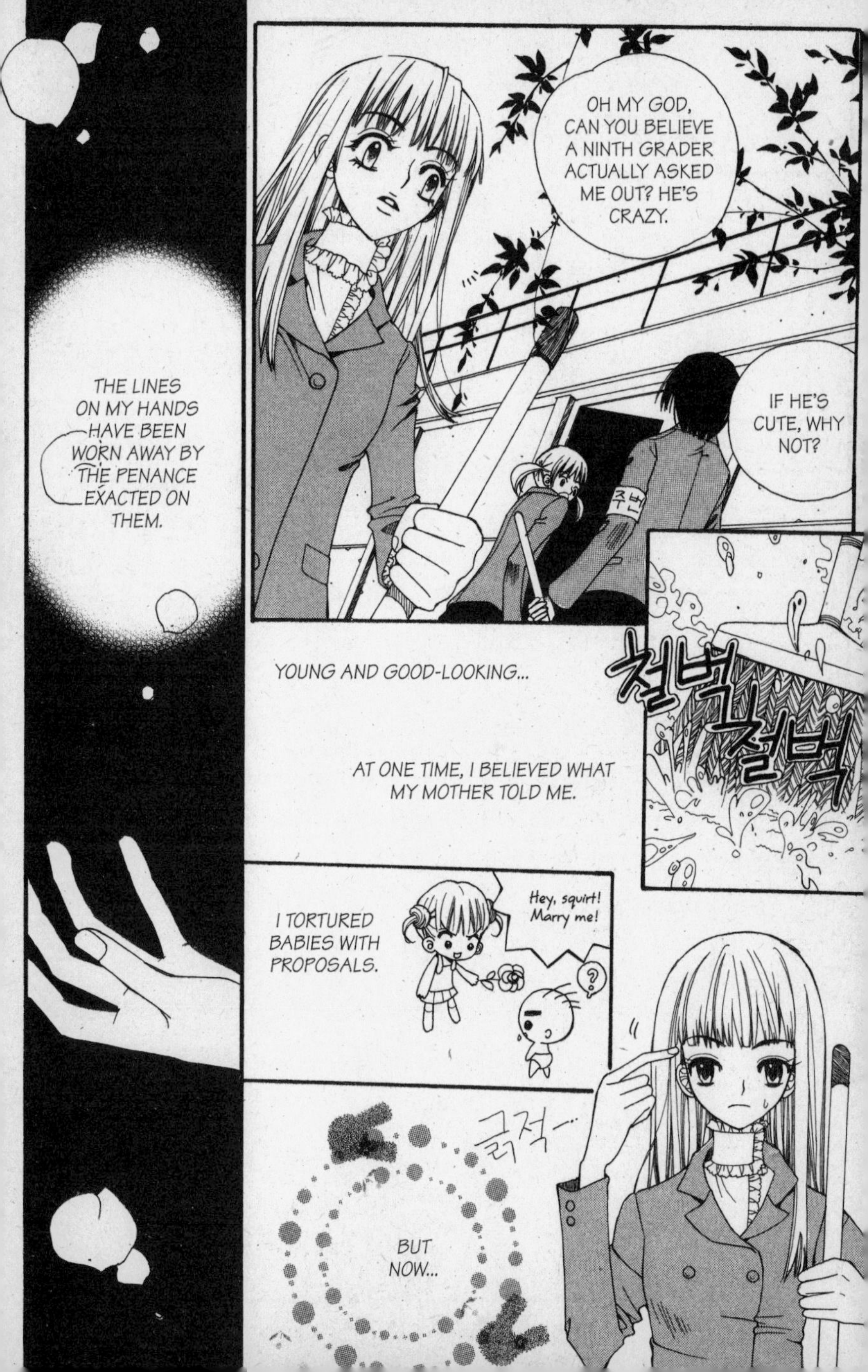
THE LINES ON MY HANDS HAVE BEEN WORN AWAY BY THE PENANCE EXACTED ON THEM.
OH MY GOD, CAN YOU BELIEVE A NINTH GRADER ACTUALLY ASKED ME OUT? HE'S CRAZY.
IF HE'S CUTE, WHY NOT?
주번
YOUNG AND GOOD-LOOKING...
철벅 철벅
AT ONE TIME, I BELIEVED WHAT MY MOTHER TOLD ME.
I TORTURED BABIES WITH PROPOSALS.
Hey, squirt! Marry me!
?
긁적—
BUT NOW...

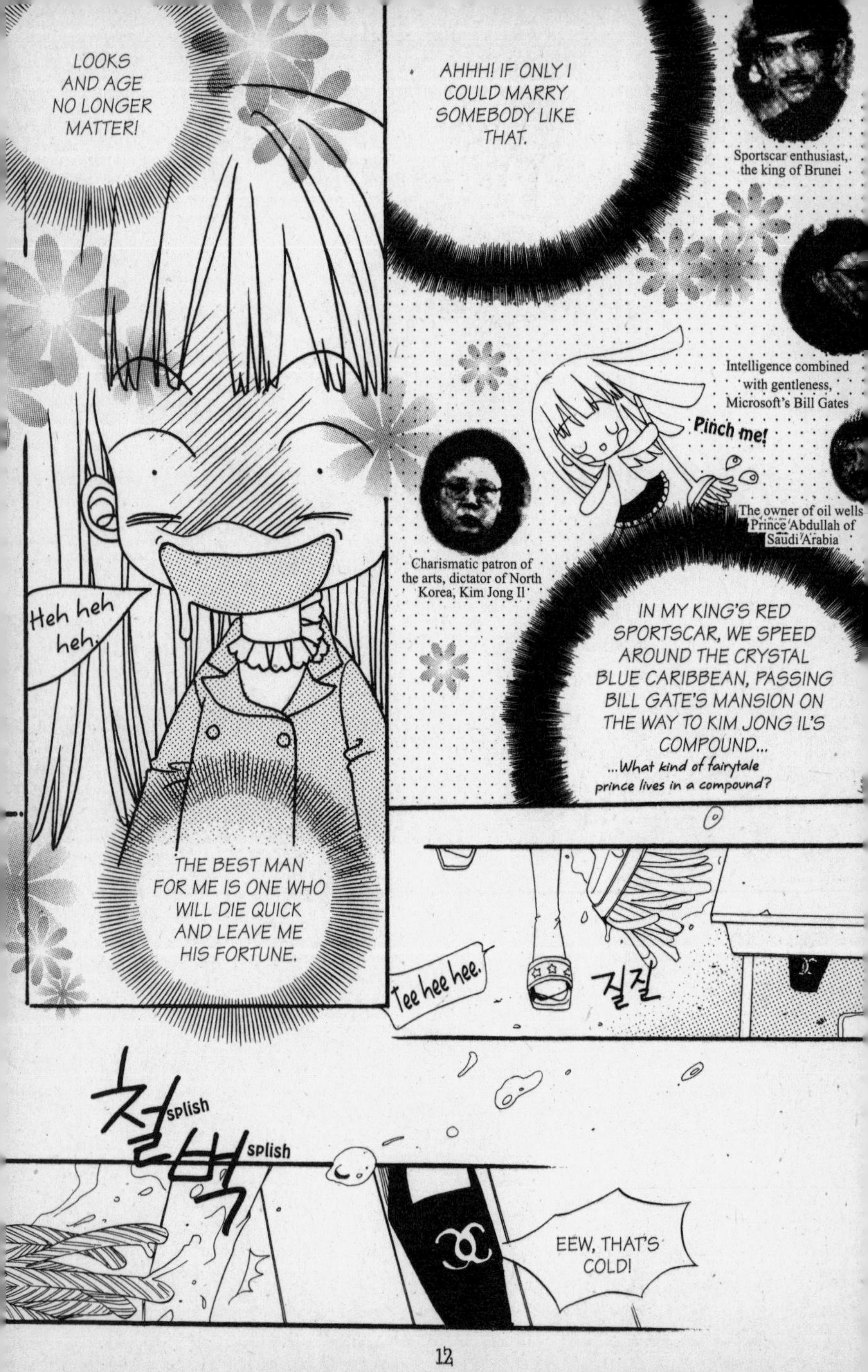
LOOKS AND AGE NO LONGER MATTER!
Heh heh heh.
THE BEST MAN FOR ME IS ONE WHO WILL DIE QUICK AND LEAVE ME HIS FORTUNE.
AHHH! IF ONLY I COULD MARRY SOMEBODY LIKE THAT.
Sportscar enthusiast, the king of Brunei
Intelligence combined with gentleness, Microsoft's Bill Gates
Pinch me!
Charismatic patron of the arts, dictator of North Korea, Kim Jong Il
The owner of oil wells Prince Abdullah of Saudi Arabia
IN MY KING'S RED SPORTSCAR, WE SPEED AROUND THE CRYSTAL BLUE CARIBBEAN, PASSING BILL GATE'S MANSION ON THE WAY TO KIM JONG IL'S COMPOUND...
...What kind of fairytale prince lives in a compound?
Tee hee hee.
질질
철벅
splish
splish
EEW, THAT'S COLD!

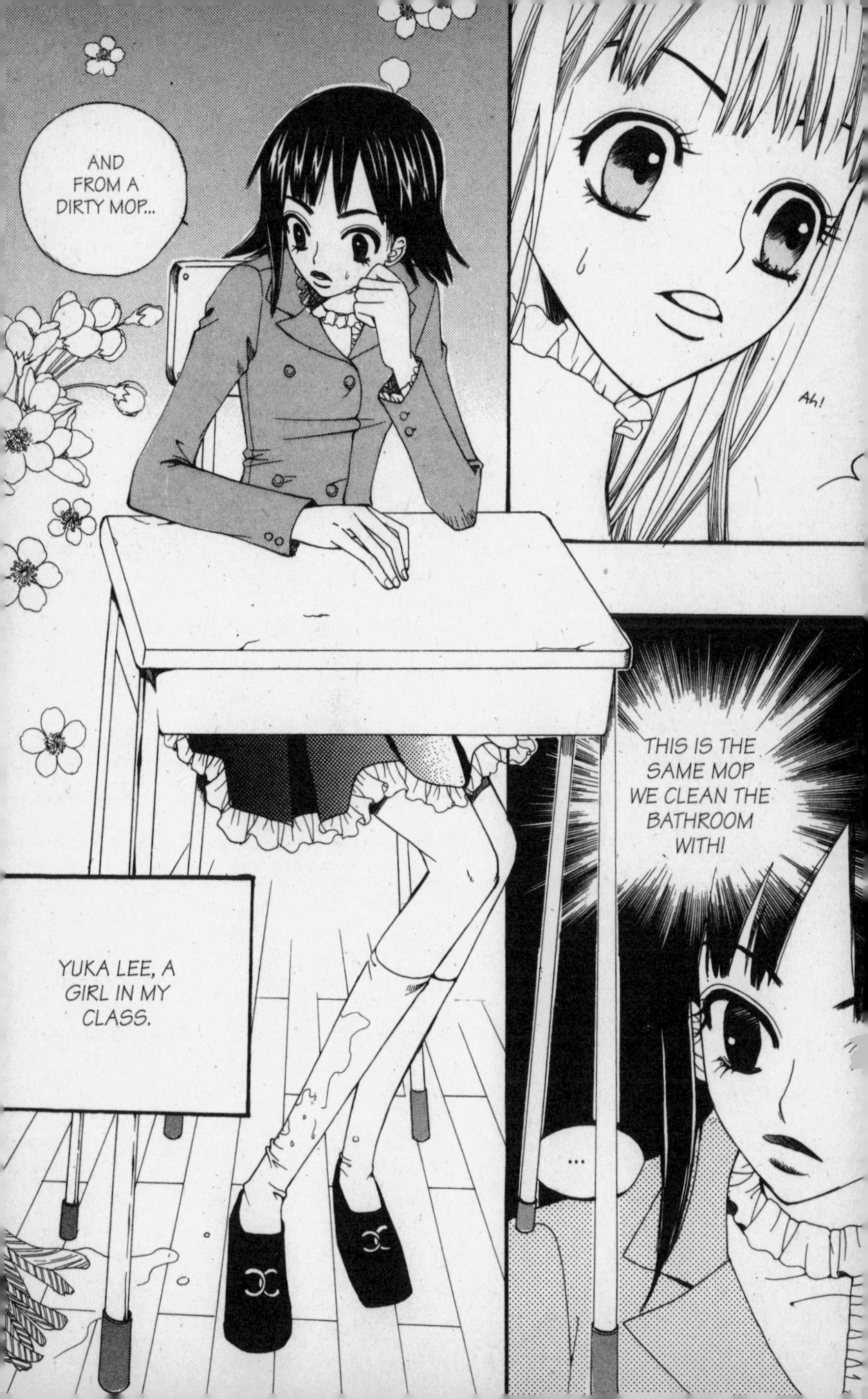
AND FROM A DIRTY MOP...
YUKA LEE, A GIRL IN MY CLASS.
Ah!
THIS IS THE SAME MOP WE CLEAN THE BATHROOM WITH!
...

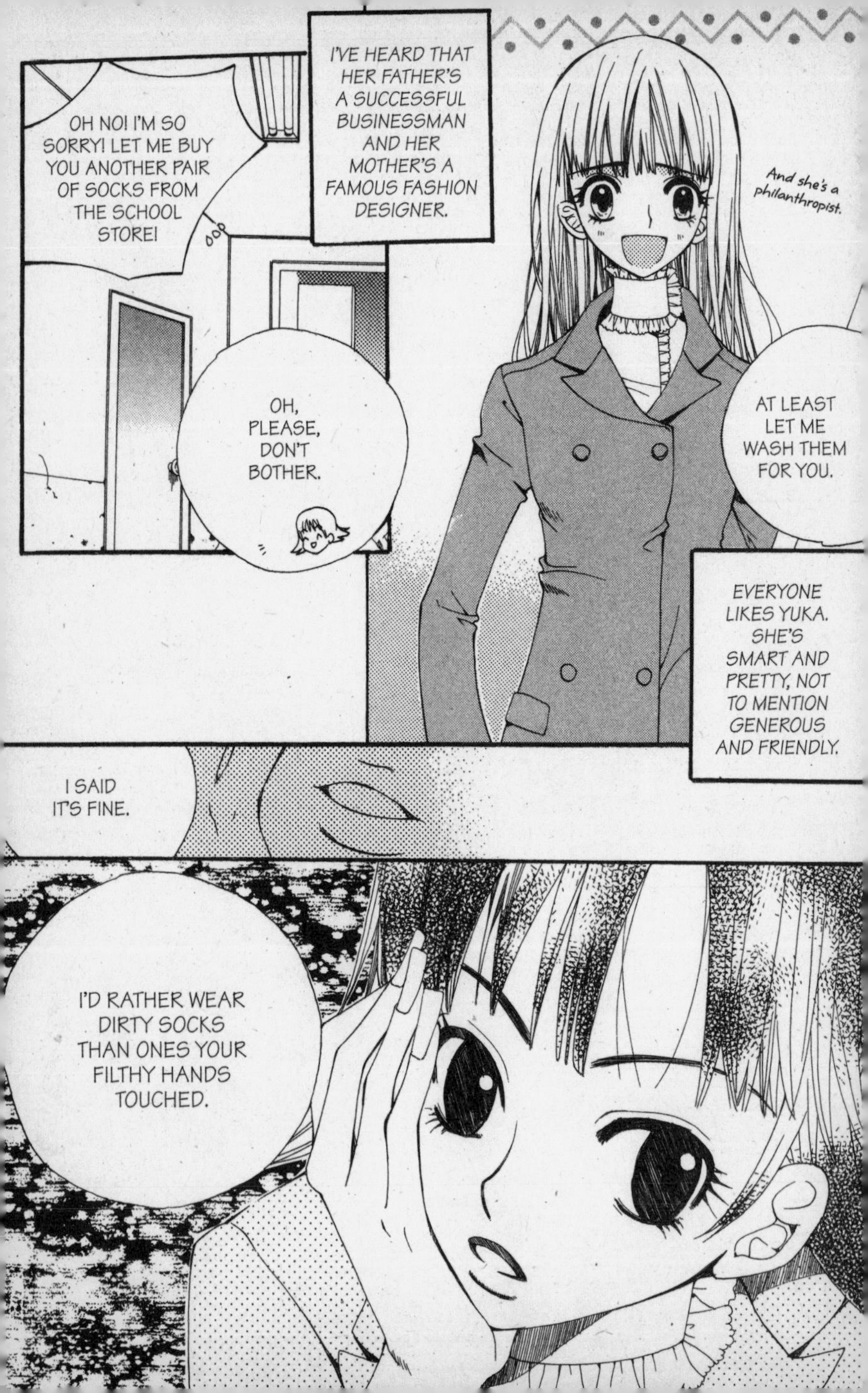
OH NO! I'M SO SORRY! LET ME BUY YOU ANOTHER PAIR OF SOCKS FROM THE SCHOOL STORE!
I'VE HEARD THAT HER FATHER'S A SUCCESSFUL BUSINESSMAN AND HER MOTHER'S A FAMOUS FASHION DESIGNER.
OH, PLEASE, DON'T BOTHER.
And she's a philanthropist.
AT LEAST LET ME WASH THEM FOR YOU.
EVERYONE LIKES YUKA. SHE'S SMART AND PRETTY, NOT TO MENTION GENEROUS AND FRIENDLY.
I SAID IT'S FINE.
I'D RATHER WEAR DIRTY SOCKS THAN ONES YOUR FILTHY HANDS TOUCHED.

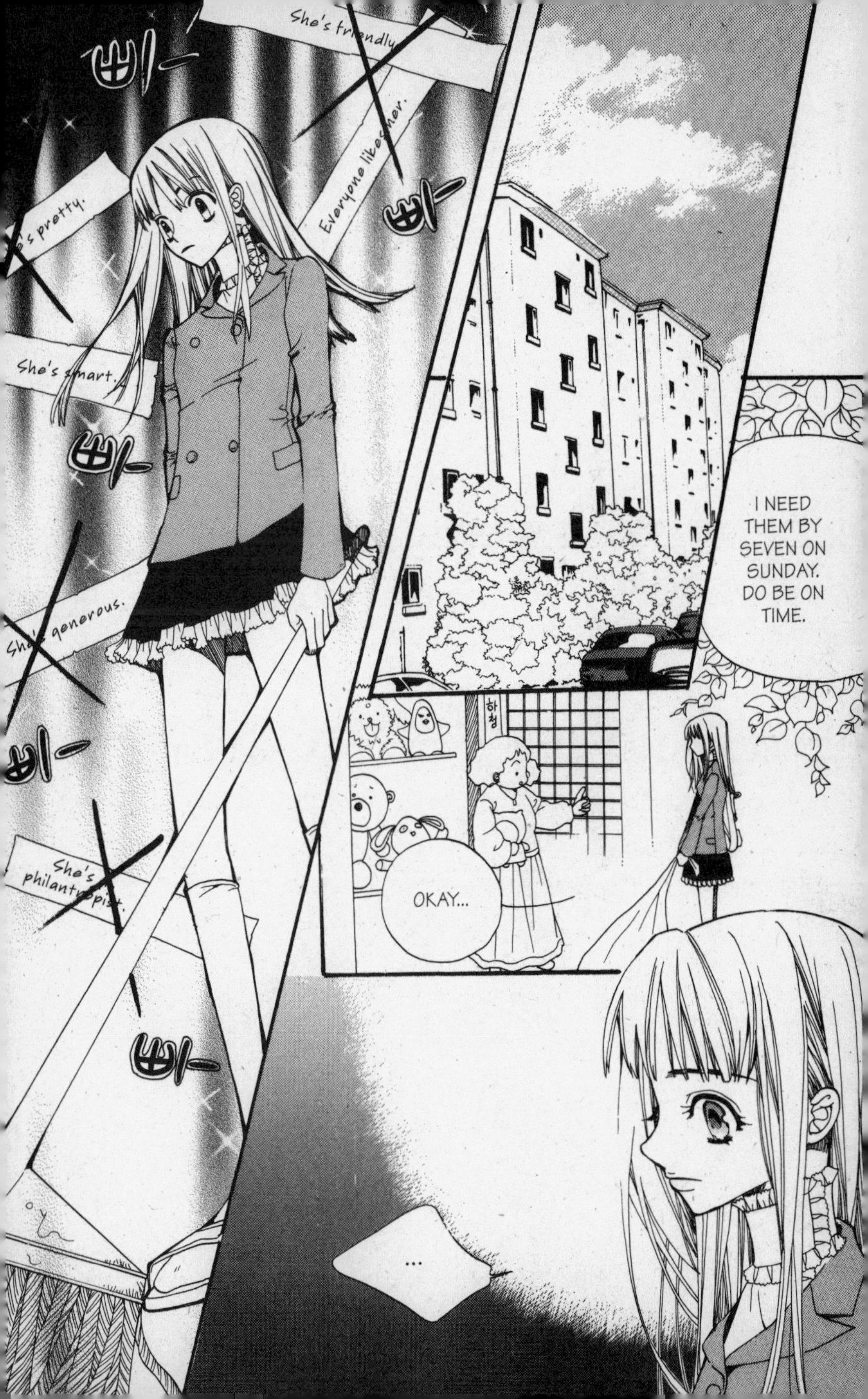
She's friendly.
Everyone likes her.
She's pretty.
She's smart.
She's generous.
She's philantropist.
I NEED THEM BY SEVEN ON SUNDAY. DO BE ON TIME.
OKAY...
...

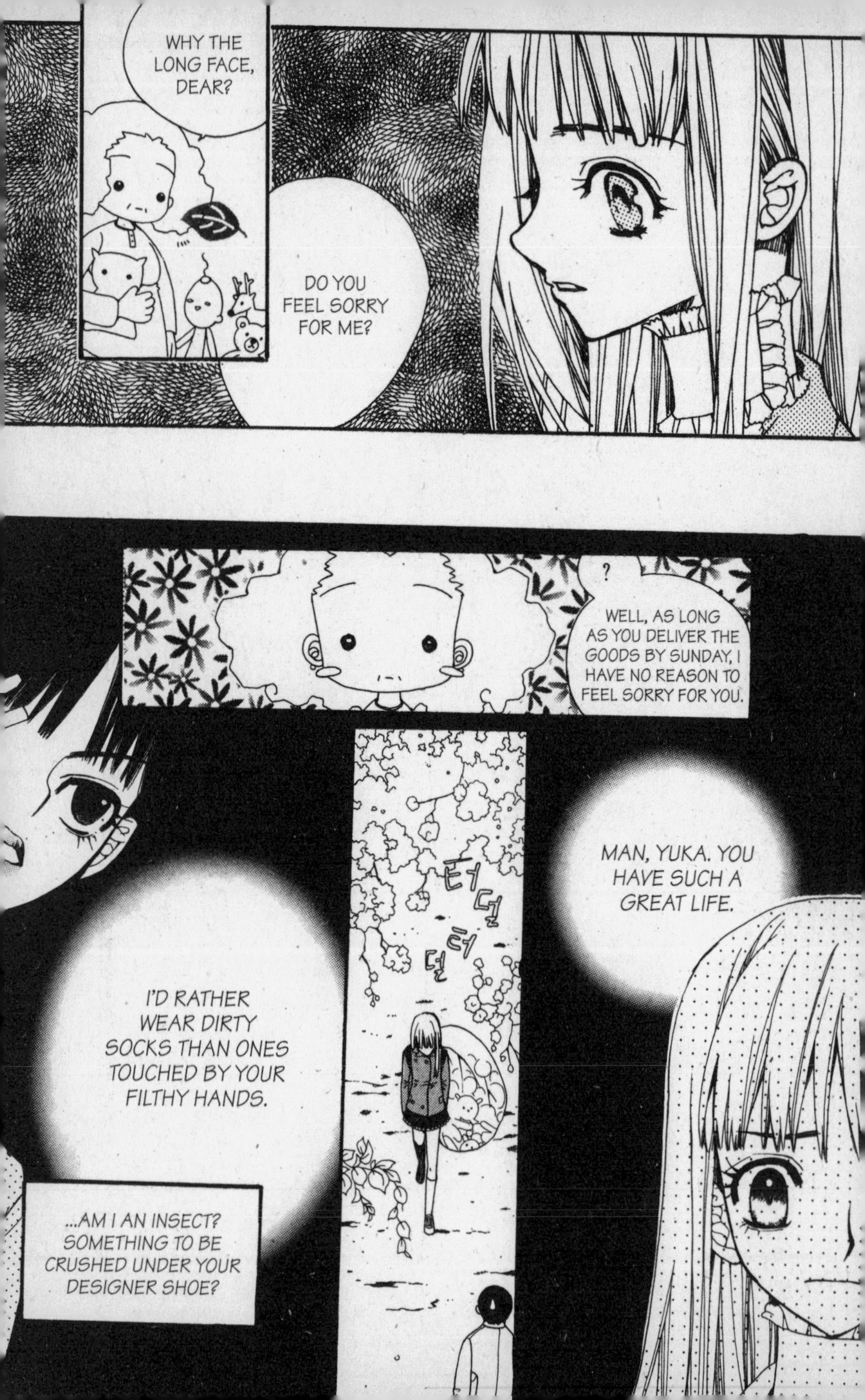
WHY THE LONG FACE, DEAR?
DO YOU FEEL SORRY FOR ME?
?
WELL, AS LONG AS YOU DELIVER THE GOODS BY SUNDAY, I HAVE NO REASON TO FEEL SORRY FOR YOU.
I'D RATHER WEAR DIRTY SOCKS THAN ONES TOUCHED BY YOUR FILTHY HANDS.
...AM I AN INSECT? SOMETHING TO BE CRUSHED UNDER YOUR DESIGNER SHOE?
터덜터덜
MAN, YUKA. YOU HAVE SUCH A GREAT LIFE.

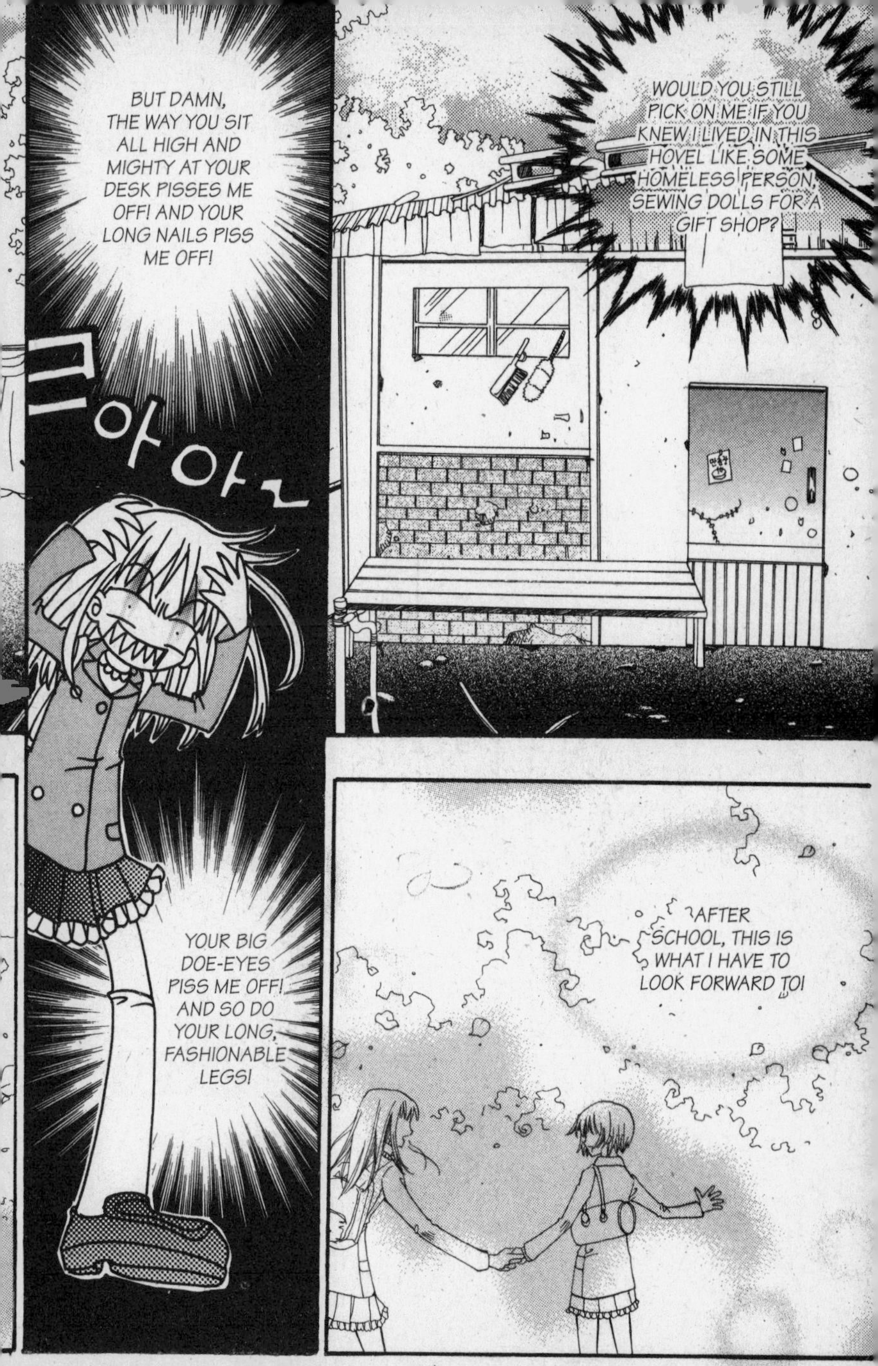
BUT DAMN, THE WAY YOU SIT ALL HIGH AND MIGHTY AT YOUR DESK PISSES ME OFF! AND YOUR LONG NAILS PISS ME OFF!
YOUR BIG DOE-EYES PISS ME OFF! AND SO DO YOUR LONG, FASHIONABLE LEGS!
WOULD YOU STILL PICK ON ME IF YOU KNEW I LIVED IN THIS HOVEL LIKE SOME HOMELESS PERSON, SEWING DOLLS FOR A GIFT SHOP?
AFTER SCHOOL, THIS IS WHAT I HAVE TO LOOK FORWARD TO!

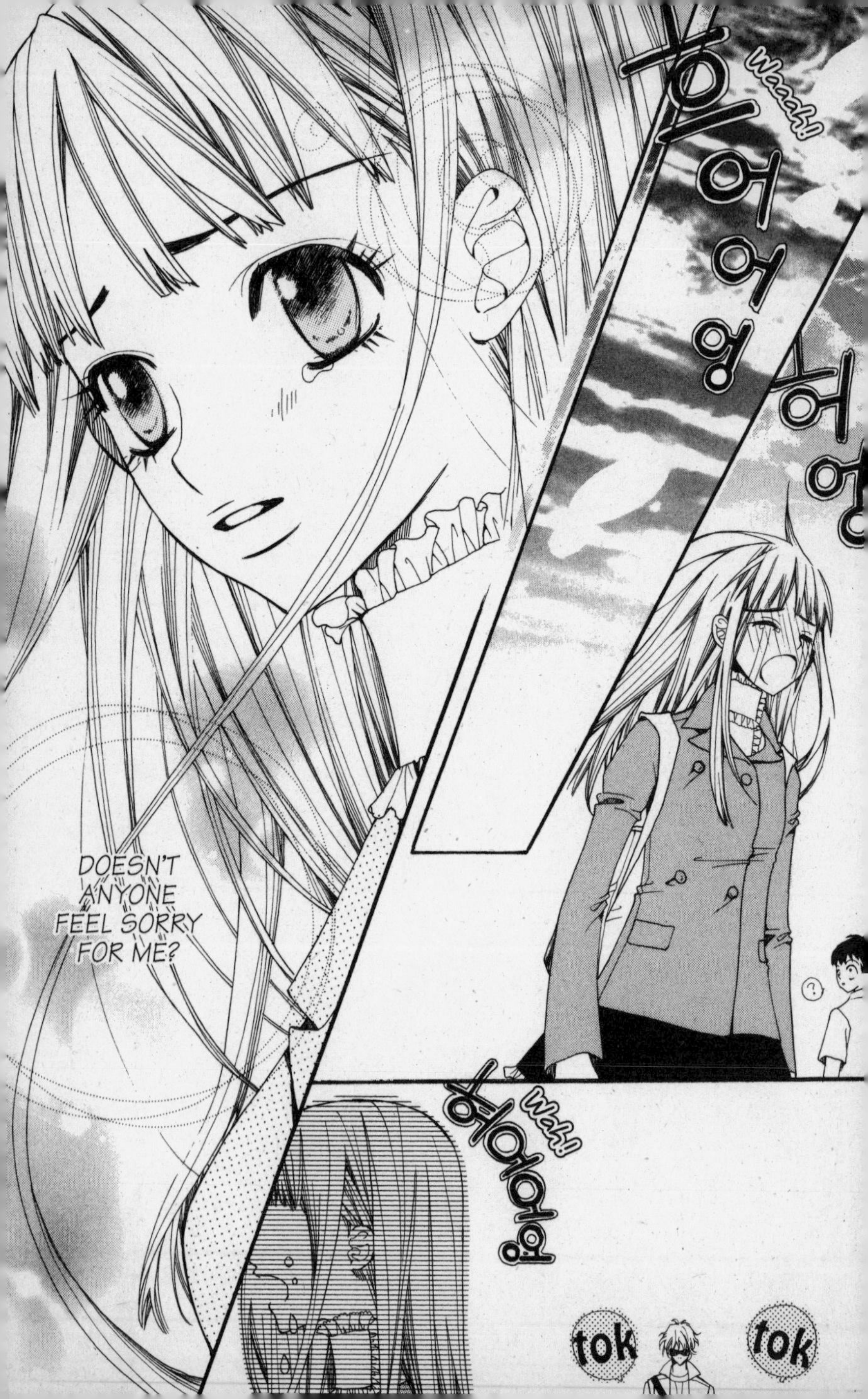
DOESN'T ANYONE FEEL SORRY FOR ME?
Waaah!
?
Wah!
tok
tok

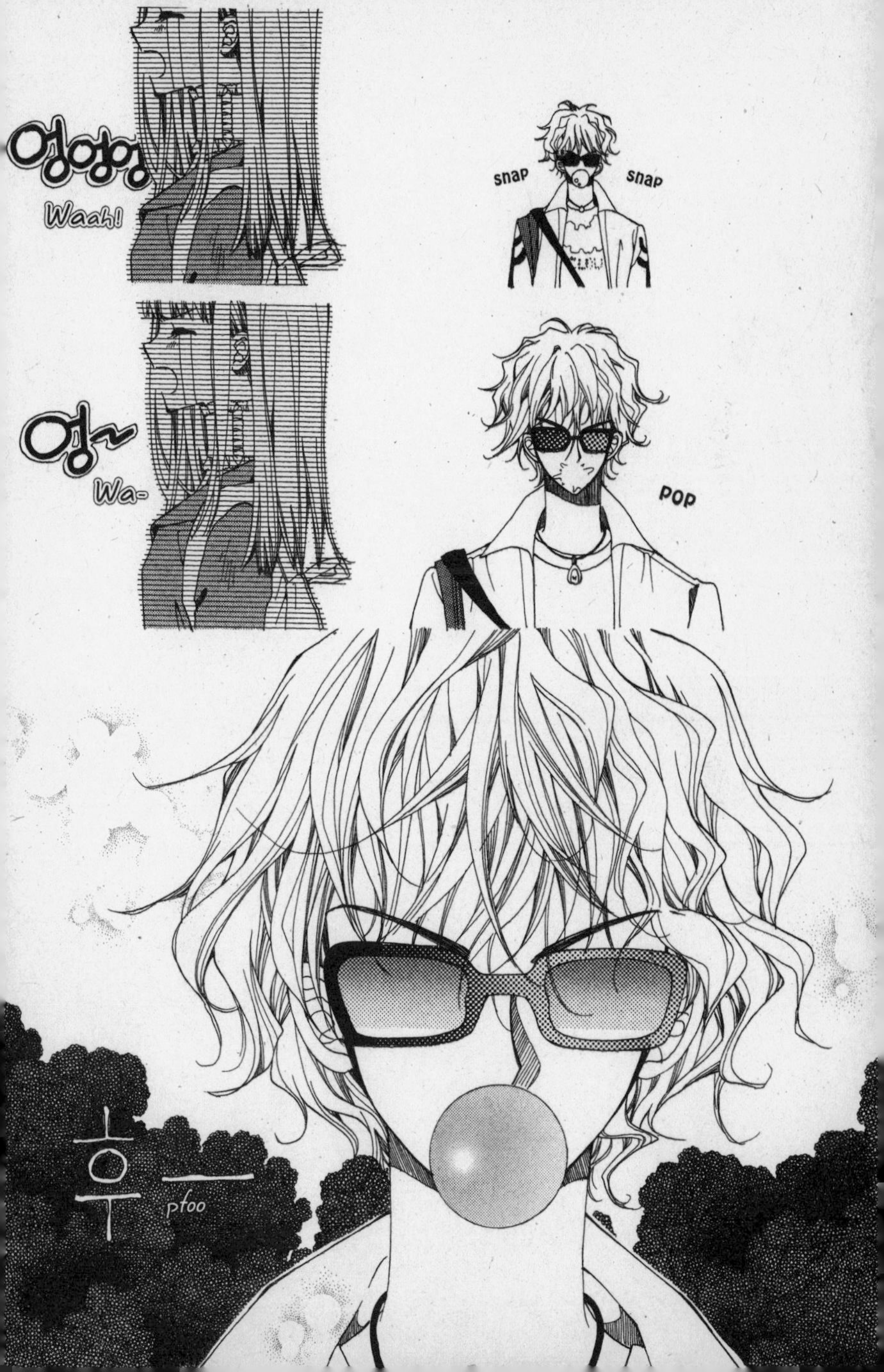

엉엉엉
Waah!
snap
snap
엉~
Wa-
pop
후
pfoo

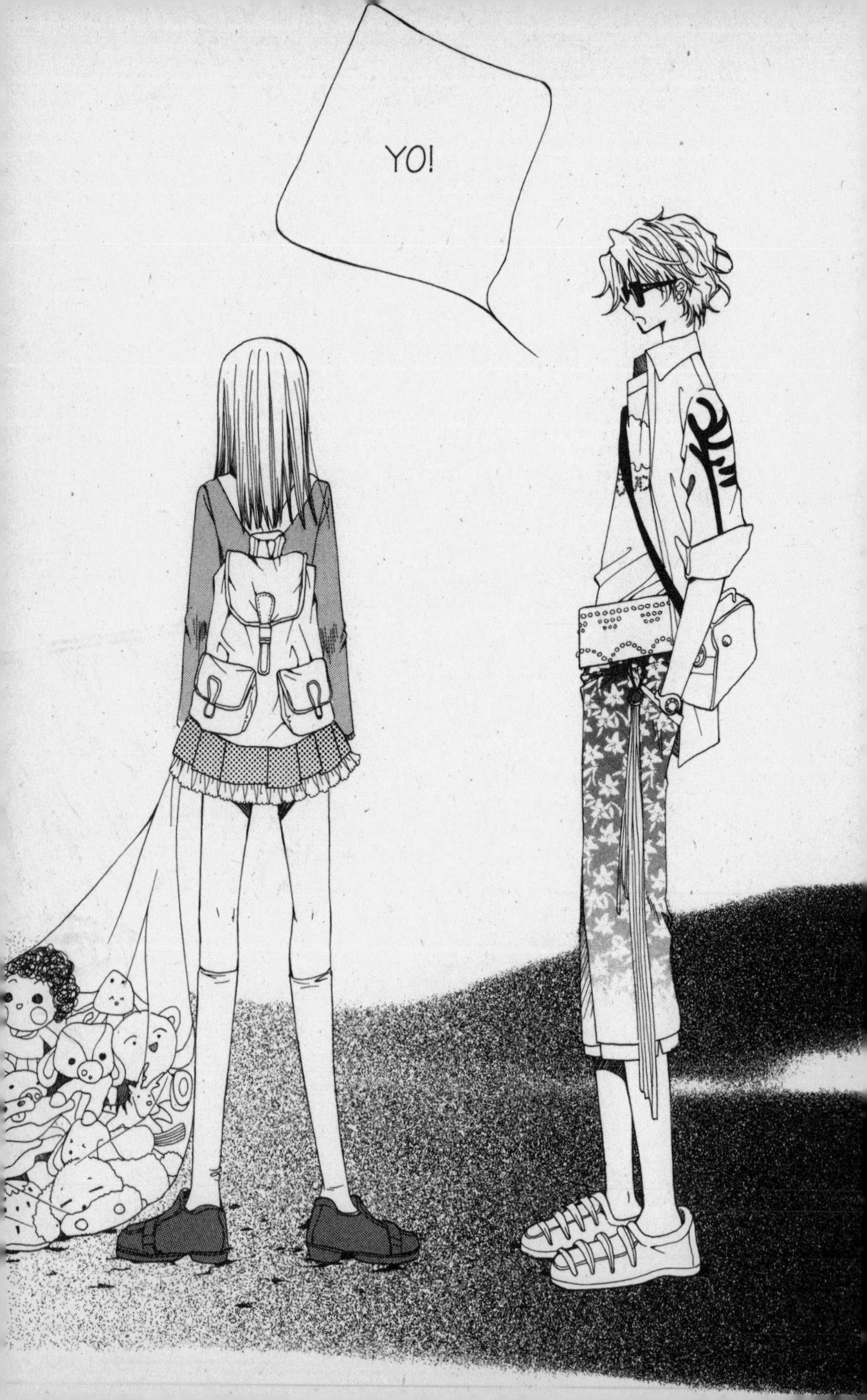
YO!

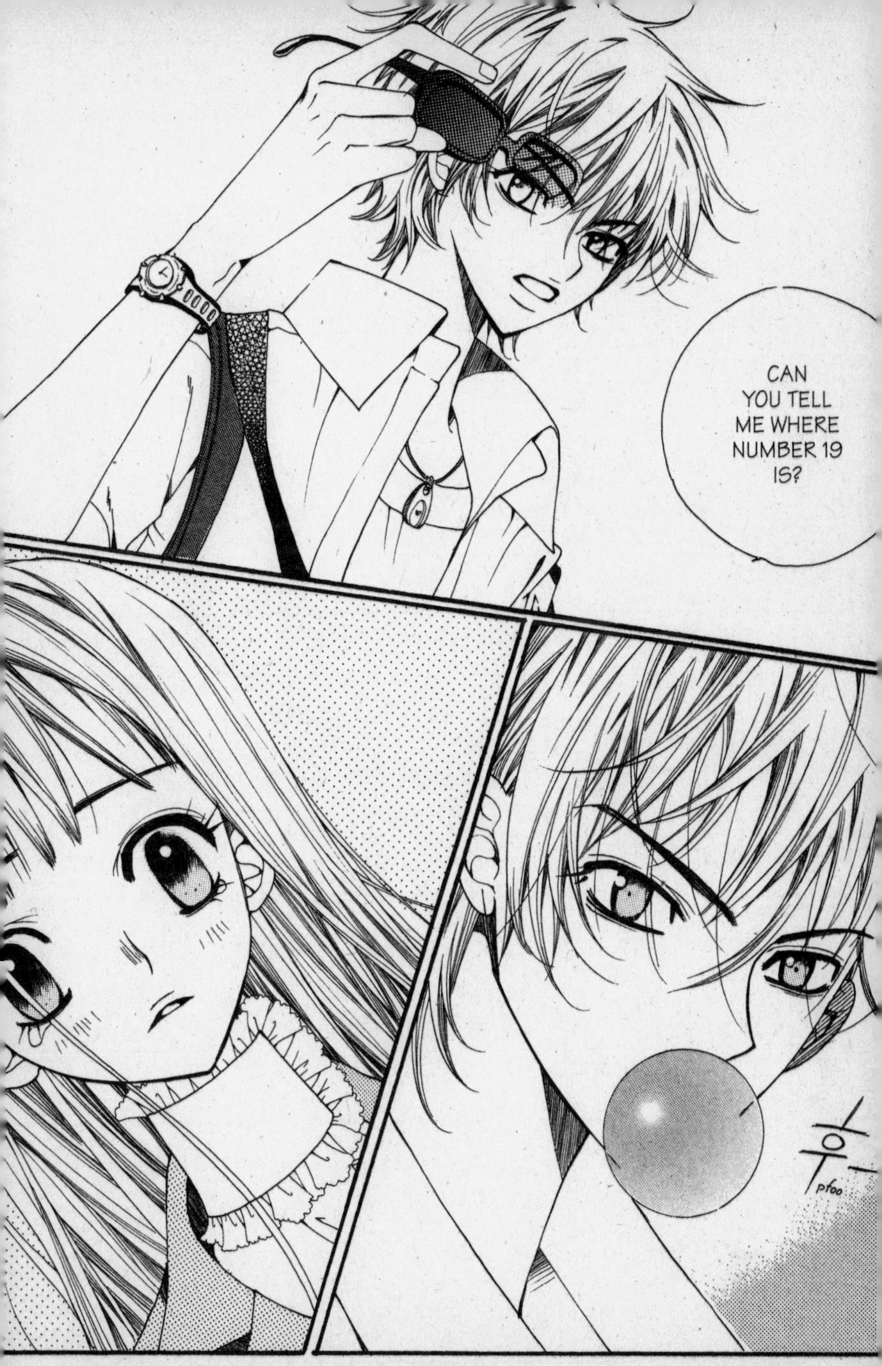
CAN YOU TELL ME WHERE NUMBER 19 IS?
pfoo

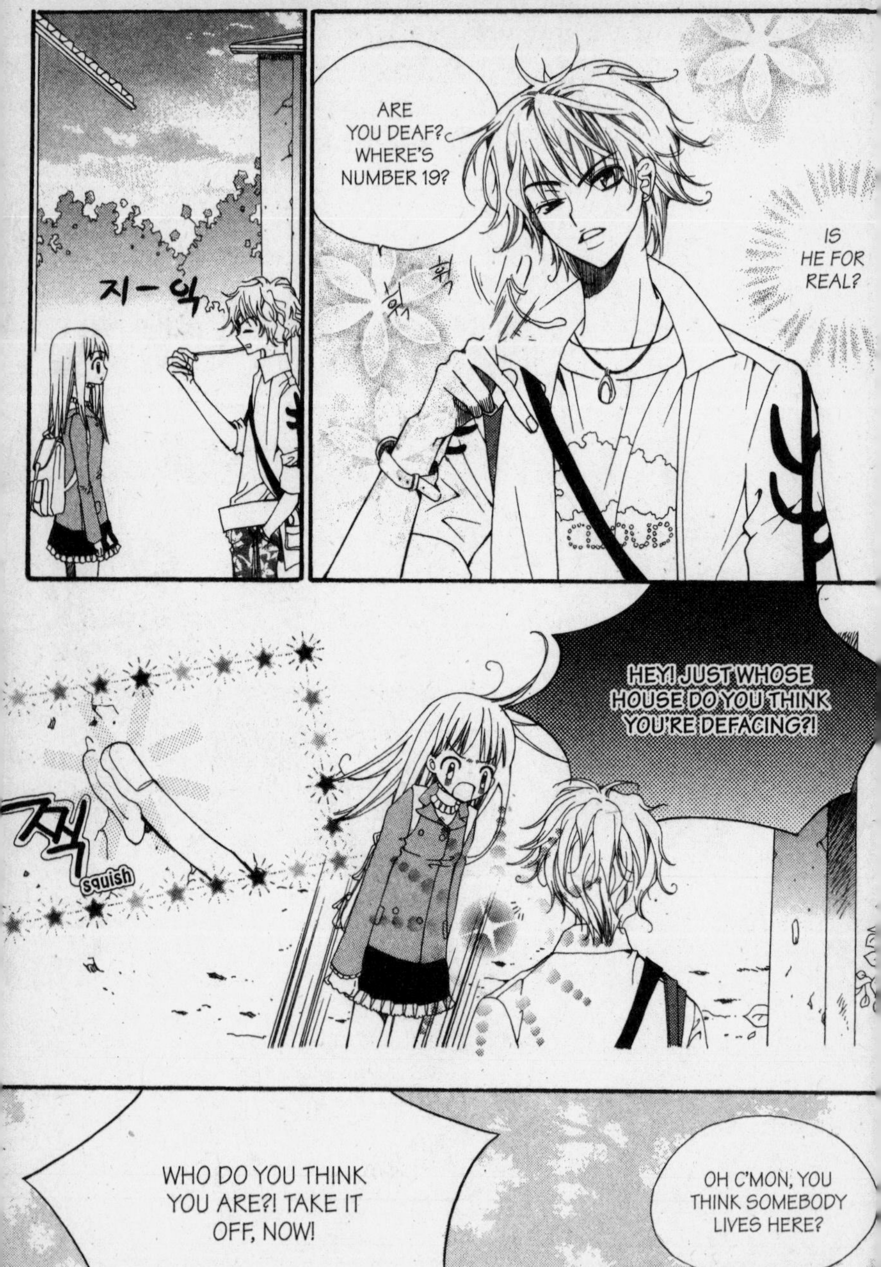
지-익
ARE YOU DEAF? WHERE'S NUMBER 19?
IS HE FOR REAL?
squish
HEY! JUST WHOSE HOUSE DO YOU THINK YOU'RE DEFACING?!
WHO DO YOU THINK YOU ARE?! TAKE IT OFF, NOW!
OH C'MON, YOU THINK SOMEBODY LIVES HERE?

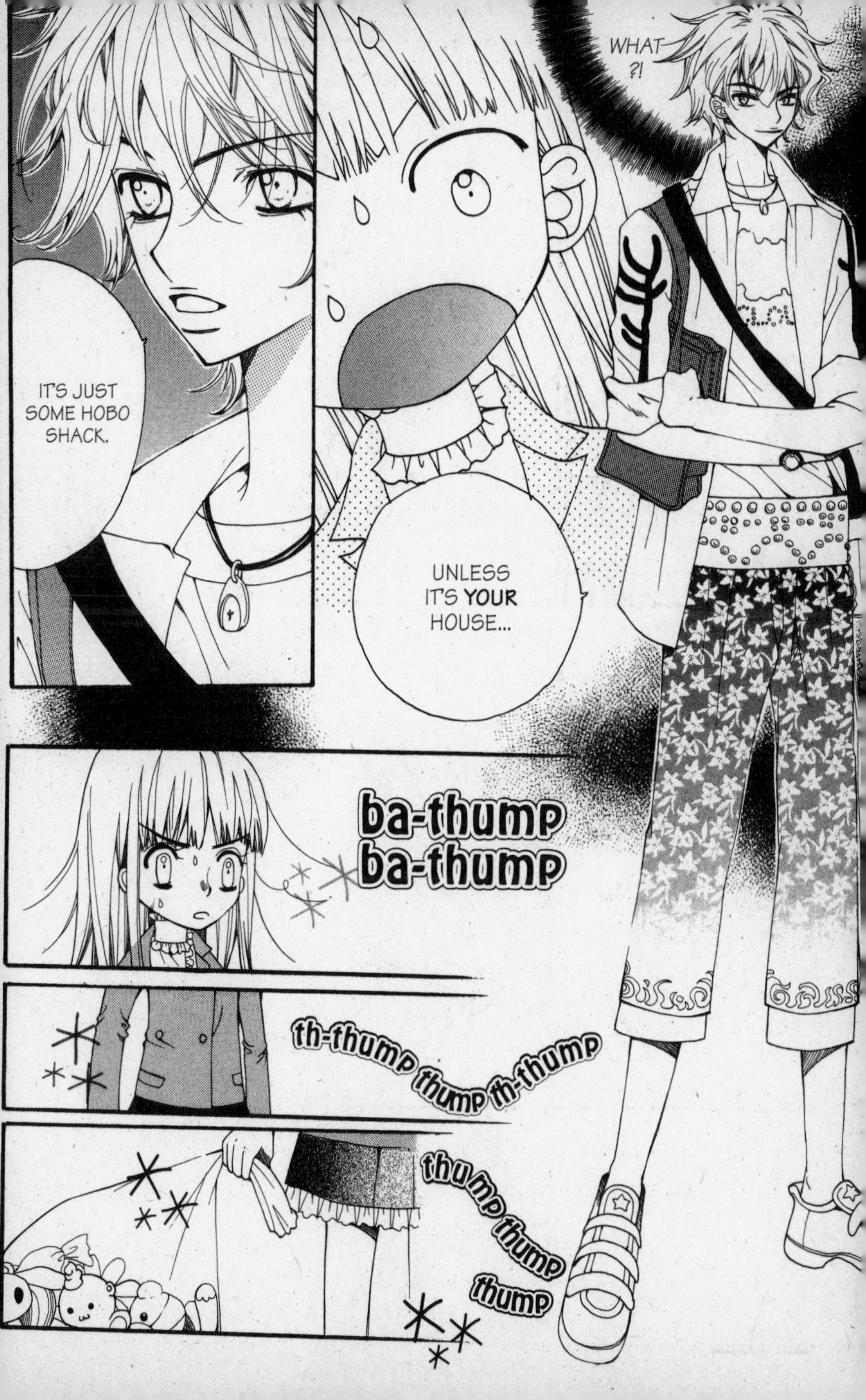
IT'S JUST SOME HOBO SHACK.
UNLESS IT'S YOUR HOUSE...
WHAT ?!
ba-thump ba-thump
th-thump thump th-thump
thump thump thump

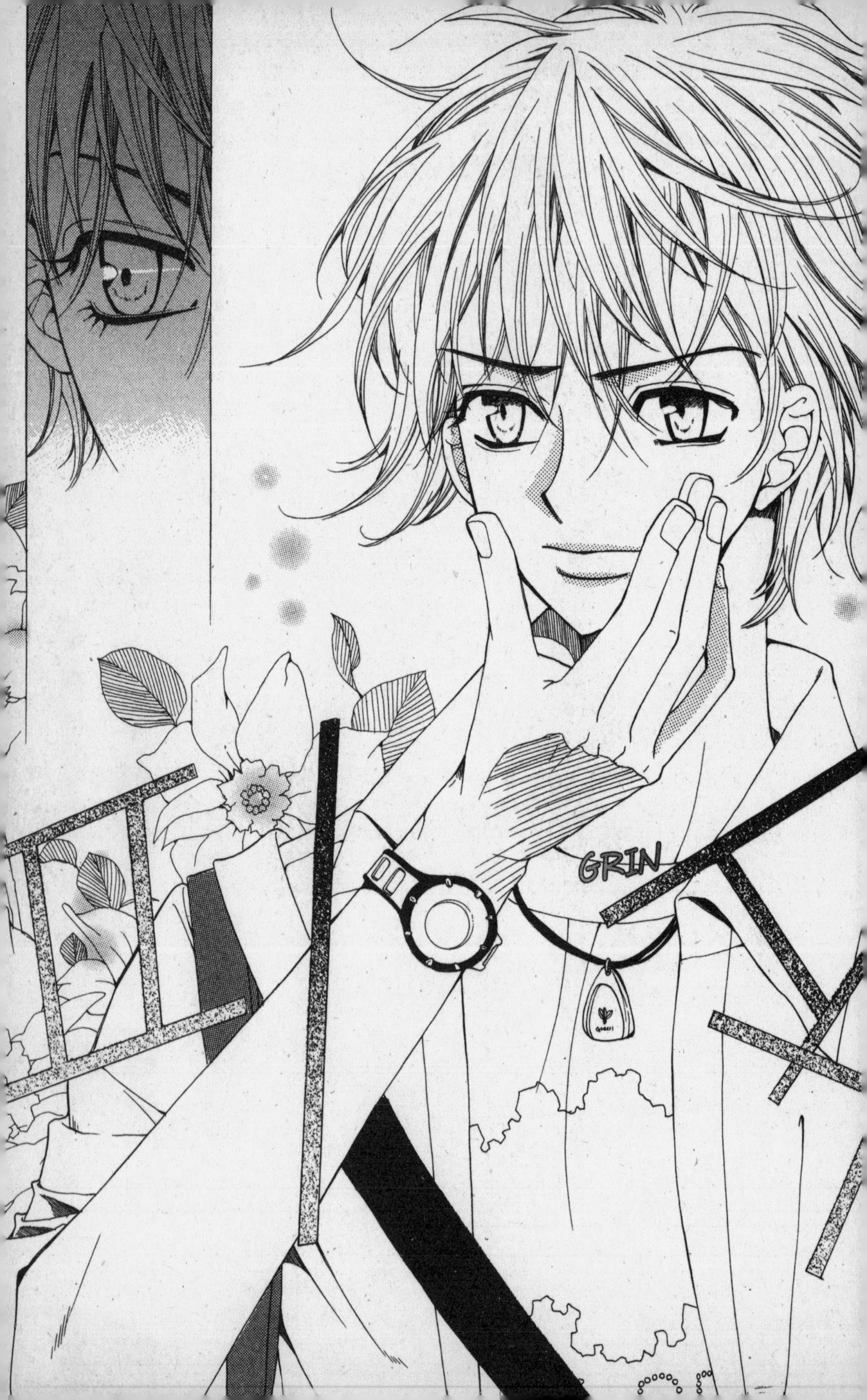
GRIN

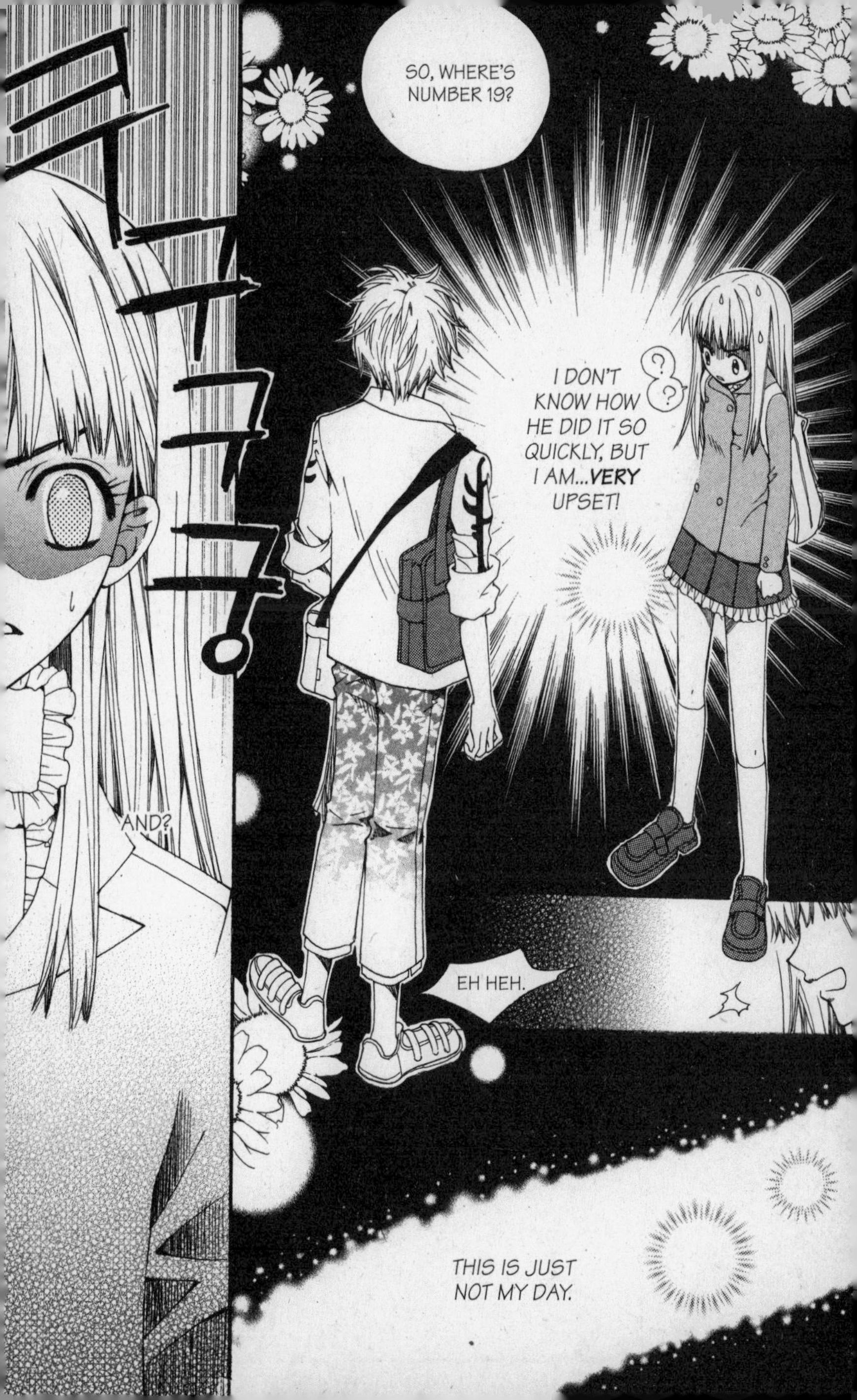
AND?
SO, WHERE'S NUMBER 19?
I DON'T KNOW HOW HE DID IT SO QUICKLY, BUT I AM...**VERY** UPSET!
EH HEH.
THIS IS JUST NOT MY DAY.

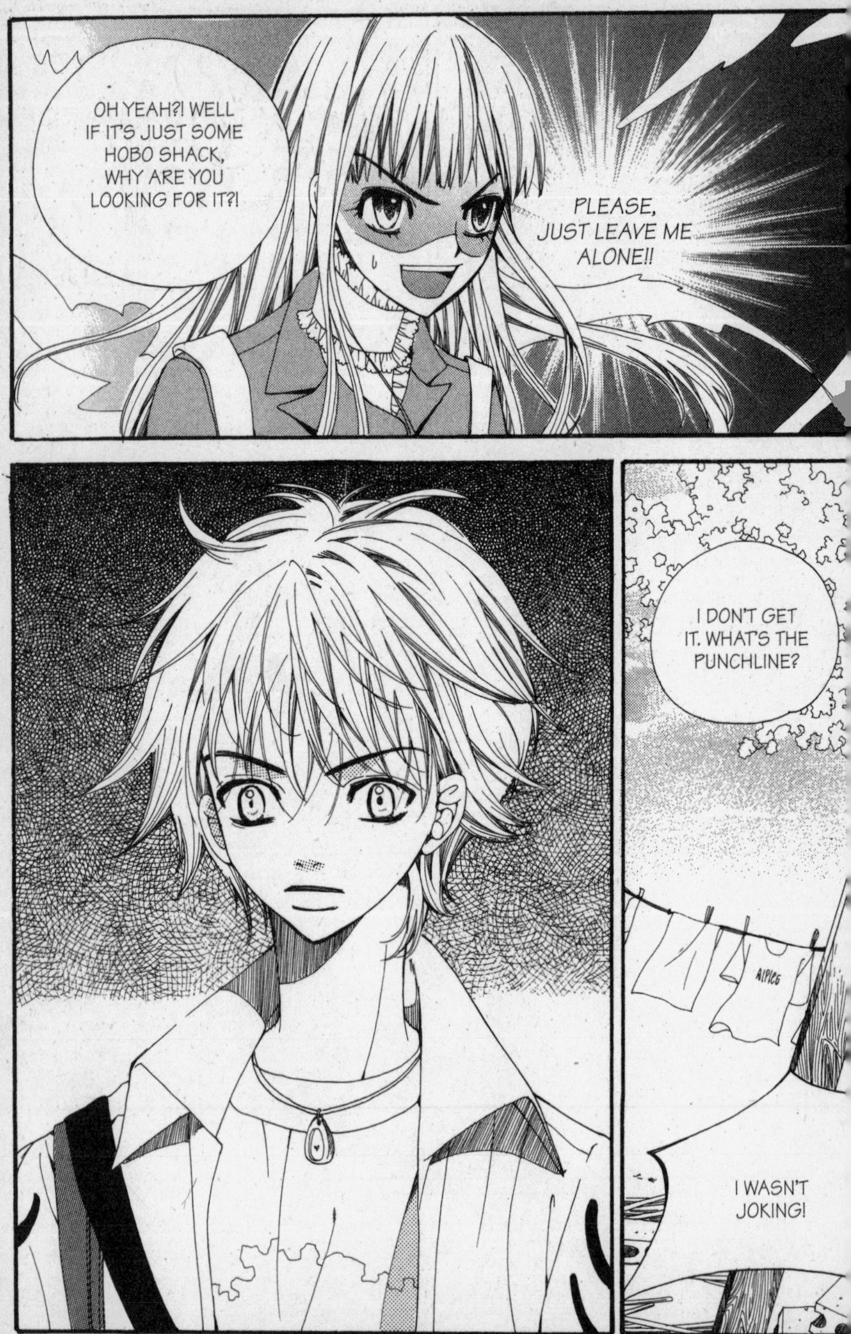
OH YEAH?! WELL IF IT'S JUST SOME HOBO SHACK, WHY ARE YOU LOOKING FOR IT?!
PLEASE, JUST LEAVE ME ALONE!!
I DON'T GET IT. WHAT'S THE PUNCHLINE?
I WASN'T JOKING!

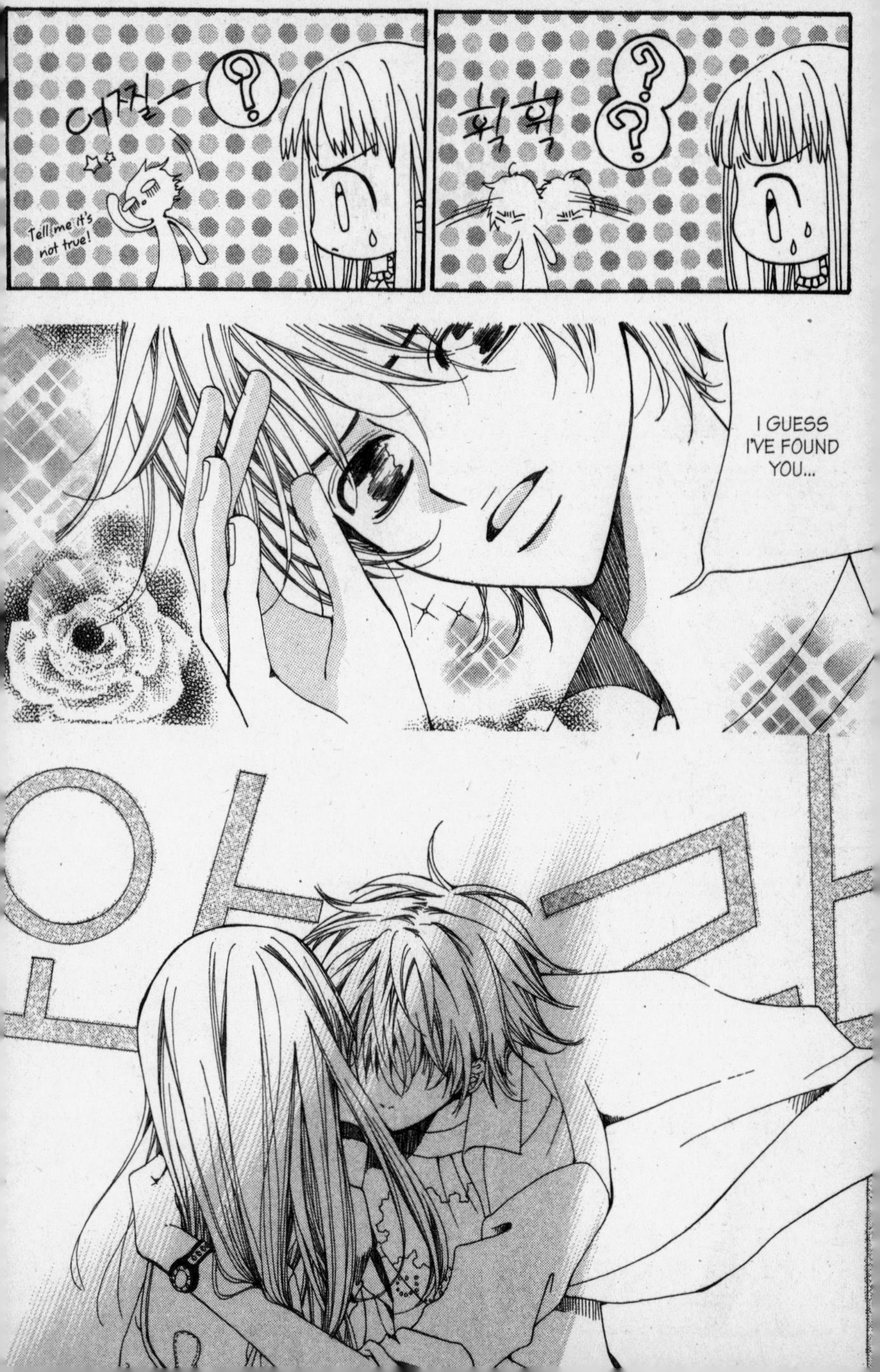
Tell me it's not true!
휙휙
I GUESS I'VE FOUND YOU...

...DAUGHTER!!

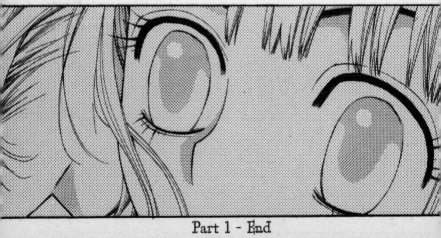

Part 1 - End

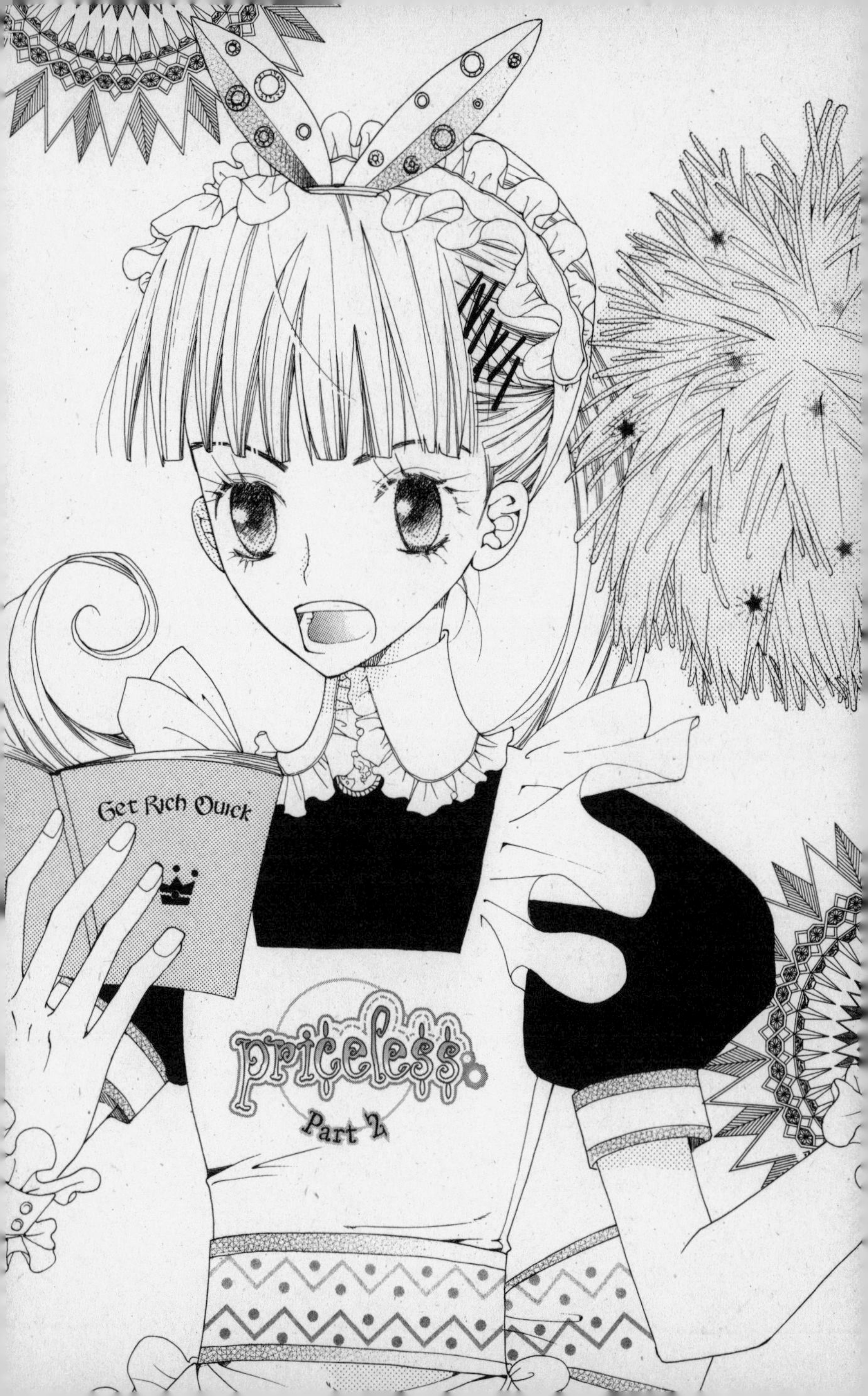
Get Rich Quick
priceless
Part 2

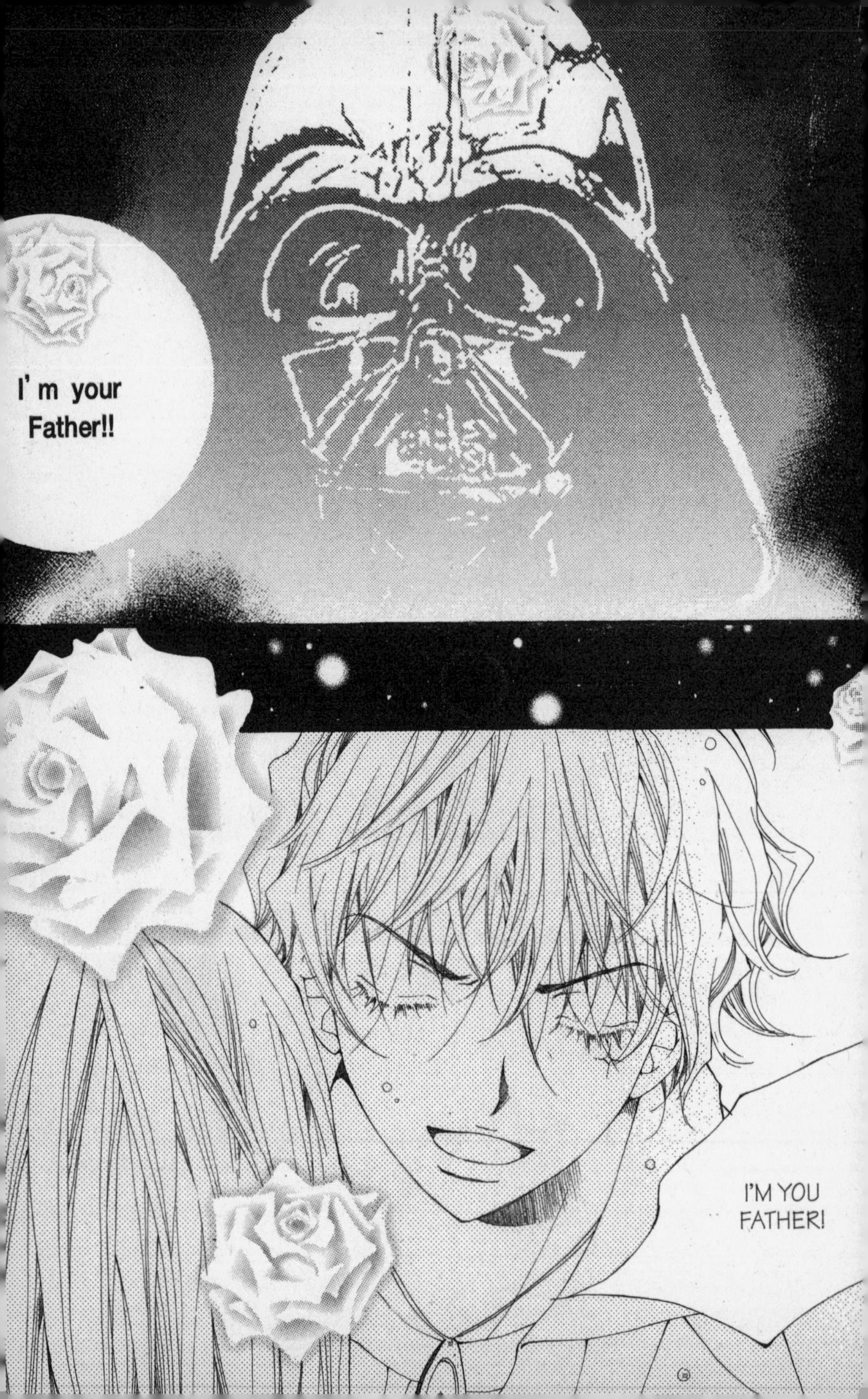
I' m your Father!!
I'M YOU FATHER!

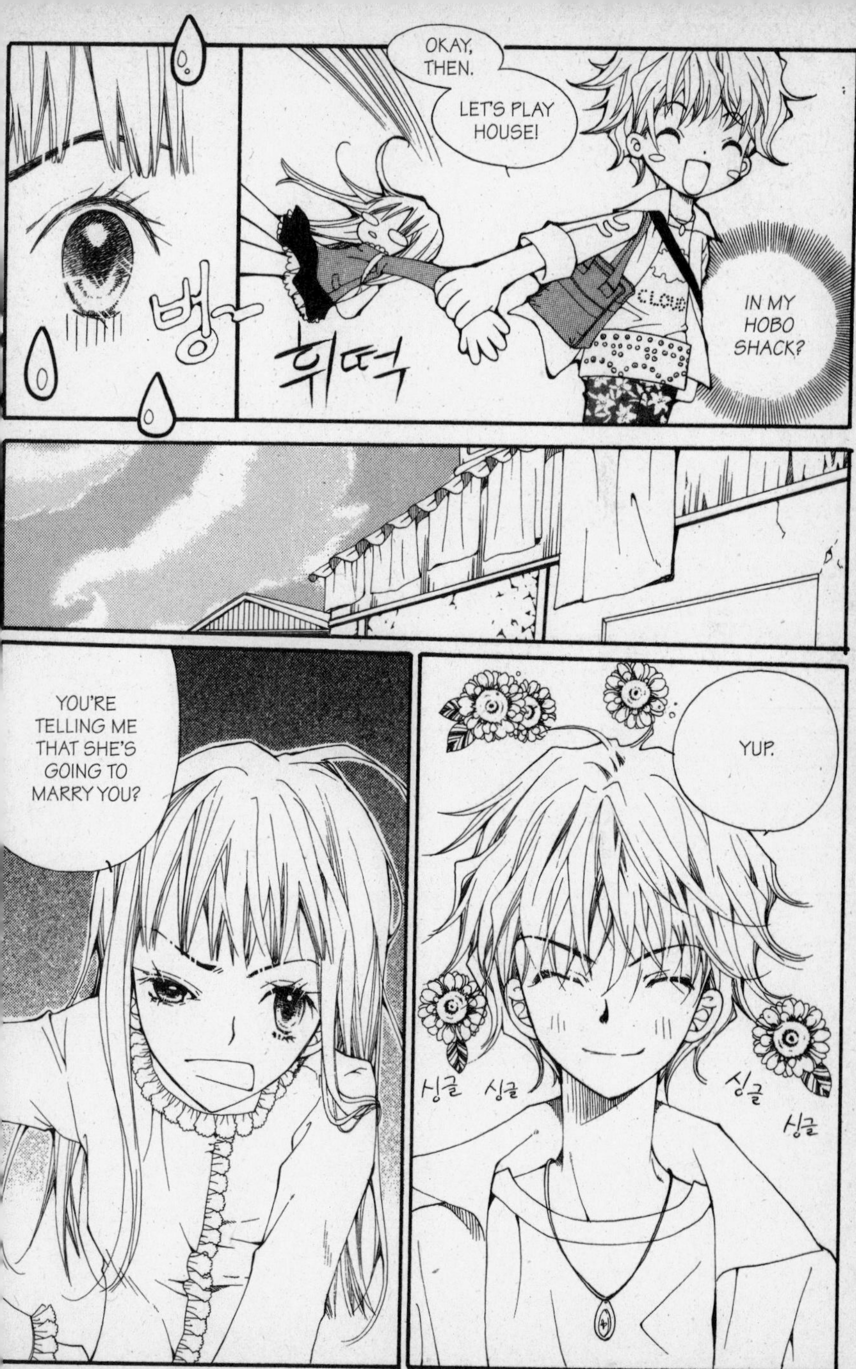

방~
휘떡
OKAY, THEN.
LET'S PLAY HOUSE!
IN MY HOBO SHACK?
CLOUD
YOU'RE TELLING ME THAT SHE'S GOING TO MARRY YOU?
YUP.
싱글 싱글
싱글
싱글

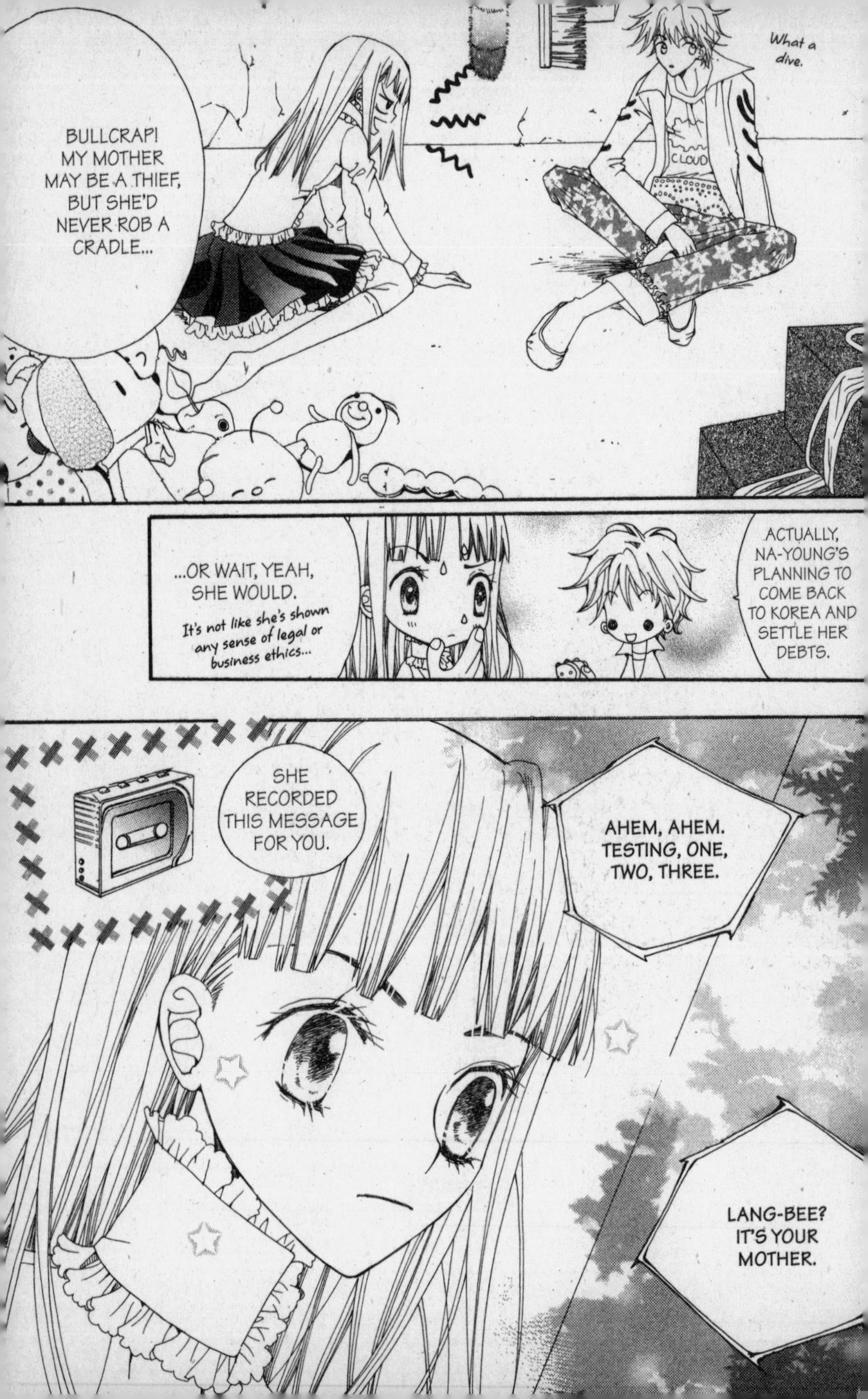
BULLCRAP! MY MOTHER MAY BE A THIEF, BUT SHE'D NEVER ROB A CRADLE...
What a dive.
...OR WAIT, YEAH, SHE WOULD.
It's not like she's shown any sense of legal or business ethics...
ACTUALLY, NA-YOUNG'S PLANNING TO COME BACK TO KOREA AND SETTLE HER DEBTS.
SHE RECORDED THIS MESSAGE FOR YOU.
AHEM, AHEM. TESTING, ONE, TWO, THREE.
LANG-BEE? IT'S YOUR MOTHER.

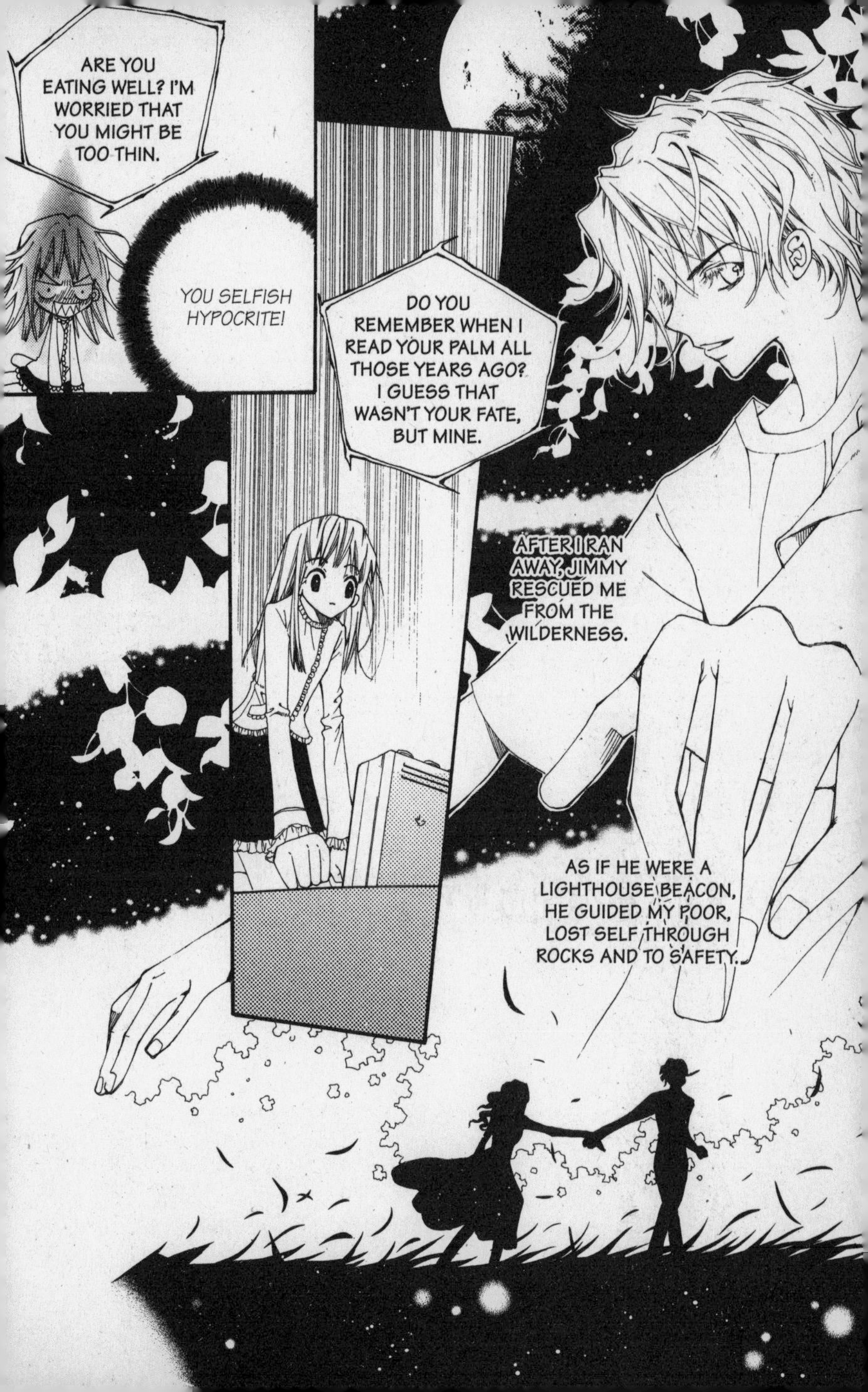
ARE YOU EATING WELL? I'M WORRIED THAT YOU MIGHT BE TOO THIN.
YOU SELFISH HYPOCRITE!
DO YOU REMEMBER WHEN I READ YOUR PALM ALL THOSE YEARS AGO? I GUESS THAT WASN'T YOUR FATE, BUT MINE.
AFTER I RAN AWAY, JIMMY RESCUED ME FROM THE WILDERNESS.
AS IF HE WERE A LIGHTHOUSE BEACON, HE GUIDED MY POOR, LOST SELF THROUGH ROCKS AND TO SAFETY.

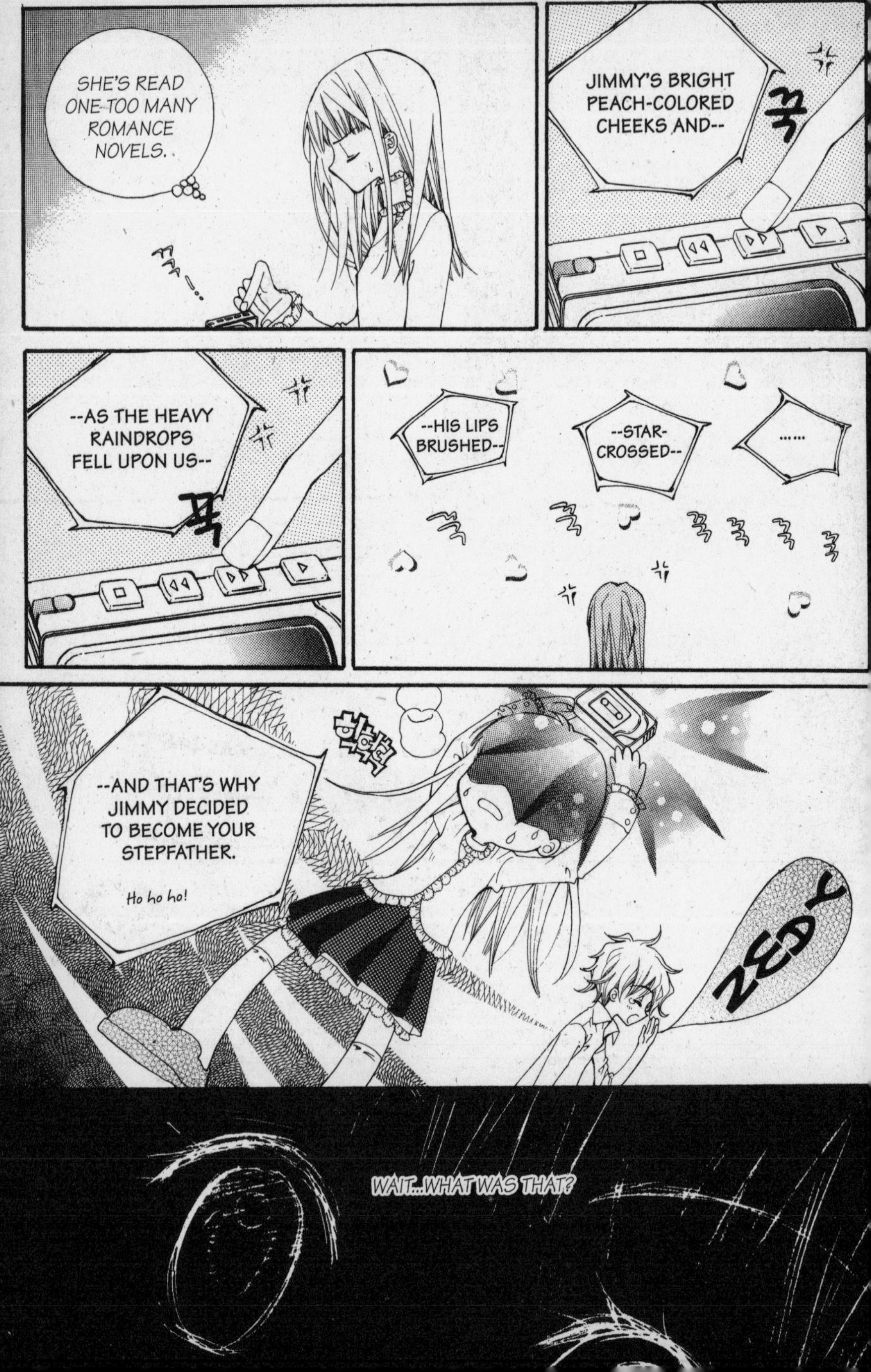

SHE'S READ ONE TOO MANY ROMANCE NOVELS.
JIMMY'S BRIGHT PEACH-COLORED CHEEKS AND--
--AS THE HEAVY RAINDROPS FELL UPON US--
--HIS LIPS BRUSHED--
--STAR-CROSSED--
......
--AND THAT'S WHY JIMMY DECIDED TO BECOME YOUR STEPFATHER.
Ho ho ho!
WAIT...WHAT WAS THAT?

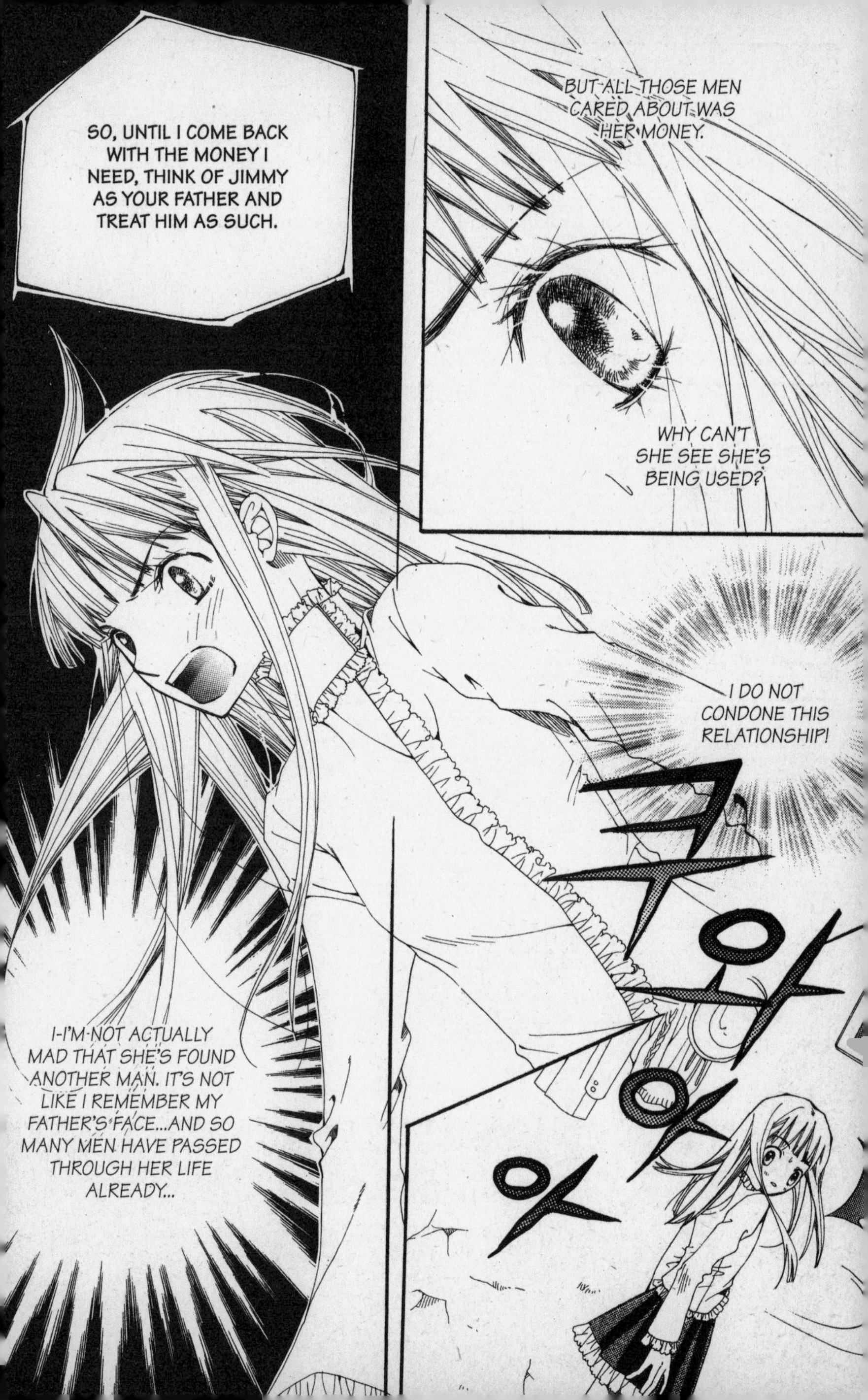
SO, UNTIL I COME BACK WITH THE MONEY I NEED, THINK OF JIMMY AS YOUR FATHER AND TREAT HIM AS SUCH.
I-I'M NOT ACTUALLY MAD THAT SHE'S FOUND ANOTHER MAN. IT'S NOT LIKE I REMEMBER MY FATHER'S FACE...AND SO MANY MEN HAVE PASSED THROUGH HER LIFE ALREADY...
BUT ALL THOSE MEN CARED ABOUT WAS HER MONEY.
WHY CAN'T SHE SEE SHE'S BEING USED?
I DO NOT CONDONE THIS RELATIONSHIP!
크와아아

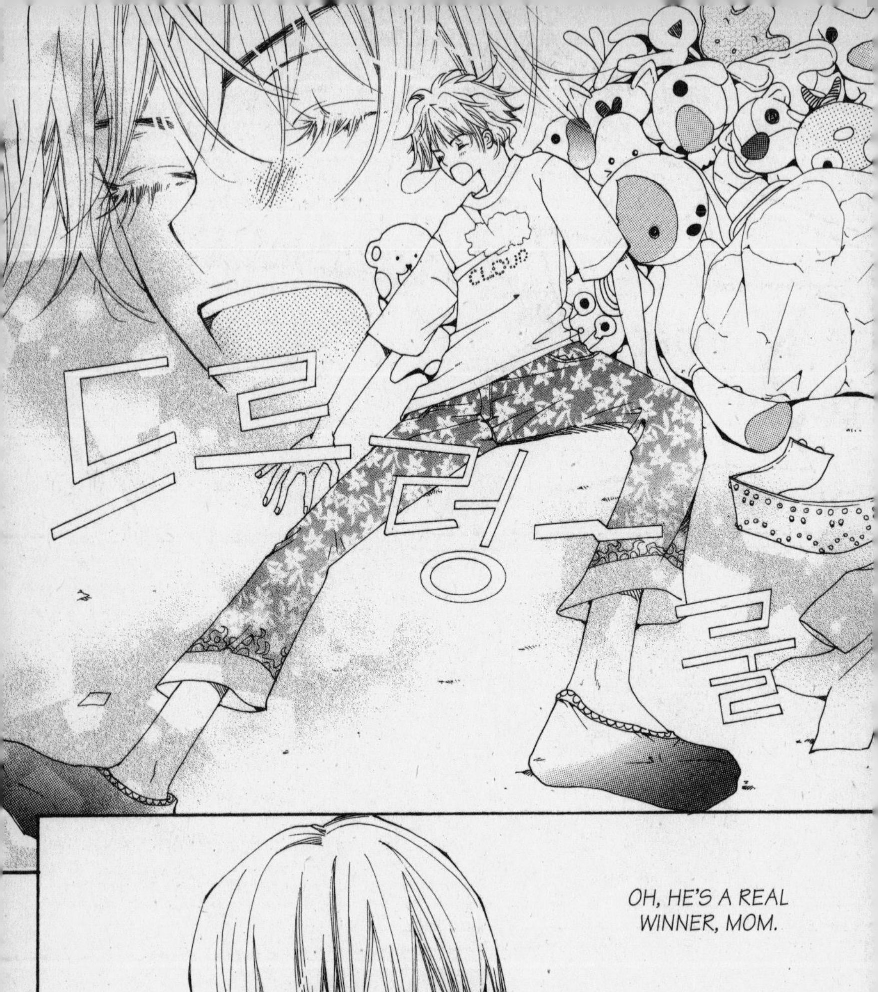
드르렁
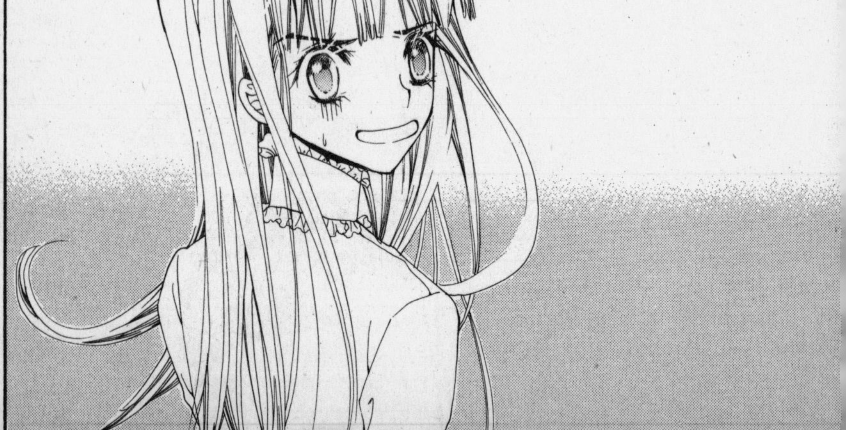
OH, HE'S A REAL
WINNER, MOM.

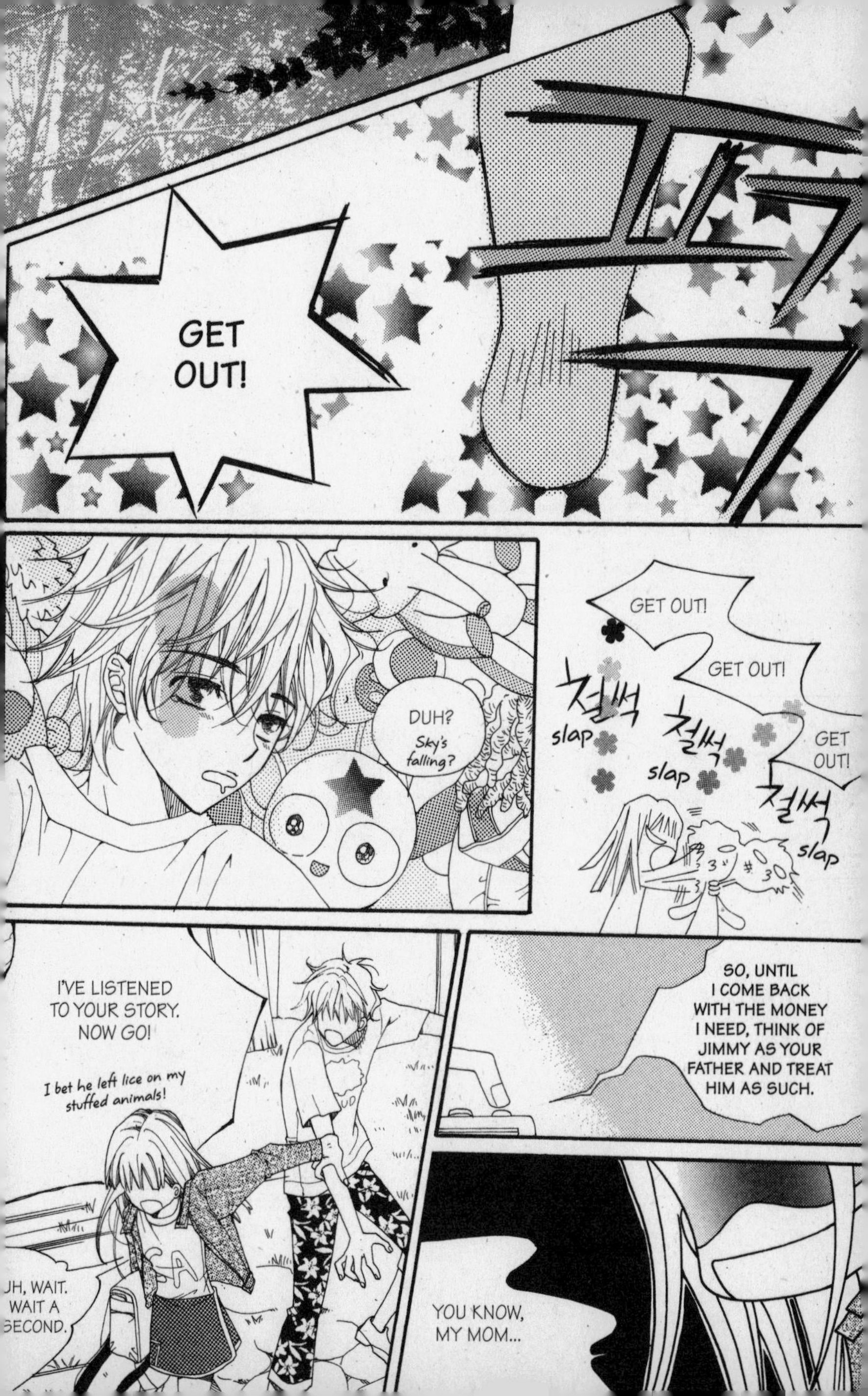
GET OUT!
DUH? Sky's falling?
GET OUT!
GET OUT!
GET OUT!
철썩
slap
철썩
slap
철썩
slap
I'VE LISTENED TO YOUR STORY. NOW GO!
I bet he left lice on my stuffed animals!
UH, WAIT. WAIT A SECOND.
SO, UNTIL I COME BACK WITH THE MONEY I NEED, THINK OF JIMMY AS YOUR FATHER AND TREAT HIM AS SUCH.
YOU KNOW, MY MOM...

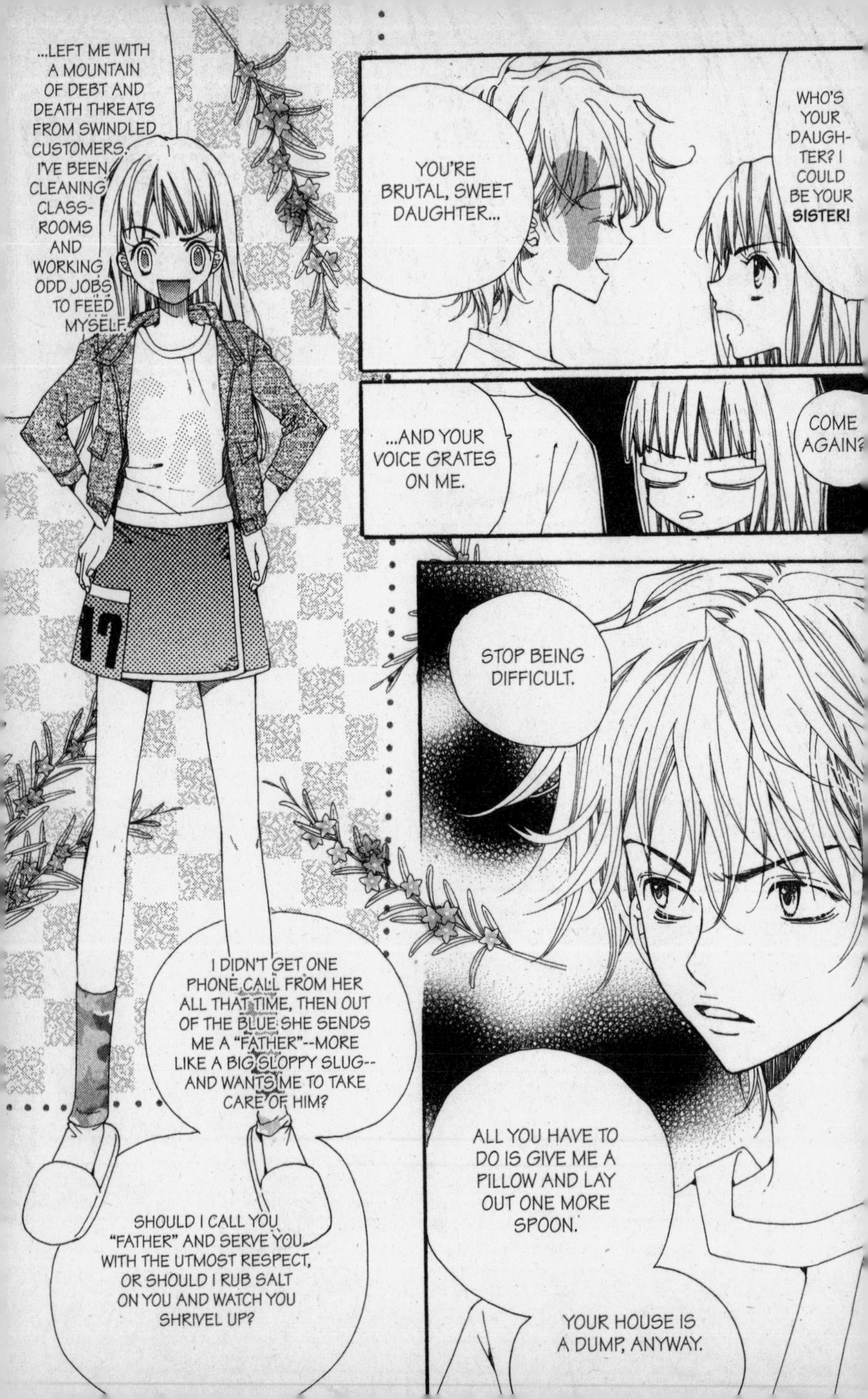
...LEFT ME WITH A MOUNTAIN OF DEBT AND DEATH THREATS FROM SWINDLED CUSTOMERS.
I'VE BEEN CLEANING CLASSROOMS AND WORKING ODD JOBS TO FEED MYSELF.
I DIDN'T GET ONE PHONE CALL FROM HER ALL THAT TIME, THEN OUT OF THE BLUE SHE SENDS ME A "FATHER"--MORE LIKE A BIG SLOPPY SLUG--AND WANTS ME TO TAKE CARE OF HIM?
SHOULD I CALL YOU "FATHER" AND SERVE YOU WITH THE UTMOST RESPECT, OR SHOULD I RUB SALT ON YOU AND WATCH YOU SHRIVEL UP?
YOU'RE BRUTAL, SWEET DAUGHTER...
WHO'S YOUR DAUGHTER? I COULD BE YOUR **SISTER!**
...AND YOUR VOICE GRATES ON ME.
COME AGAIN?
STOP BEING DIFFICULT.
ALL YOU HAVE TO DO IS GIVE ME A PILLOW AND LAY OUT ONE MORE SPOON.
YOUR HOUSE IS A DUMP, ANYWAY.

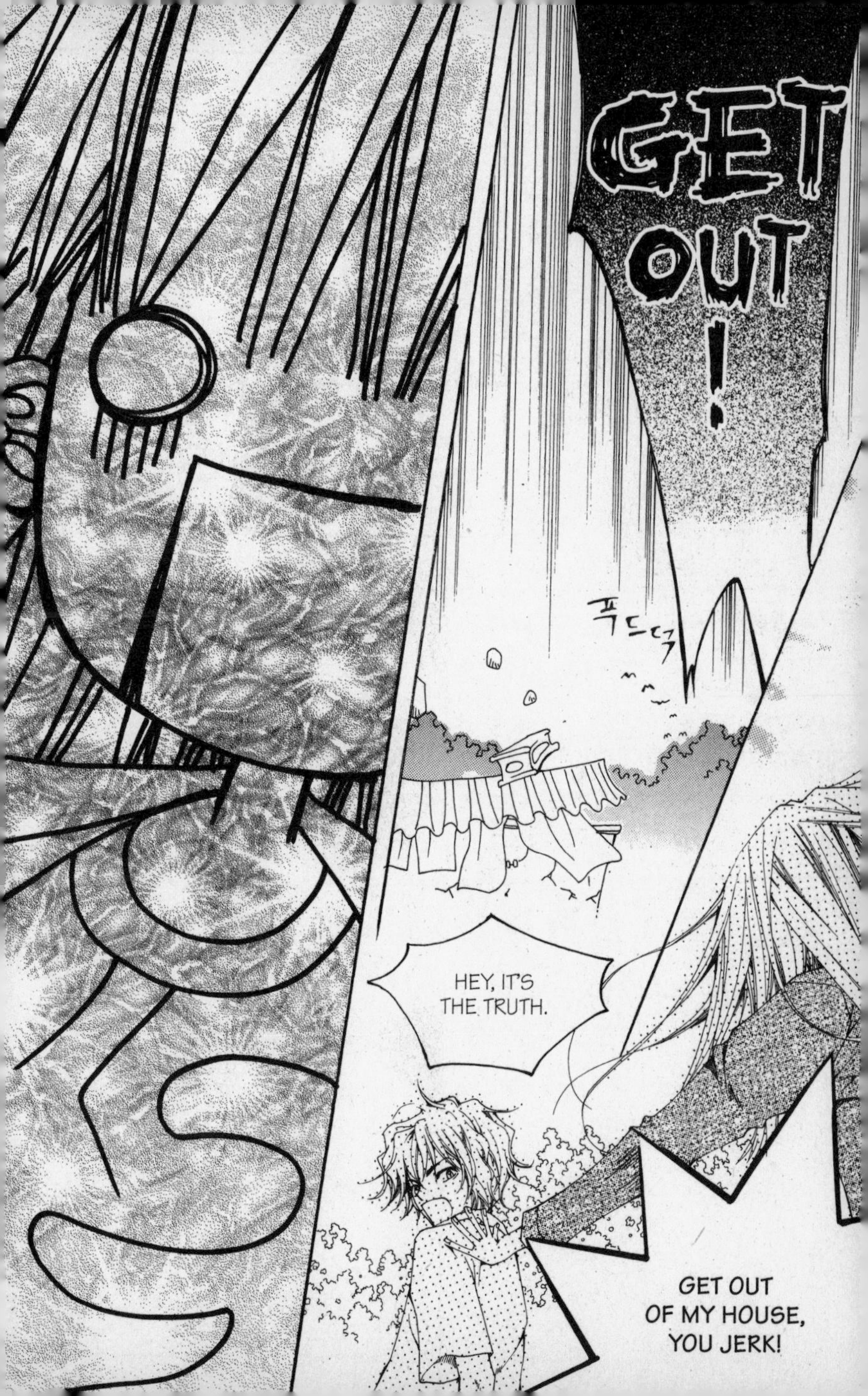
GET OUT!
푸드덕
HEY, IT'S THE TRUTH.
GET OUT OF MY HOUSE, YOU JERK!

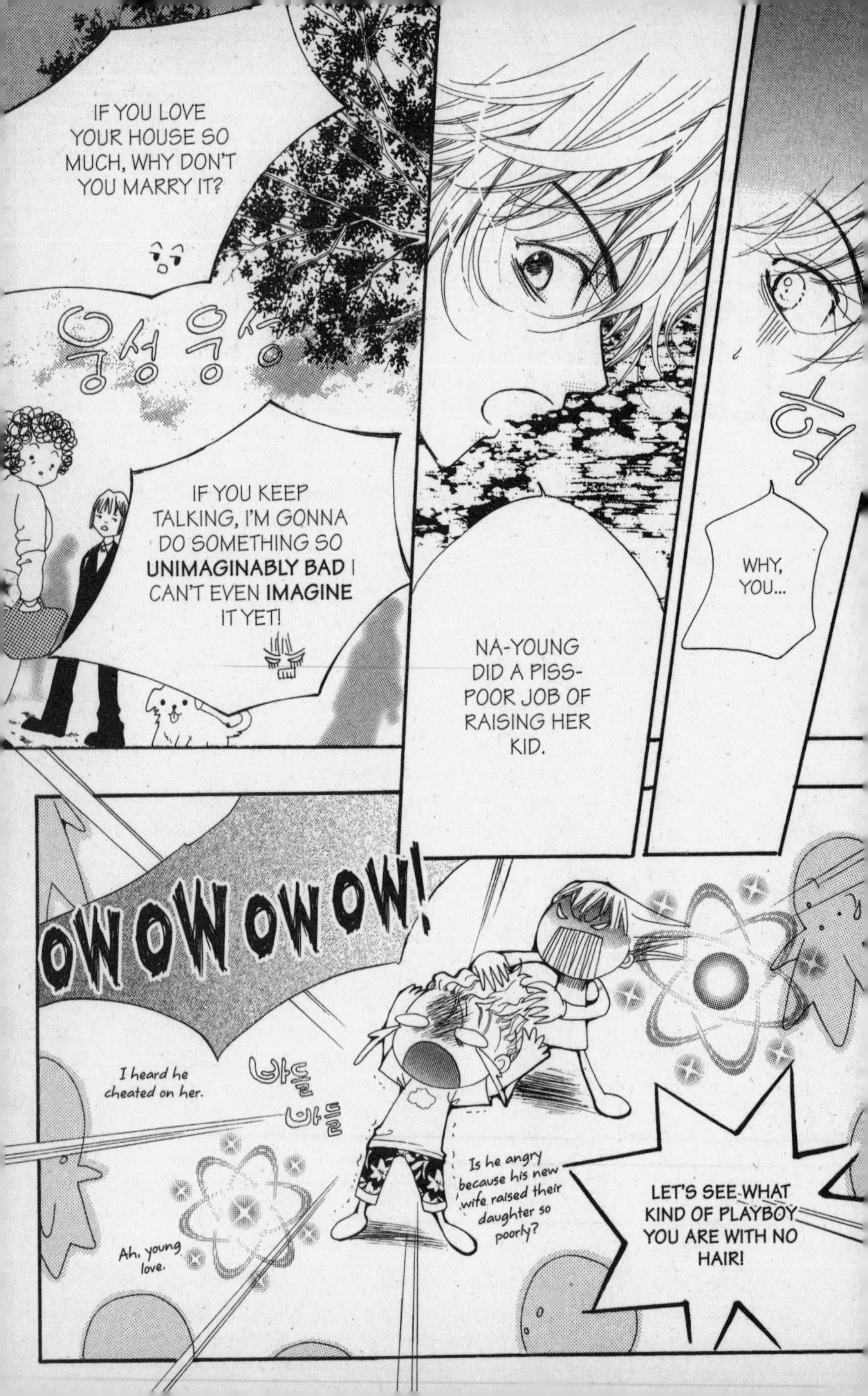

IF YOU LOVE YOUR HOUSE SO MUCH, WHY DON'T YOU MARRY IT?
웅성웅
IF YOU KEEP TALKING, I'M GONNA DO SOMETHING SO **UNIMAGINABLY BAD** I CAN'T EVEN **IMAGINE** IT YET!
NA-YOUNG DID A PISS-POOR JOB OF RAISING HER KID.
헉
WHY, YOU...
OW OW OW OW!
I heard he cheated on her.
바들 바들
Ah, young love.
Is he angry because his new wife raised their daughter so poorly?
LET'S SEE WHAT KIND OF PLAYBOY YOU ARE WITH NO HAIR!

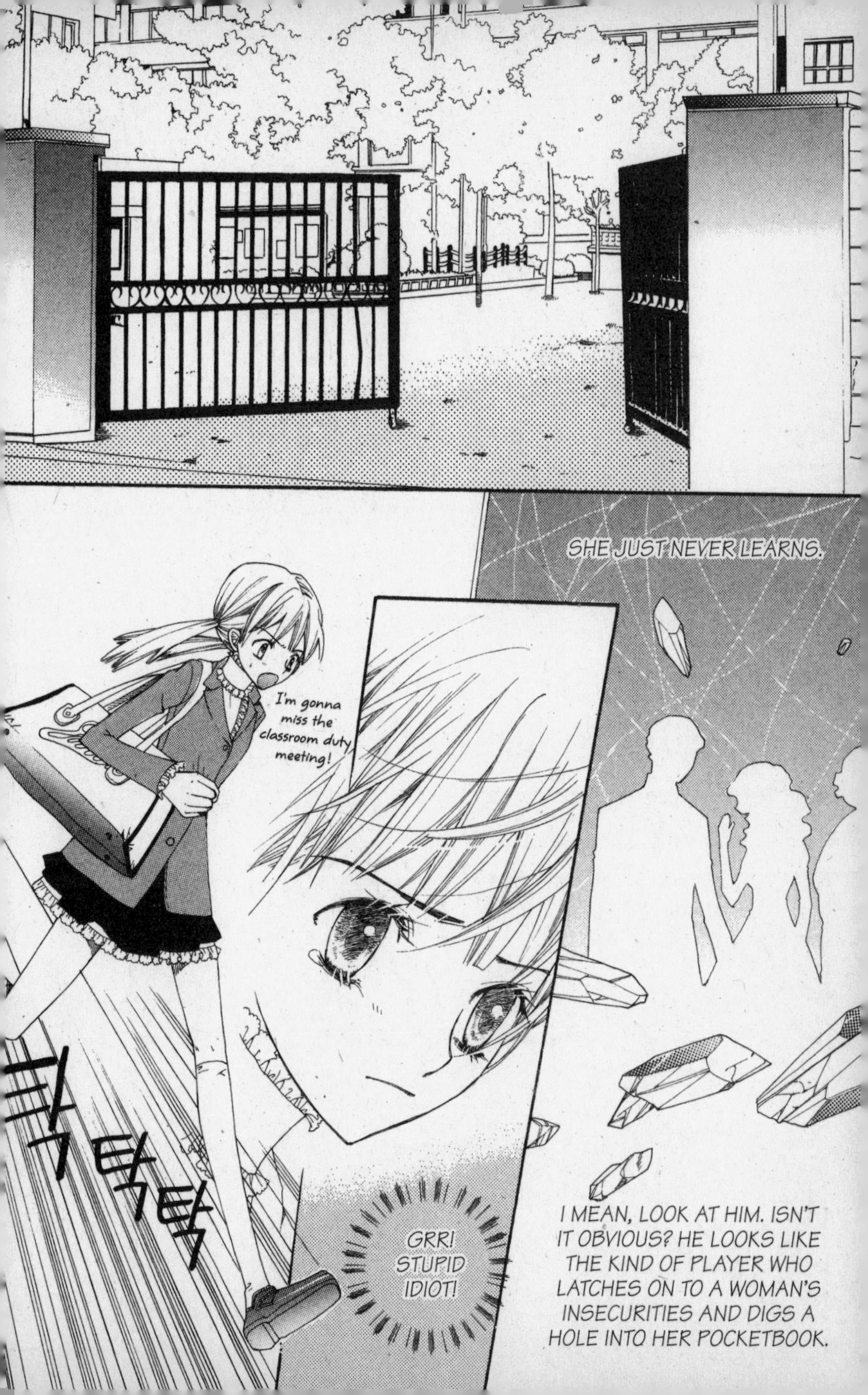
I'm gonna miss the classroom duty meeting!
SHE JUST NEVER LEARNS.
GRR! STUPID IDIOT!
I MEAN, LOOK AT HIM. ISN'T IT OBVIOUS? HE LOOKS LIKE THE KIND OF PLAYER WHO LATCHES ON TO A WOMAN'S INSECURITIES AND DIGS A HOLE INTO HER POCKETBOOK.

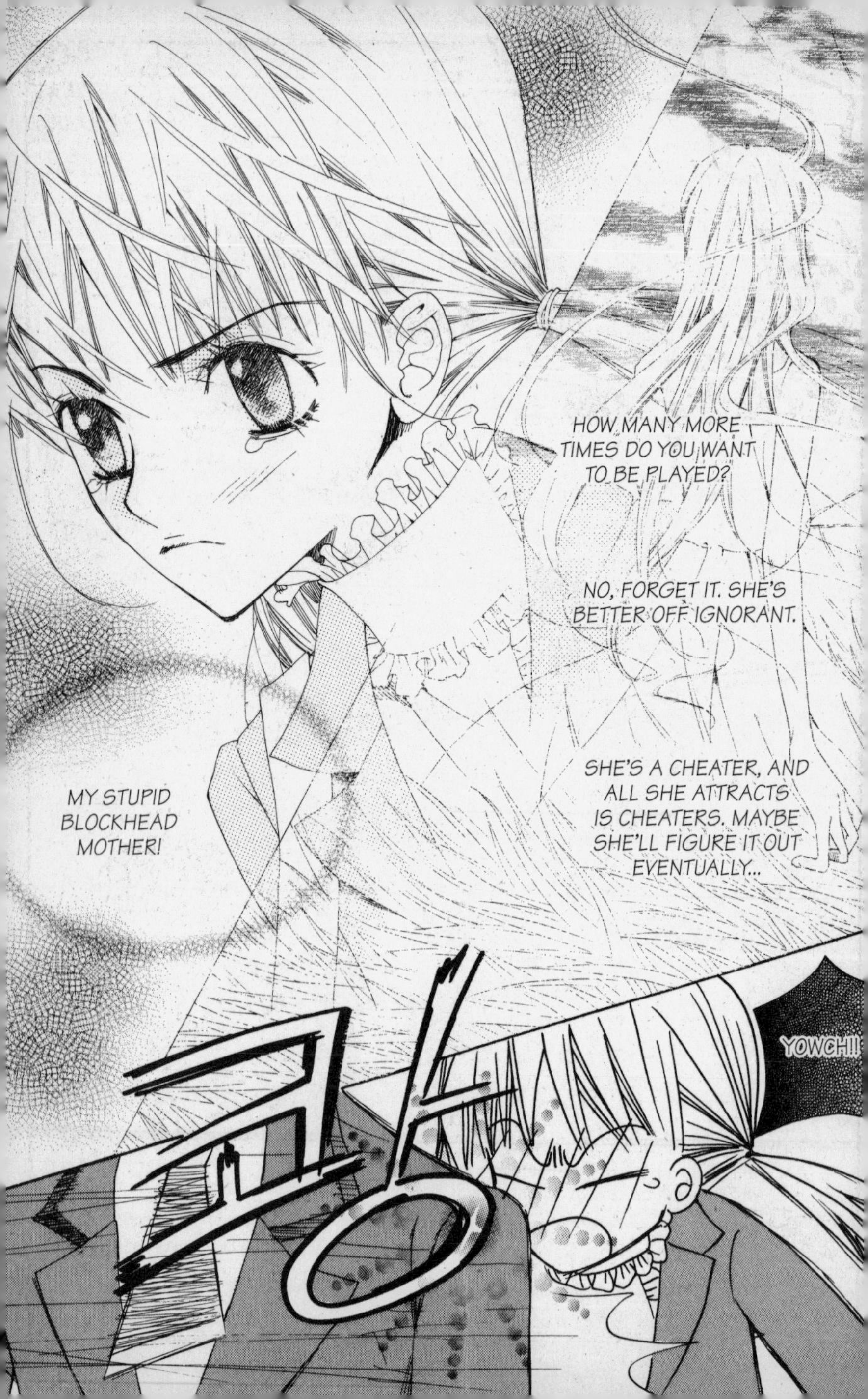
MY STUPID BLOCKHEAD MOTHER!
HOW MANY MORE TIMES DO YOU WANT TO BE PLAYED?
NO, FORGET IT. SHE'S BETTER OFF IGNORANT.
SHE'S A CHEATER, AND ALL SHE ATTRACTS IS CHEATERS. MAYBE SHE'LL FIGURE IT OUT EVENTUALLY...
YOWCH!!

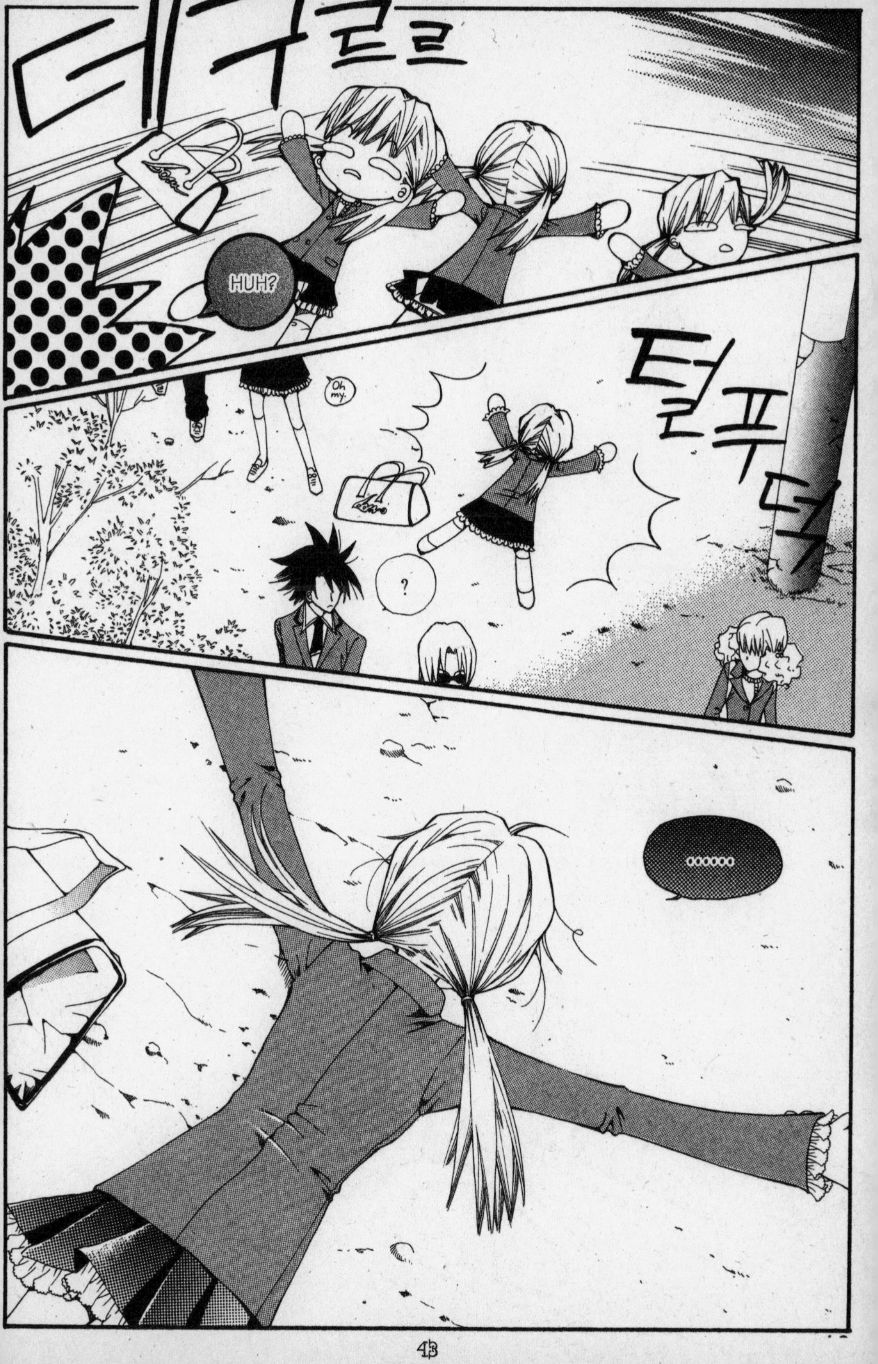
데구르르
HUH?
Oh my.
?
털푸덕
......

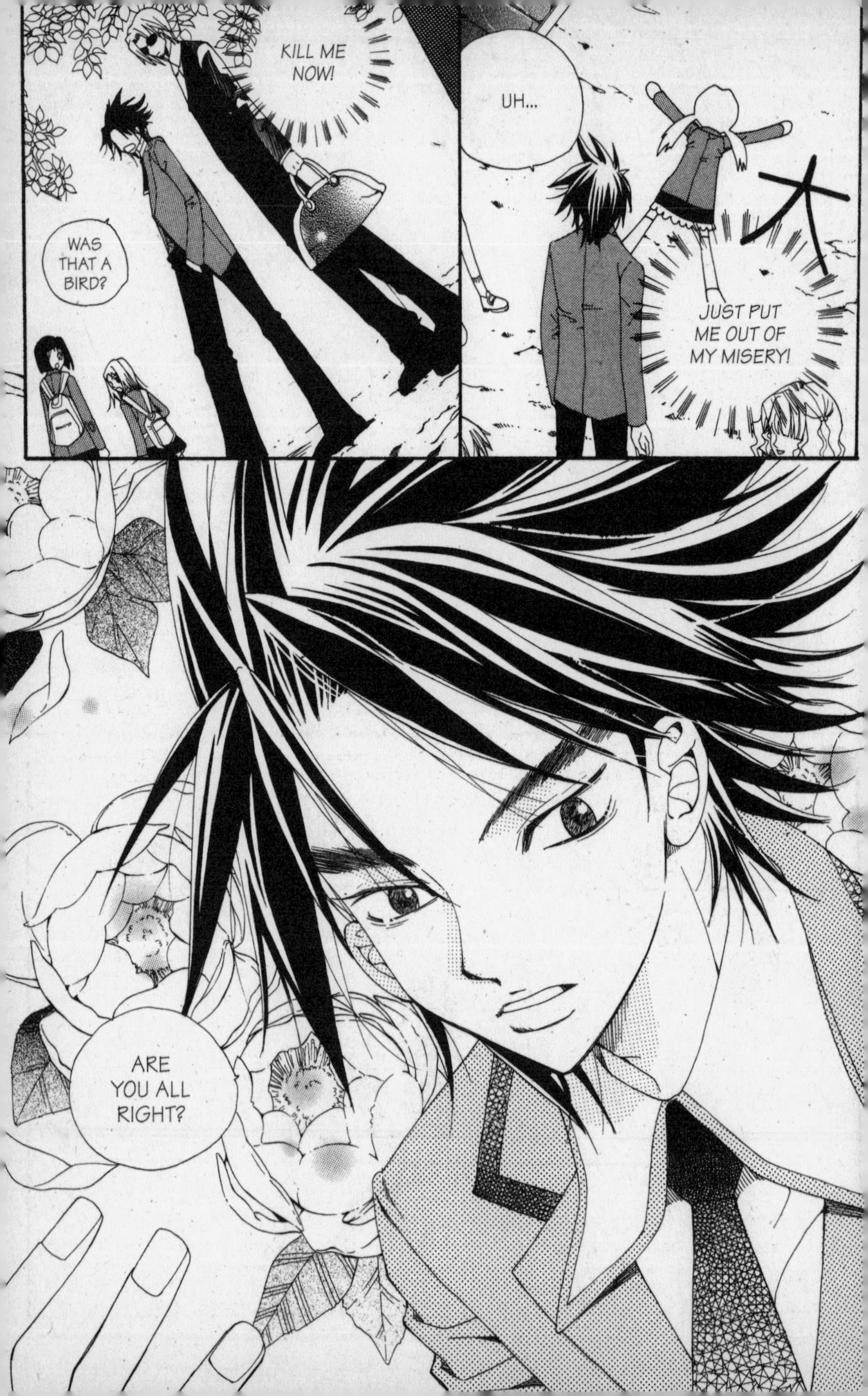
KILL ME NOW!
WAS THAT A BIRD?
UH...
大
JUST PUT ME OUT OF MY MISERY!
ARE YOU ALL RIGHT?

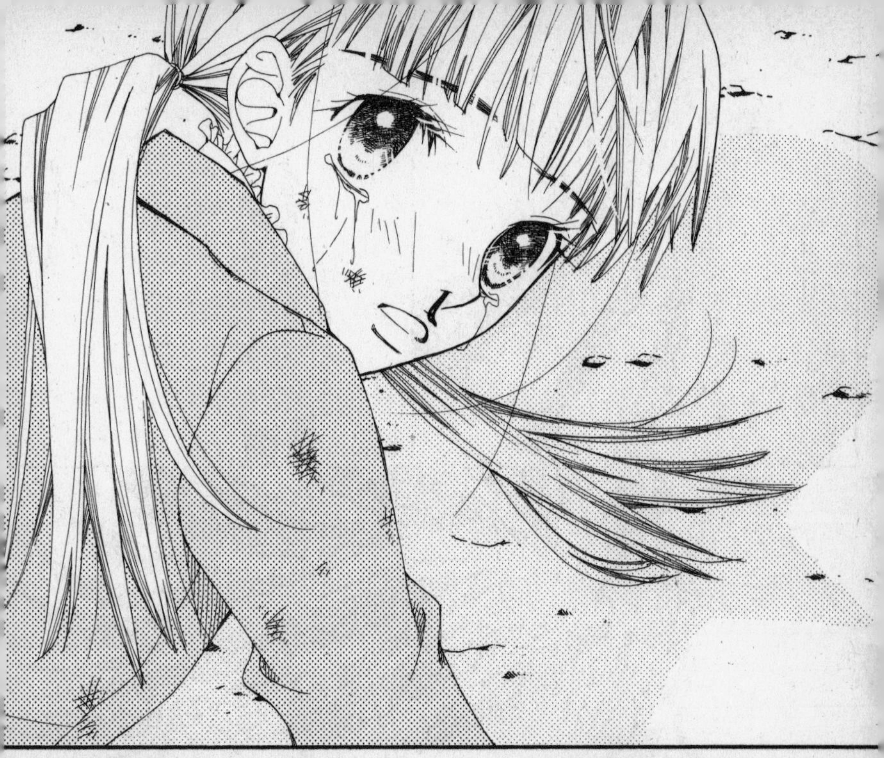

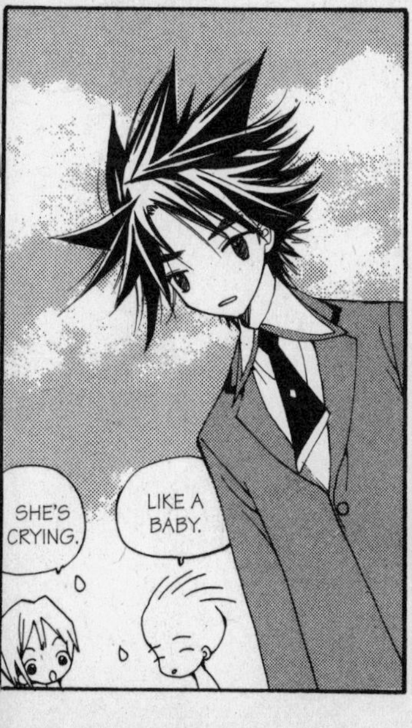
SHE'S CRYING.
LIKE A BABY.

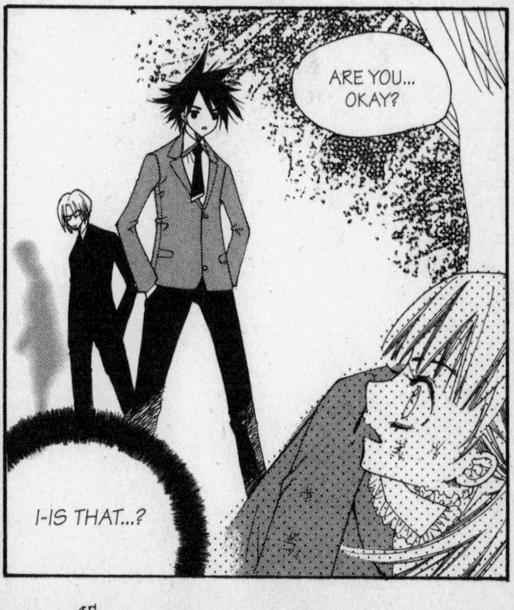
ARE YOU... OKAY?
I-IS THAT...?

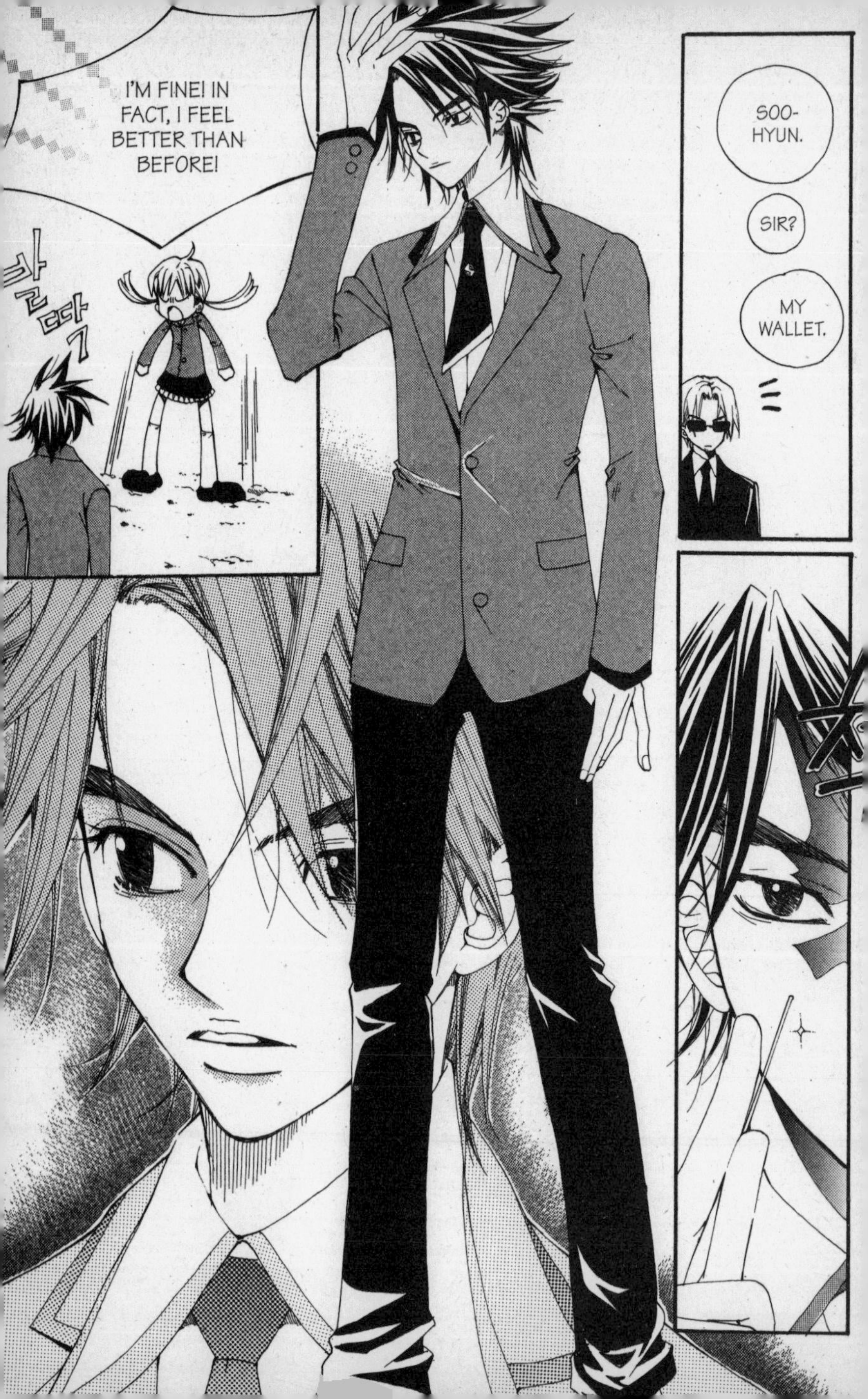
I'M FINE! IN FACT, I FEEL BETTER THAN BEFORE!
SOO-HYUN.
SIR?
MY WALLET.

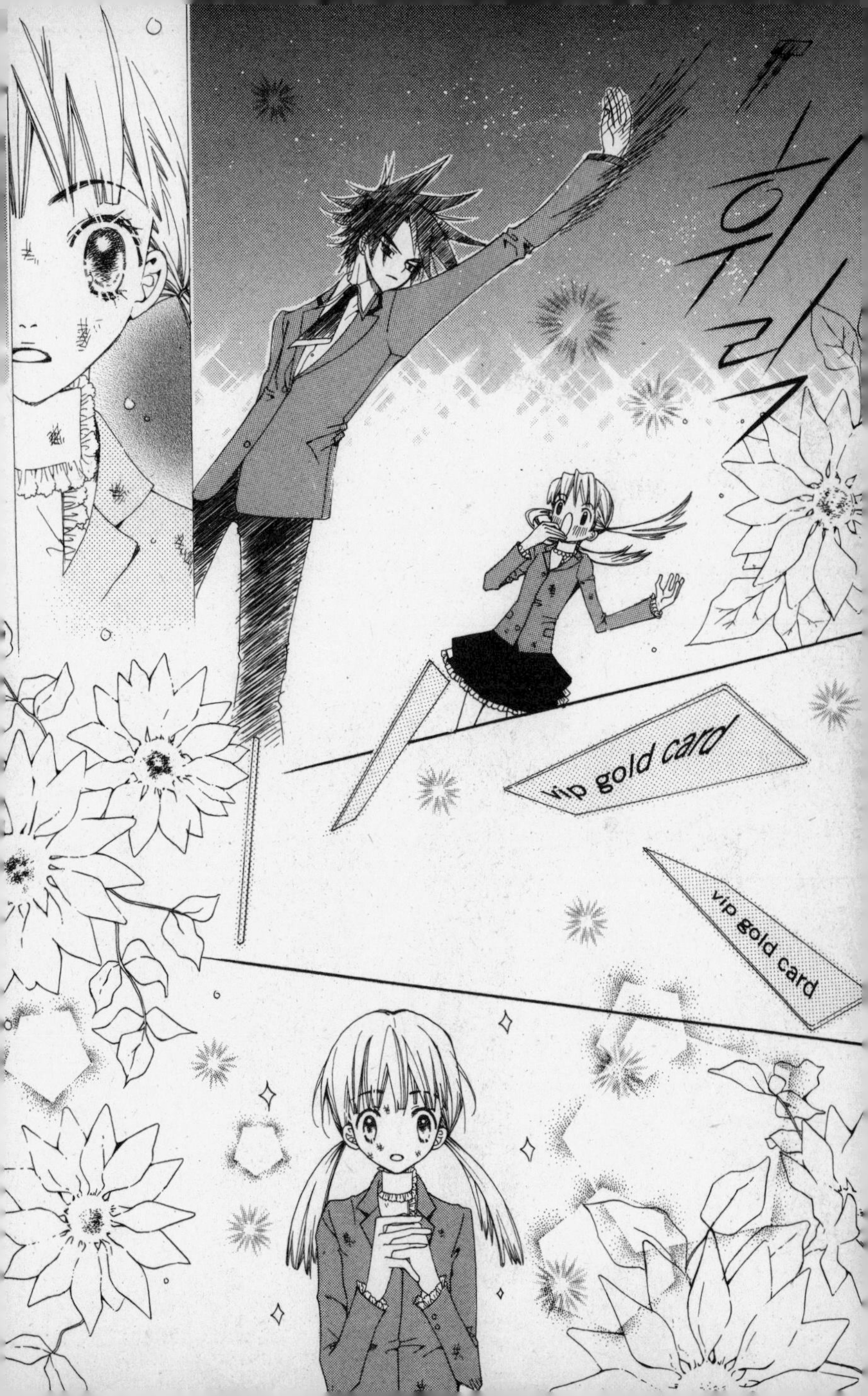
vip gold card
vip gold card

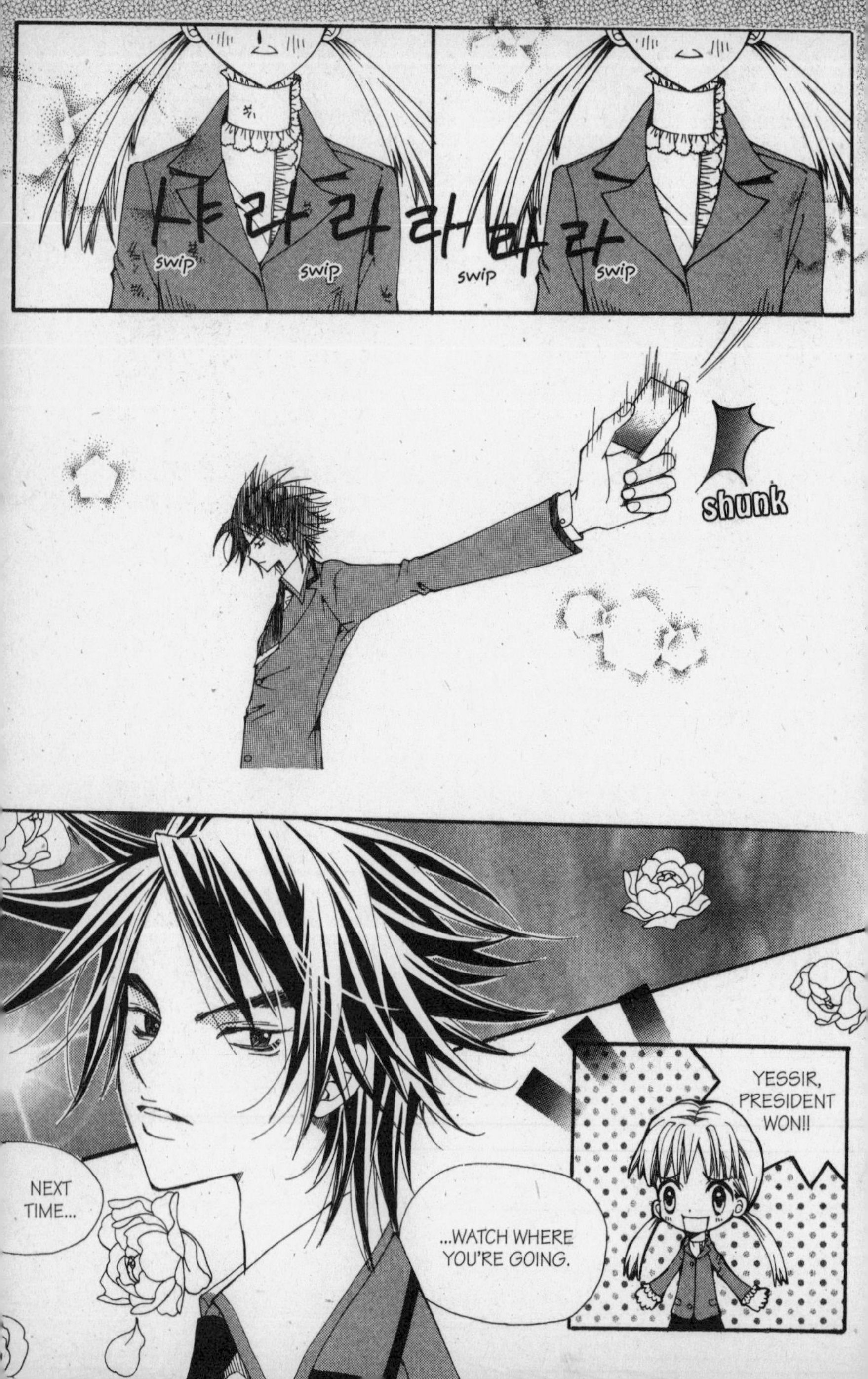
샤라라라빠라
swip
swip
swip
swip
shunk
NEXT TIME...
...WATCH WHERE YOU'RE GOING.
YESSIR, PRESIDENT WON!!

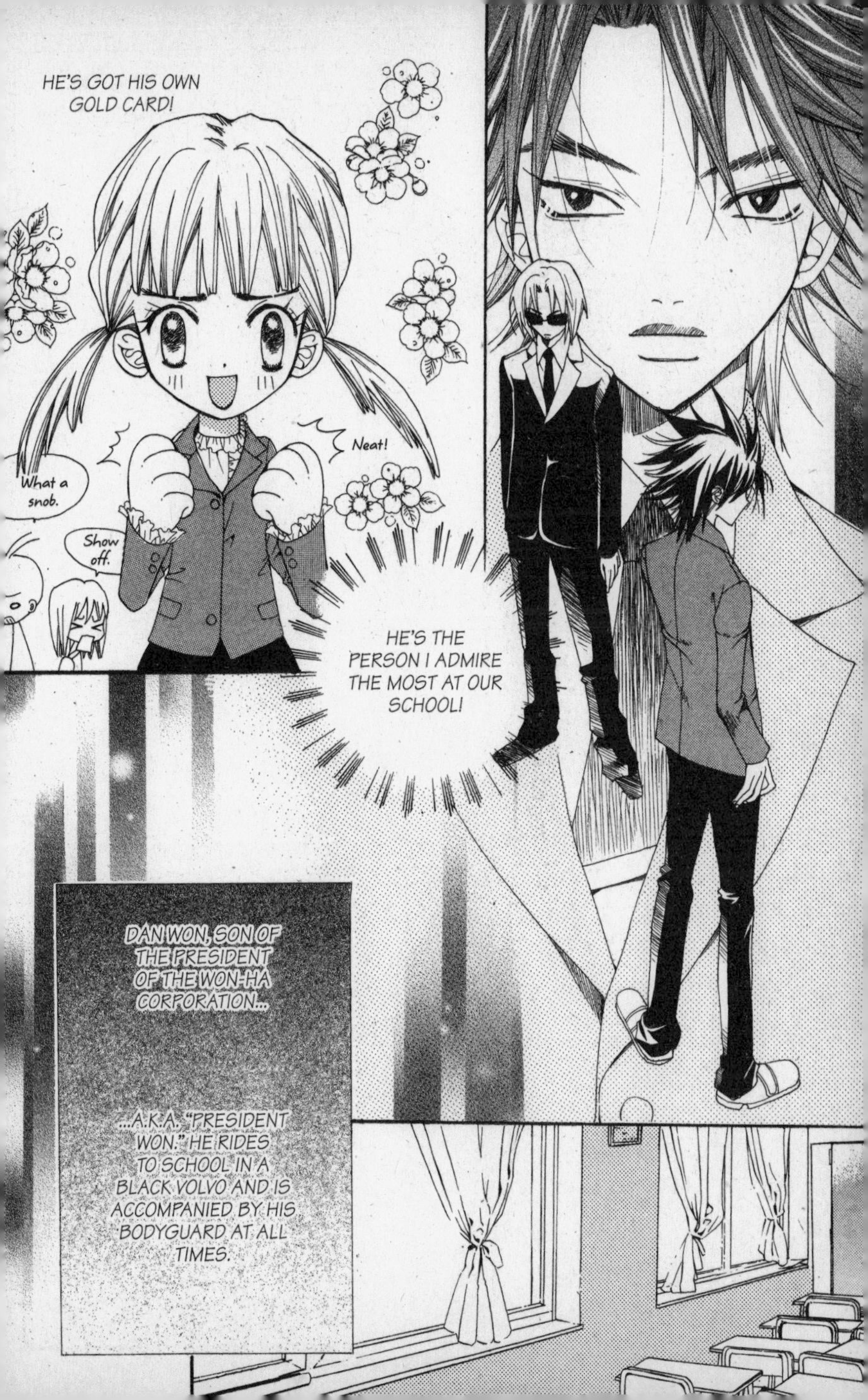
HE'S GOT HIS OWN GOLD CARD!
What a snob.
Show off.
Neat!
HE'S THE PERSON I ADMIRE THE MOST AT OUR SCHOOL!
DAN WON, SON OF THE PRESIDENT OF THE WON-HA CORPORATION...
...A.K.A. "PRESIDENT WON." HE RIDES TO SCHOOL IN A BLACK VOLVO AND IS ACCOMPANIED BY HIS BODYGUARD AT ALL TIMES.

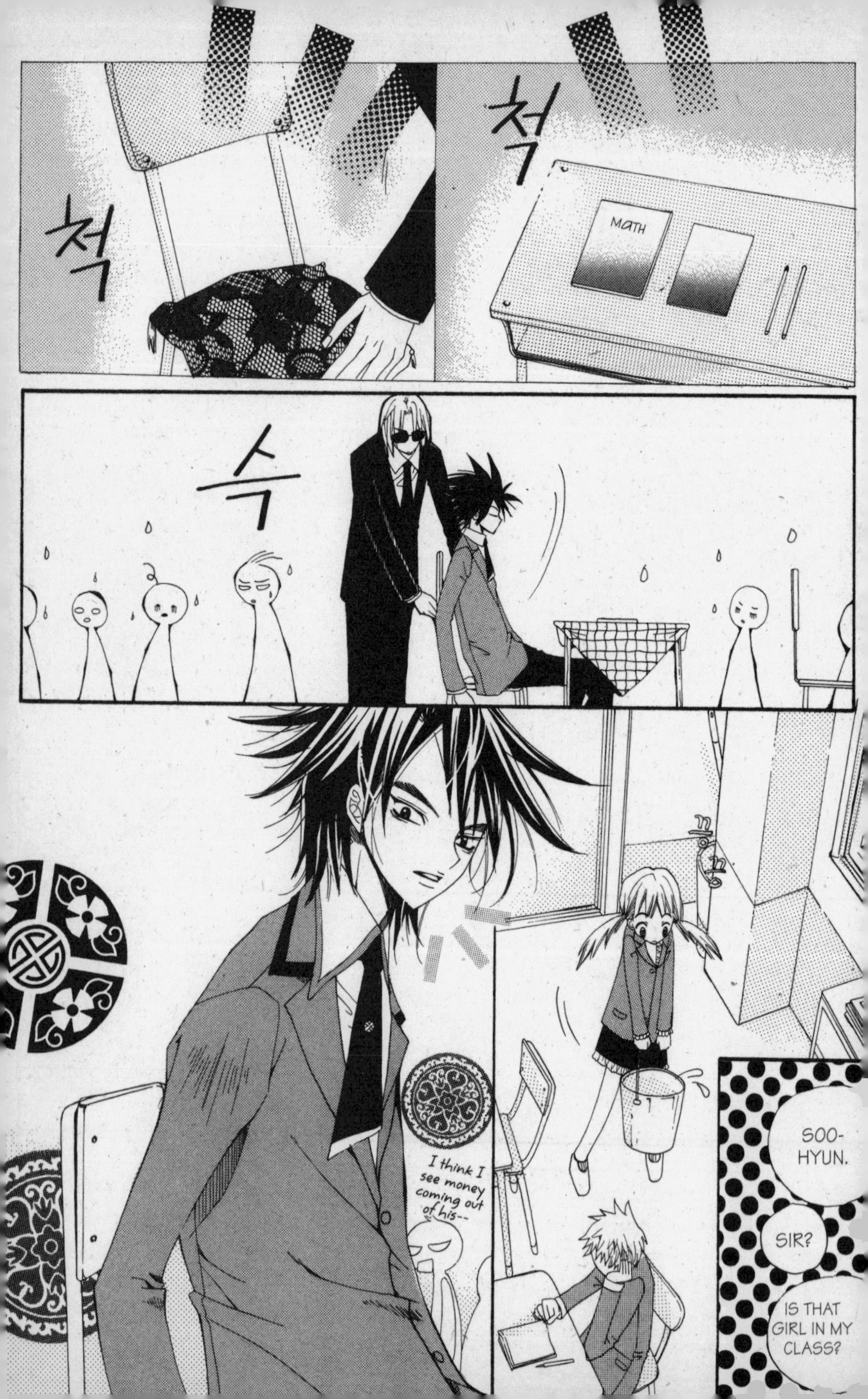
척
척
MATH
슥
I think I see money coming out of his--
SOO-HYUN.
SIR?
IS THAT GIRL IN MY CLASS?

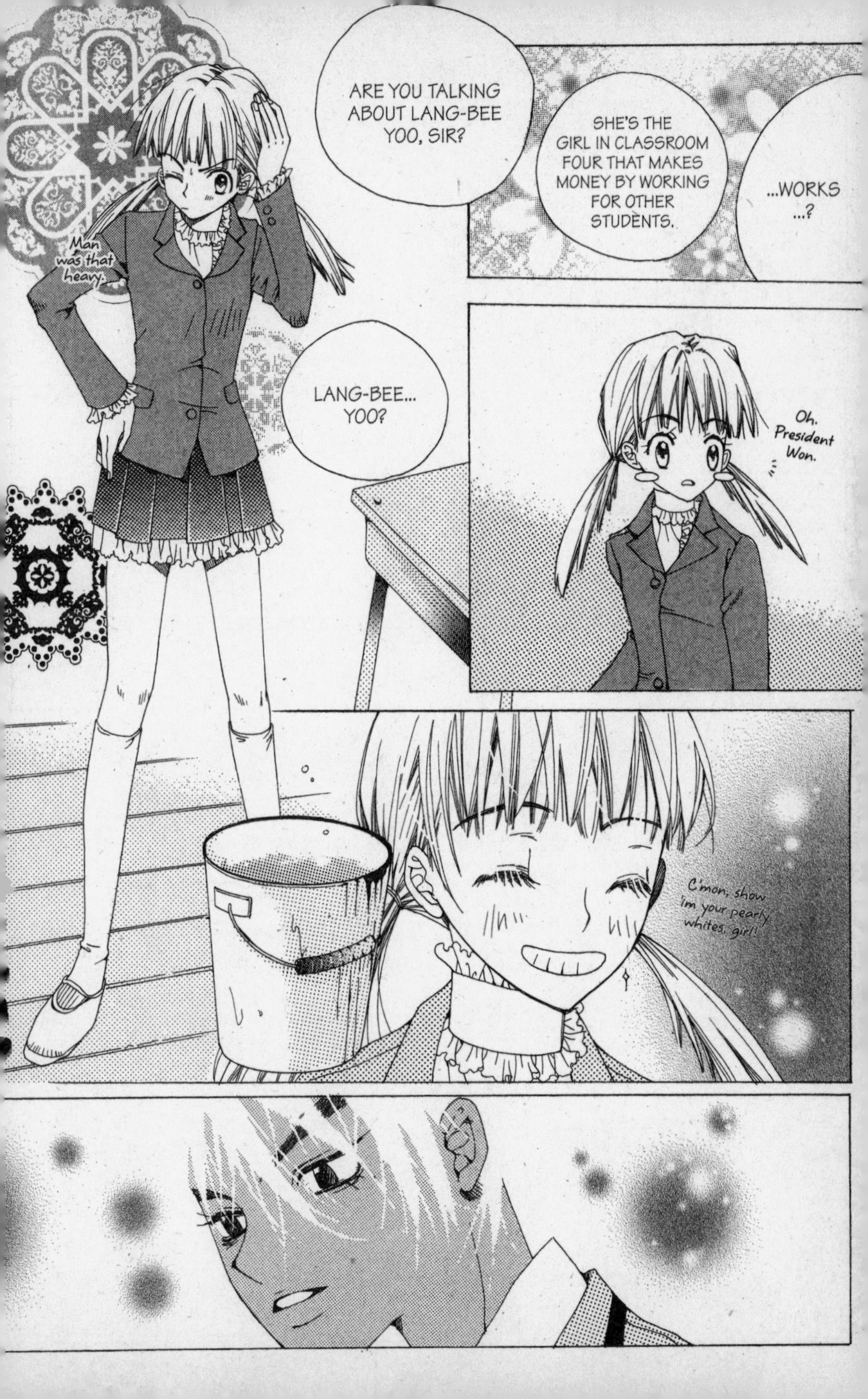
Man was that heavy.
ARE YOU TALKING ABOUT LANG-BEE YOO, SIR?
SHE'S THE GIRL IN CLASSROOM FOUR THAT MAKES MONEY BY WORKING FOR OTHER STUDENTS.
...WORKS ...?
LANG-BEE... YOO?
Oh. President Won.
C'mon, show 'im your pearly whites, girl!

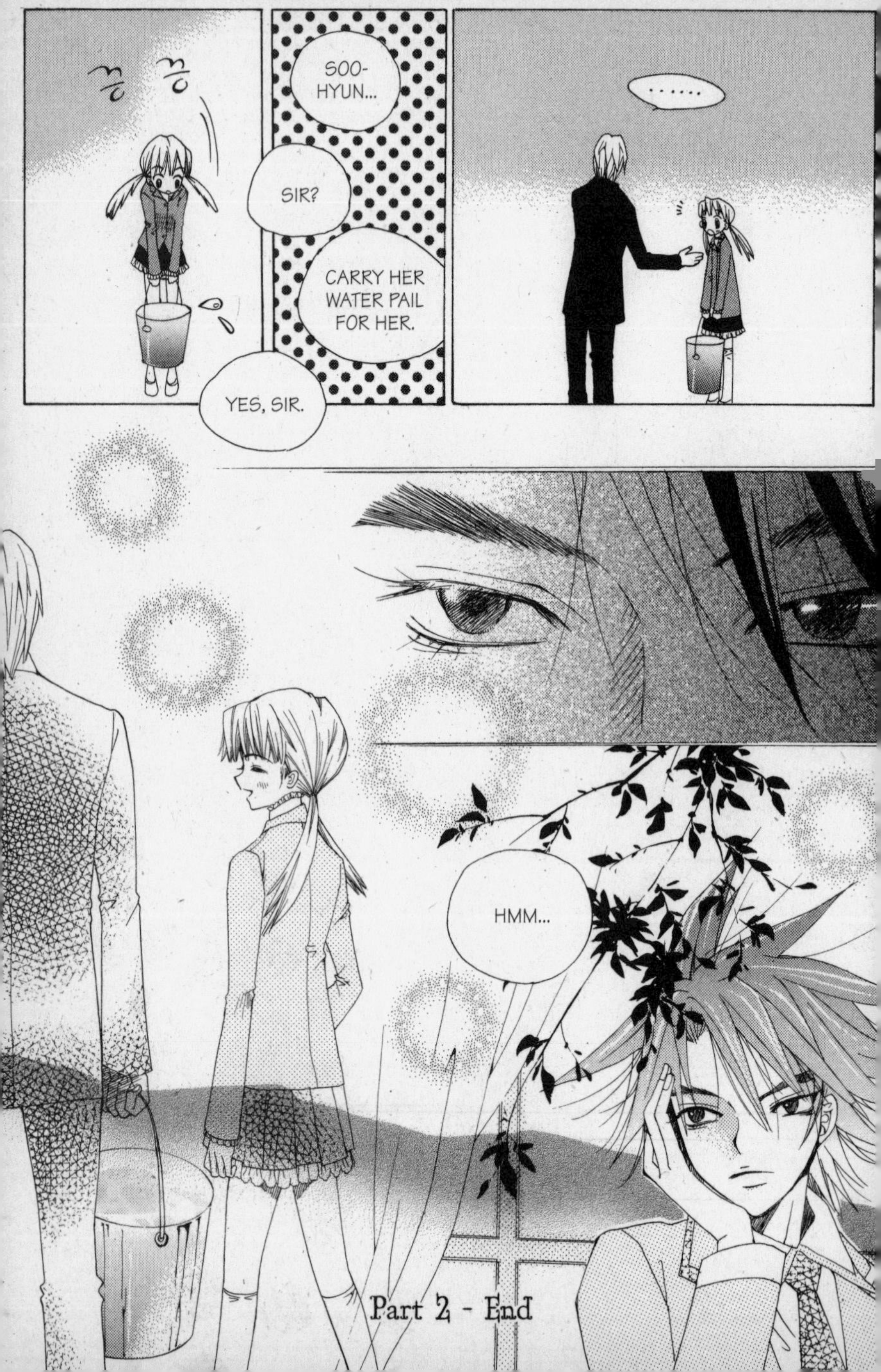
SOO-HYUN...
SIR?
CARRY HER WATER PAIL FOR HER.
YES, SIR.
......
HMM...
Part 2 - End

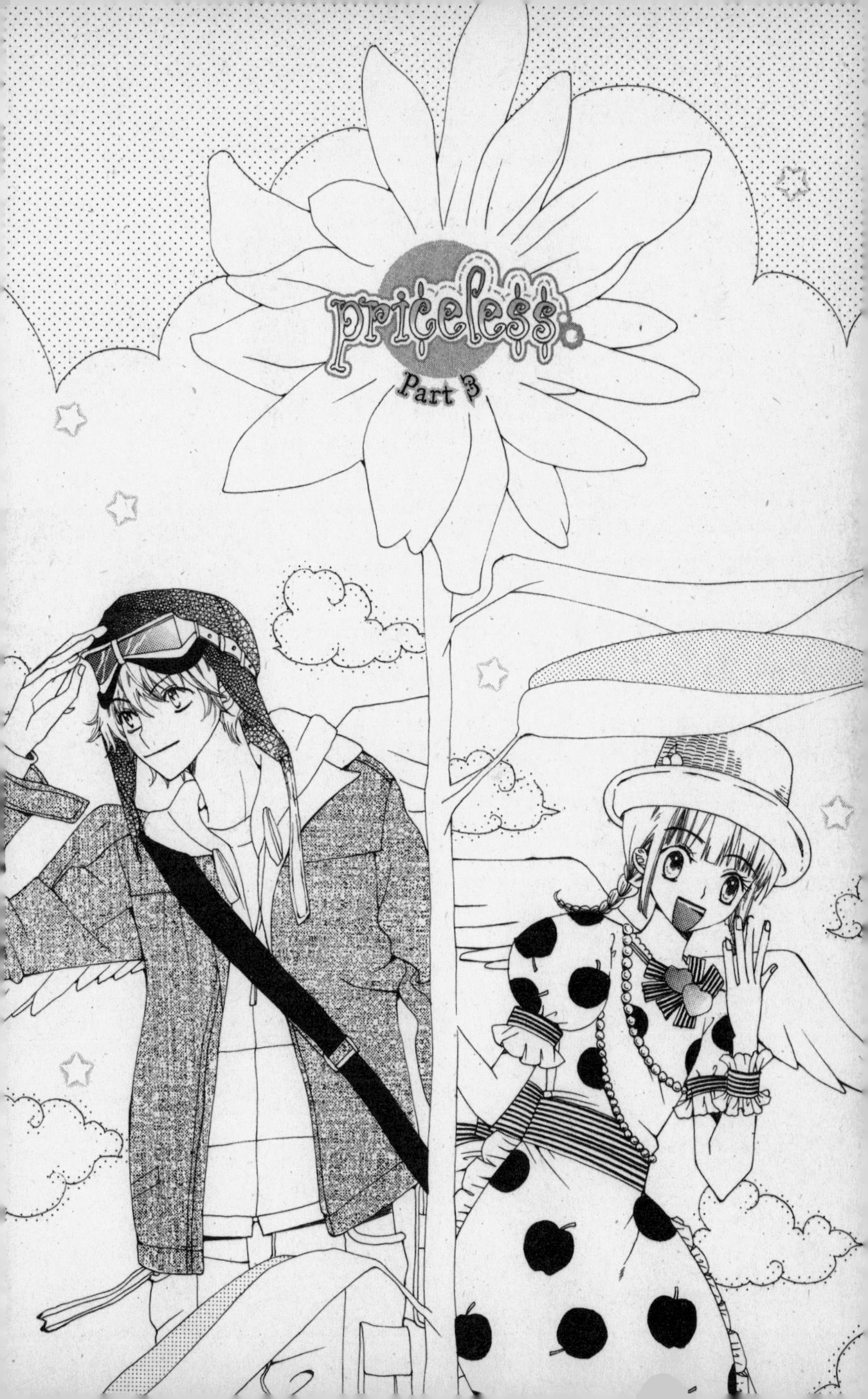
priceless.
Part 3

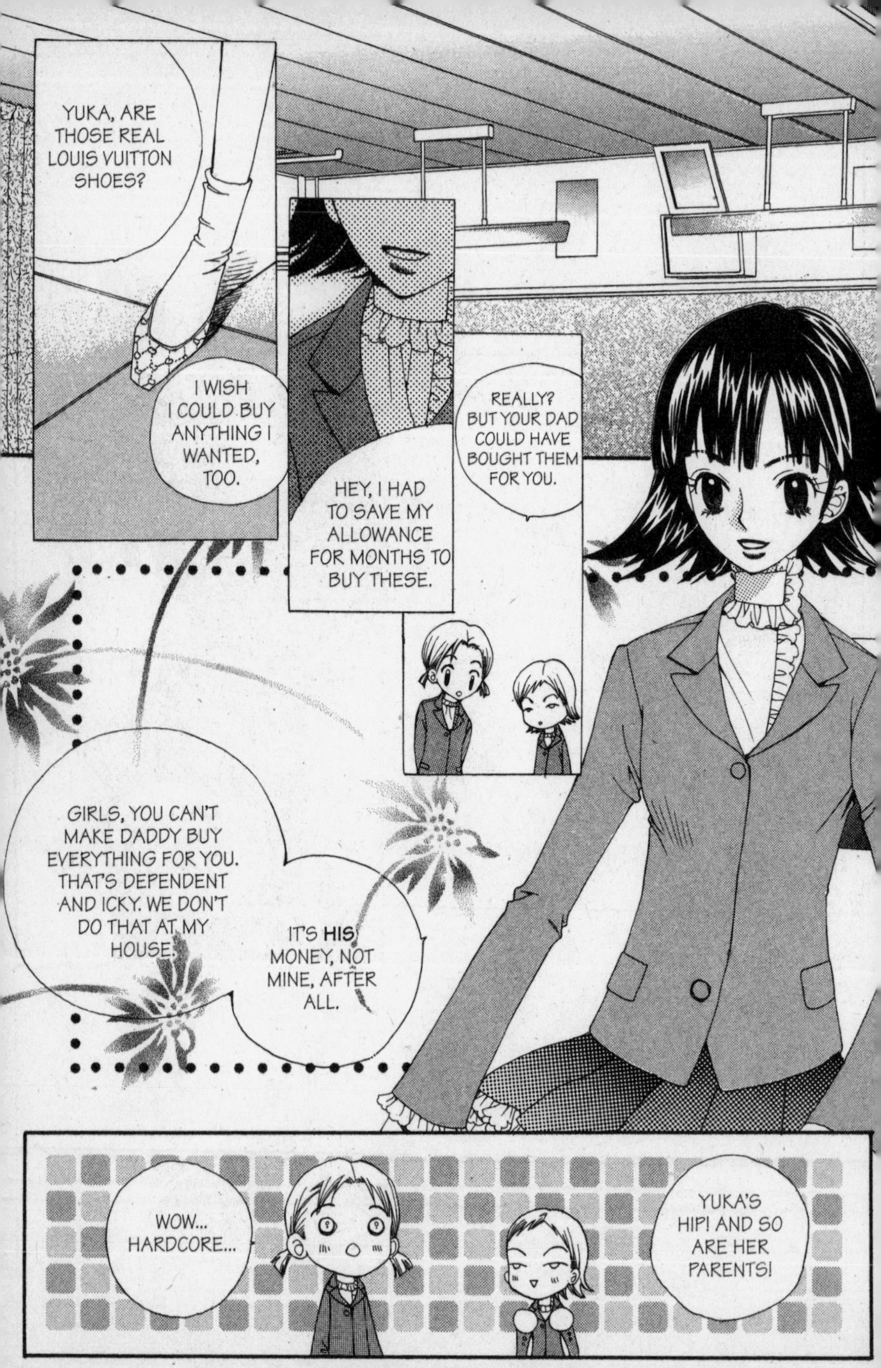

YUKA, ARE THOSE REAL LOUIS VUITTON SHOES?
I WISH I COULD BUY ANYTHING I WANTED, TOO.
HEY, I HAD TO SAVE MY ALLOWANCE FOR MONTHS TO BUY THESE.
REALLY? BUT YOUR DAD COULD HAVE BOUGHT THEM FOR YOU.
GIRLS, YOU CAN'T MAKE DADDY BUY EVERYTHING FOR YOU. THAT'S DEPENDENT AND ICKY. WE DON'T DO THAT AT MY HOUSE.
IT'S **HIS** MONEY, NOT MINE, AFTER ALL.
WOW... HARDCORE...
YUKA'S HIP! AND SO ARE HER PARENTS!

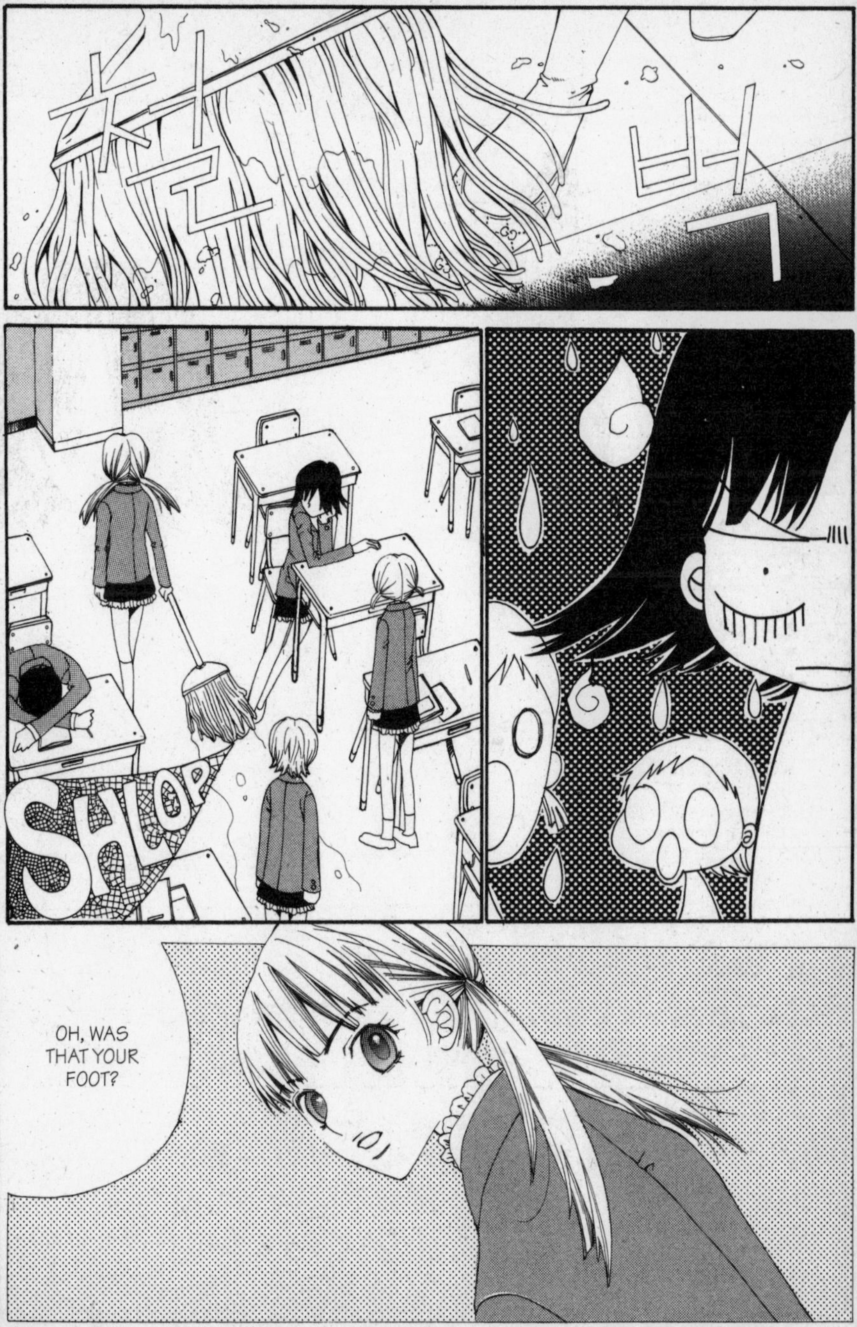
SHLOP
OH, WAS THAT YOUR FOOT?

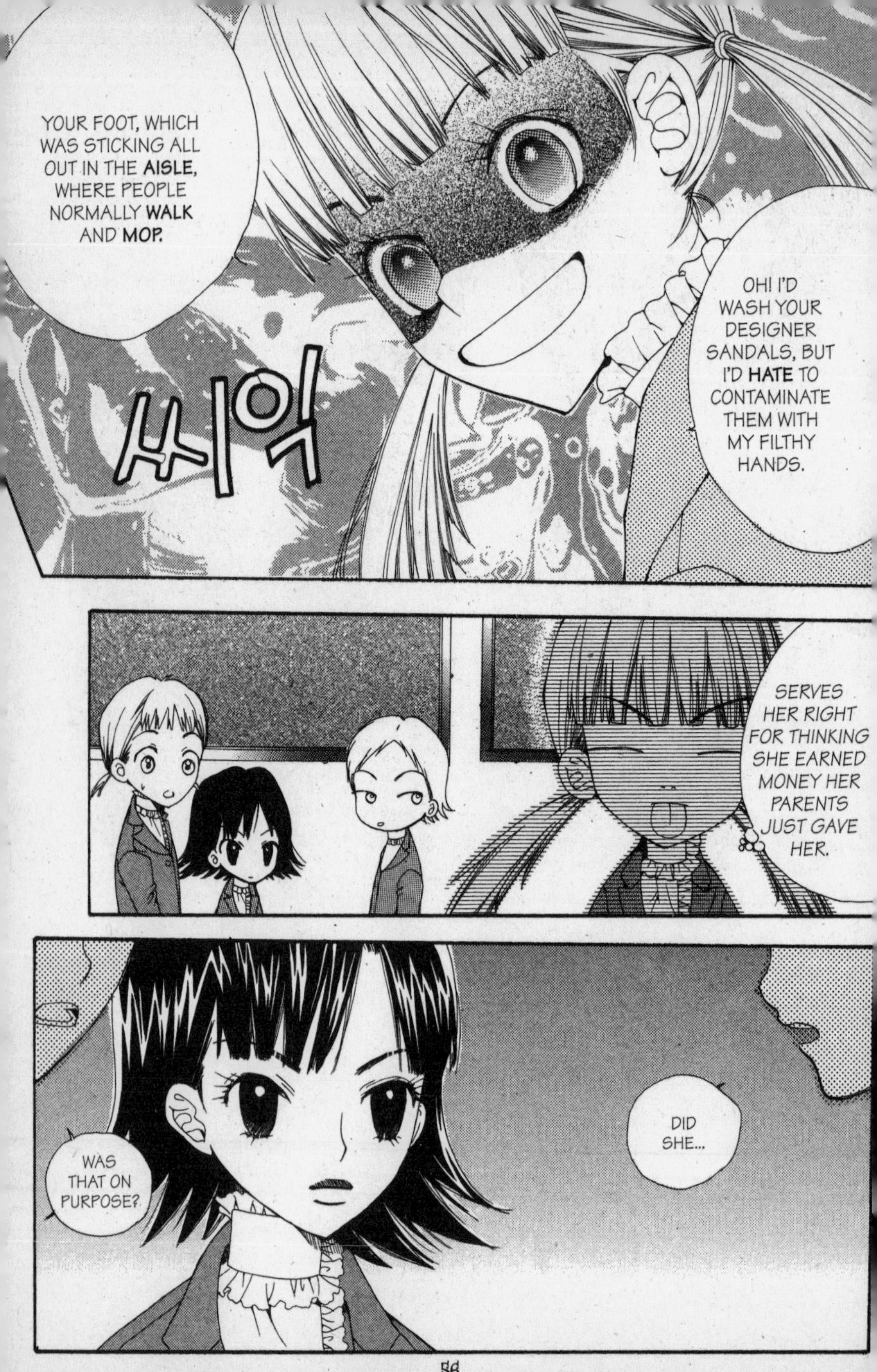
YOUR FOOT, WHICH WAS STICKING ALL OUT IN THE AISLE, WHERE PEOPLE NORMALLY WALK AND MOP.
쓰윽
OH! I'D WASH YOUR DESIGNER SANDALS, BUT I'D HATE TO CONTAMINATE THEM WITH MY FILTHY HANDS.
SERVES HER RIGHT FOR THINKING SHE EARNED MONEY HER PARENTS JUST GAVE HER.
WAS THAT ON PURPOSE?
DID SHE...

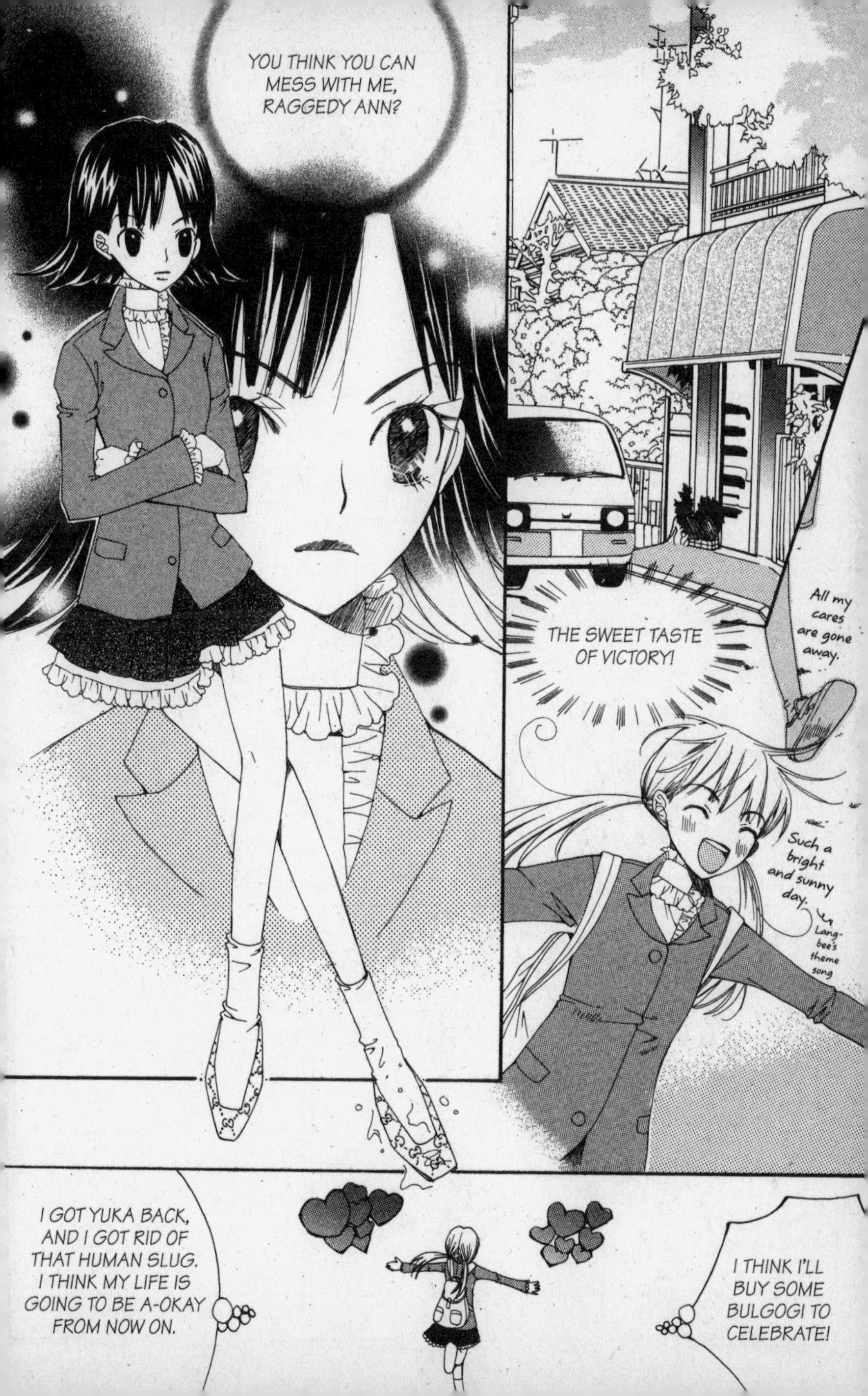
YOU THINK YOU CAN MESS WITH ME, RAGGEDY ANN?
THE SWEET TASTE OF VICTORY!
All my cares are gone away.
Such a bright and sunny day.
Lang-bee's theme song
I GOT YUKA BACK, AND I GOT RID OF THAT HUMAN SLUG. I THINK MY LIFE IS GOING TO BE A-OKAY FROM NOW ON.
I THINK I'LL BUY SOME BULGOGI TO CELEBRATE!

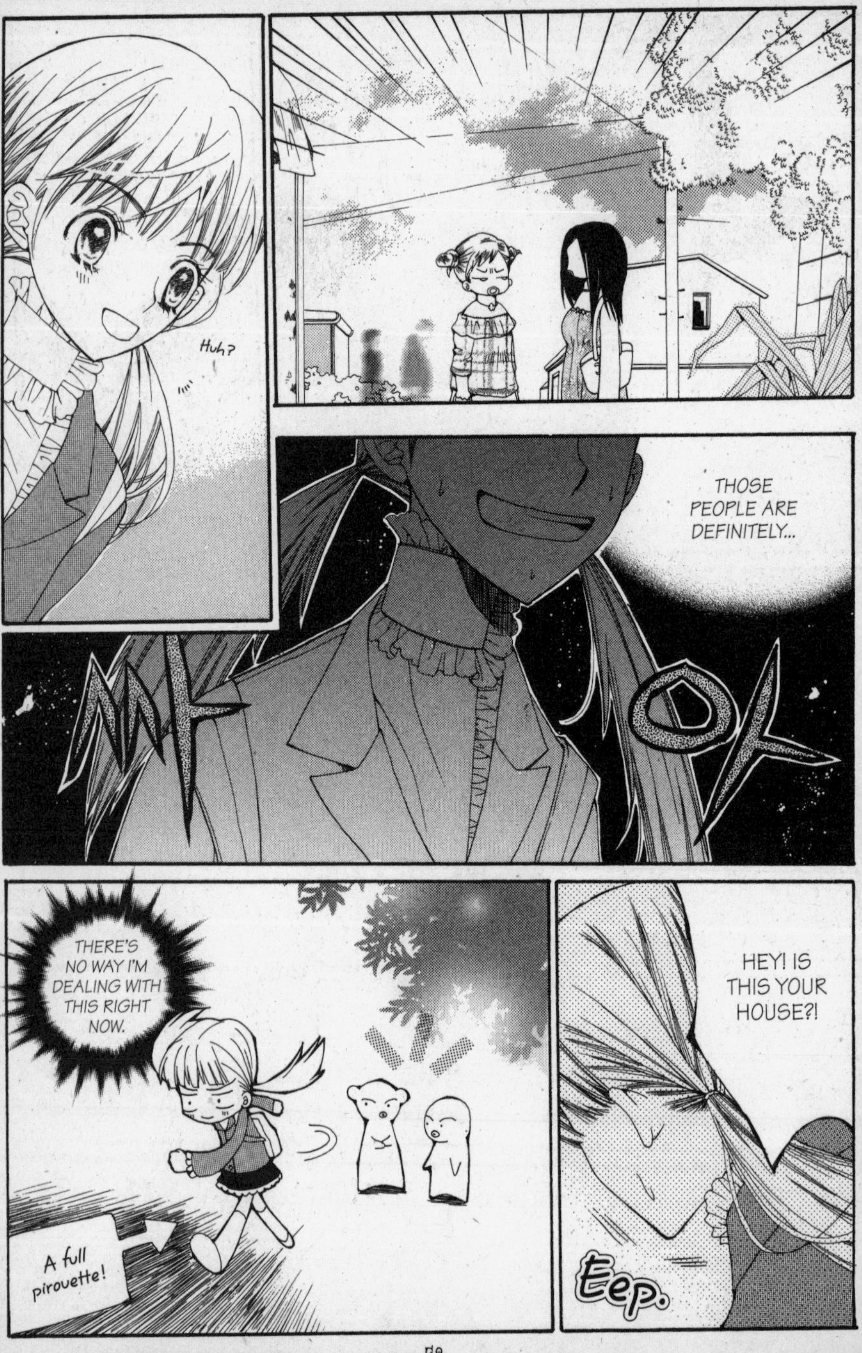
Huh?
THOSE PEOPLE ARE DEFINITELY...
THERE'S NO WAY I'M DEALING WITH THIS RIGHT NOW.
A full pirouette!
HEY! IS THIS YOUR HOUSE?!
Eep.

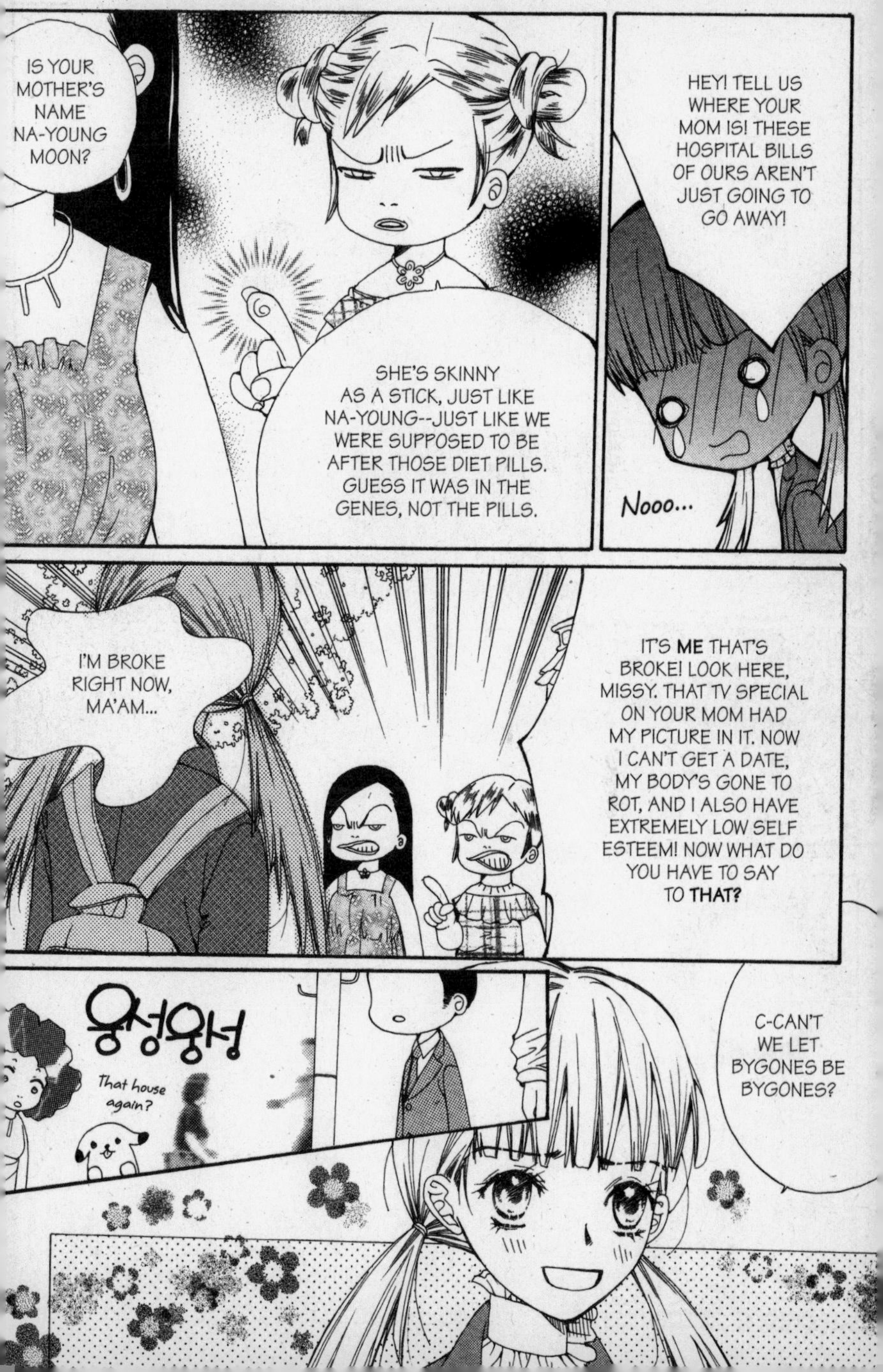
IS YOUR MOTHER'S NAME NA-YOUNG MOON?
SHE'S SKINNY AS A STICK, JUST LIKE NA-YOUNG--JUST LIKE WE WERE SUPPOSED TO BE AFTER THOSE DIET PILLS. GUESS IT WAS IN THE GENES, NOT THE PILLS.
HEY! TELL US WHERE YOUR MOM IS! THESE HOSPITAL BILLS OF OURS AREN'T JUST GOING TO GO AWAY!
Nooo...
I'M BROKE RIGHT NOW, MA'AM...
IT'S ME THAT'S BROKE! LOOK HERE, MISSY. THAT TV SPECIAL ON YOUR MOM HAD MY PICTURE IN IT. NOW I CAN'T GET A DATE, MY BODY'S GONE TO ROT, AND I ALSO HAVE EXTREMELY LOW SELF ESTEEM! NOW WHAT DO YOU HAVE TO SAY TO THAT?
웅성웅성
That house again?
C-CAN'T WE LET BYGONES BE BYGONES?

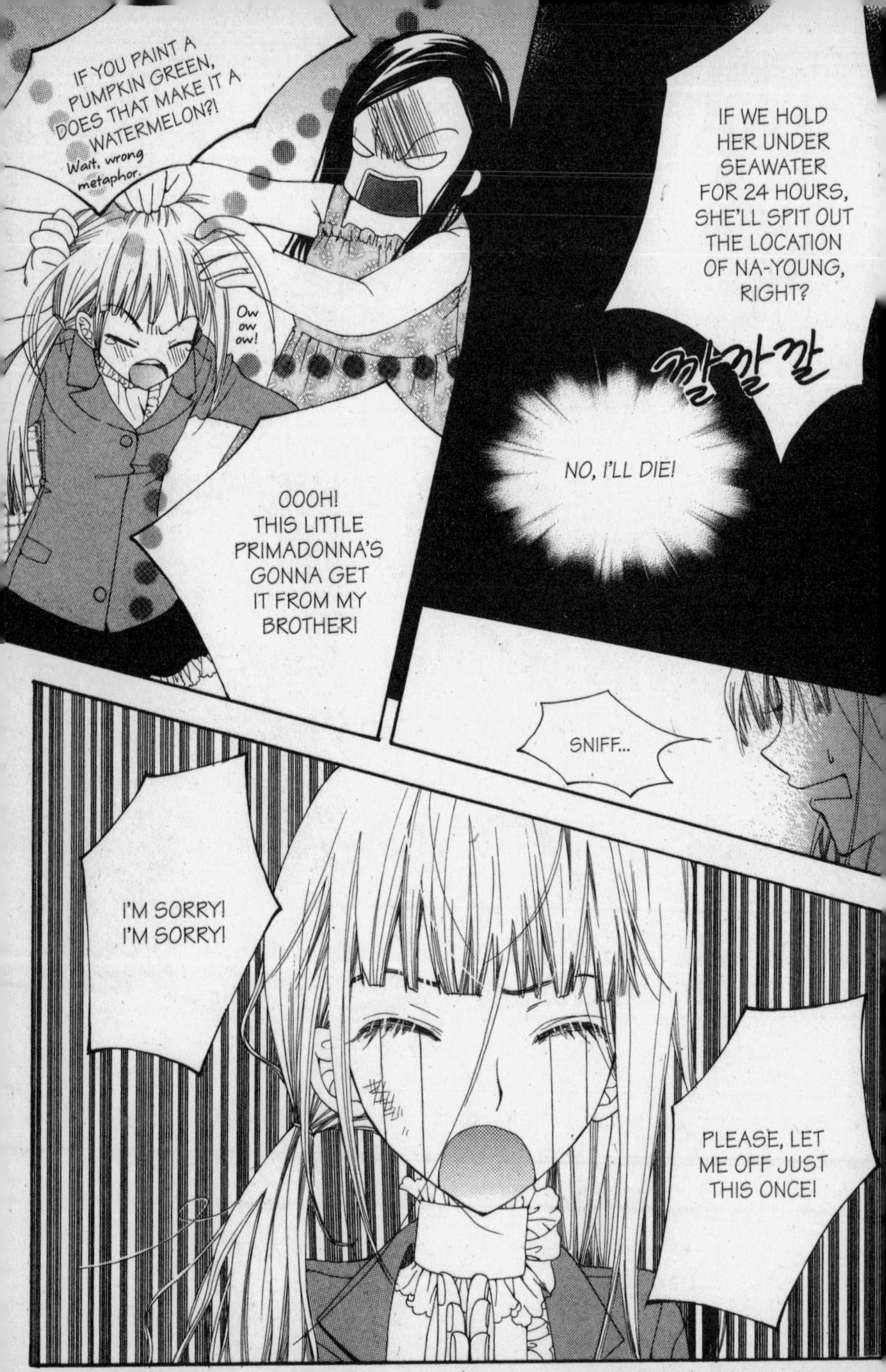
IF YOU PAINT A PUMPKIN GREEN, DOES THAT MAKE IT A WATERMELON?!
Wait, wrong metaphor.
Ow ow ow!
OOOH! THIS LITTLE PRIMADONNA'S GONNA GET IT FROM MY BROTHER!
IF WE HOLD HER UNDER SEAWATER FOR 24 HOURS, SHE'LL SPIT OUT THE LOCATION OF NA-YOUNG, RIGHT?
깔깔깔
NO, I'LL DIE!
SNIFF...
I'M SORRY! I'M SORRY!
PLEASE, LET ME OFF JUST THIS ONCE!

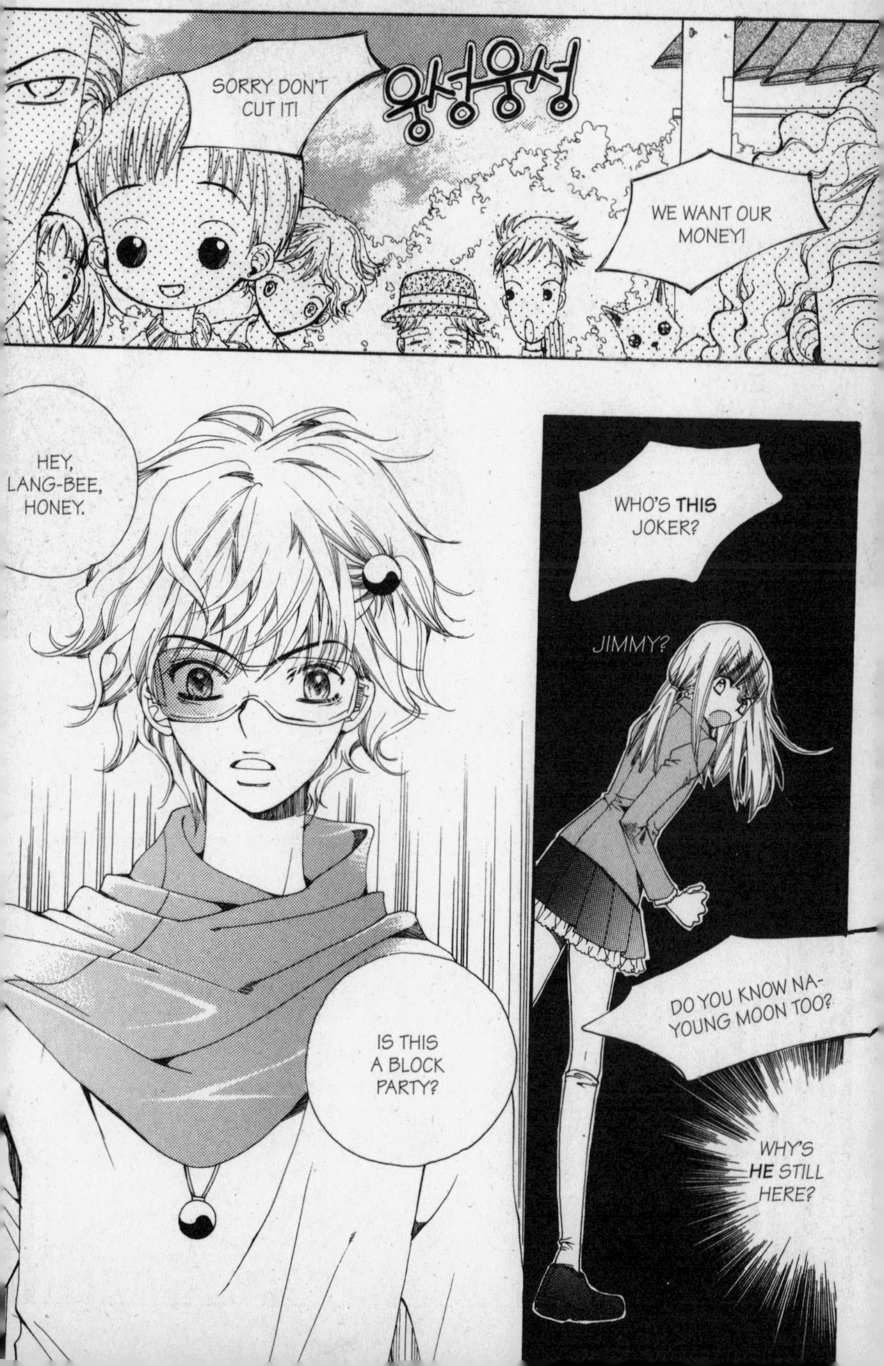
SORRY DON'T CUT IT!
웅성웅성
WE WANT OUR MONEY!
HEY, LANG-BEE, HONEY.
IS THIS A BLOCK PARTY?
WHO'S **THIS** JOKER?
JIMMY?
DO YOU KNOW NA-YOUNG MOON TOO?
WHY'S **HE** STILL HERE?

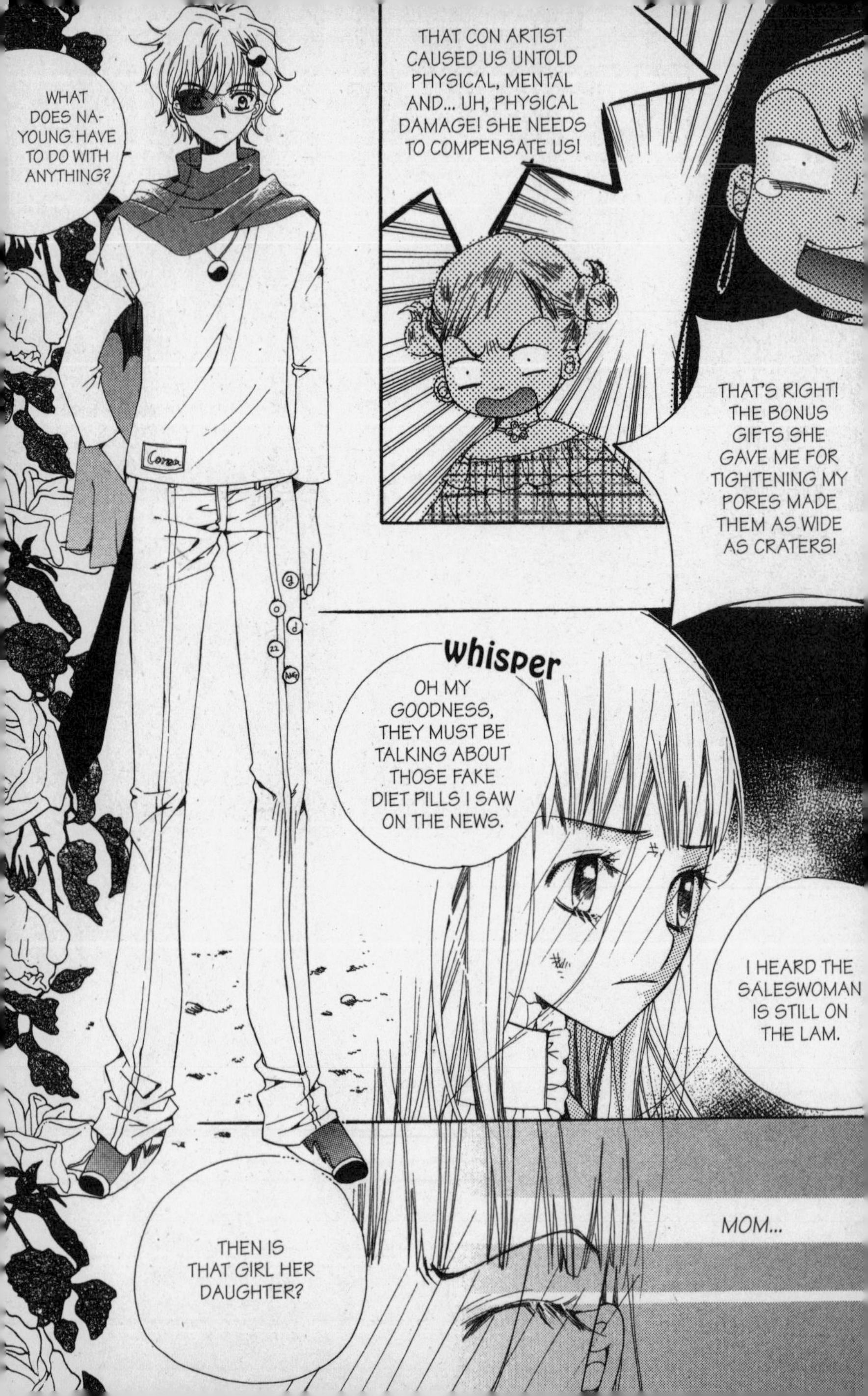
WHAT DOES NA-YOUNG HAVE TO DO WITH ANYTHING?
THEN IS THAT GIRL HER DAUGHTER?
THAT CON ARTIST CAUSED US UNTOLD PHYSICAL, MENTAL AND... UH, PHYSICAL DAMAGE! SHE NEEDS TO COMPENSATE US!
THAT'S RIGHT! THE BONUS GIFTS SHE GAVE ME FOR TIGHTENING MY PORES MADE THEM AS WIDE AS CRATERS!
whisper
OH MY GOODNESS, THEY MUST BE TALKING ABOUT THOSE FAKE DIET PILLS I SAW ON THE NEWS.
I HEARD THE SALESWOMAN IS STILL ON THE LAM.
MOM...

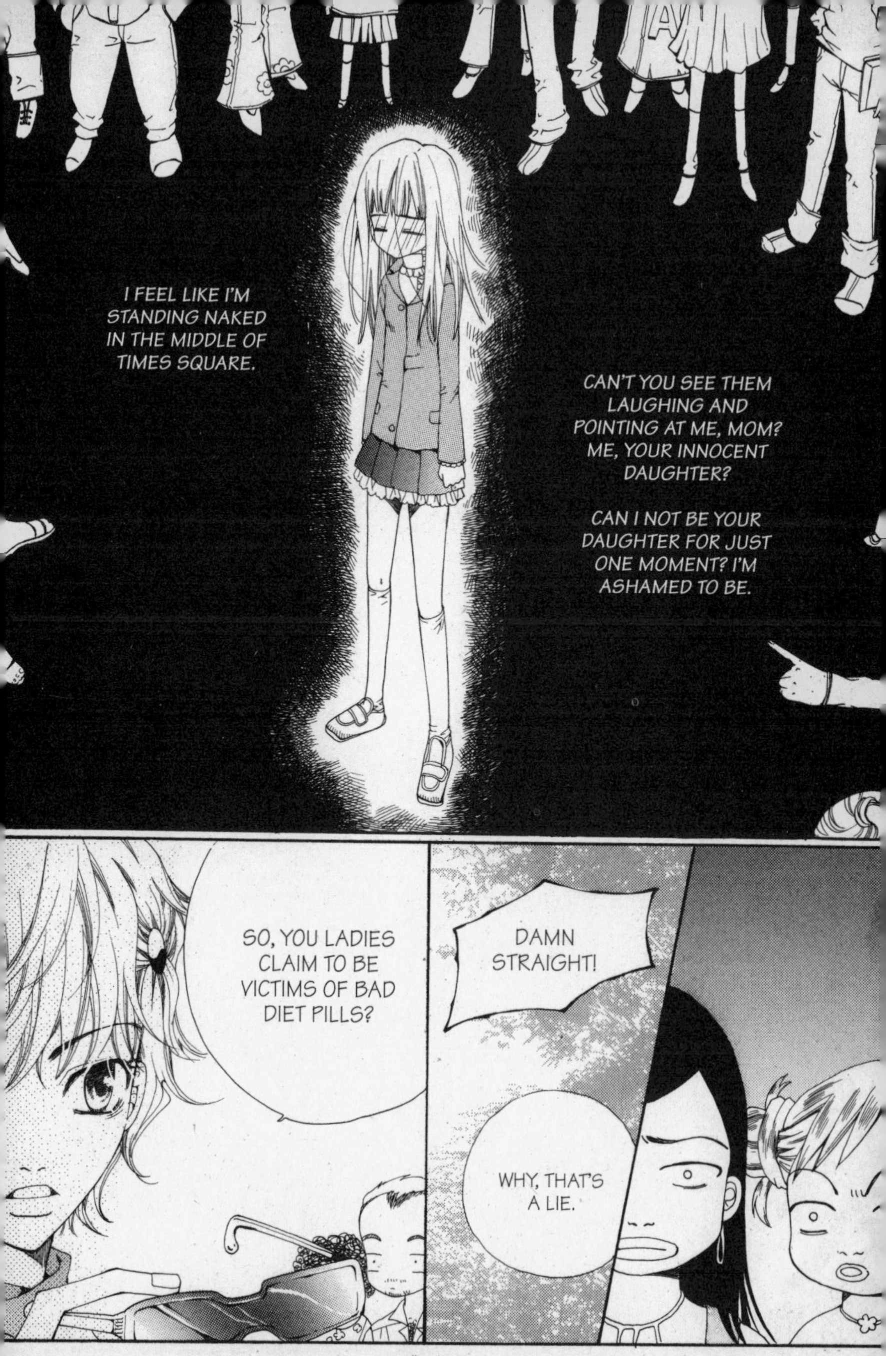
I FEEL LIKE I'M STANDING NAKED IN THE MIDDLE OF TIMES SQUARE.
CAN'T YOU SEE THEM LAUGHING AND POINTING AT ME, MOM? ME, YOUR INNOCENT DAUGHTER?
CAN I NOT BE YOUR DAUGHTER FOR JUST ONE MOMENT? I'M ASHAMED TO BE.
SO, YOU LADIES CLAIM TO BE VICTIMS OF BAD DIET PILLS?
DAMN STRAIGHT!
WHY, THAT'S A LIE.

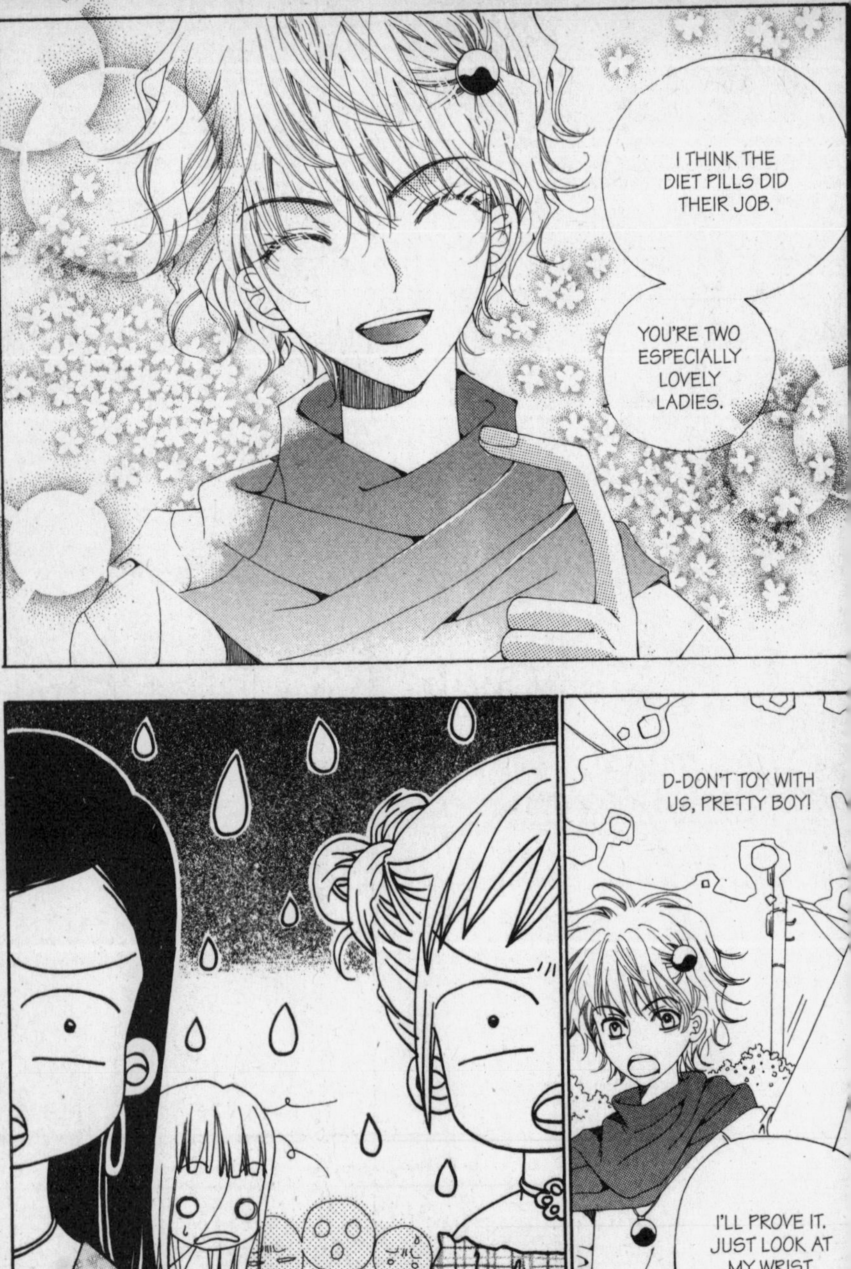
I THINK THE DIET PILLS DID THEIR JOB.
YOU'RE TWO ESPECIALLY LOVELY LADIES.
D-DON'T TOY WITH US, PRETTY BOY!
I'LL PROVE IT. JUST LOOK AT MY WRIST.

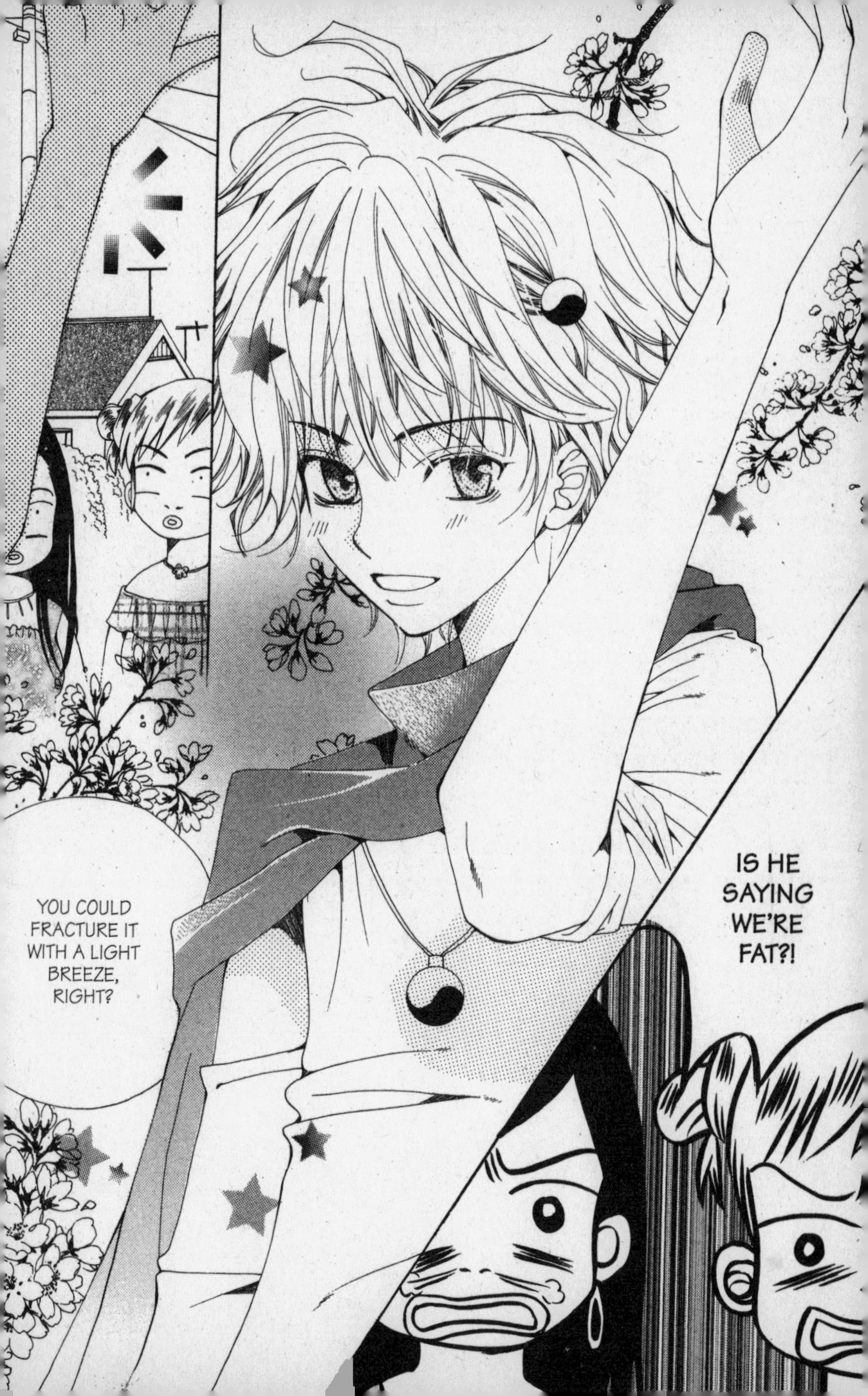
YOU COULD FRACTURE IT WITH A LIGHT BREEZE, RIGHT?
IS HE SAYING WE'RE FAT?!

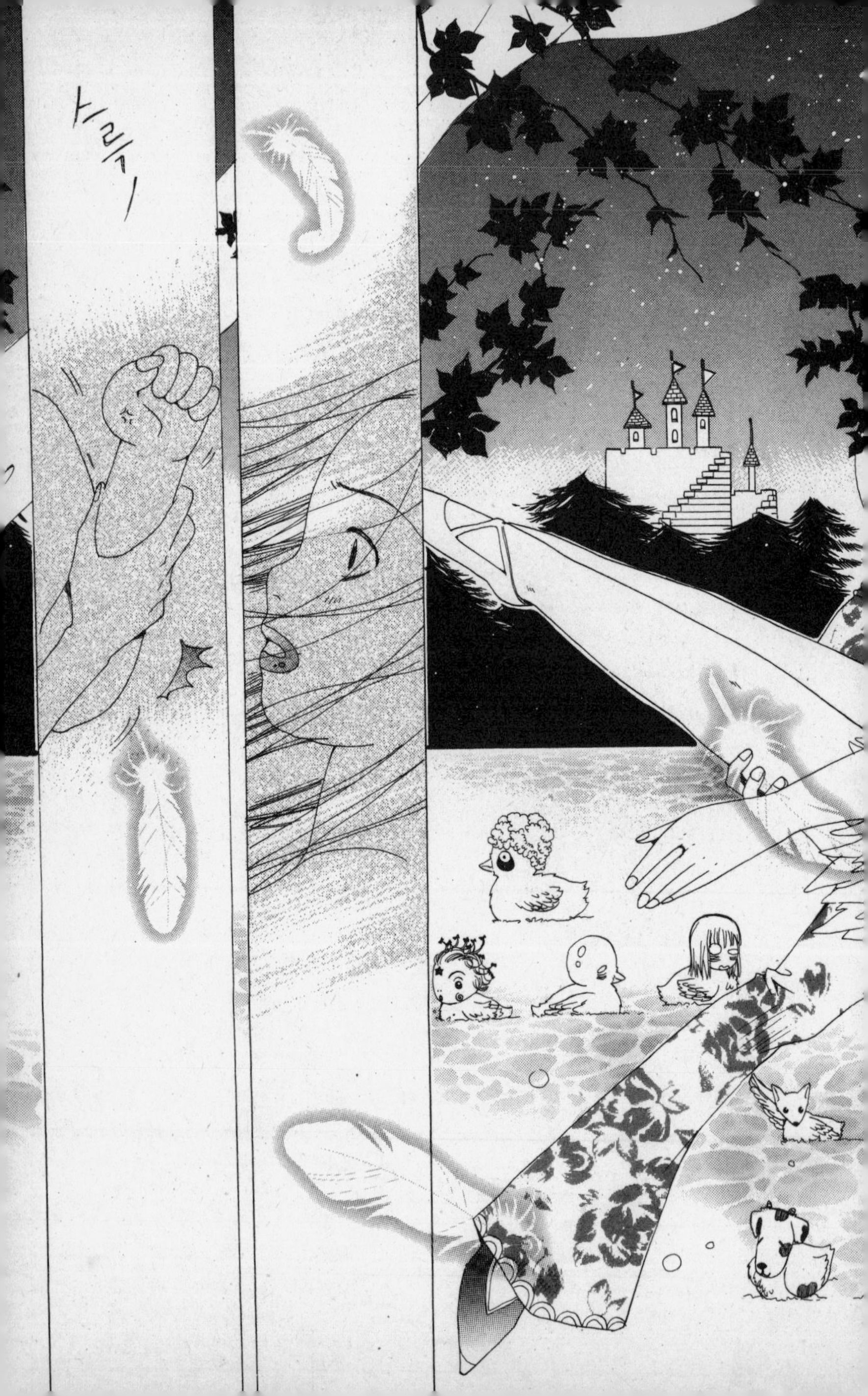
스르륵

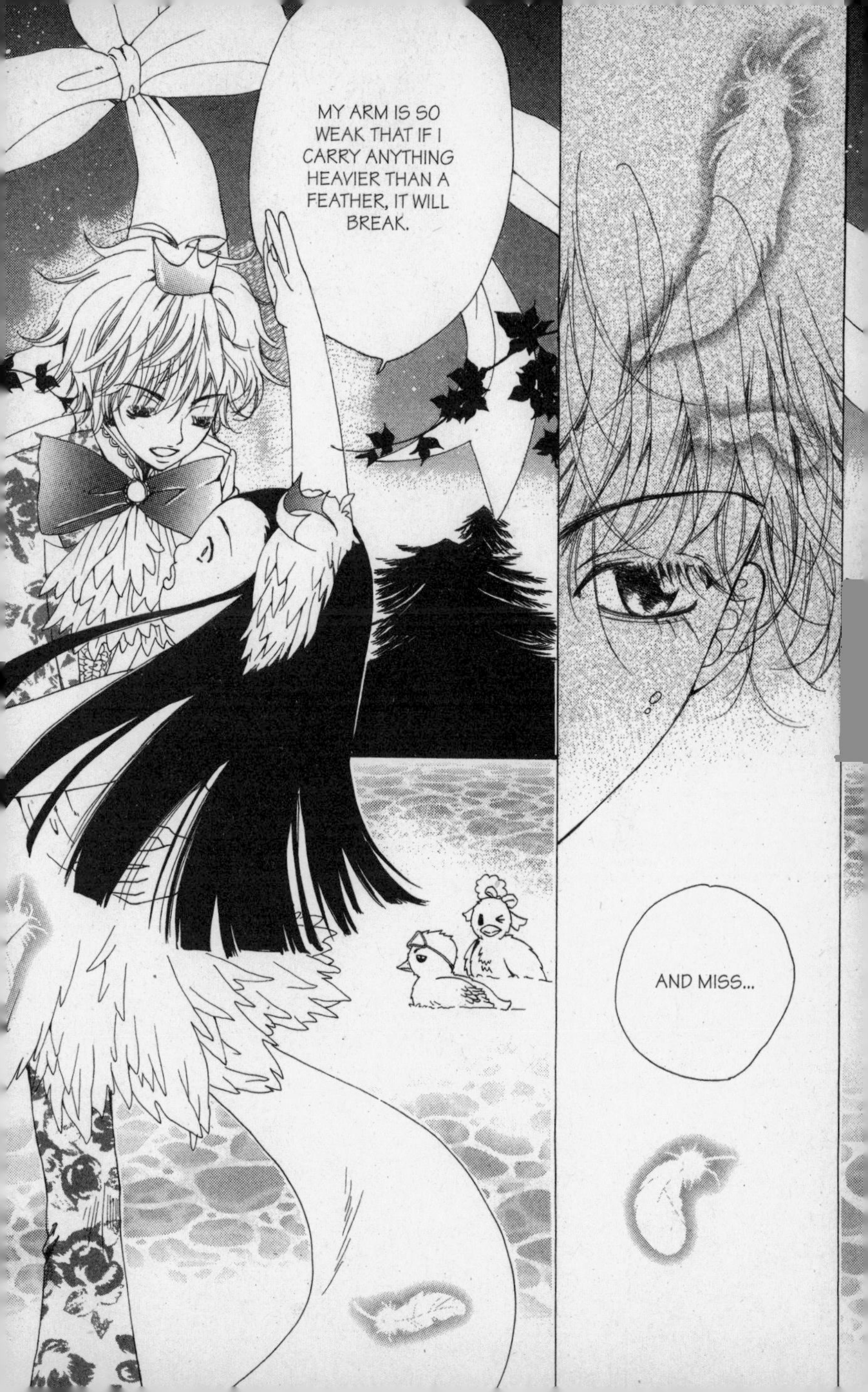
MY ARM IS SO WEAK THAT IF I CARRY ANYTHING HEAVIER THAN A FEATHER, IT WILL BREAK.
AND MISS...

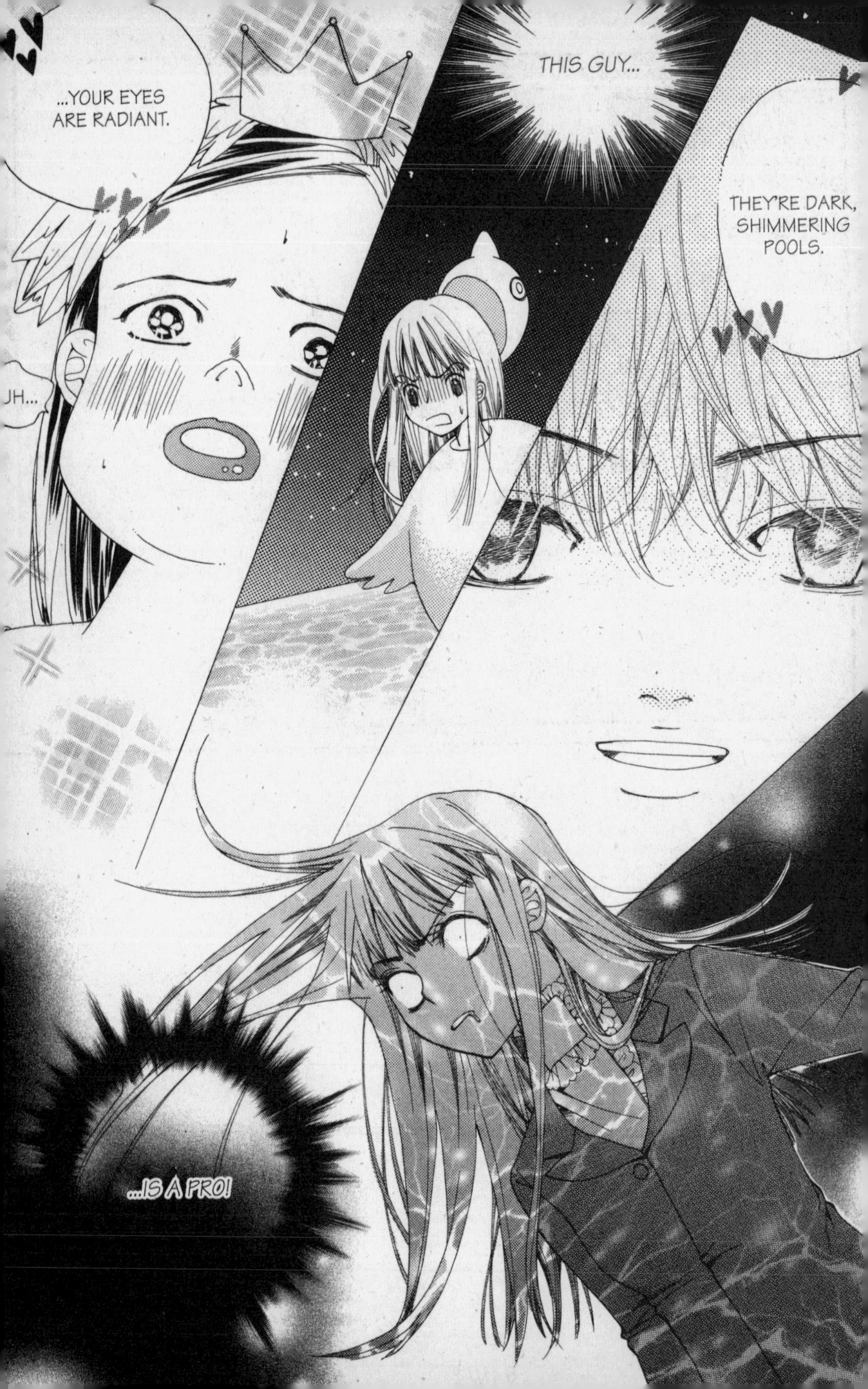

...YOUR EYES ARE RADIANT.
UH...
THIS GUY...
THEY'RE DARK, SHIMMERING POOLS.
...IS A PRO!

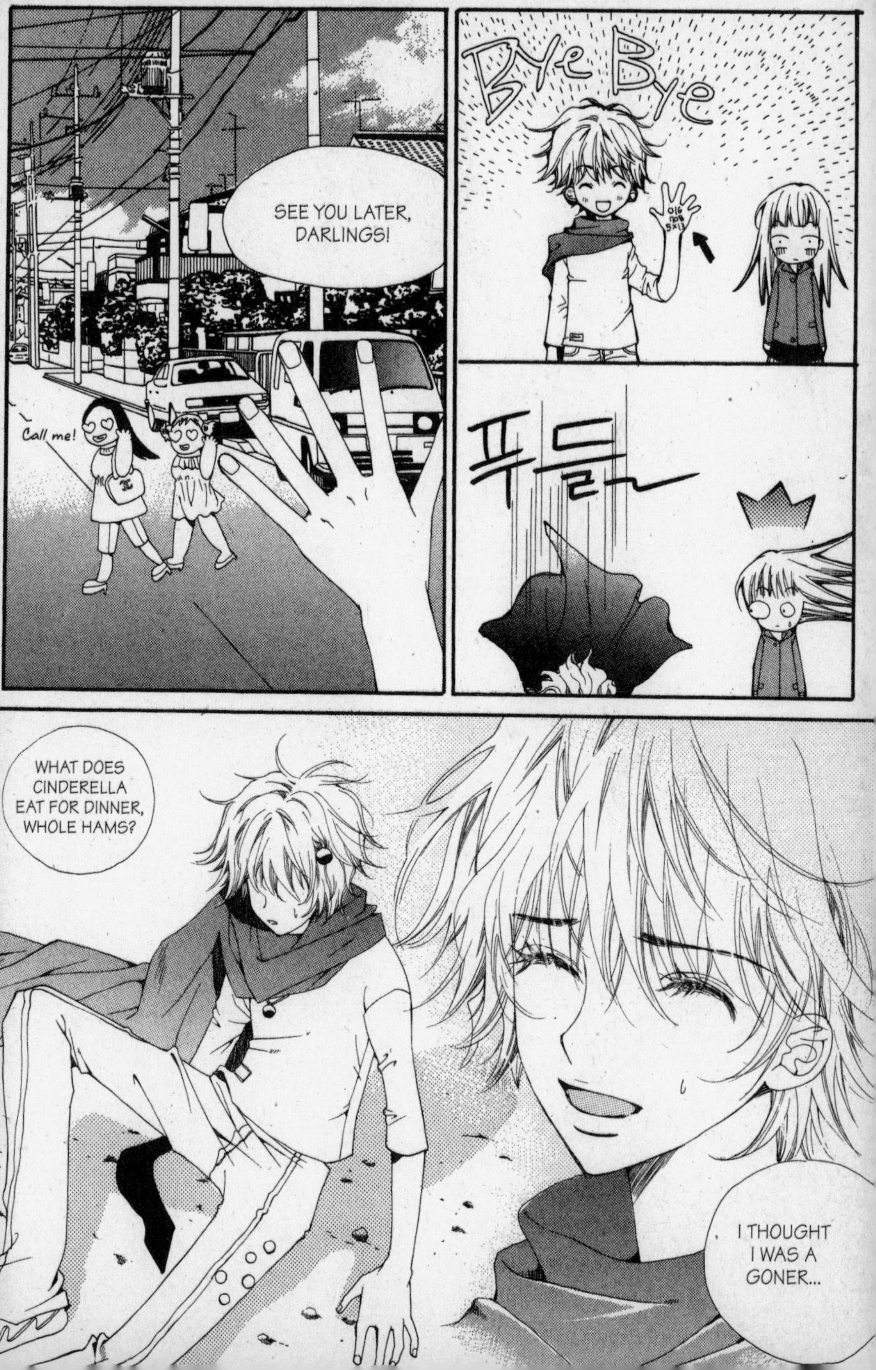
SEE YOU LATER, DARLINGS!
Call me!
Bye Bye
푸들~
WHAT DOES CINDERELLA EAT FOR DINNER, WHOLE HAMS?
I THOUGHT I WAS A GONER...

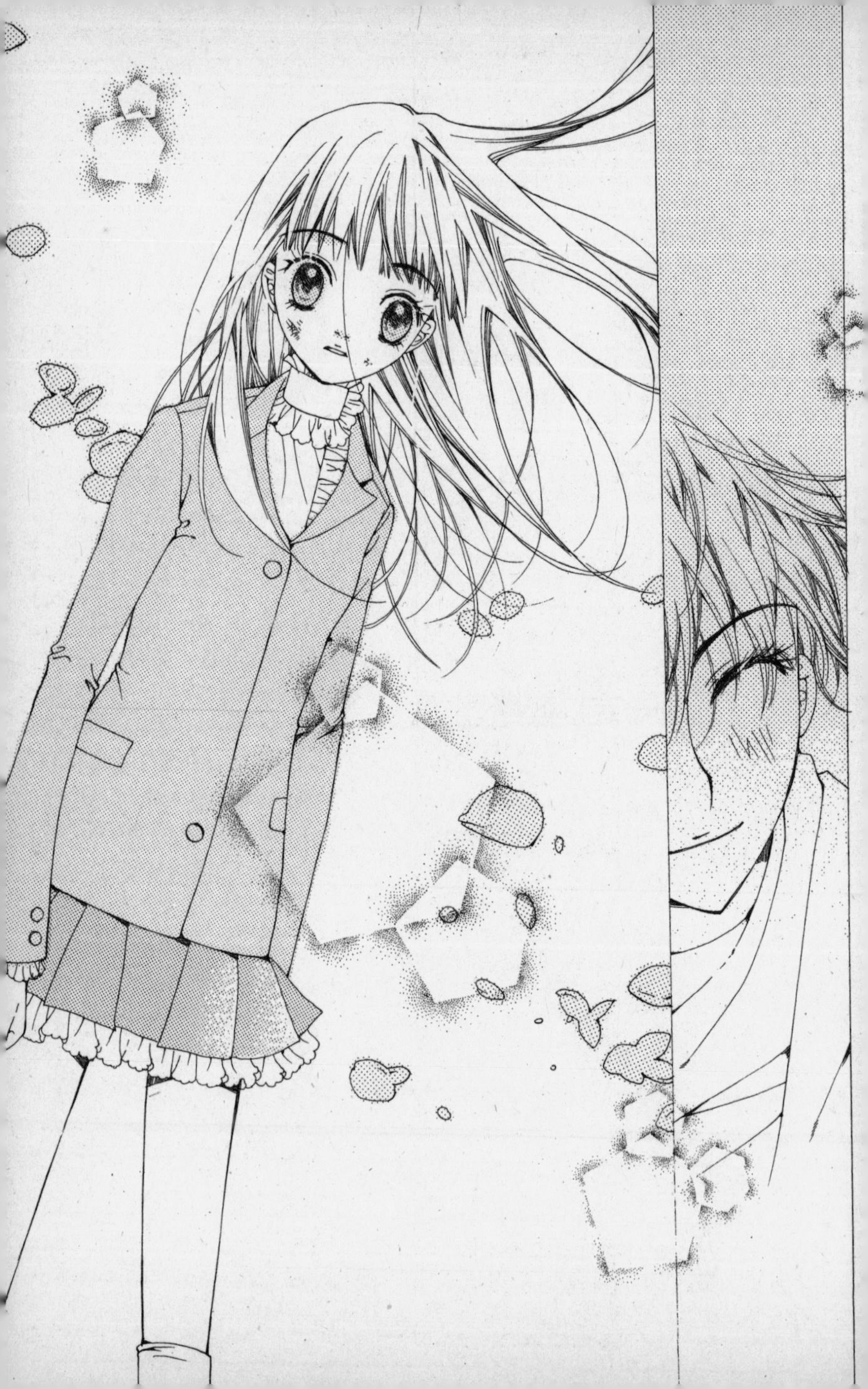

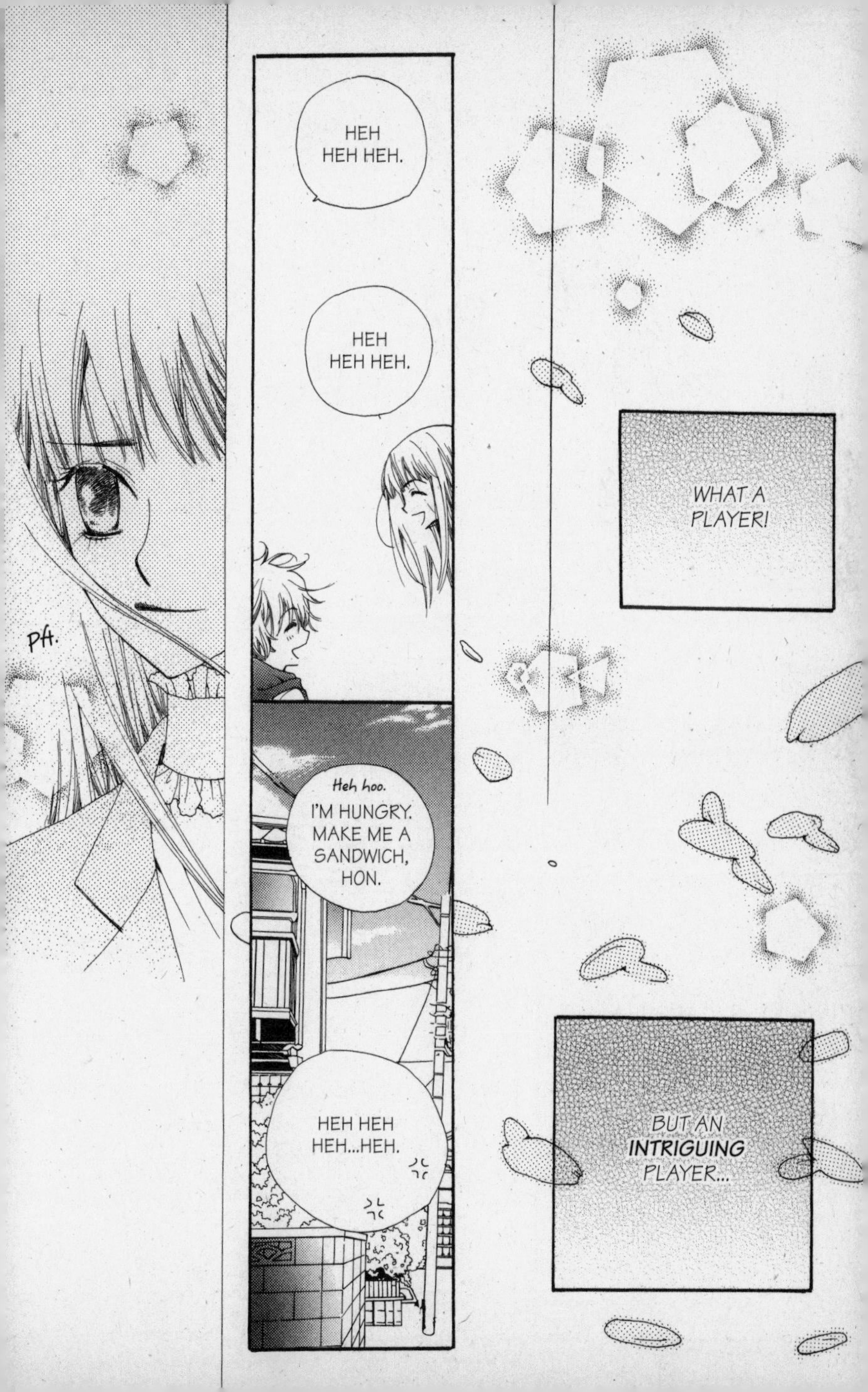
Pft.
HEH HEH HEH.
HEH HEH HEH.
Heh hoo.
I'M HUNGRY. MAKE ME A SANDWICH, HON.
HEH HEH HEH...HEH.
WHAT A PLAYER!
BUT AN **INTRIGUING** PLAYER...

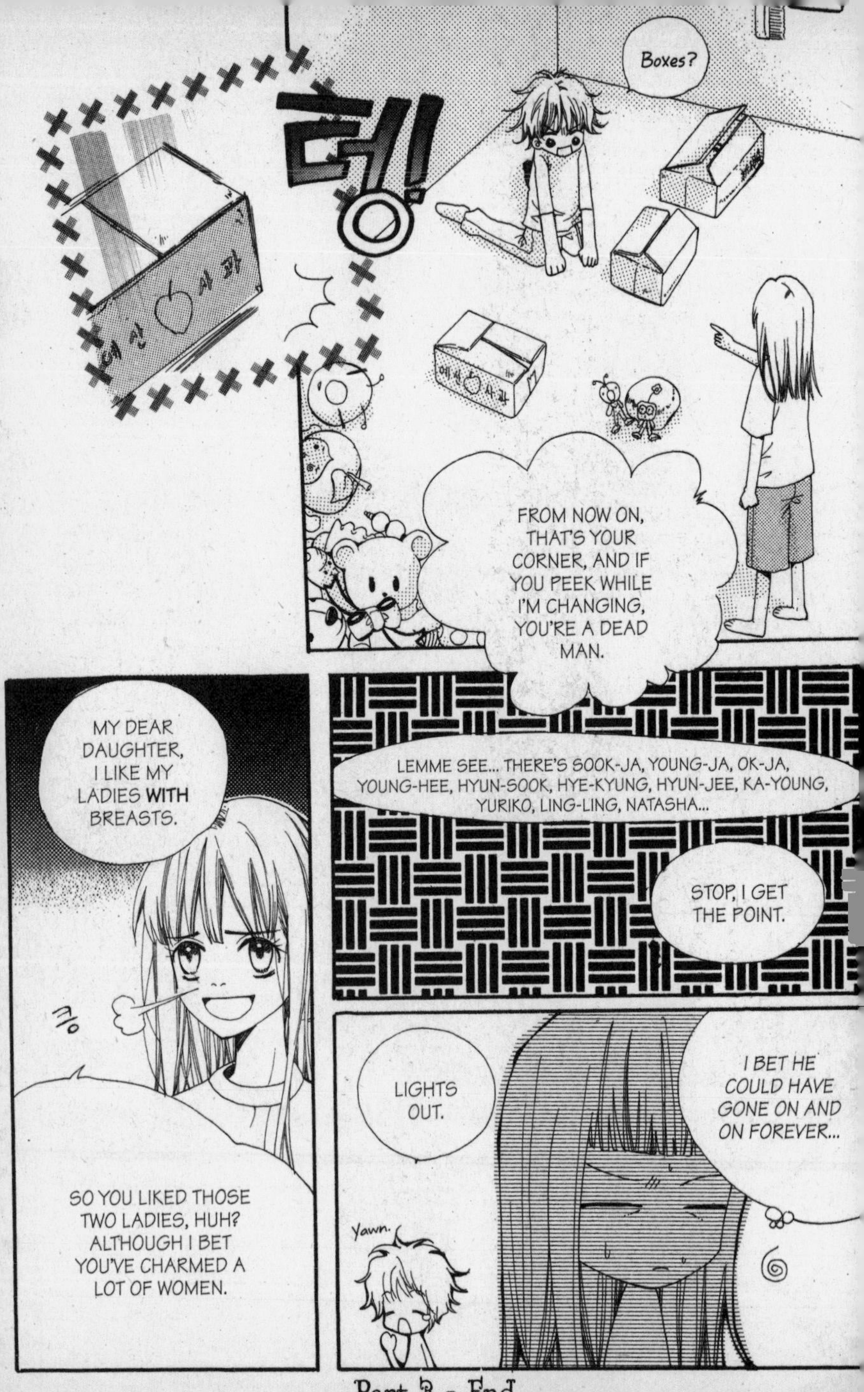
Boxes?
FROM NOW ON, THAT'S YOUR CORNER, AND IF YOU PEEK WHILE I'M CHANGING, YOU'RE A DEAD MAN.
MY DEAR DAUGHTER, I LIKE MY LADIES **WITH** BREASTS.
SO YOU LIKED THOSE TWO LADIES, HUH? ALTHOUGH I BET YOU'VE CHARMED A LOT OF WOMEN.
LEMME SEE... THERE'S SOOK-JA, YOUNG-JA, OK-JA, YOUNG-HEE, HYUN-SOOK, HYE-KYUNG, HYUN-JEE, KA-YOUNG, YURIKO, LING-LING, NATASHA...
STOP, I GET THE POINT.
LIGHTS OUT.
I BET HE COULD HAVE GONE ON AND ON FOREVER...
Yawn.

Part 3 - End

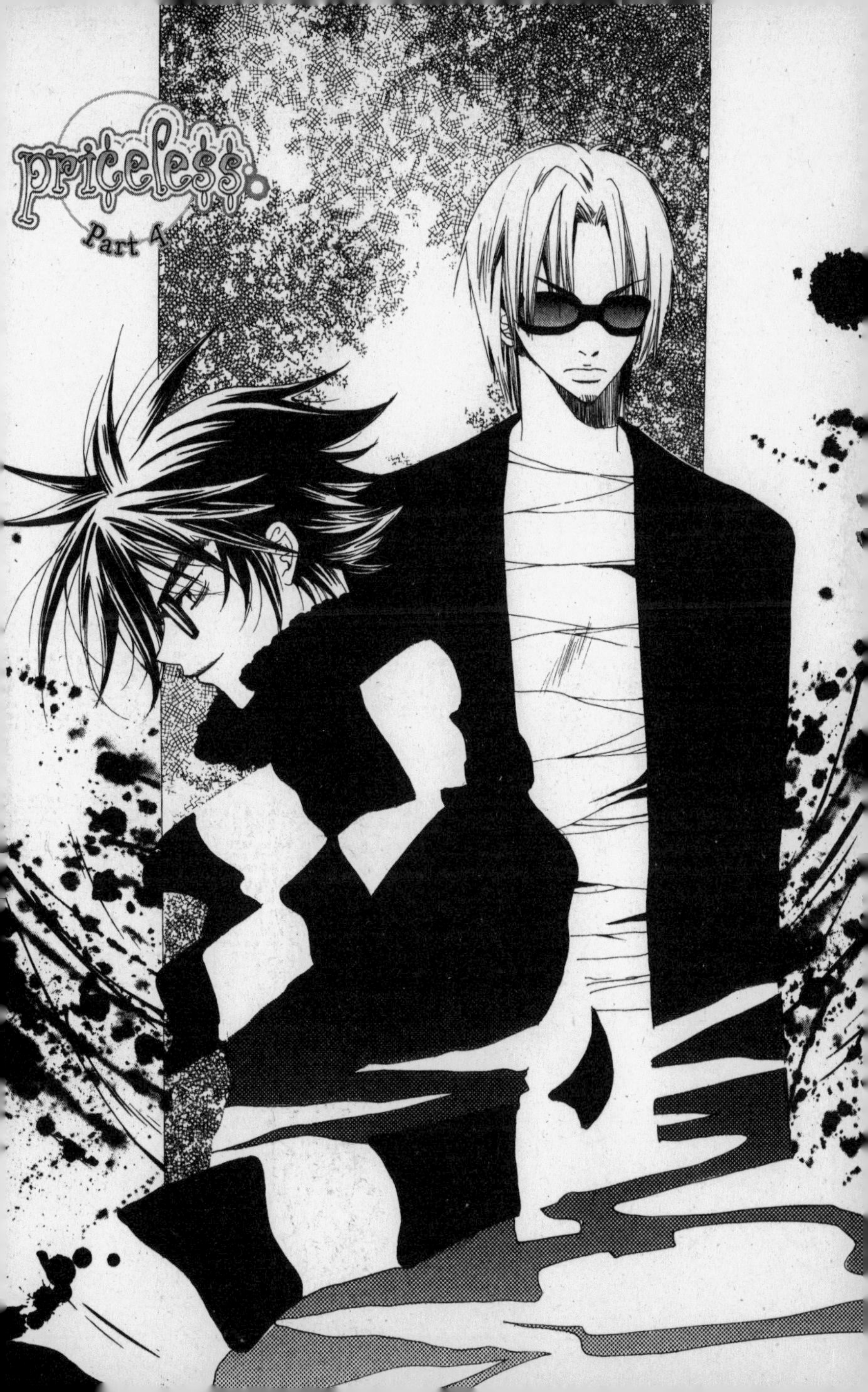
priceless
Part 4

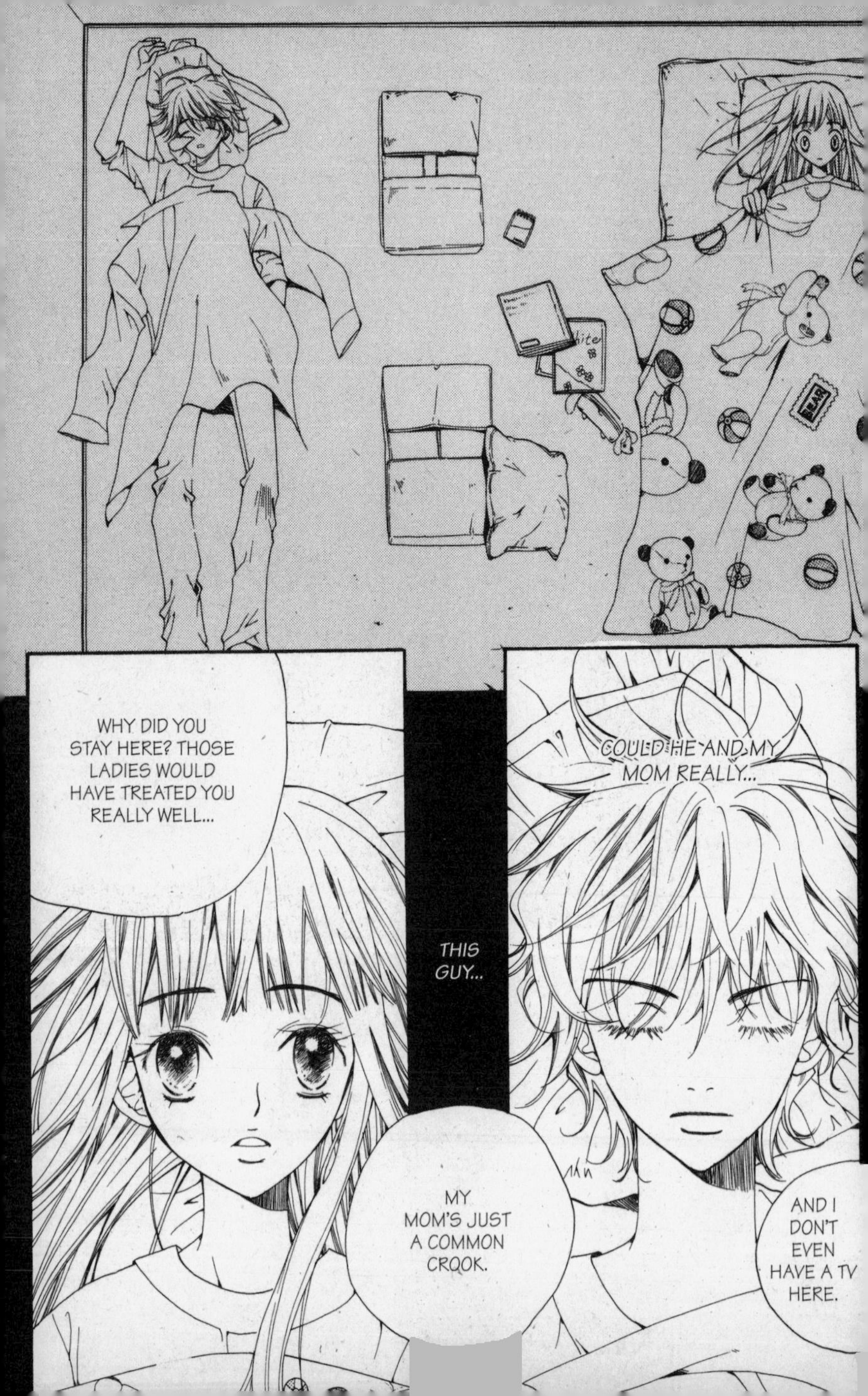

WHY DID YOU STAY HERE? THOSE LADIES WOULD HAVE TREATED YOU REALLY WELL...
THIS GUY...
COULD HE AND MY MOM REALLY...
MY MOM'S JUST A COMMON CROOK.
AND I DON'T EVEN HAVE A TV HERE.

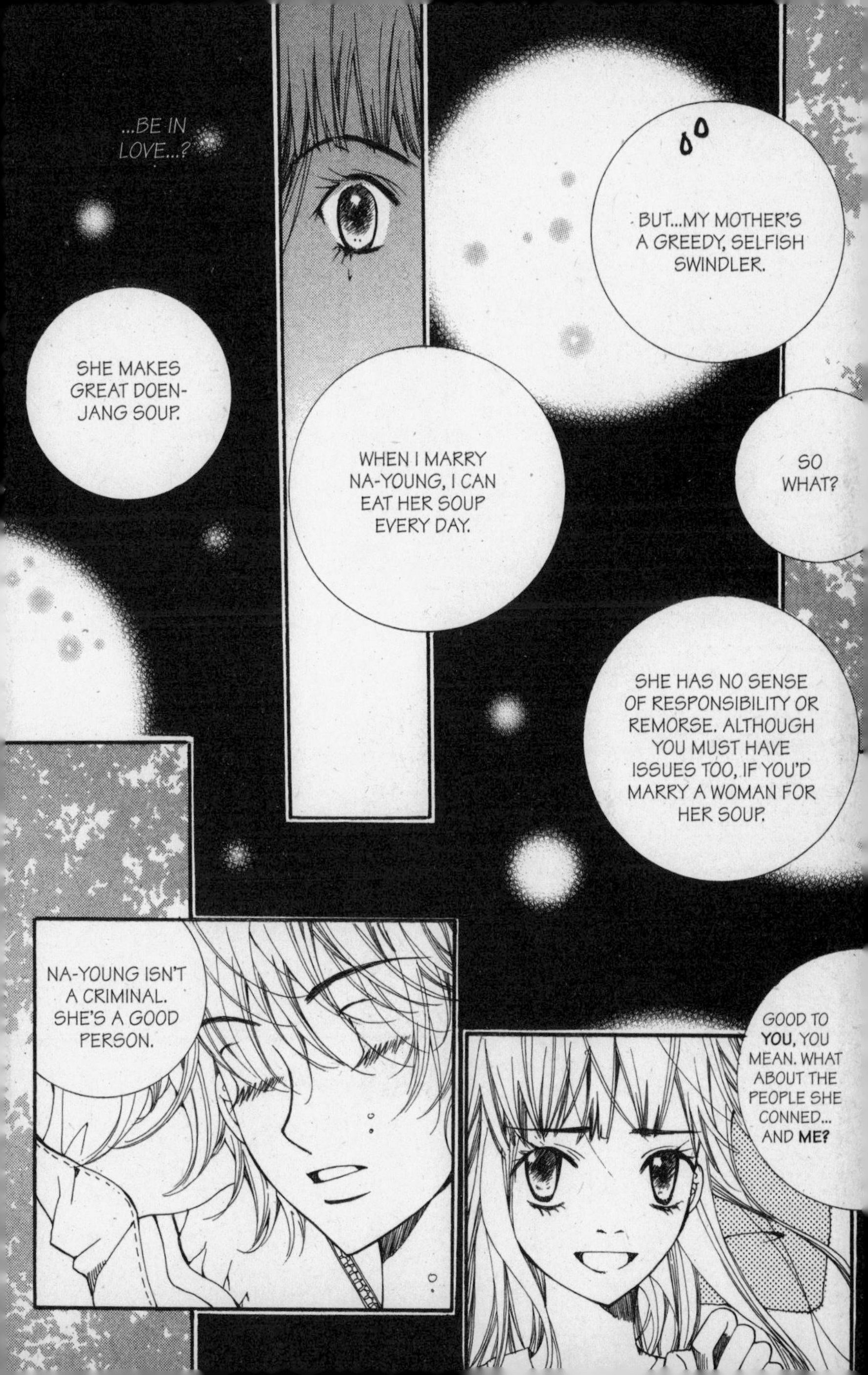
...BE IN LOVE...?
SHE MAKES GREAT DOEN-JANG SOUP.
WHEN I MARRY NA-YOUNG, I CAN EAT HER SOUP EVERY DAY.
BUT...MY MOTHER'S A GREEDY, SELFISH SWINDLER.
SO WHAT?
SHE HAS NO SENSE OF RESPONSIBILITY OR REMORSE. ALTHOUGH YOU MUST HAVE ISSUES TOO, IF YOU'D MARRY A WOMAN FOR HER SOUP.
NA-YOUNG ISN'T A CRIMINAL. SHE'S A GOOD PERSON.
GOOD TO **YOU**, YOU MEAN. WHAT ABOUT THE PEOPLE SHE CONNED... AND **ME?**

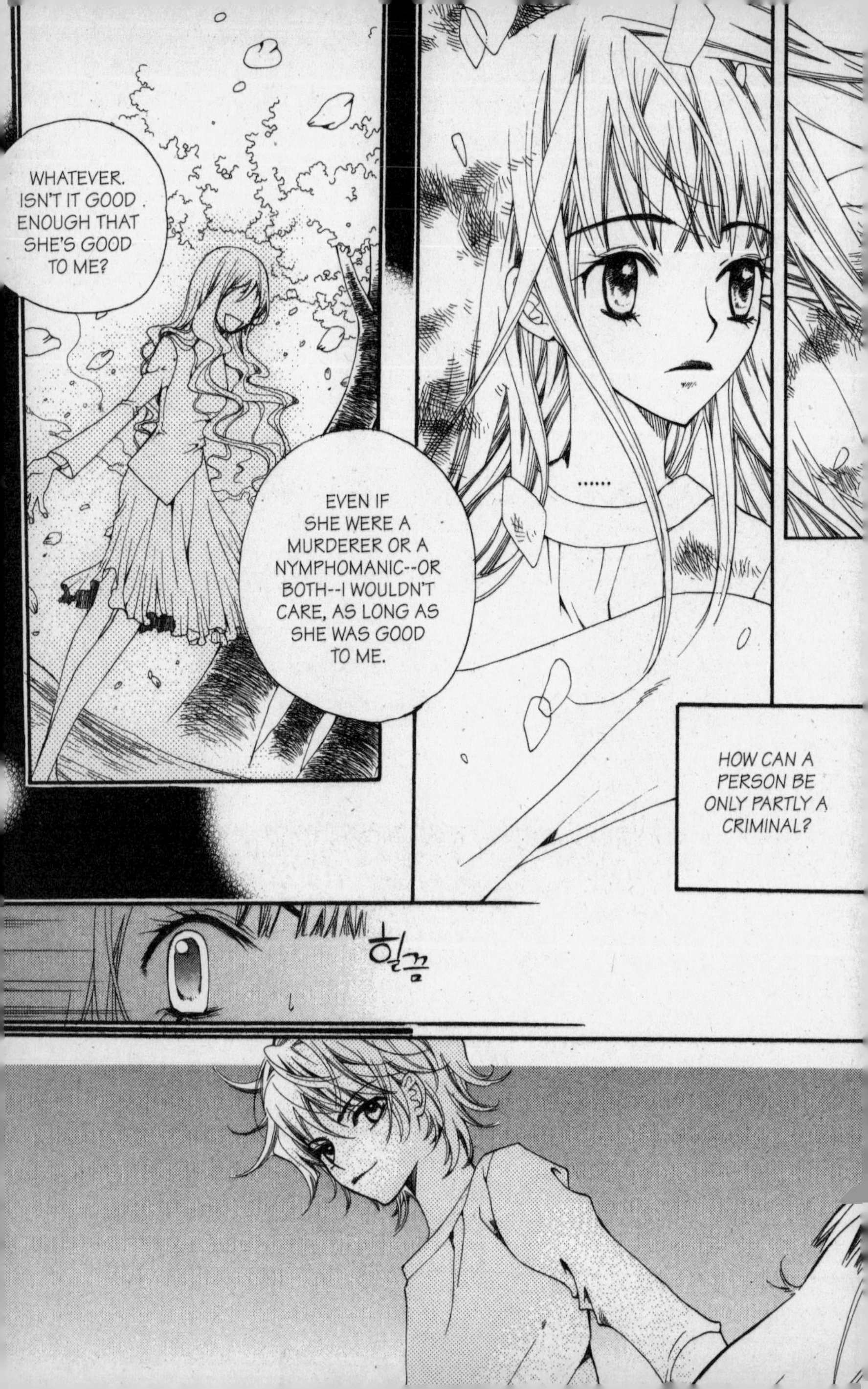

WHATEVER. ISN'T IT GOOD ENOUGH THAT SHE'S GOOD TO ME?
EVEN IF SHE WERE A MURDERER OR A NYMPHOMANIC--OR BOTH--I WOULDN'T CARE, AS LONG AS SHE WAS GOOD TO ME.
......
HOW CAN A PERSON BE ONLY PARTLY A CRIMINAL?
힐끔

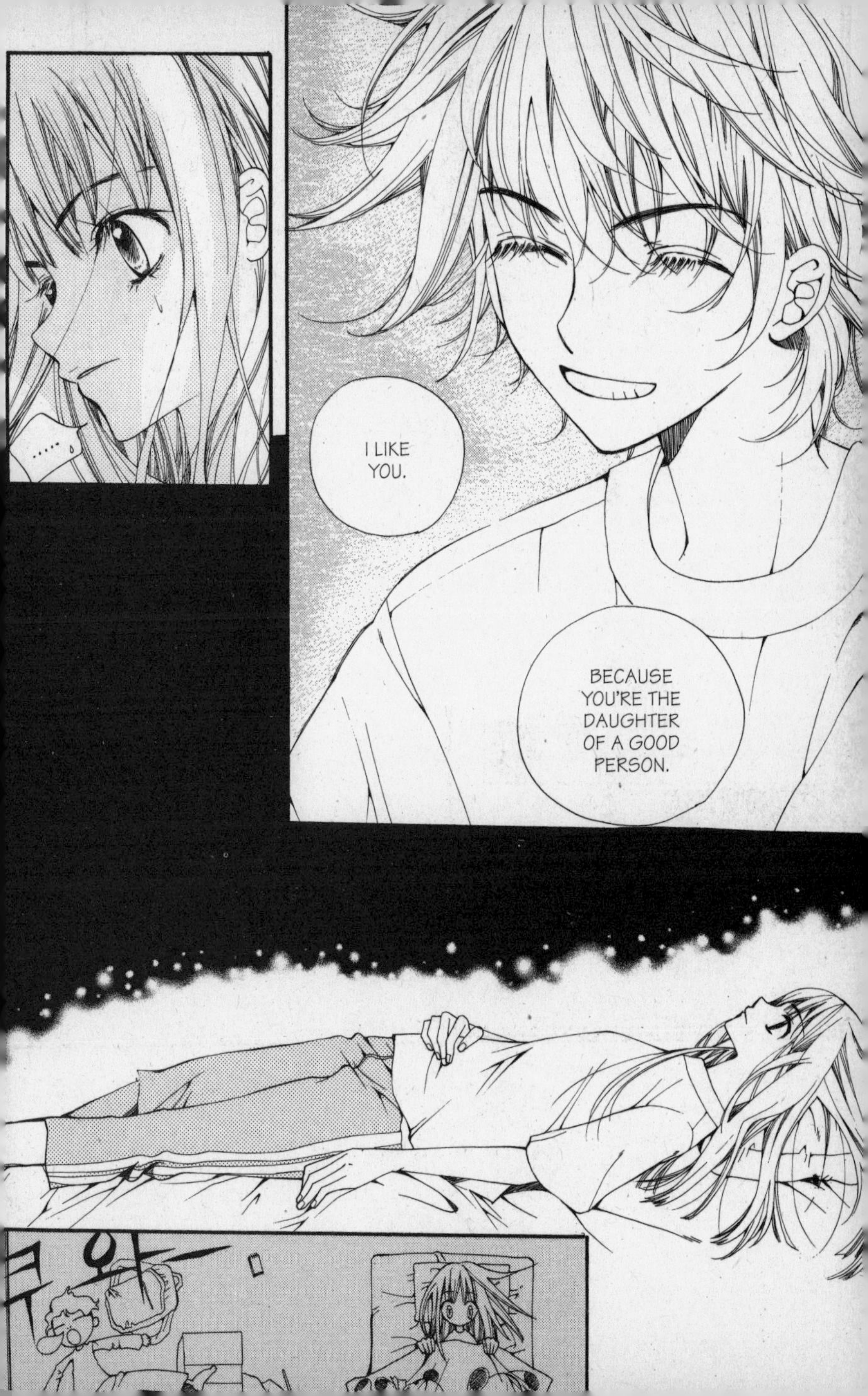
.....
I LIKE YOU.
BECAUSE YOU'RE THE DAUGHTER OF A GOOD PERSON.

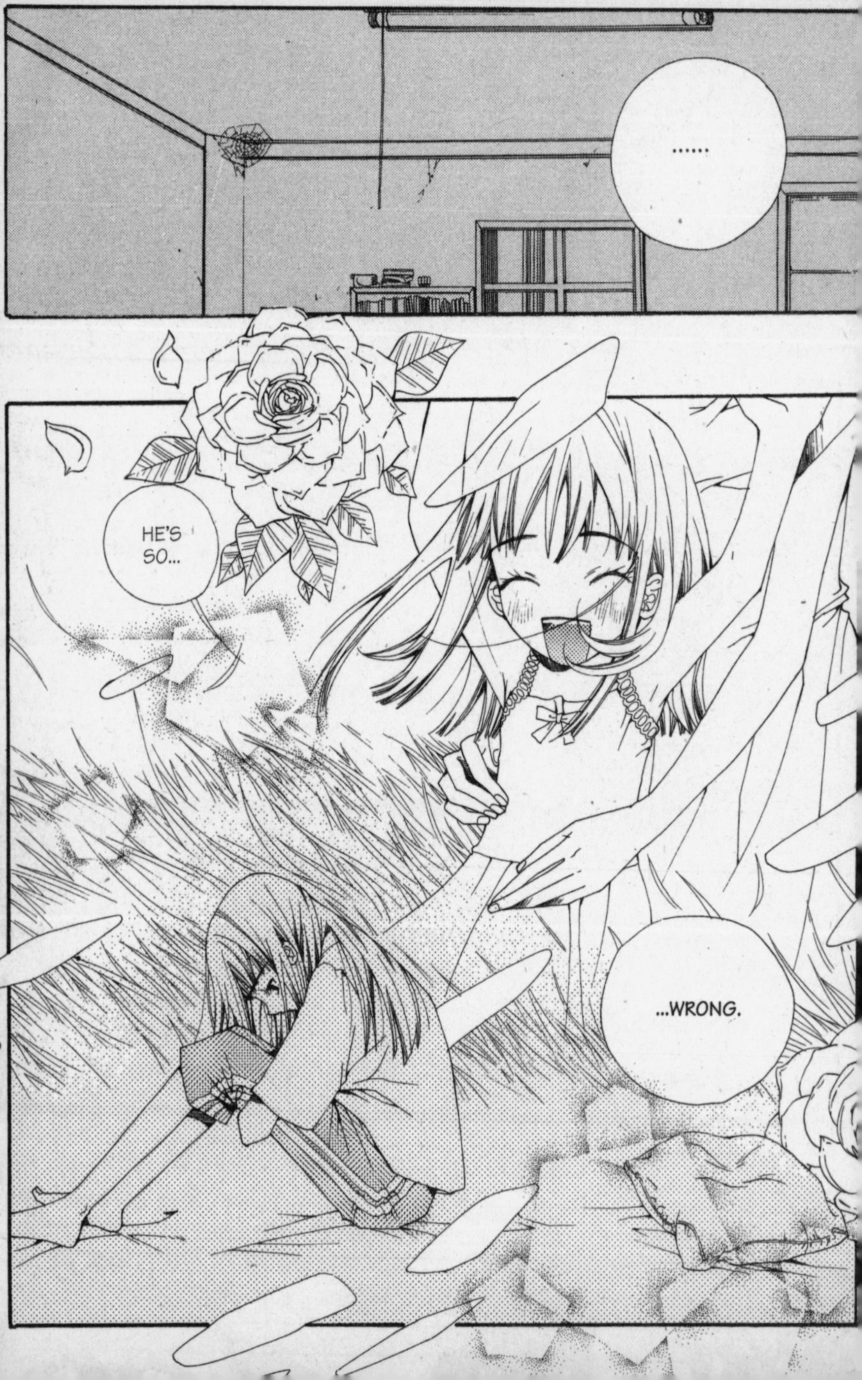
......
HE'S SO...
...WRONG.

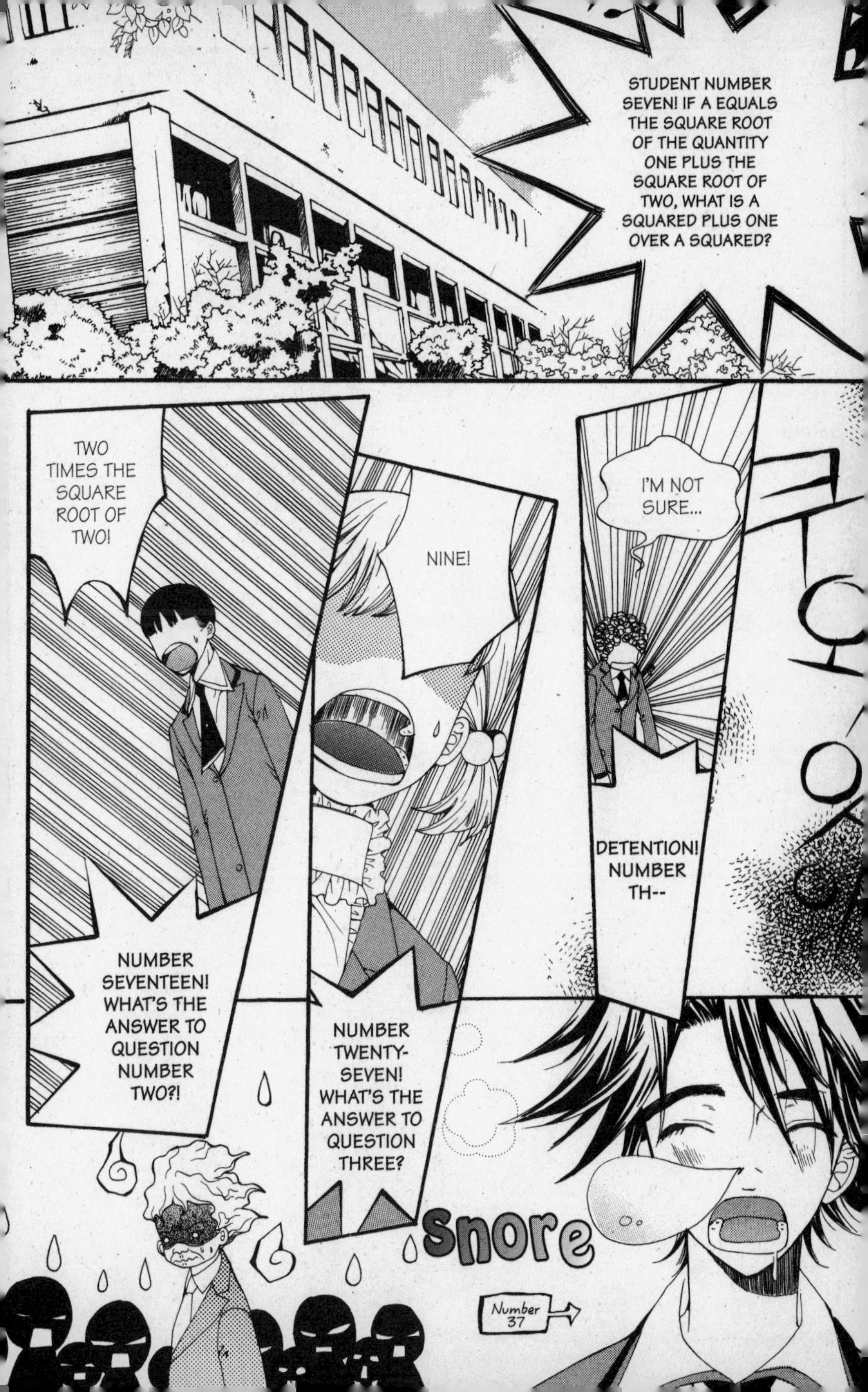
STUDENT NUMBER SEVEN! IF A EQUALS THE SQUARE ROOT OF THE QUANTITY ONE PLUS THE SQUARE ROOT OF TWO, WHAT IS A SQUARED PLUS ONE OVER A SQUARED?
TWO TIMES THE SQUARE ROOT OF TWO!
NUMBER SEVENTEEN! WHAT'S THE ANSWER TO QUESTION NUMBER TWO?!
NINE!
NUMBER TWENTY-SEVEN! WHAT'S THE ANSWER TO QUESTION THREE?
I'M NOT SURE...
DETENTION! NUMBER TH--
SNORE
Number 37

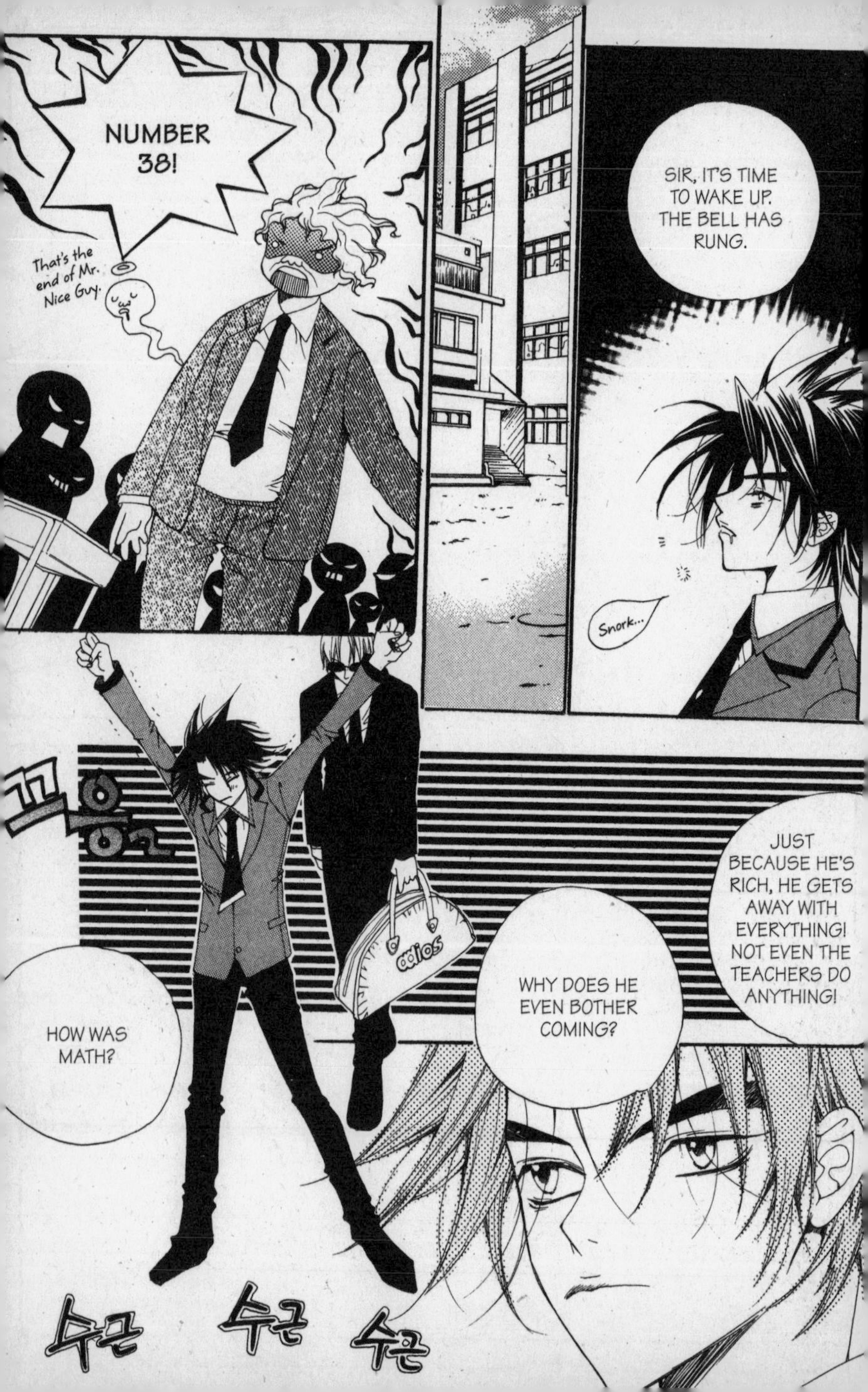
NUMBER 38!
That's the end of Mr. Nice Guy.
SIR, IT'S TIME TO WAKE UP. THE BELL HAS RUNG.
Snork...
HOW WAS MATH?
WHY DOES HE EVEN BOTHER COMING?
JUST BECAUSE HE'S RICH, HE GETS AWAY WITH EVERYTHING! NOT EVEN THE TEACHERS DO ANYTHING!
수군 수군 수군

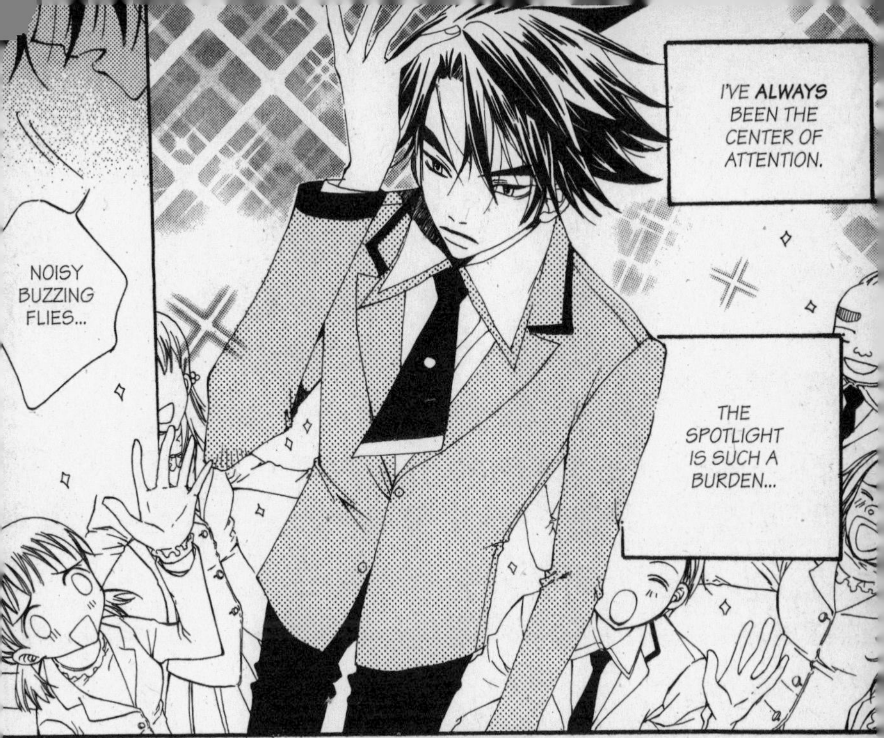
I'VE **ALWAYS** BEEN THE CENTER OF ATTENTION.
NOISY BUZZING FLIES...
THE SPOTLIGHT IS SUCH A BURDEN...

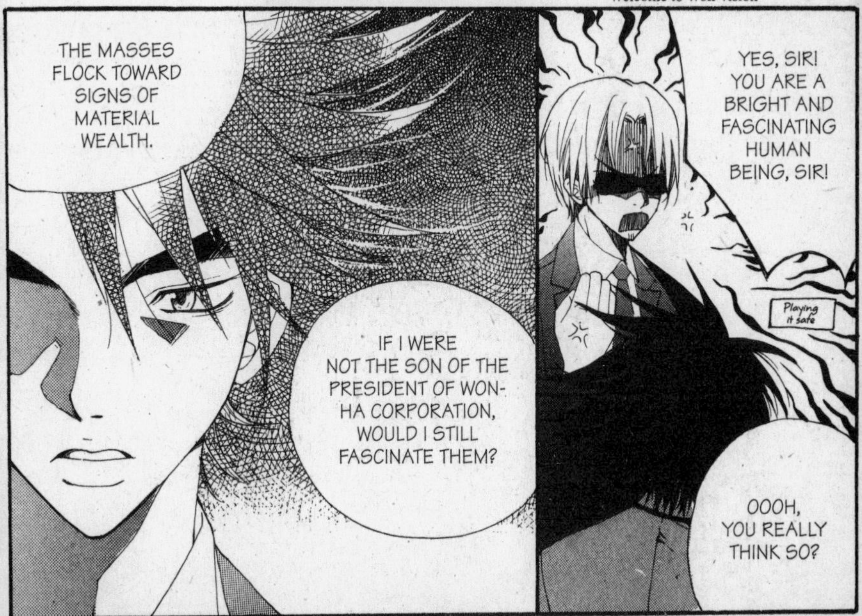
THE MASSES FLOCK TOWARD SIGNS OF MATERIAL WEALTH.
IF I WERE NOT THE SON OF THE PRESIDENT OF WON-HA CORPORATION, WOULD I STILL FASCINATE THEM?
YES, SIR! YOU ARE A BRIGHT AND FASCINATING HUMAN BEING, SIR!
Playing it safe
OOOH, YOU REALLY THINK SO?

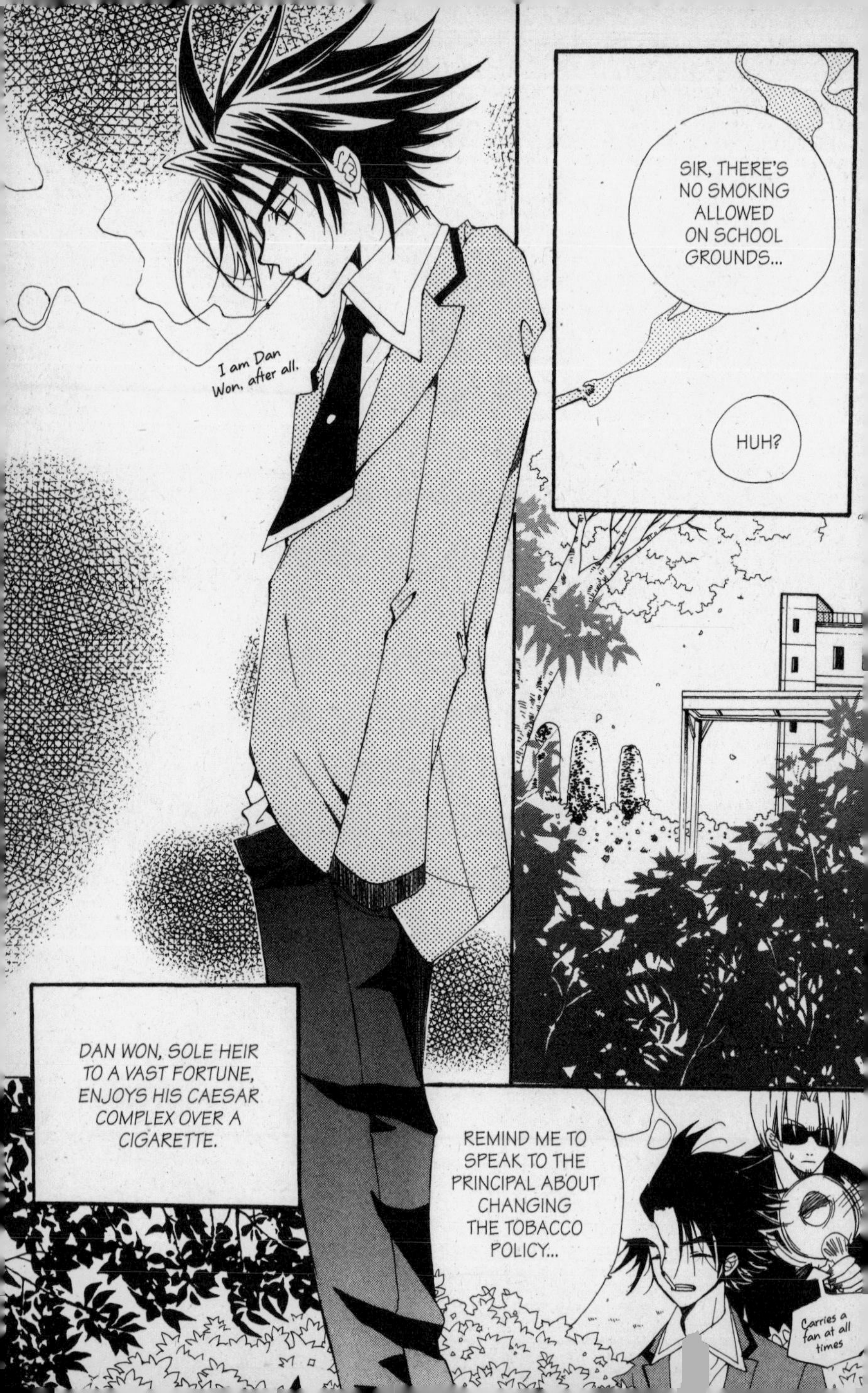
I am Dan Won, after all.
DAN WON, SOLE HEIR TO A VAST FORTUNE, ENJOYS HIS CAESAR COMPLEX OVER A CIGARETTE.
SIR, THERE'S NO SMOKING ALLOWED ON SCHOOL GROUNDS...
HUH?
REMIND ME TO SPEAK TO THE PRINCIPAL ABOUT CHANGING THE TOBACCO POLICY...
Carries a fan at all times

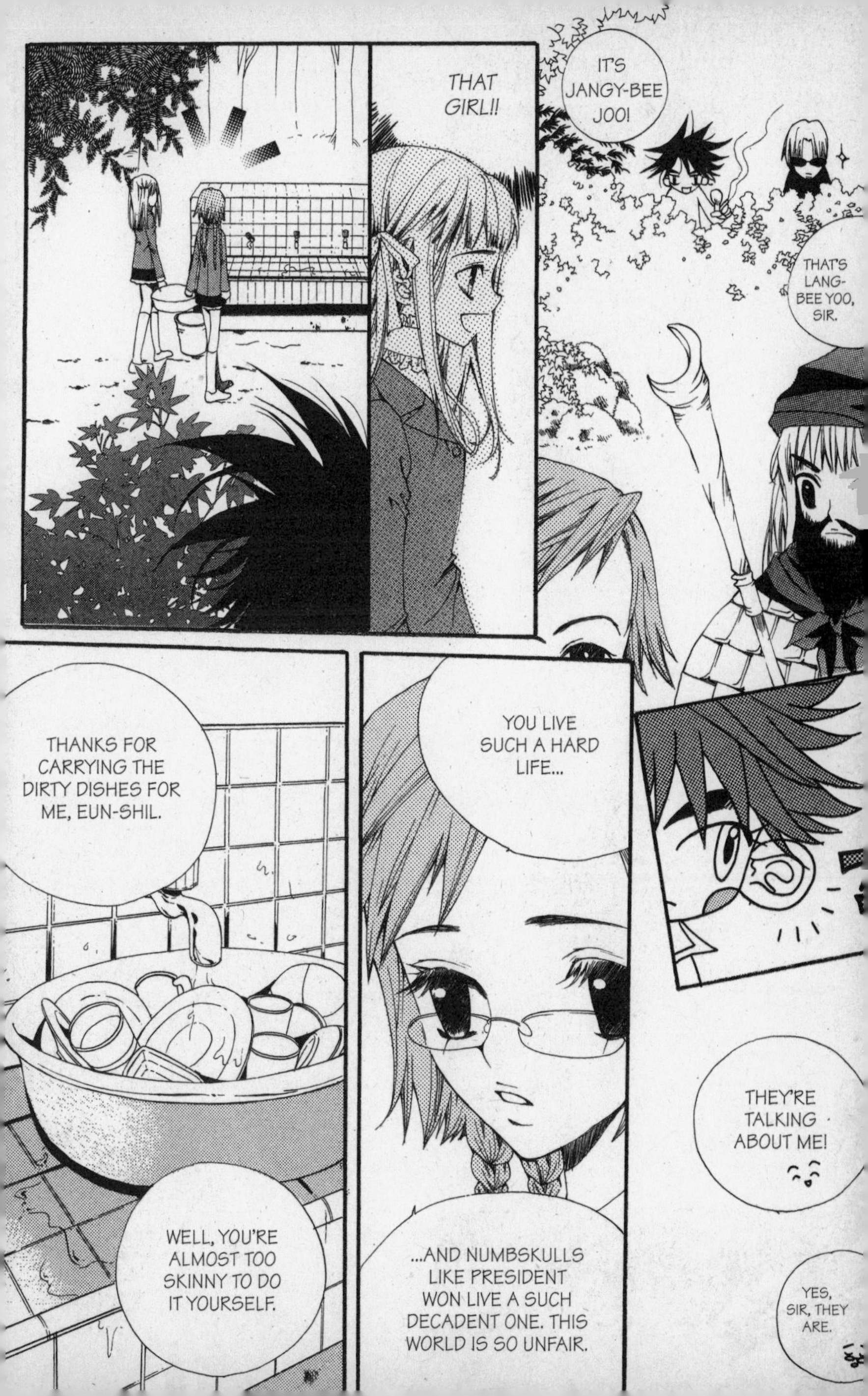
THAT GIRL!!
IT'S JANGY-BEE JOO!
THAT'S LANG-BEE YOO, SIR.
THANKS FOR CARRYING THE DIRTY DISHES FOR ME, EUN-SHIL.
WELL, YOU'RE ALMOST TOO SKINNY TO DO IT YOURSELF.
YOU LIVE SUCH A HARD LIFE...
...AND NUMBSKULLS LIKE PRESIDENT WON LIVE A SUCH DECADENT ONE. THIS WORLD IS SO UNFAIR.
THEY'RE TALKING ABOUT ME!
YES, SIR, THEY ARE.

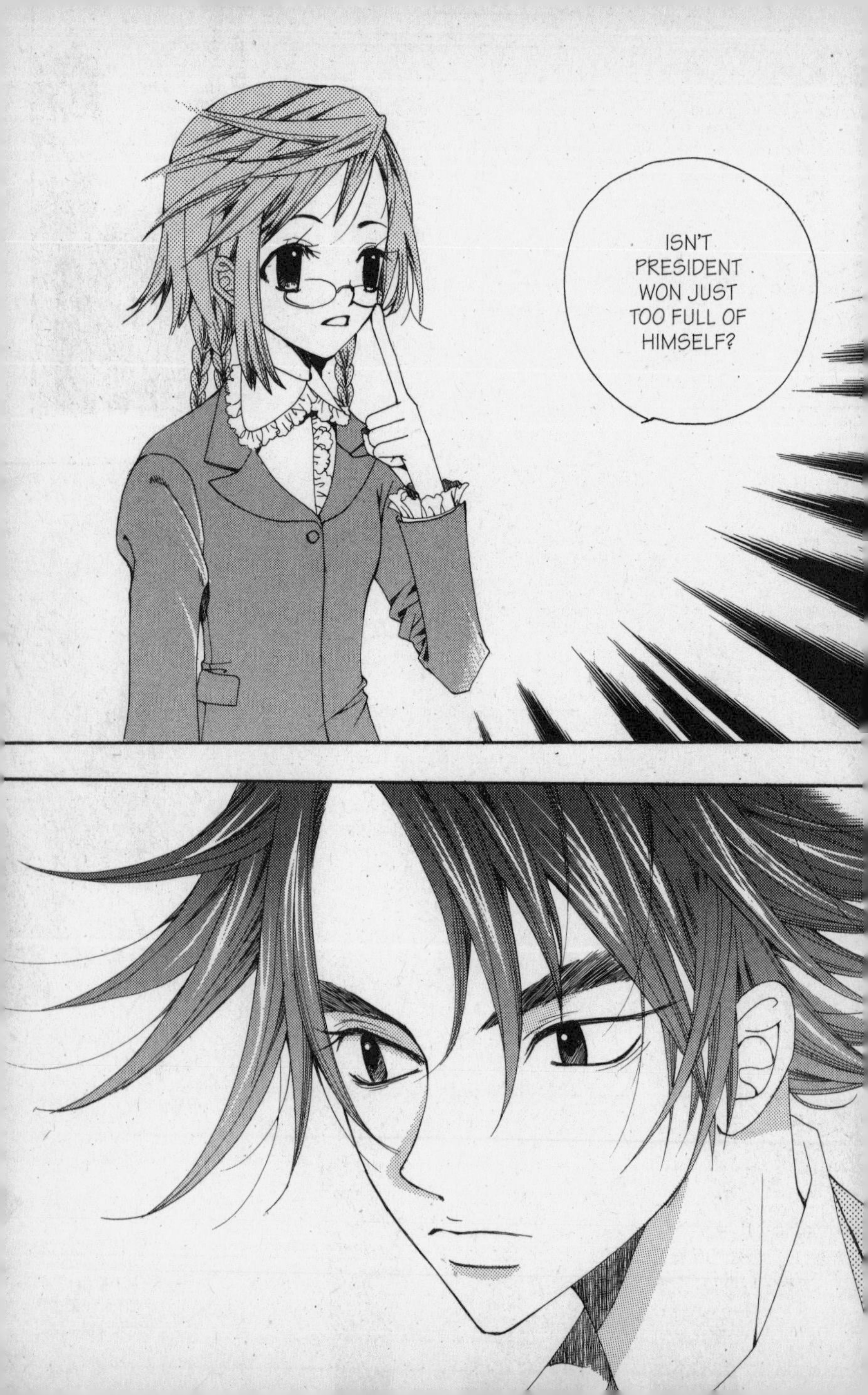
ISN'T PRESIDENT WON JUST TOO FULL OF HIMSELF?

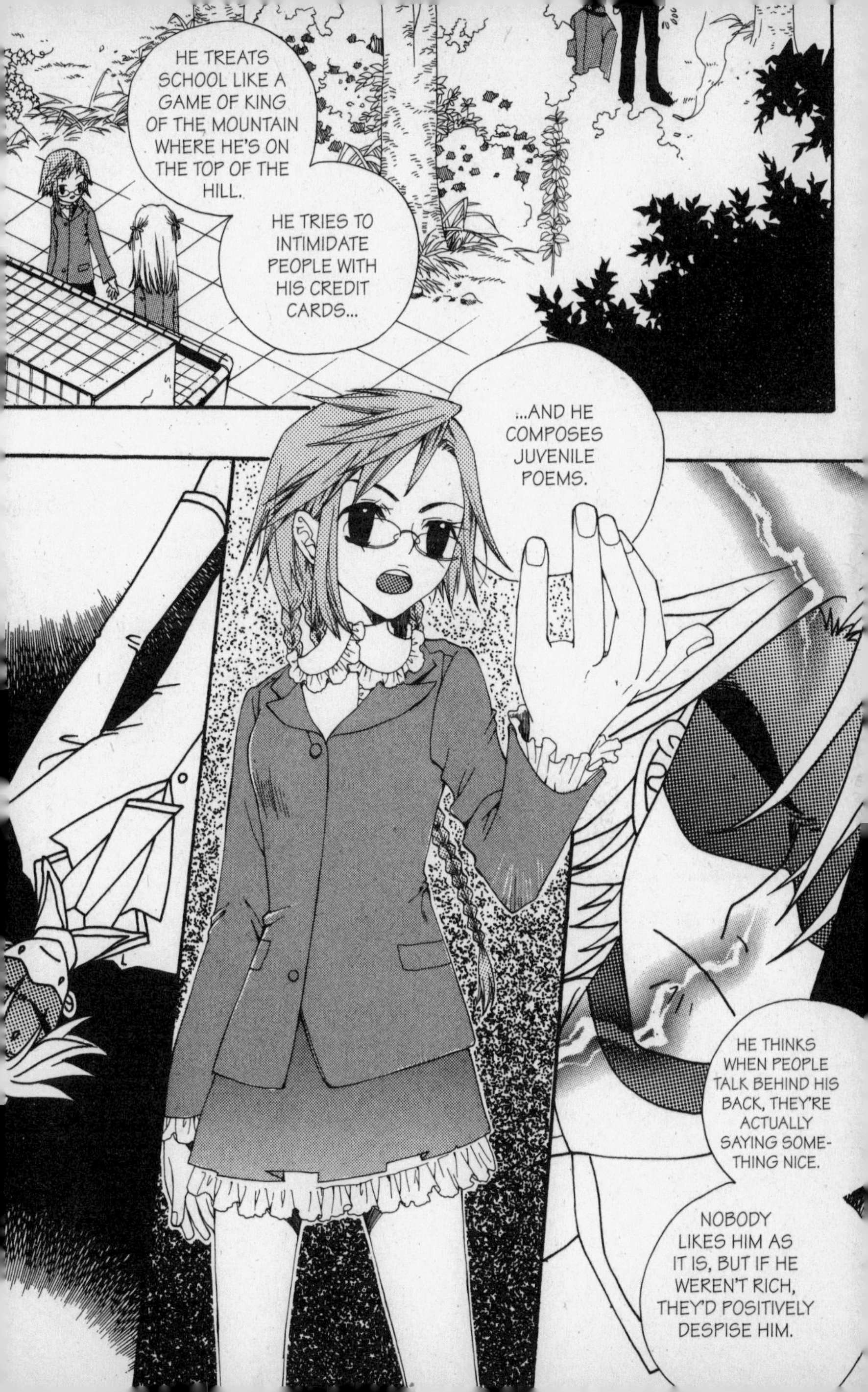
HE TREATS SCHOOL LIKE A GAME OF KING OF THE MOUNTAIN WHERE HE'S ON THE TOP OF THE HILL.
HE TRIES TO INTIMIDATE PEOPLE WITH HIS CREDIT CARDS...
...AND HE COMPOSES JUVENILE POEMS.
HE THINKS WHEN PEOPLE TALK BEHIND HIS BACK, THEY'RE ACTUALLY SAYING SOME-THING NICE.
NOBODY LIKES HIM AS IT IS, BUT IF HE WEREN'T RICH, THEY'D POSITIVELY DESPISE HIM.

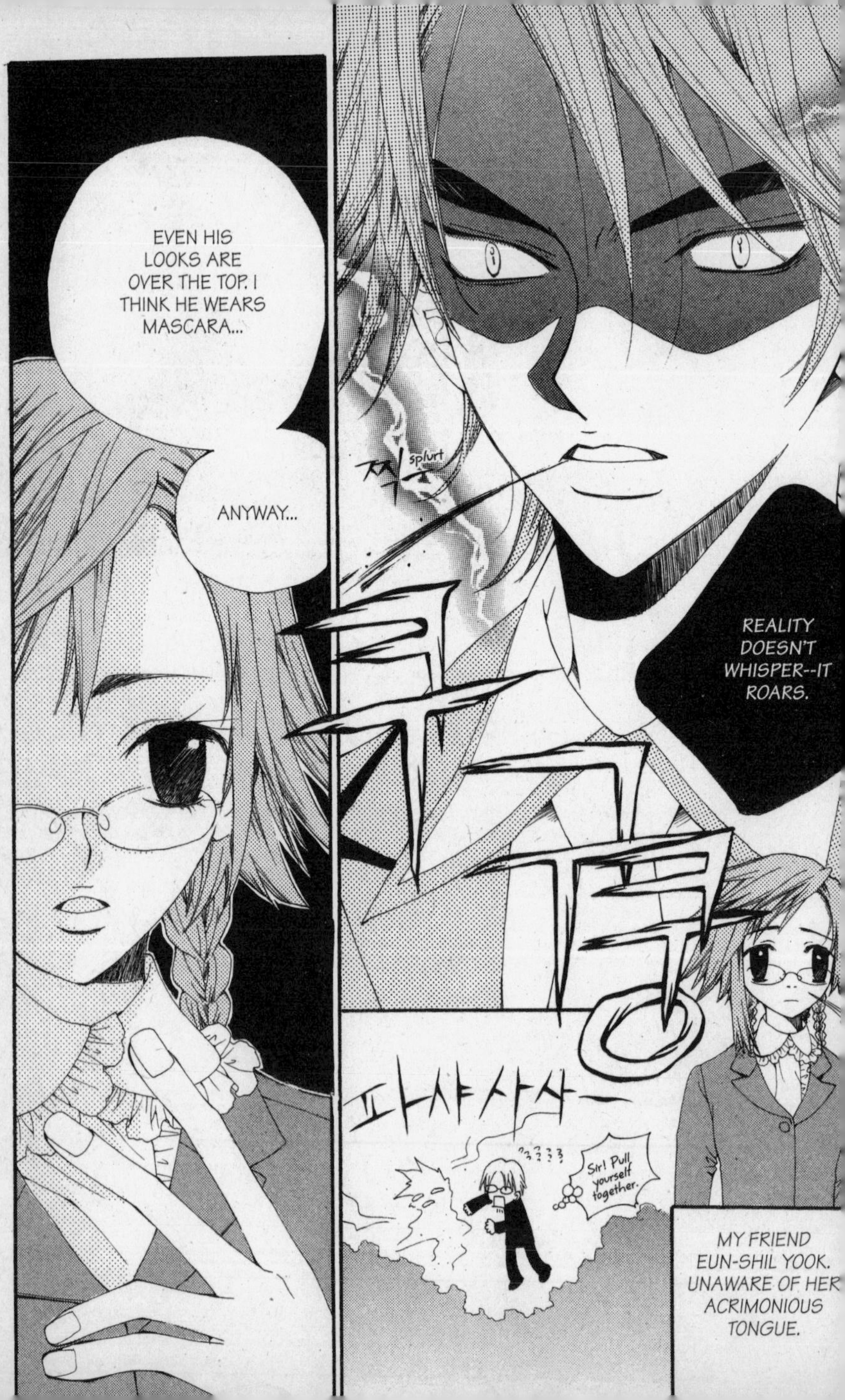
EVEN HIS LOOKS ARE OVER THE TOP. I THINK HE WEARS MASCARA...
ANYWAY...
splurt
REALITY DOESN'T WHISPER--IT ROARS.
Sir! Pull yourself together.
MY FRIEND EUN-SHIL YOOK. UNAWARE OF HER ACRIMONIOUS TONGUE.

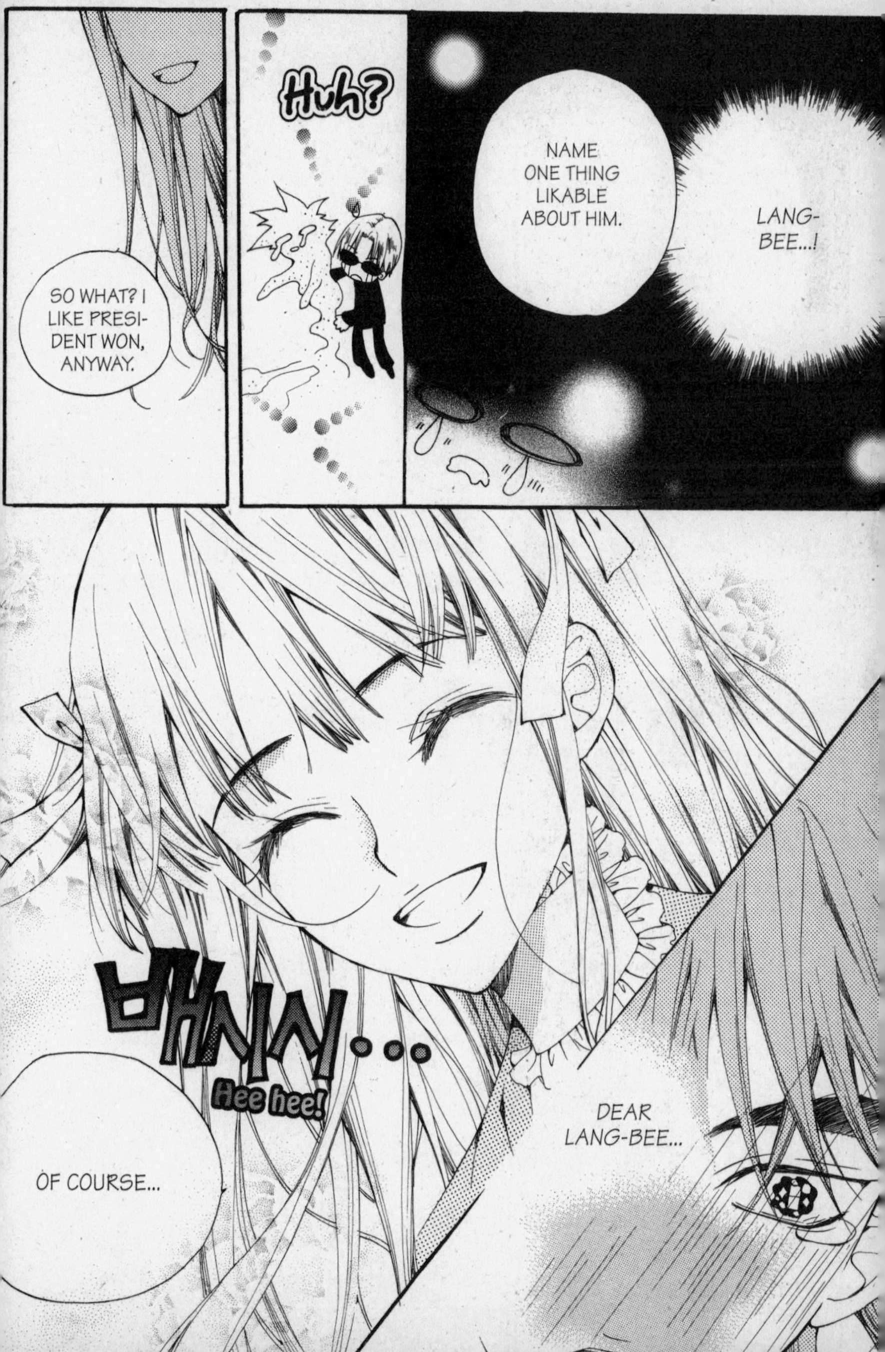
SO WHAT? I LIKE PRESI-DENT WON, ANYWAY.
Huh?
NAME ONE THING LIKABLE ABOUT HIM.
LANG-BEE...!
Hee hee!
OF COURSE...
DEAR LANG-BEE...

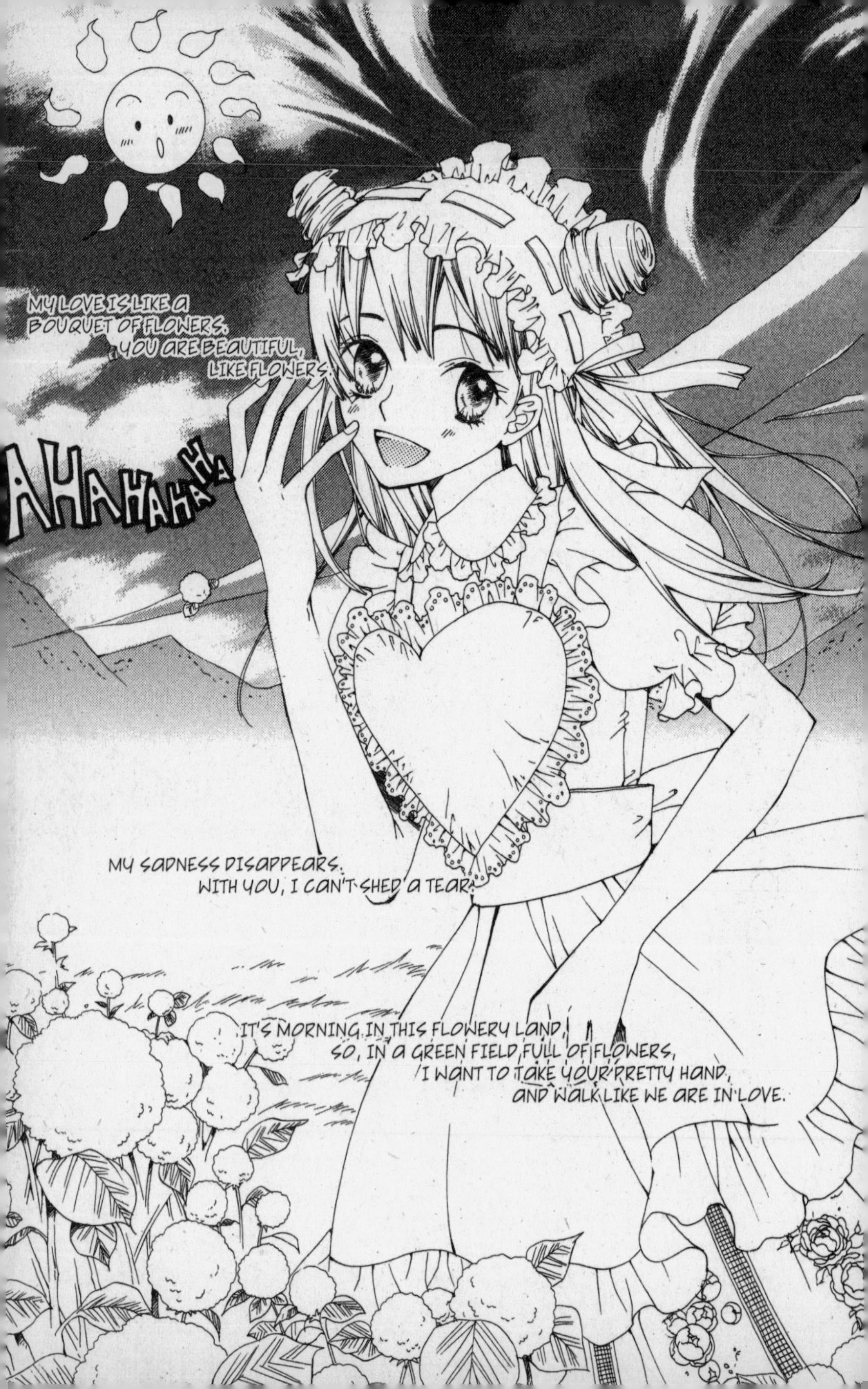

MY LOVE IS LIKE A BOUQUET OF FLOWERS. YOU ARE BEAUTIFUL, LIKE FLOWERS.
AHAHAHAHAHA
MY SADNESS DISAPPEARS. WITH YOU, I CAN'T SHED A TEAR.
IT'S MORNING IN THIS FLOWERY LAND, SO, IN A GREEN FIELD FULL OF FLOWERS, I WANT TO TAKE YOUR PRETTY HAND, AND WALK LIKE WE ARE IN LOVE.

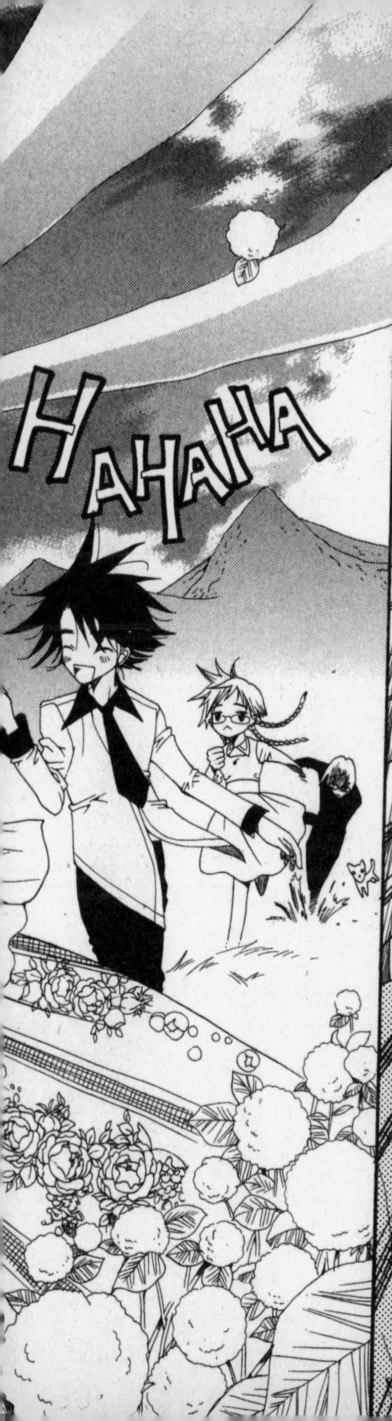
HAHAHA
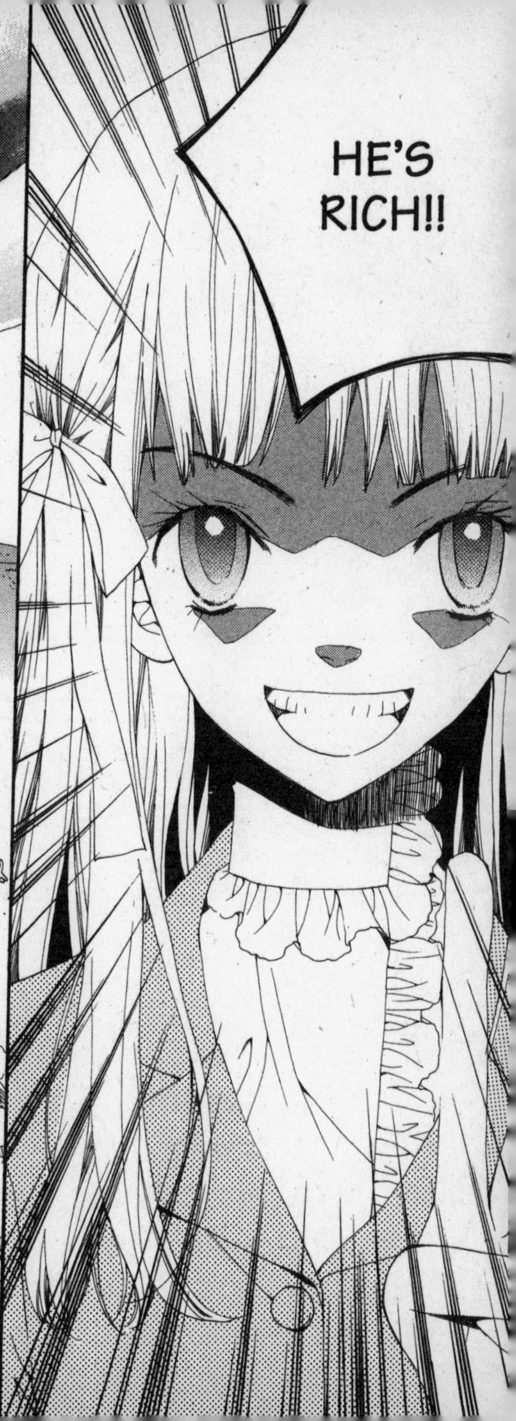
HE'S RICH!!

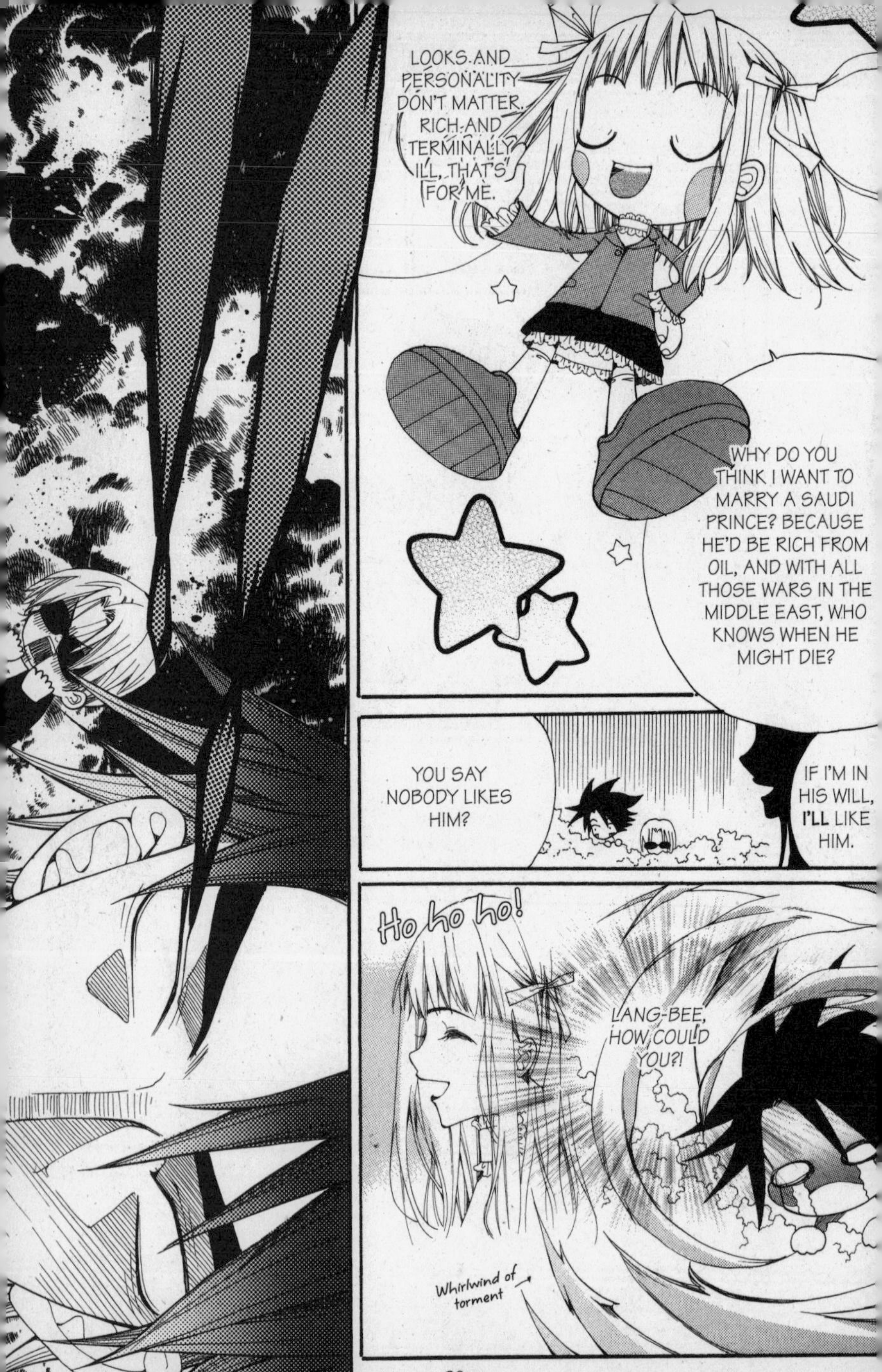
LOOKS AND PERSONALITY DON'T MATTER. RICH AND TERMINALLY ILL, THAT'S FOR ME.
WHY DO YOU THINK I WANT TO MARRY A SAUDI PRINCE? BECAUSE HE'D BE RICH FROM OIL, AND WITH ALL THOSE WARS IN THE MIDDLE EAST, WHO KNOWS WHEN HE MIGHT DIE?
YOU SAY NOBODY LIKES HIM?
IF I'M IN HIS WILL, **I'LL** LIKE HIM.
Ho ho ho!
LANG-BEE, HOW COULD YOU?!
Whirlwind of torment

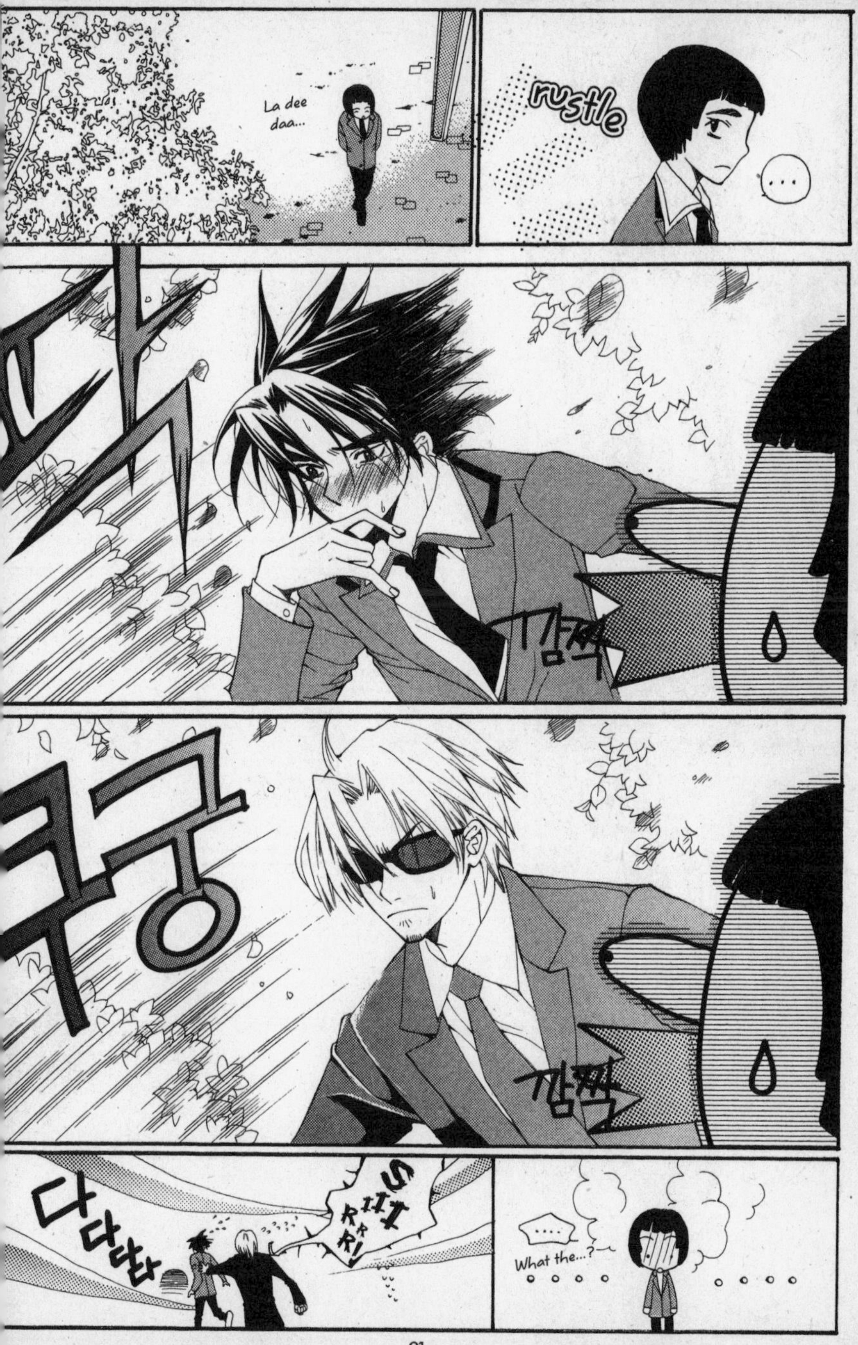
La dee daa...
rustle
...
깜짝
쿠궁
깜짝
다다닥
....
What the...?

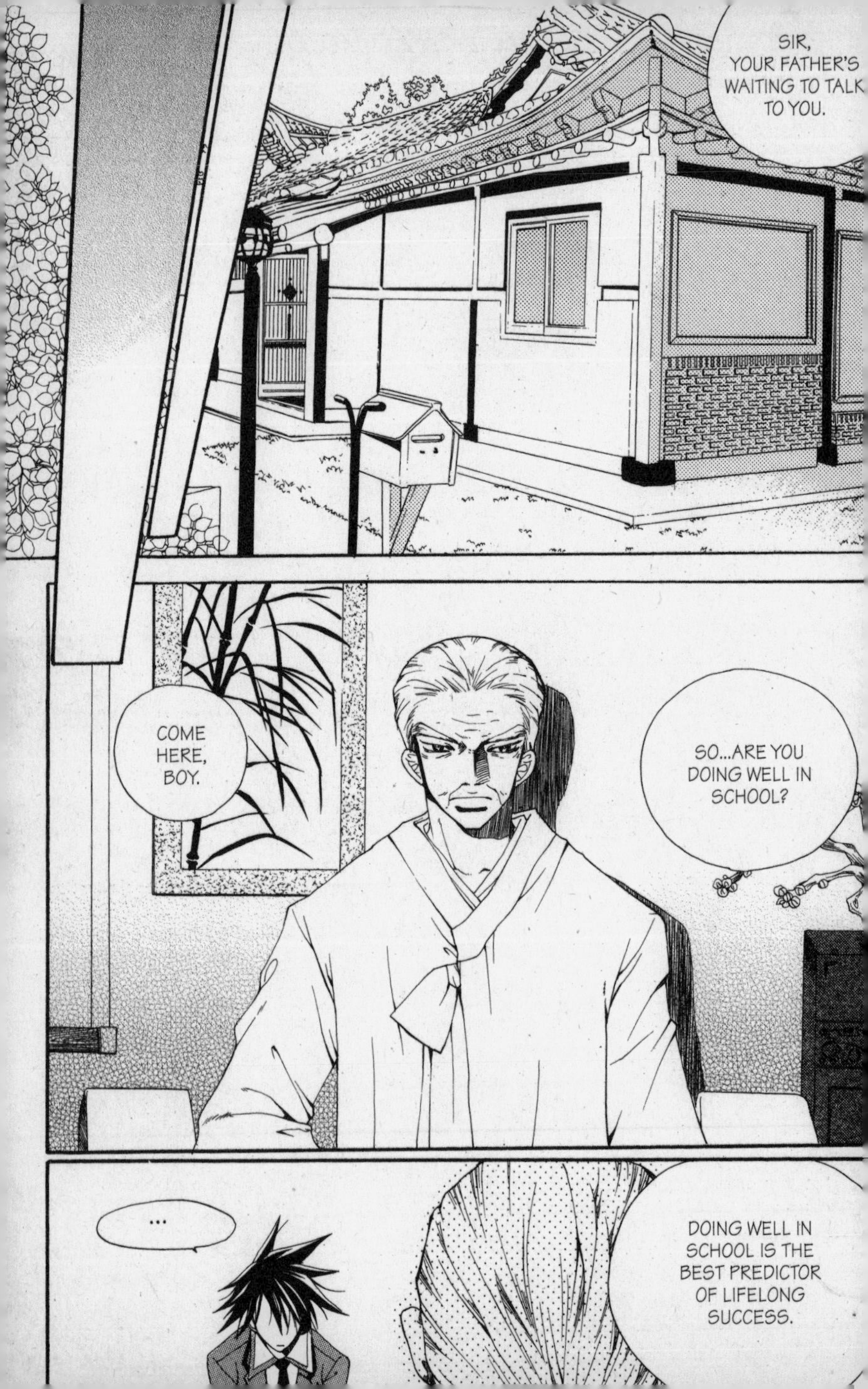
SIR, YOUR FATHER'S WAITING TO TALK TO YOU.
COME HERE, BOY.
SO...ARE YOU DOING WELL IN SCHOOL?
...
DOING WELL IN SCHOOL IS THE BEST PREDICTOR OF LIFELONG SUCCESS.

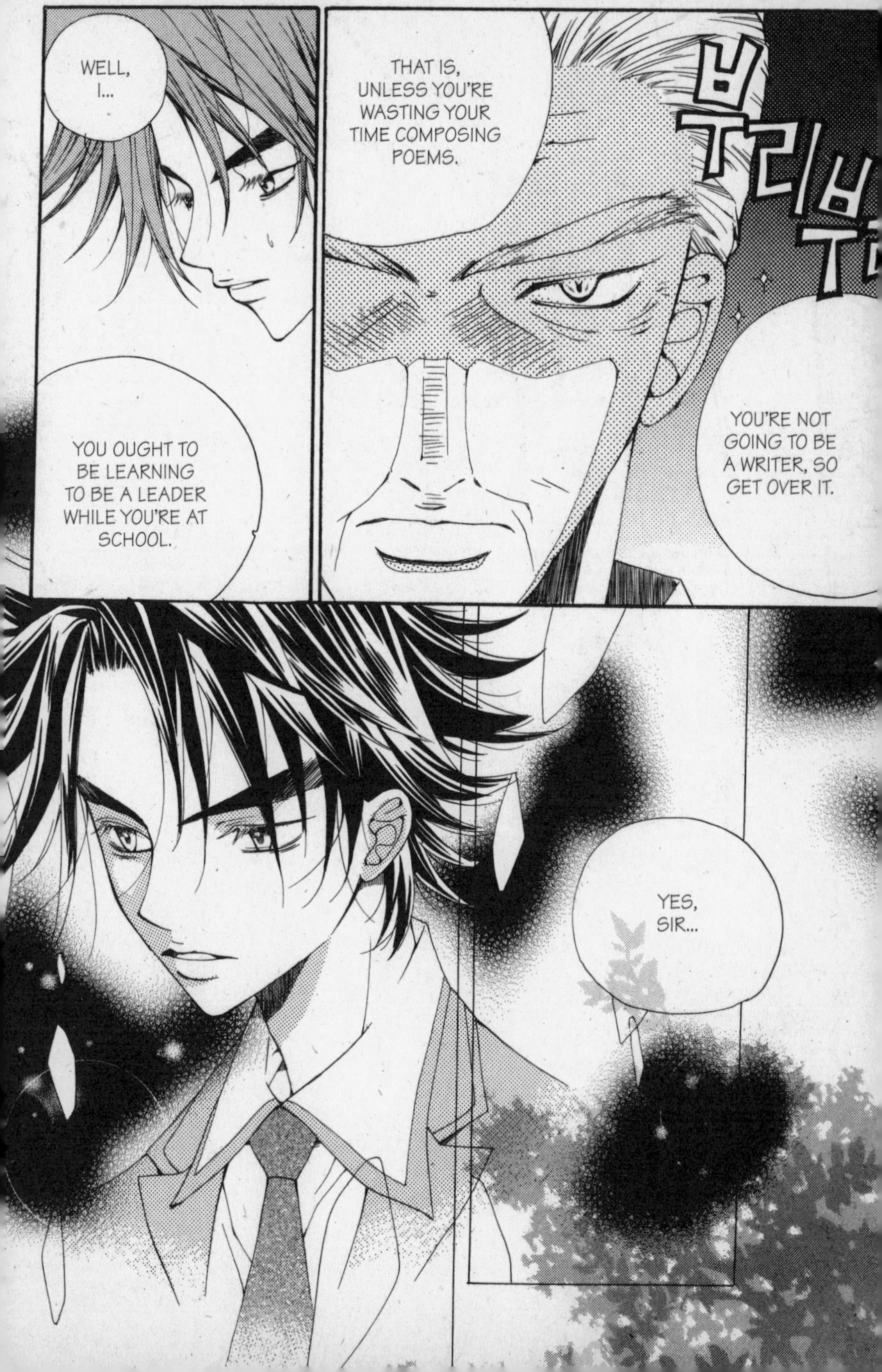
WELL, I...
YOU OUGHT TO BE LEARNING TO BE A LEADER WHILE YOU'RE AT SCHOOL.
THAT IS, UNLESS YOU'RE WASTING YOUR TIME COMPOSING POEMS.
YOU'RE NOT GOING TO BE A WRITER, SO GET OVER IT.
YES, SIR...

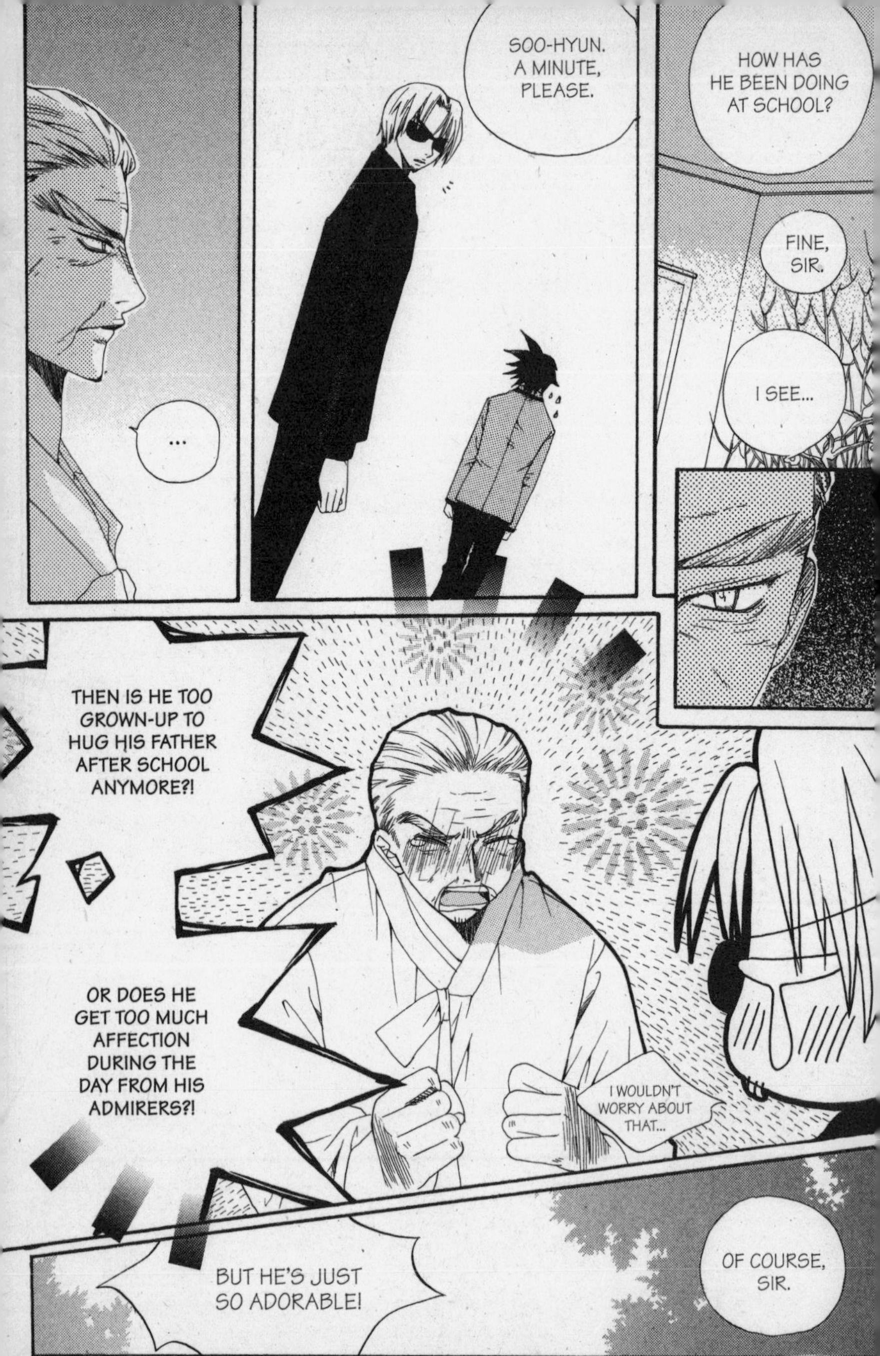
...
SOO-HYUN. A MINUTE, PLEASE.
HOW HAS HE BEEN DOING AT SCHOOL?
FINE, SIR.
I SEE...
THEN IS HE TOO GROWN-UP TO HUG HIS FATHER AFTER SCHOOL ANYMORE?!
OR DOES HE GET TOO MUCH AFFECTION DURING THE DAY FROM HIS ADMIRERS?!
I WOULDN'T WORRY ABOUT THAT...
BUT HE'S JUST SO ADORABLE!
OF COURSE, SIR.

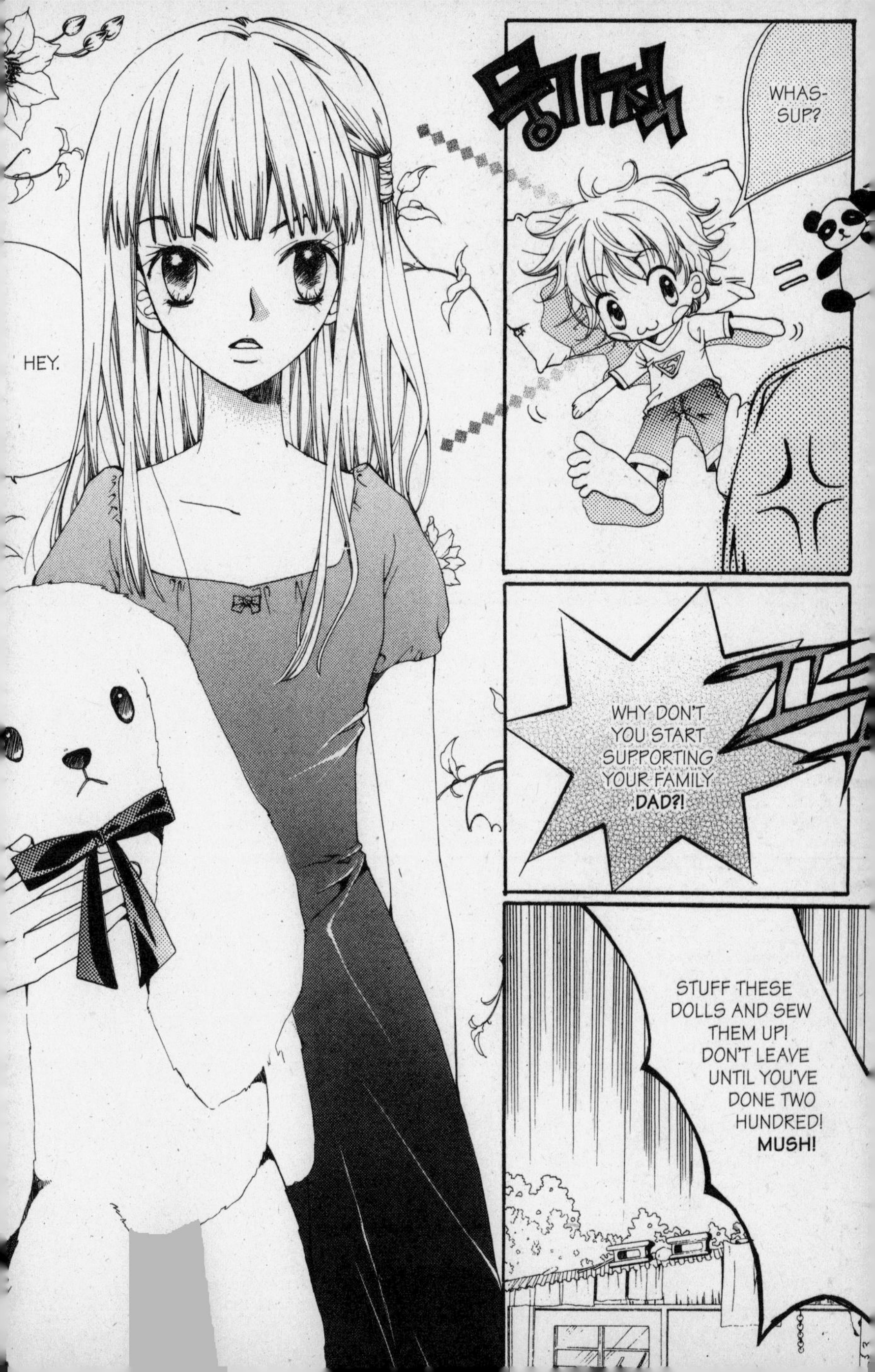
HEY.
WHAS-SUP?
WHY DON'T YOU START SUPPORTING YOUR FAMILY, **DAD?!**
STUFF THESE DOLLS AND SEW THEM UP! DON'T LEAVE UNTIL YOU'VE DONE TWO HUNDRED! **MUSH!**

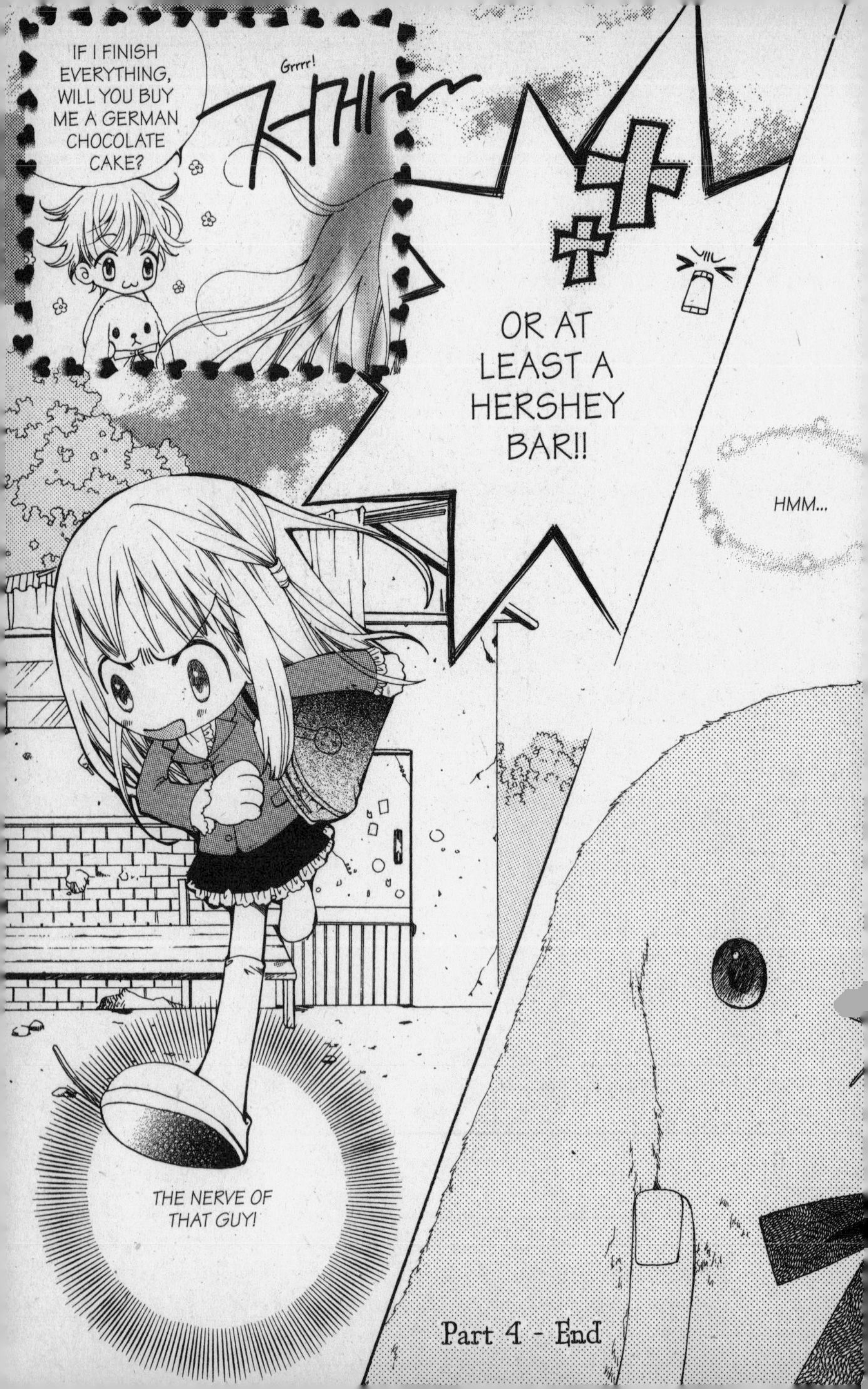
IF I FINISH EVERYTHING, WILL YOU BUY ME A GERMAN CHOCOLATE CAKE?
Grrrr!
OR AT LEAST A HERSHEY BAR!!
HMM...
THE NERVE OF THAT GUY!
Part 4 - End

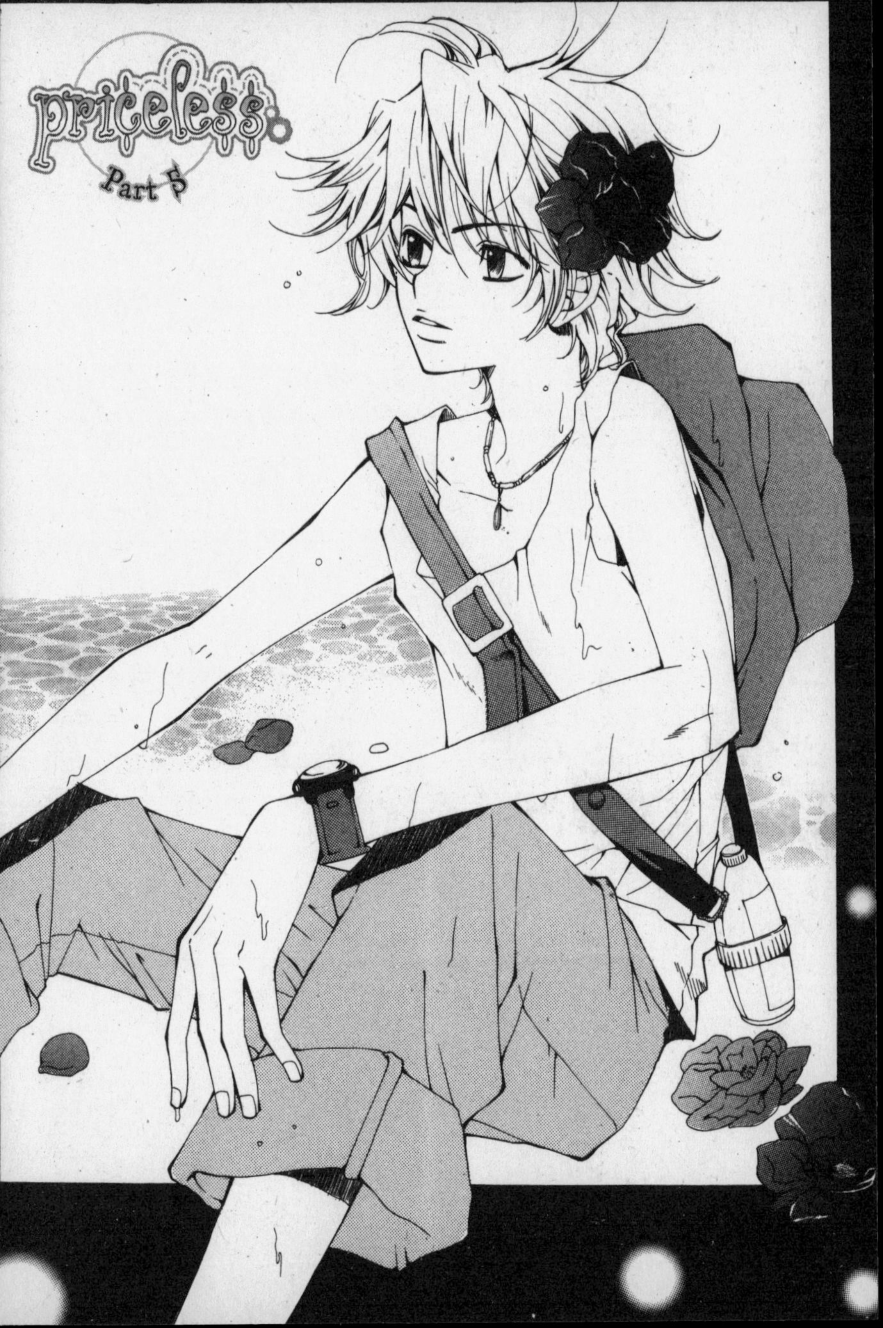
priceless
Part 5

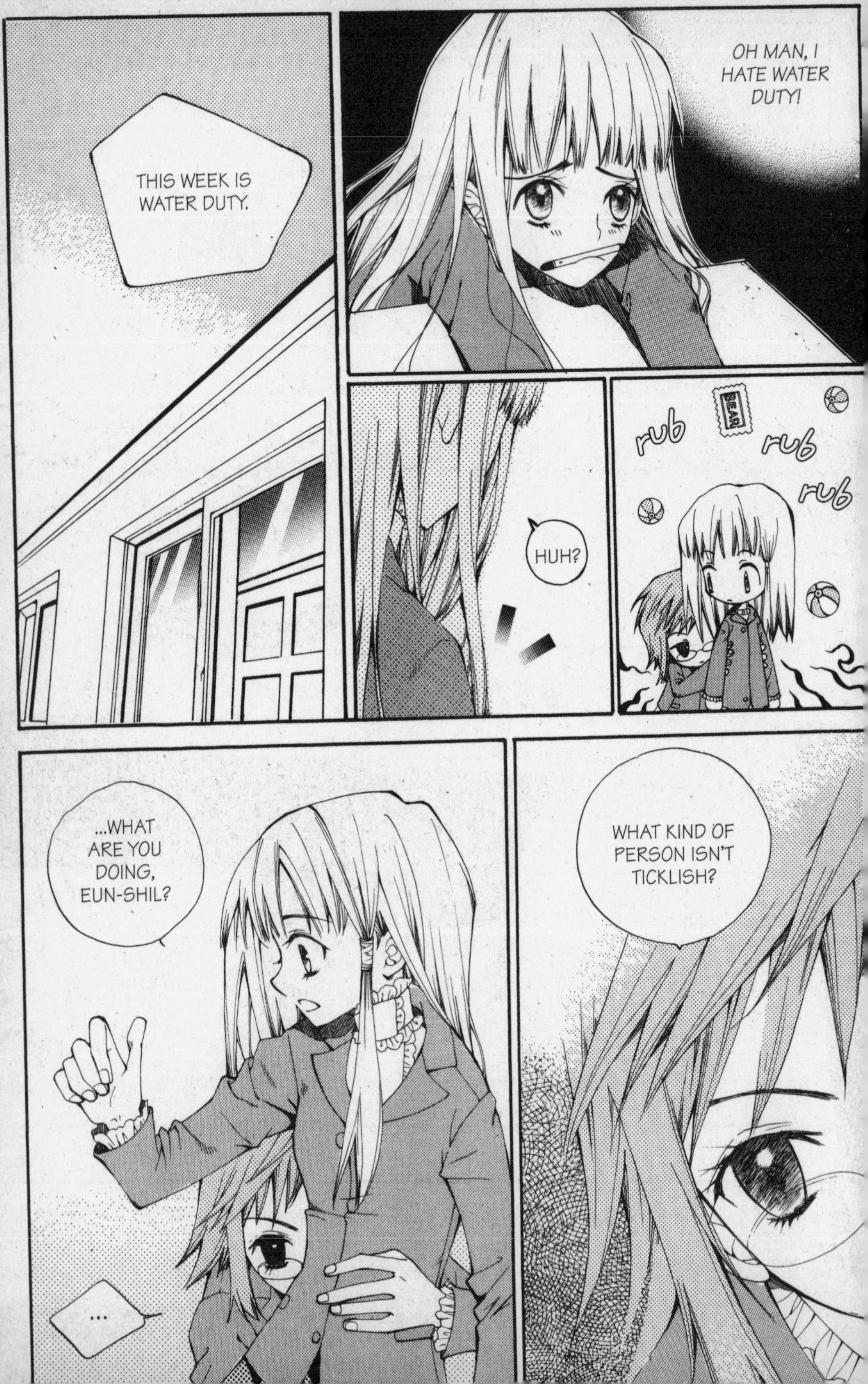
THIS WEEK IS WATER DUTY.
OH MAN, I HATE WATER DUTY!
HUH?
rub
BEAR
rub
rub
...WHAT ARE YOU DOING, EUN-SHIL?
...
WHAT KIND OF PERSON ISN'T TICKLISH?

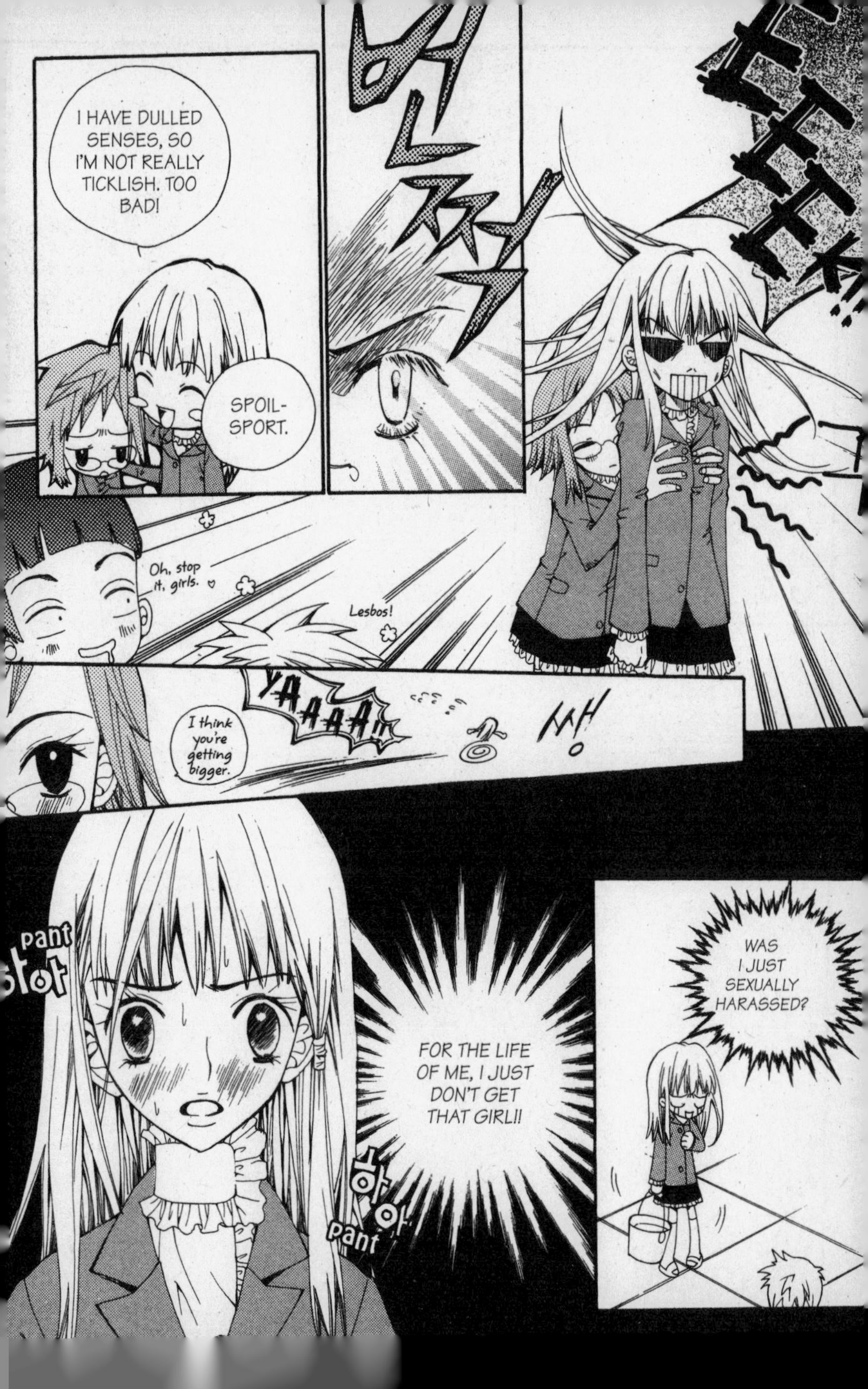

I HAVE DULLED SENSES, SO I'M NOT REALLY TICKLISH. TOO BAD!
SPOIL-SPORT.
Oh, stop it, girls.
Lesbos!
I think you're getting bigger.
YAAAAA!!
pant
pant
FOR THE LIFE OF ME, I JUST DON'T GET THAT GIRL!!
WAS I JUST SEXUALLY HARASSED?

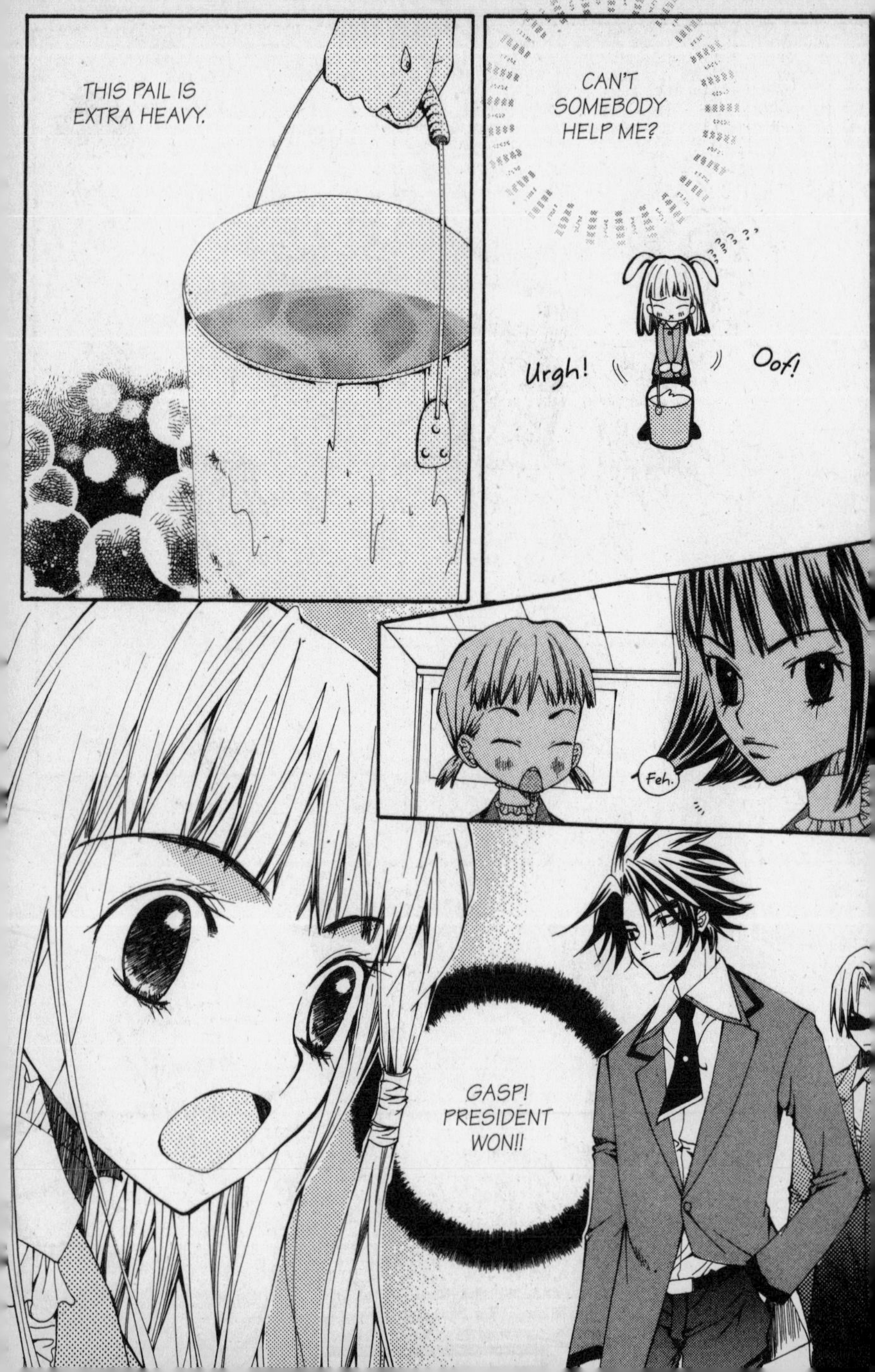
THIS PAIL IS EXTRA HEAVY.
CAN'T SOMEBODY HELP ME?
Urgh!
Oof!
Feh.
GASP! PRESIDENT WON!!

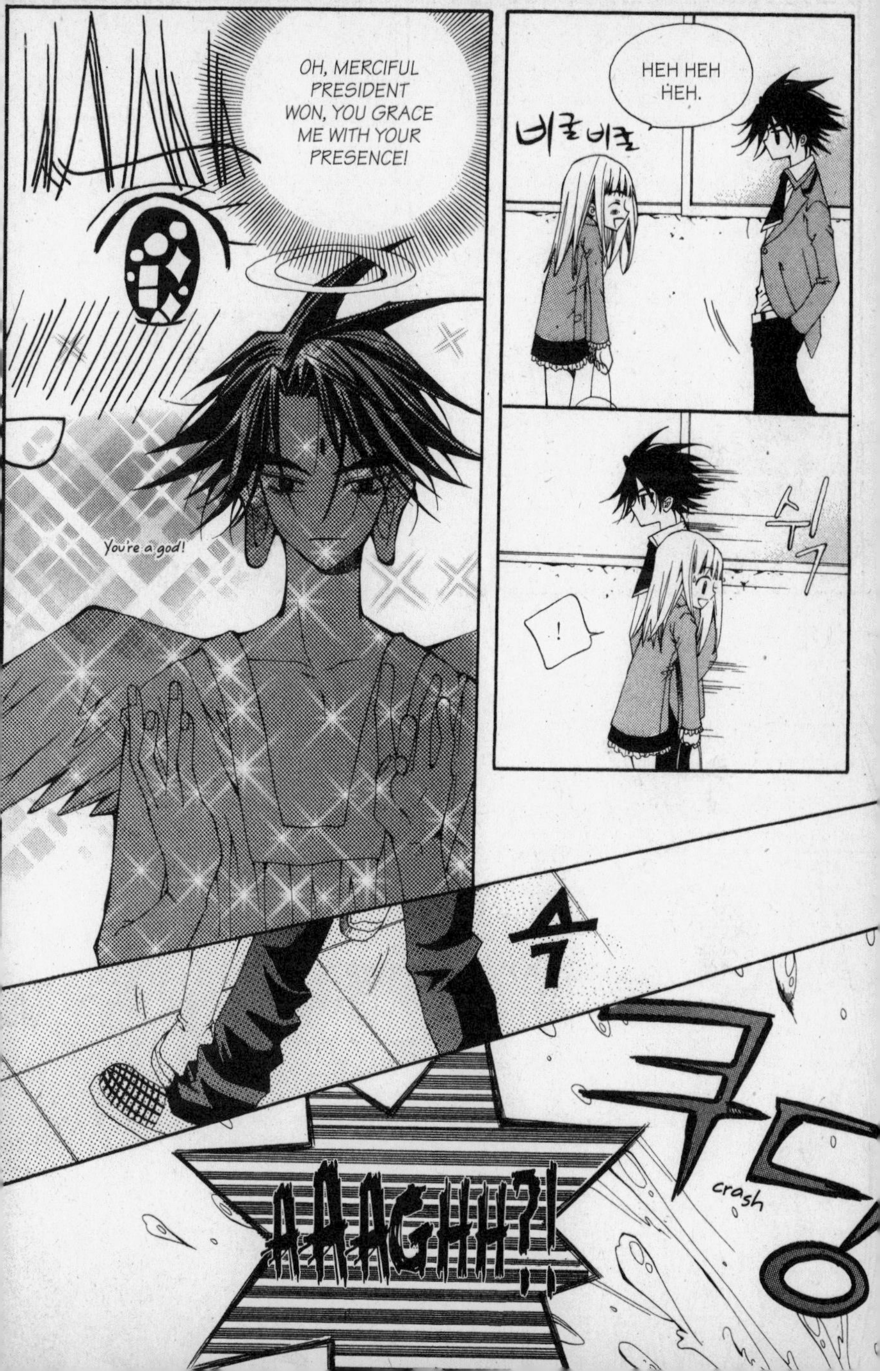

OH, MERCIFUL PRESIDENT WON, YOU GRACE ME WITH YOUR PRESENCE!
You're a god!
HEH HEH HEH.
비굴비굴
!
AAAGHH?!
crash

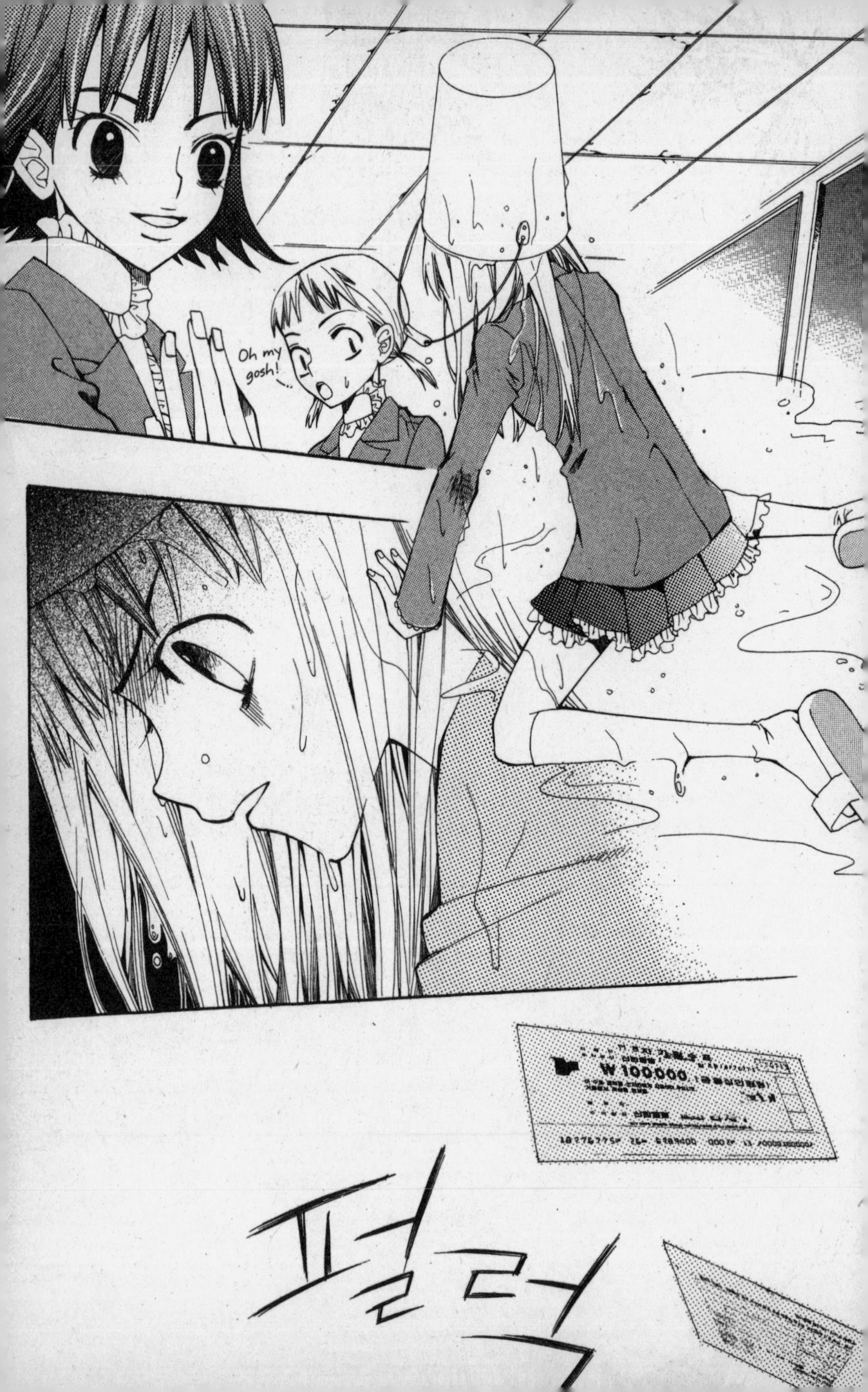

Oh my gosh!...
₩100,000
펄럭

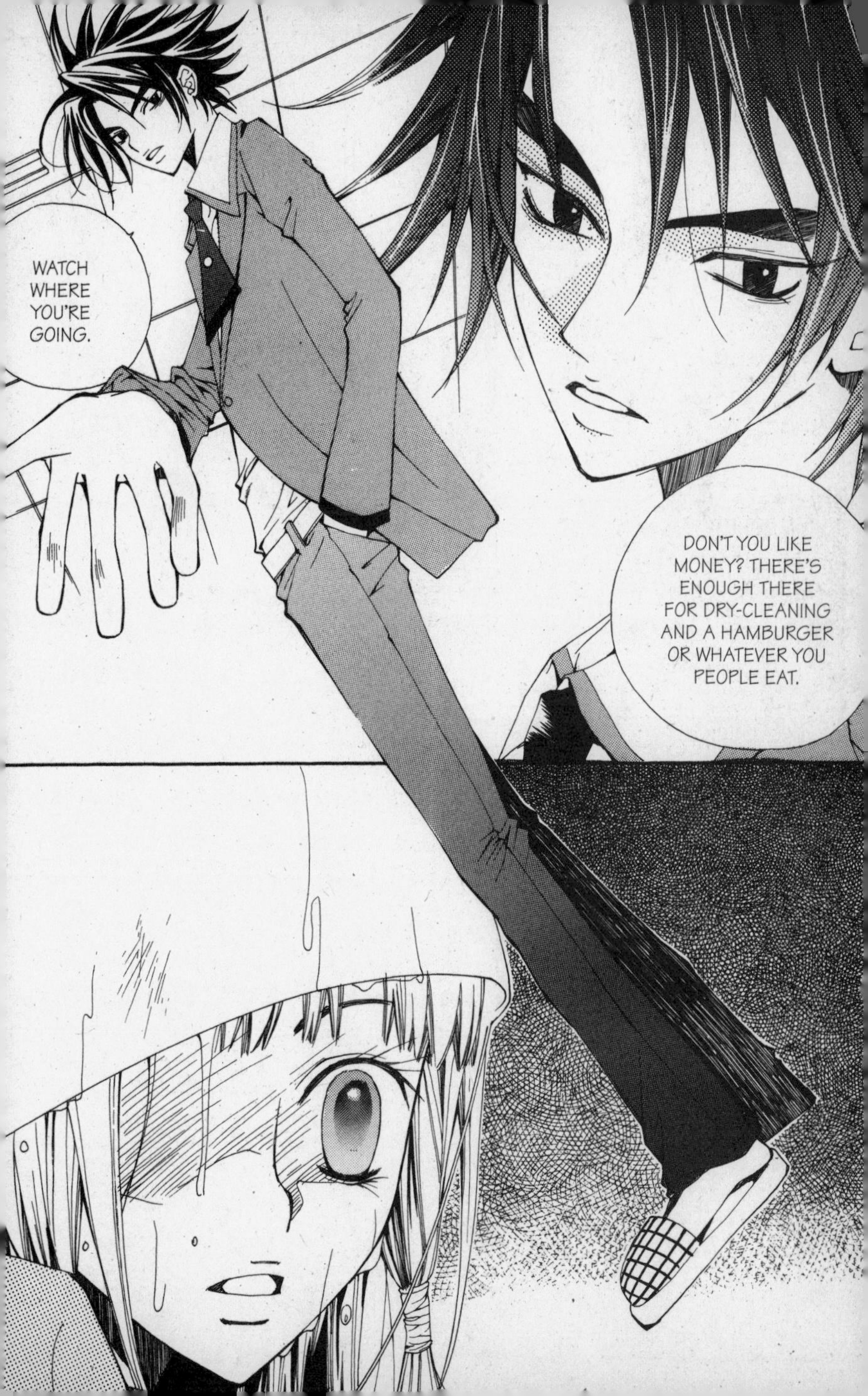
WATCH WHERE YOU'RE GOING.
DON'T YOU LIKE MONEY? THERE'S ENOUGH THERE FOR DRY-CLEANING AND A HAMBURGER OR WHATEVER YOU PEOPLE EAT.

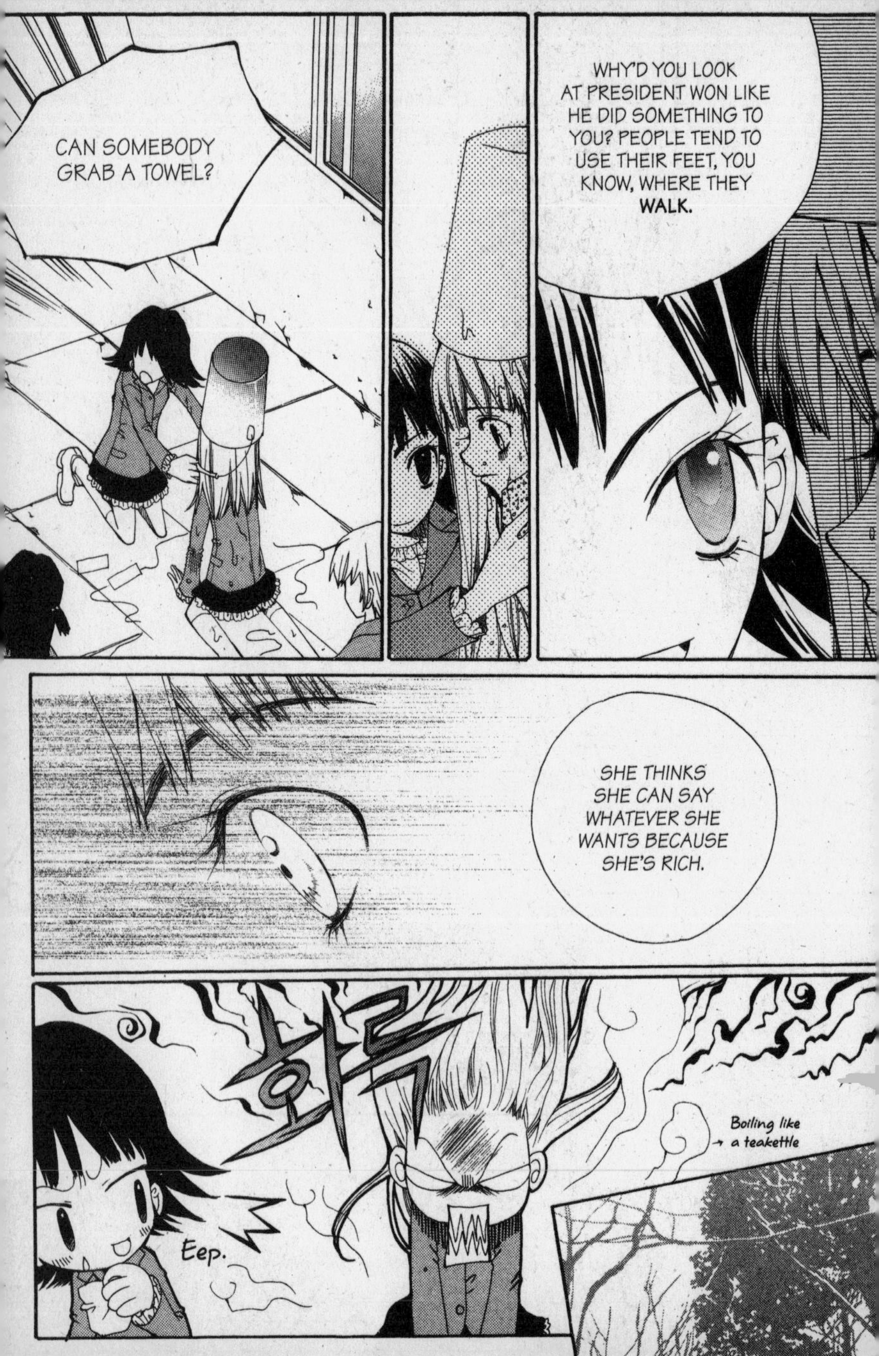

CAN SOMEBODY GRAB A TOWEL?
WHY'D YOU LOOK AT PRESIDENT WON LIKE HE DID SOMETHING TO YOU? PEOPLE TEND TO USE THEIR FEET, YOU KNOW, WHERE THEY **WALK.**
SHE THINKS SHE CAN SAY WHATEVER SHE WANTS BECAUSE SHE'S RICH.
Eep.
Boiling like a teakettle

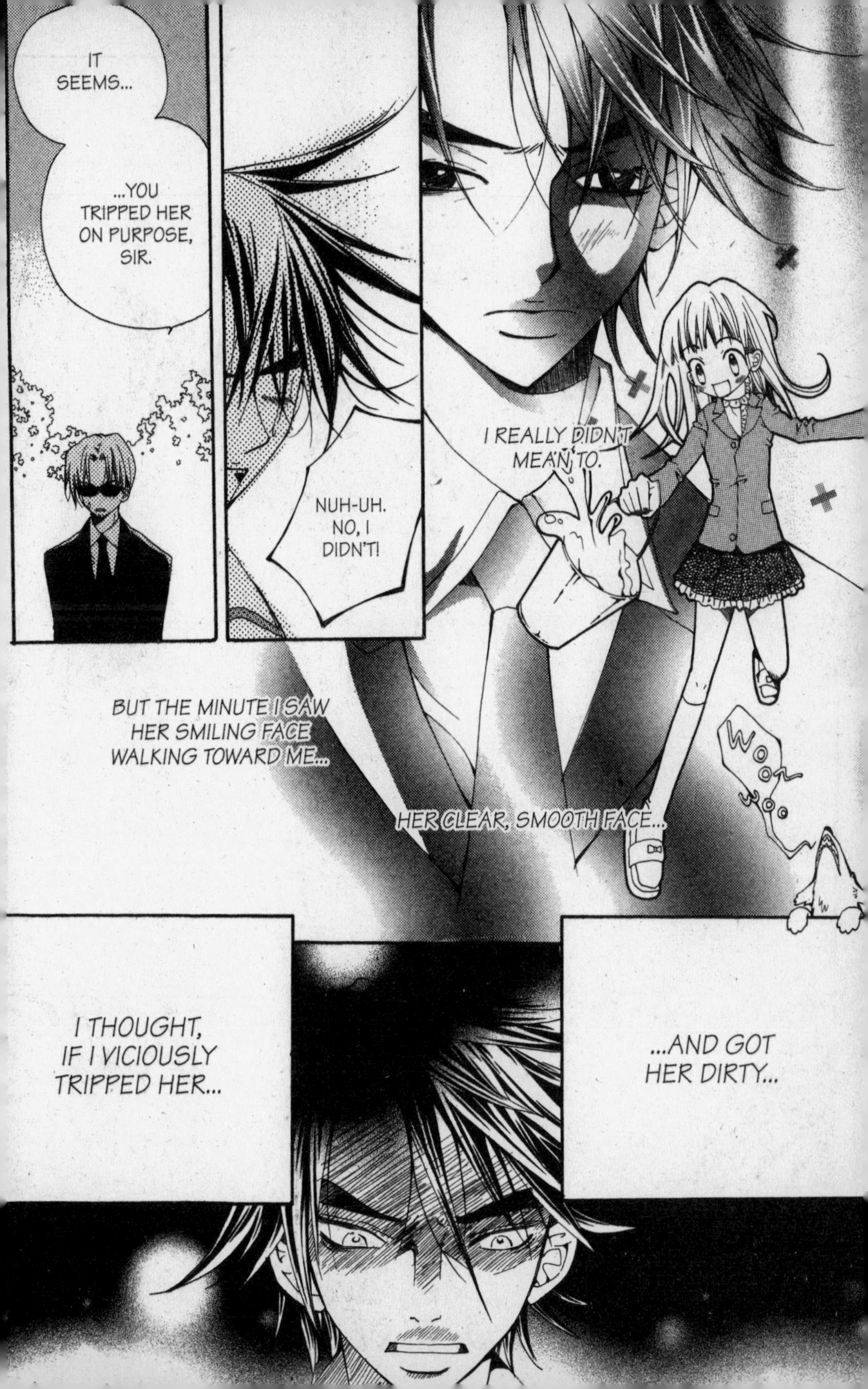
IT SEEMS...
...YOU TRIPPED HER ON PURPOSE, SIR.
NUH-UH. NO, I DIDN'T!
I REALLY DIDN'T MEAN TO.
BUT THE MINUTE I SAW HER SMILING FACE WALKING TOWARD ME...
HER CLEAR, SMOOTH FACE...
WOO WOO
I THOUGHT, IF I VICIOUSLY TRIPPED HER...
...AND GOT HER DIRTY...

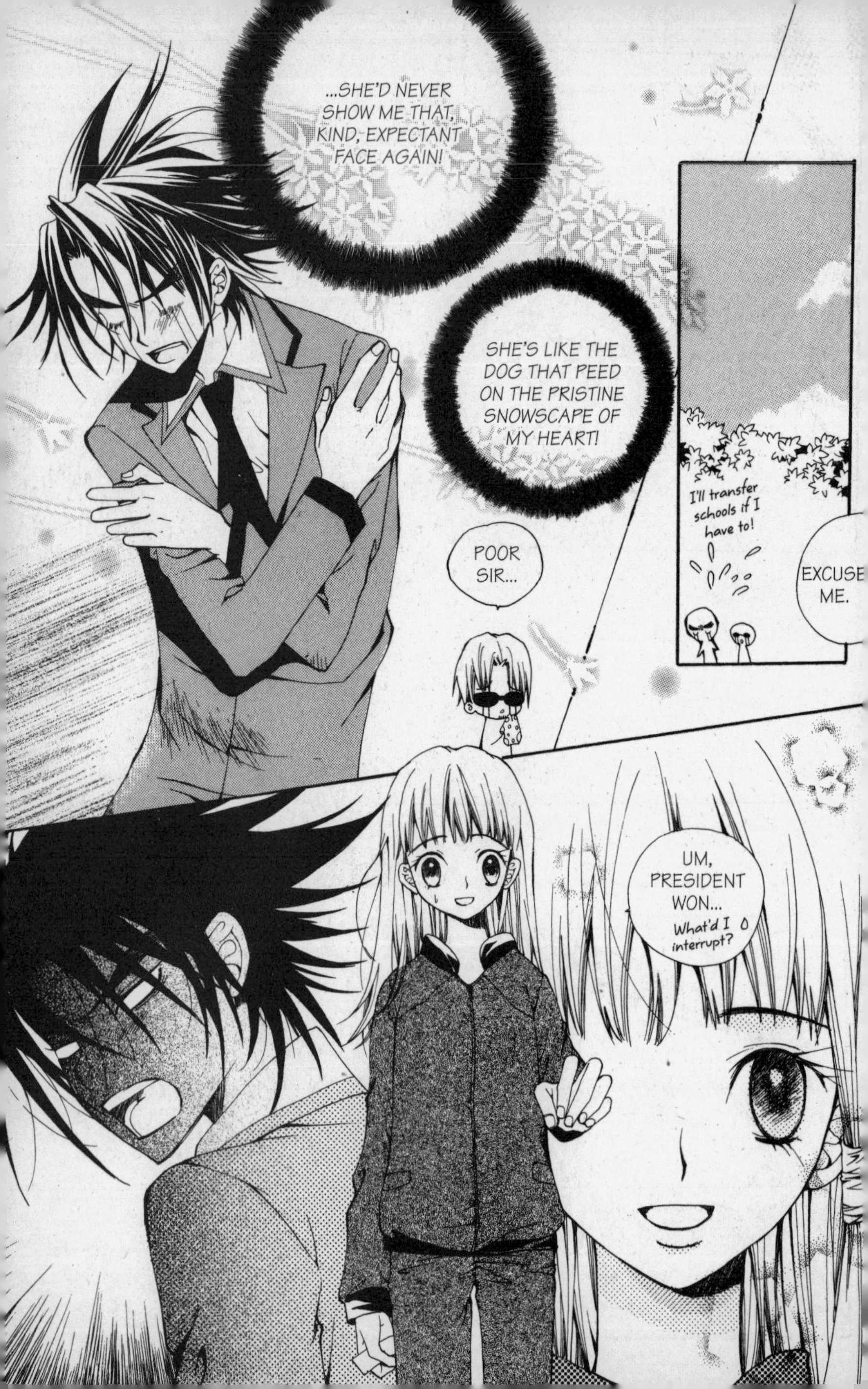
...SHE'D NEVER SHOW ME THAT, KIND, EXPECTANT FACE AGAIN!
SHE'S LIKE THE DOG THAT PEED ON THE PRISTINE SNOWSCAPE OF MY HEART!
POOR SIR...
I'll transfer schools if I have to!
EXCUSE ME.
UM, PRESIDENT WON...
What'd I interrupt?

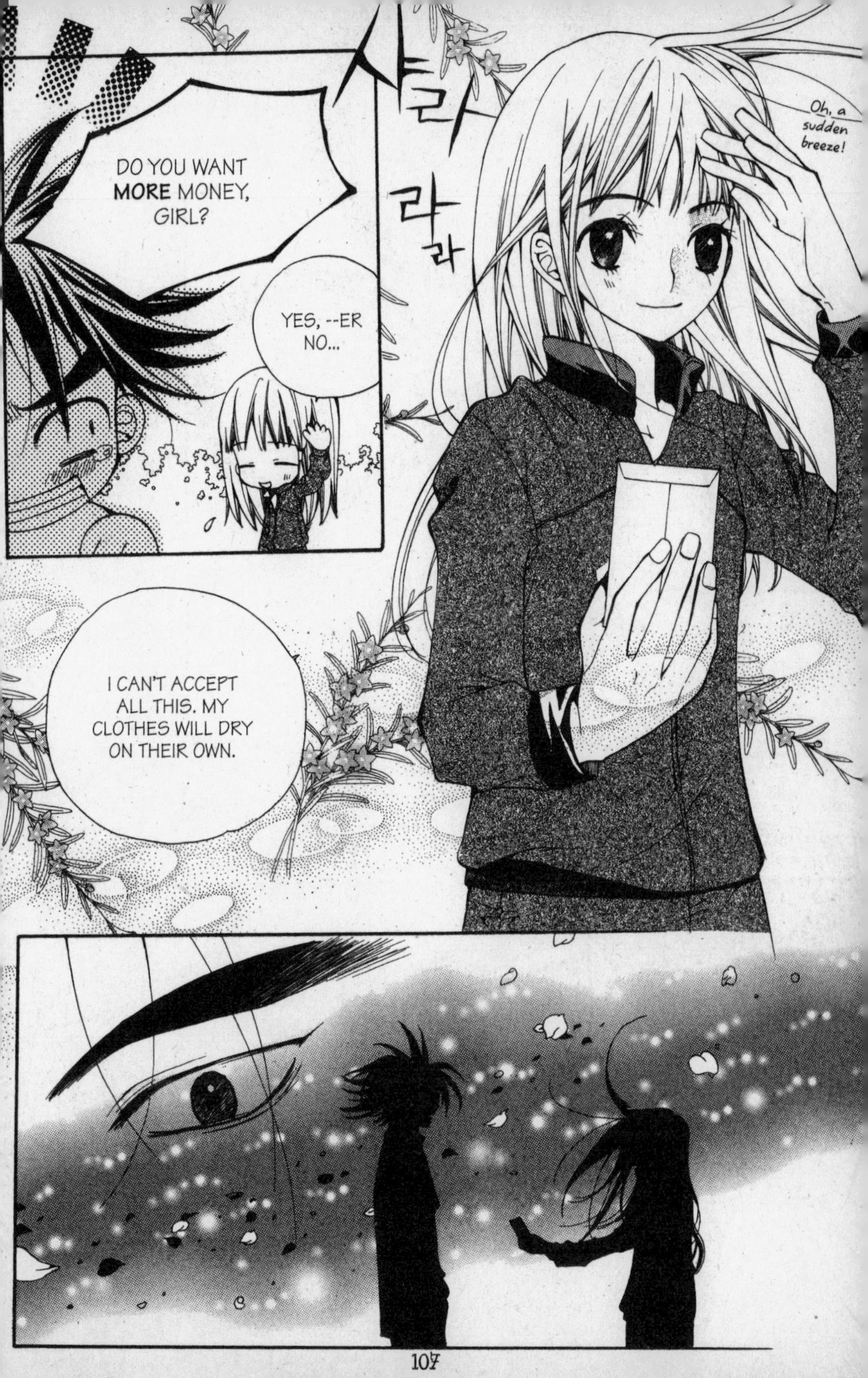
DO YOU WANT MORE MONEY, GIRL?
YES, --ER NO...
샤라라라
Oh, a sudden breeze!
I CAN'T ACCEPT ALL THIS. MY CLOTHES WILL DRY ON THEIR OWN.

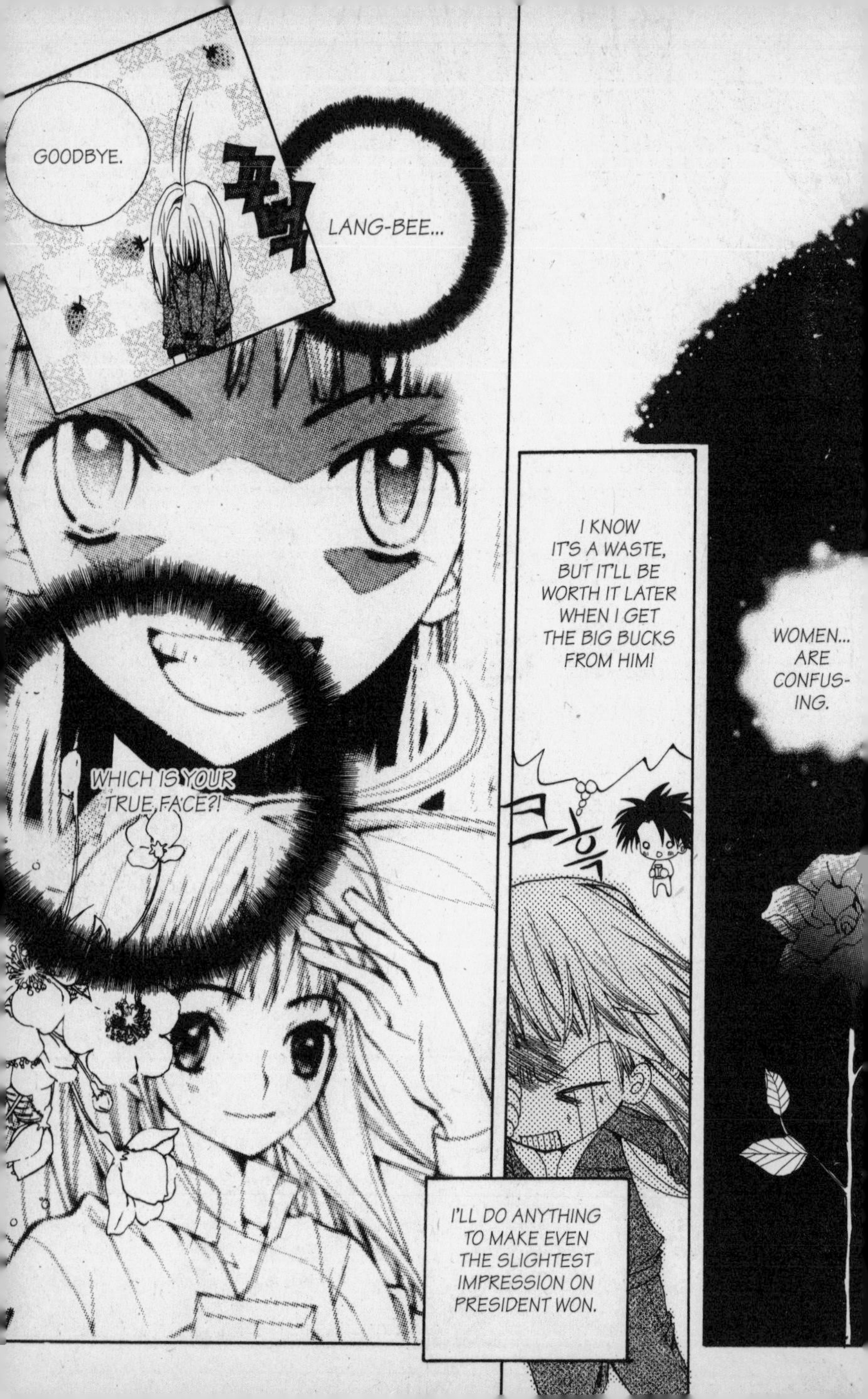
GOODBYE.
LANG-BEE...
WHICH IS YOUR TRUE FACE?!
I KNOW IT'S A WASTE, BUT IT'LL BE WORTH IT LATER WHEN I GET THE BIG BUCKS FROM HIM!
I'LL DO ANYTHING TO MAKE EVEN THE SLIGHTEST IMPRESSION ON PRESIDENT WON.
WOMEN... ARE CONFUS-ING.

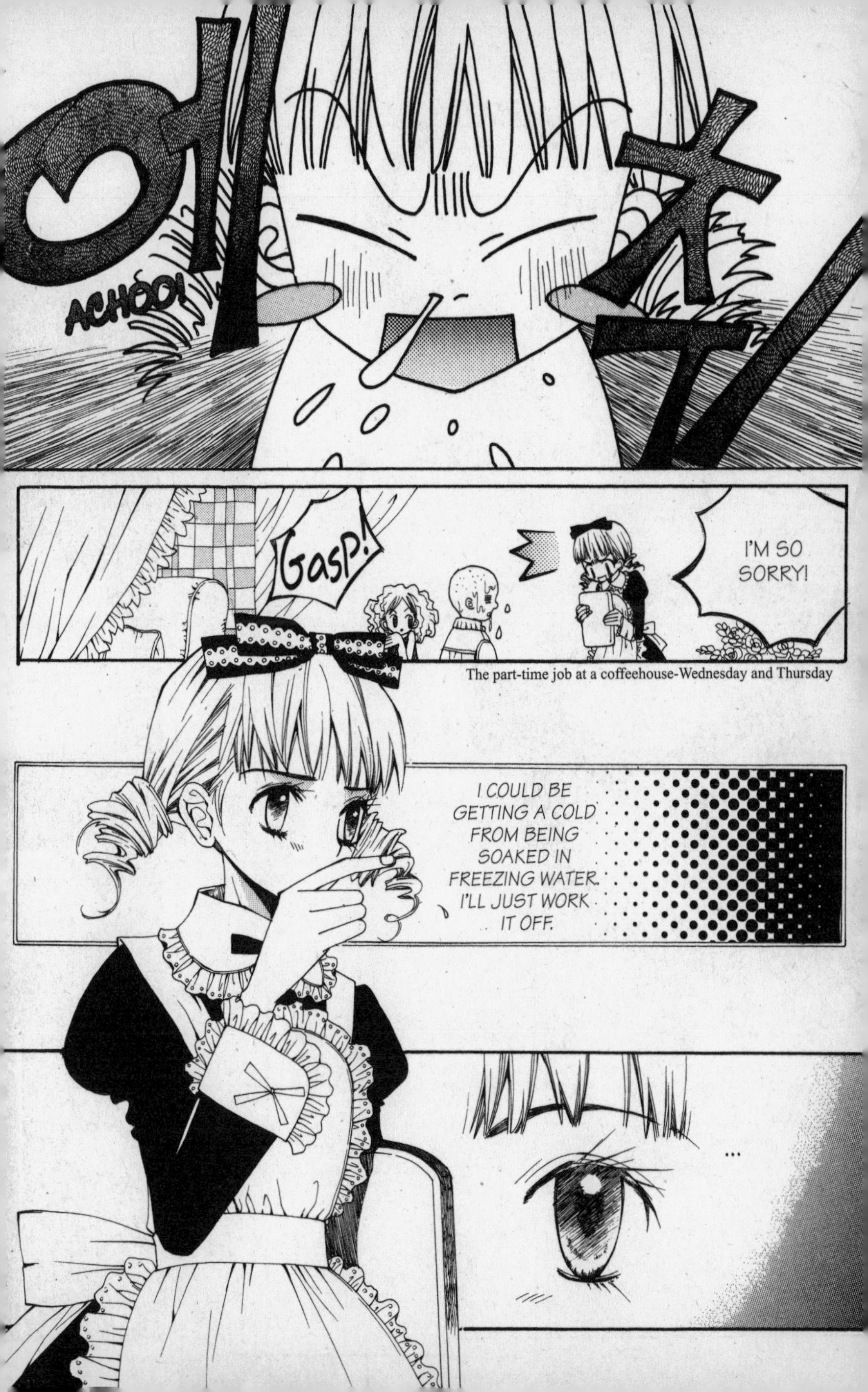
ACHOO!
Gasp!
I'M SO SORRY!
The part-time job at a coffeehouse-Wednesday and Thursday
I COULD BE GETTING A COLD FROM BEING SOAKED IN FREEZING WATER. I'LL JUST WORK IT OFF.
...

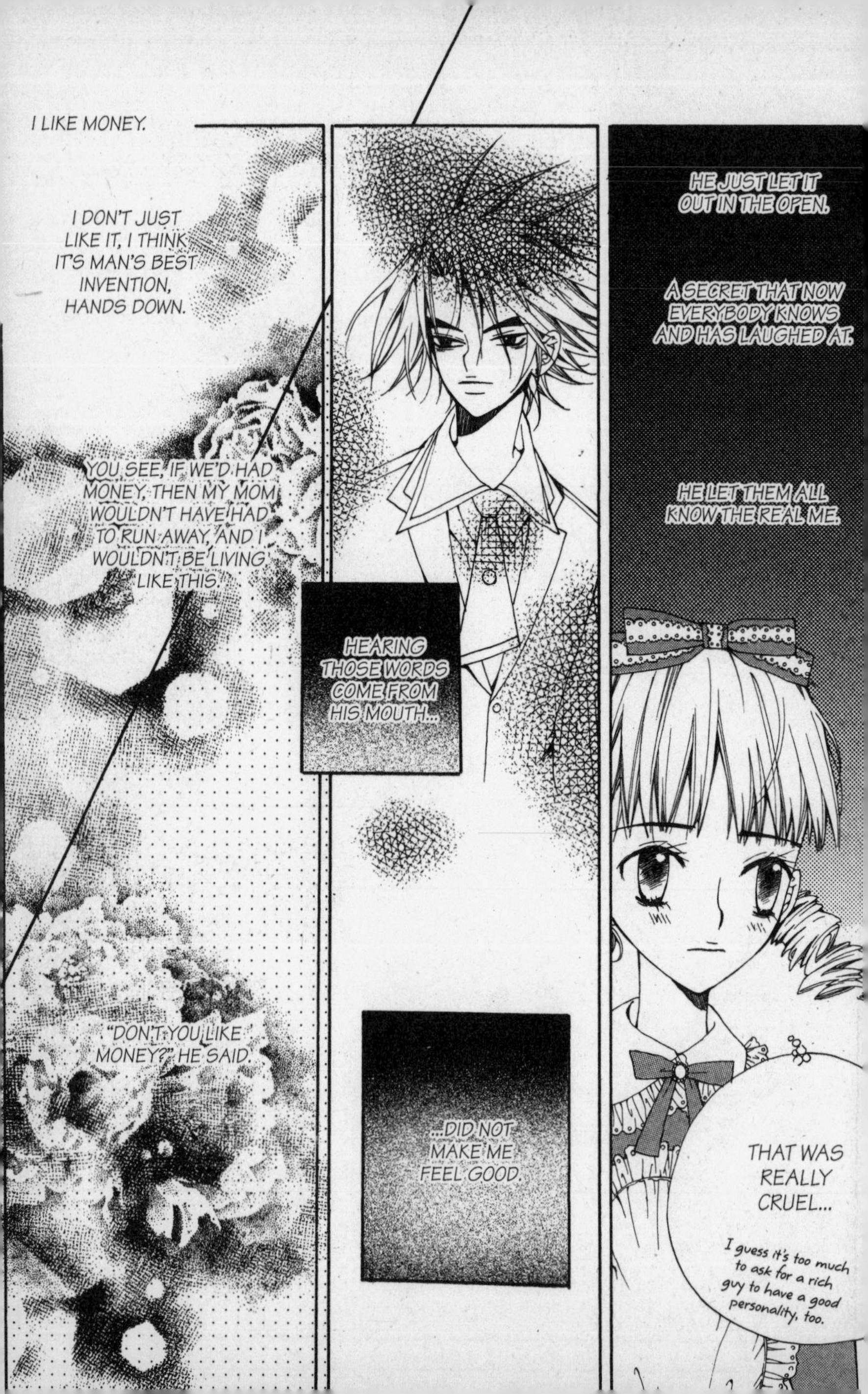
I LIKE MONEY.
I DON'T JUST LIKE IT, I THINK IT'S MAN'S BEST INVENTION, HANDS DOWN.
YOU SEE, IF WE'D HAD MONEY, THEN MY MOM WOULDN'T HAVE HAD TO RUN AWAY, AND I WOULDN'T BE LIVING LIKE THIS.
"DON'T YOU LIKE MONEY?" HE SAID.
HEARING THOSE WORDS COME FROM HIS MOUTH...
...DID NOT MAKE ME FEEL GOOD.
HE JUST LET IT OUT IN THE OPEN.
A SECRET THAT NOW EVERYBODY KNOWS AND HAS LAUGHED AT.
HE LET THEM ALL KNOW THE REAL ME.
THAT WAS REALLY CRUEL...
I guess it's too much to ask for a rich guy to have a good personality, too.

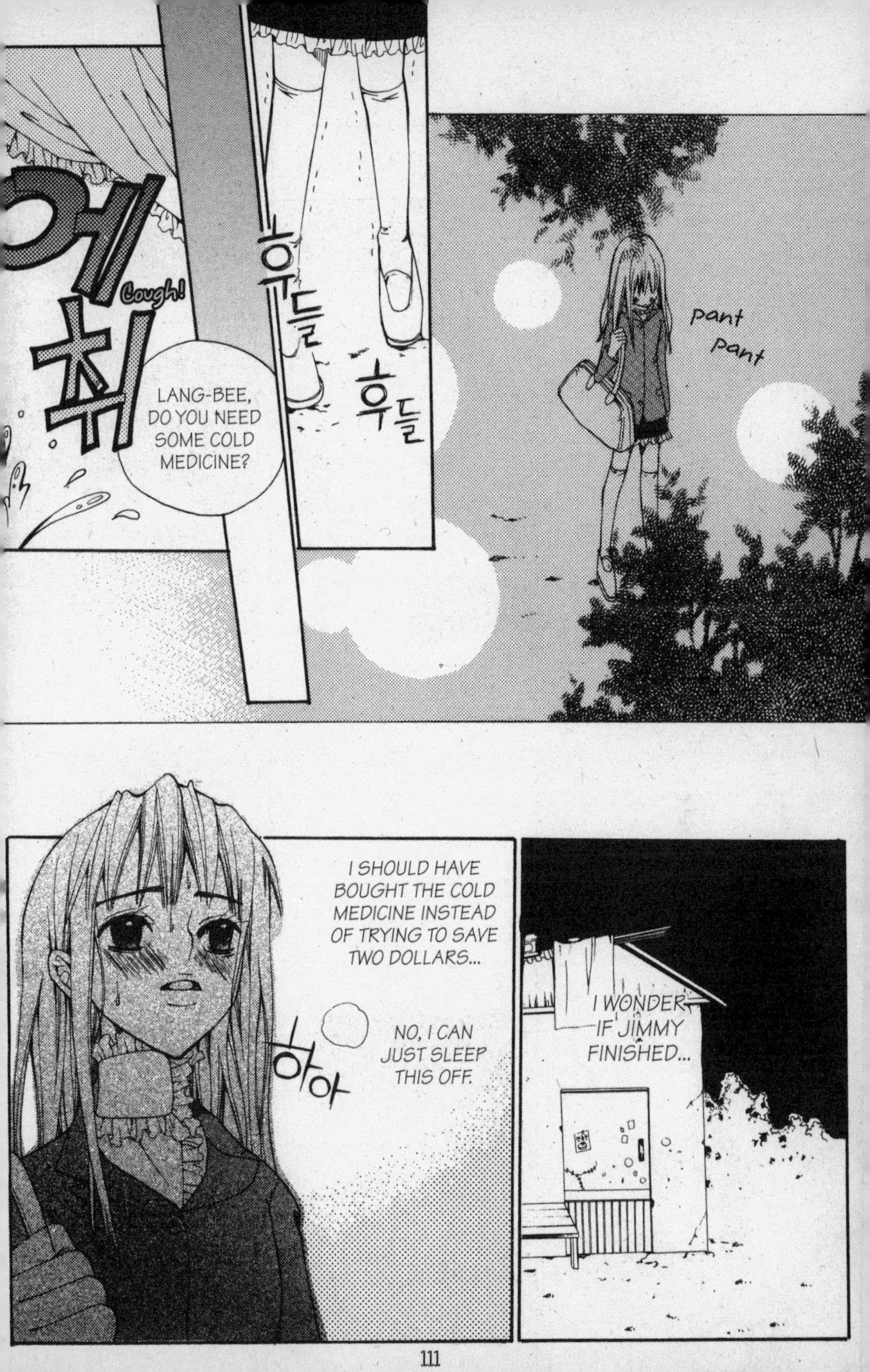

에취
Cough!
LANG-BEE, DO YOU NEED SOME COLD MEDICINE?
후들 후들
pant pant
I SHOULD HAVE BOUGHT THE COLD MEDICINE INSTEAD OF TRYING TO SAVE TWO DOLLARS...
하아
NO, I CAN JUST SLEEP THIS OFF.
I WONDER IF JIMMY FINISHED...

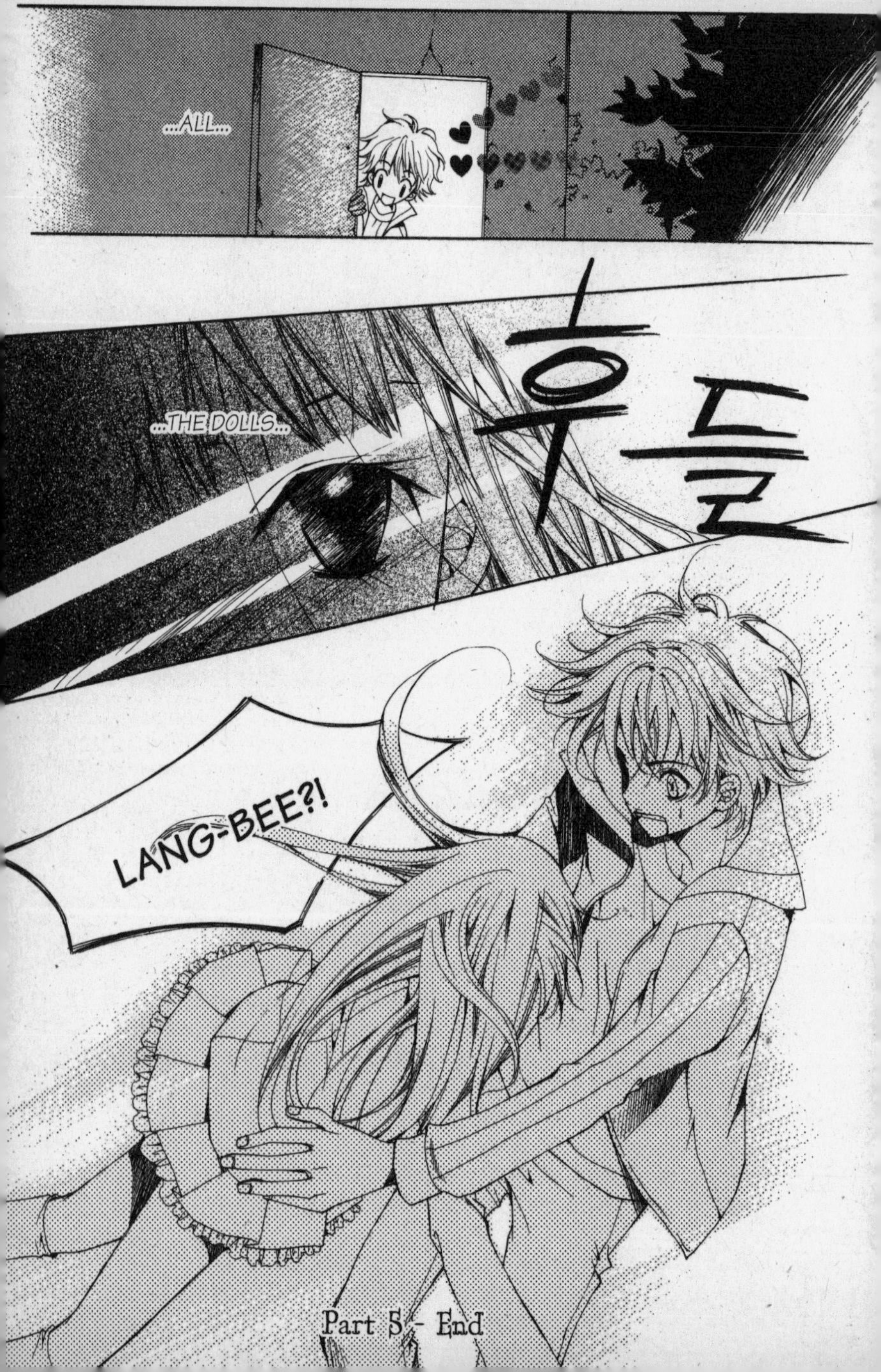
...ALL...
...THE DOLLS...
LANG-BEE?!
Part 5 - End

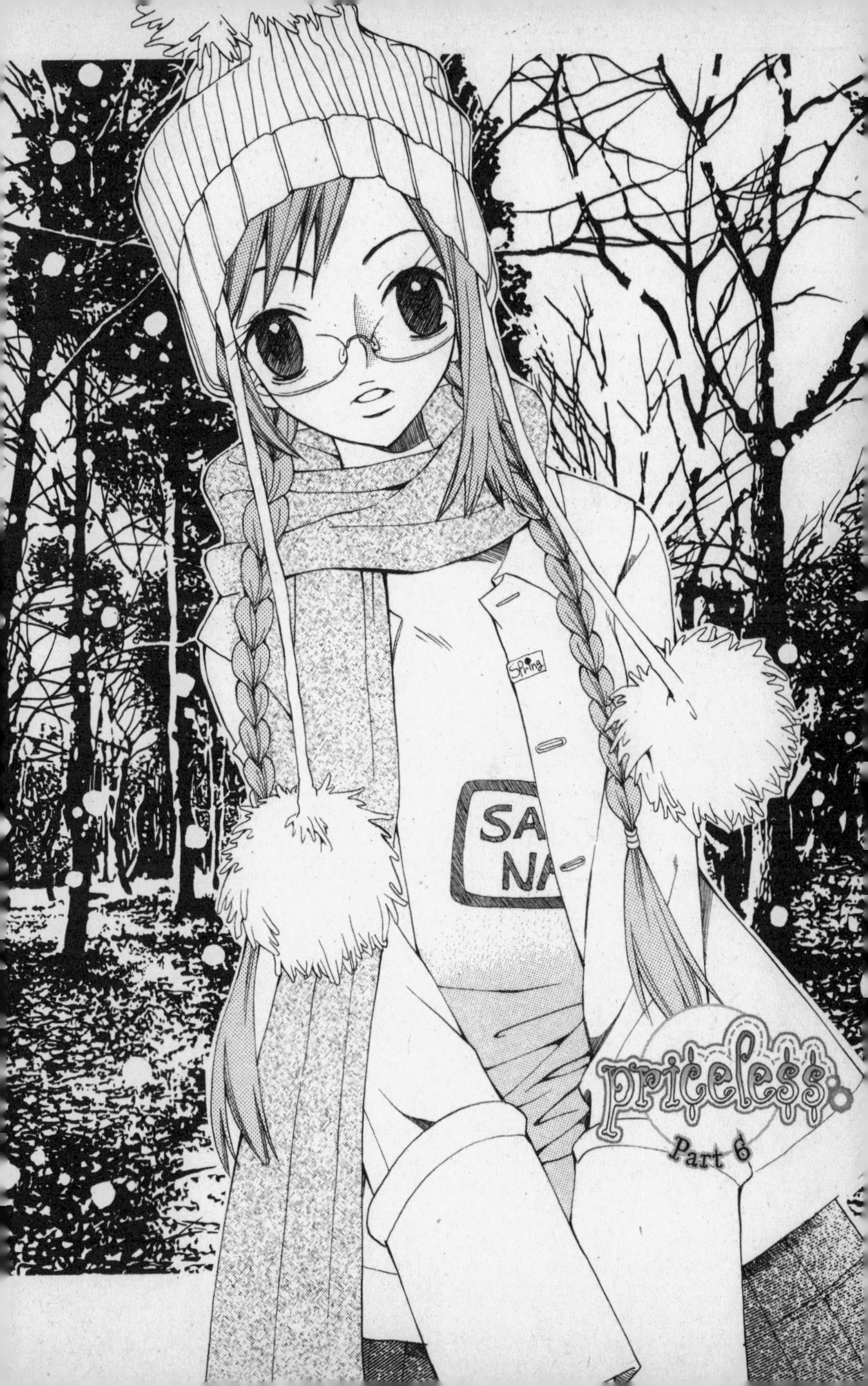
priceless
Part 6
Spring
SA
NA

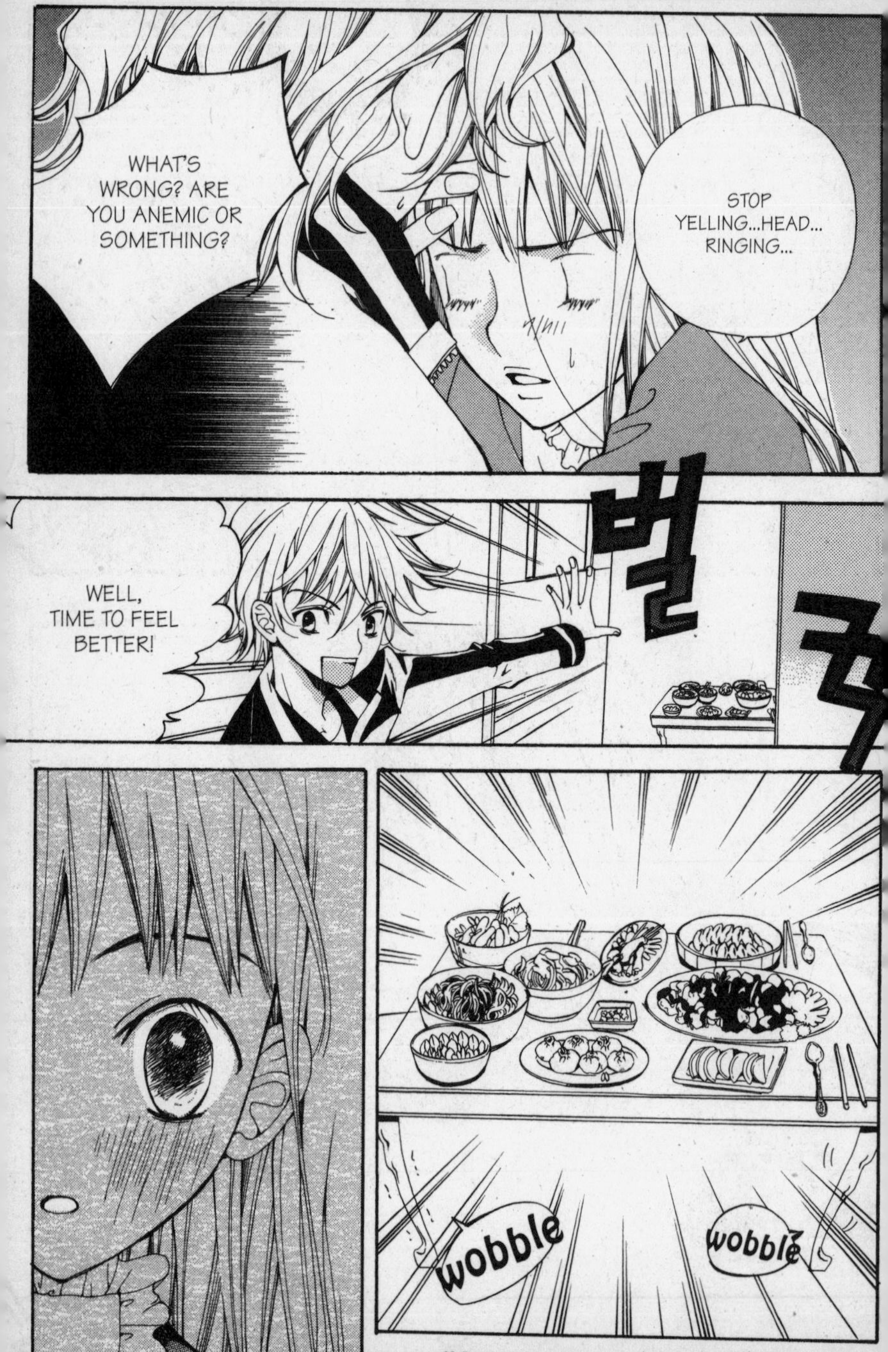
WHAT'S WRONG? ARE YOU ANEMIC OR SOMETHING?
STOP YELLING...HEAD... RINGING...
WELL, TIME TO FEEL BETTER!
벌컥
wobble
wobble

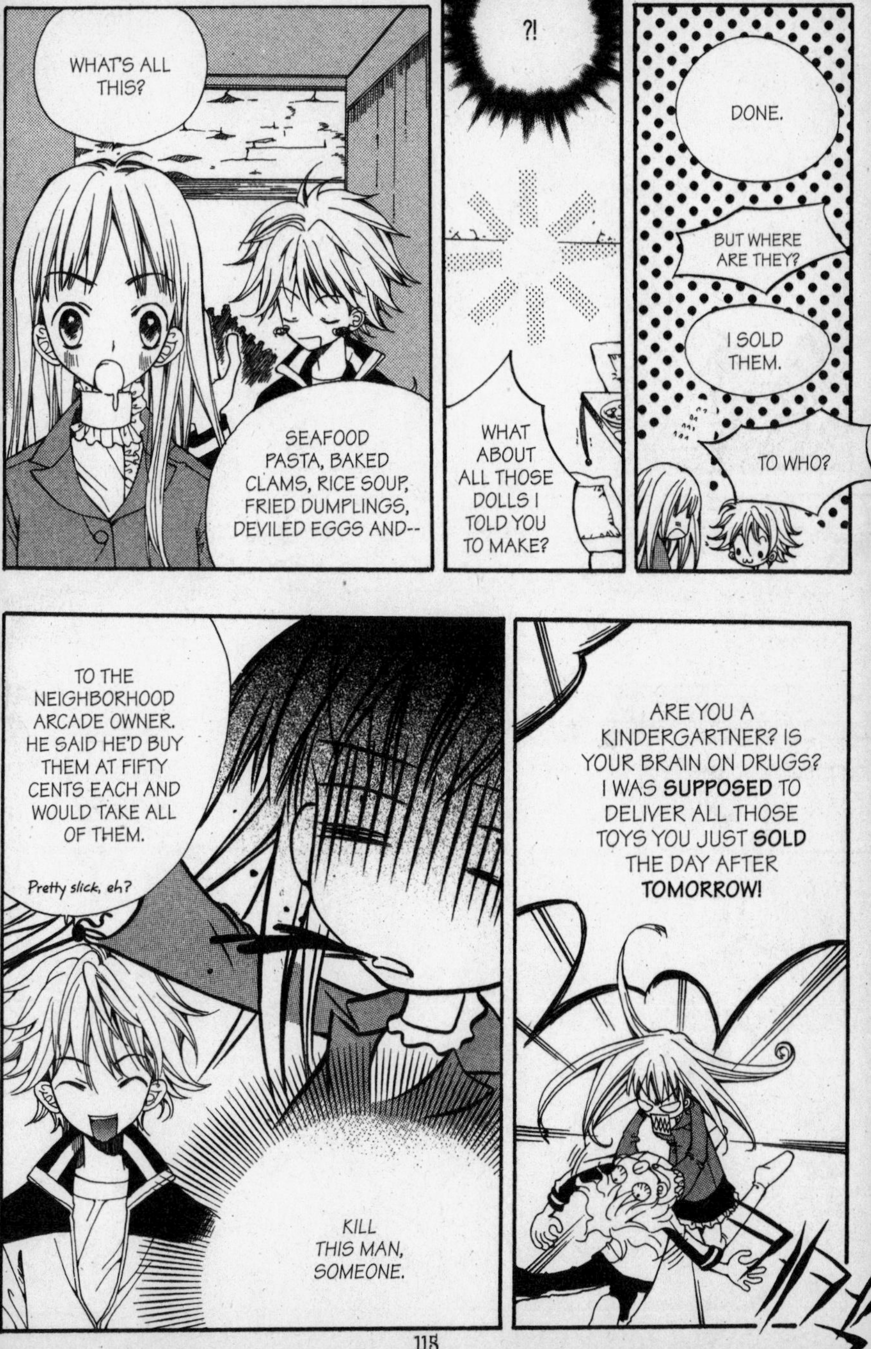
WHAT'S ALL THIS?
SEAFOOD PASTA, BAKED CLAMS, RICE SOUP, FRIED DUMPLINGS, DEVILED EGGS AND--
?!
WHAT ABOUT ALL THOSE DOLLS I TOLD YOU TO MAKE?
DONE.
BUT WHERE ARE THEY?
I SOLD THEM.
TO WHO?
TO THE NEIGHBORHOOD ARCADE OWNER. HE SAID HE'D BUY THEM AT FIFTY CENTS EACH AND WOULD TAKE ALL OF THEM.
Pretty slick, eh?
KILL THIS MAN, SOMEONE.
ARE YOU A KINDERGARTNER? IS YOUR BRAIN ON DRUGS? I WAS **SUPPOSED** TO DELIVER ALL THOSE TOYS YOU JUST **SOLD** THE DAY AFTER **TOMORROW!**

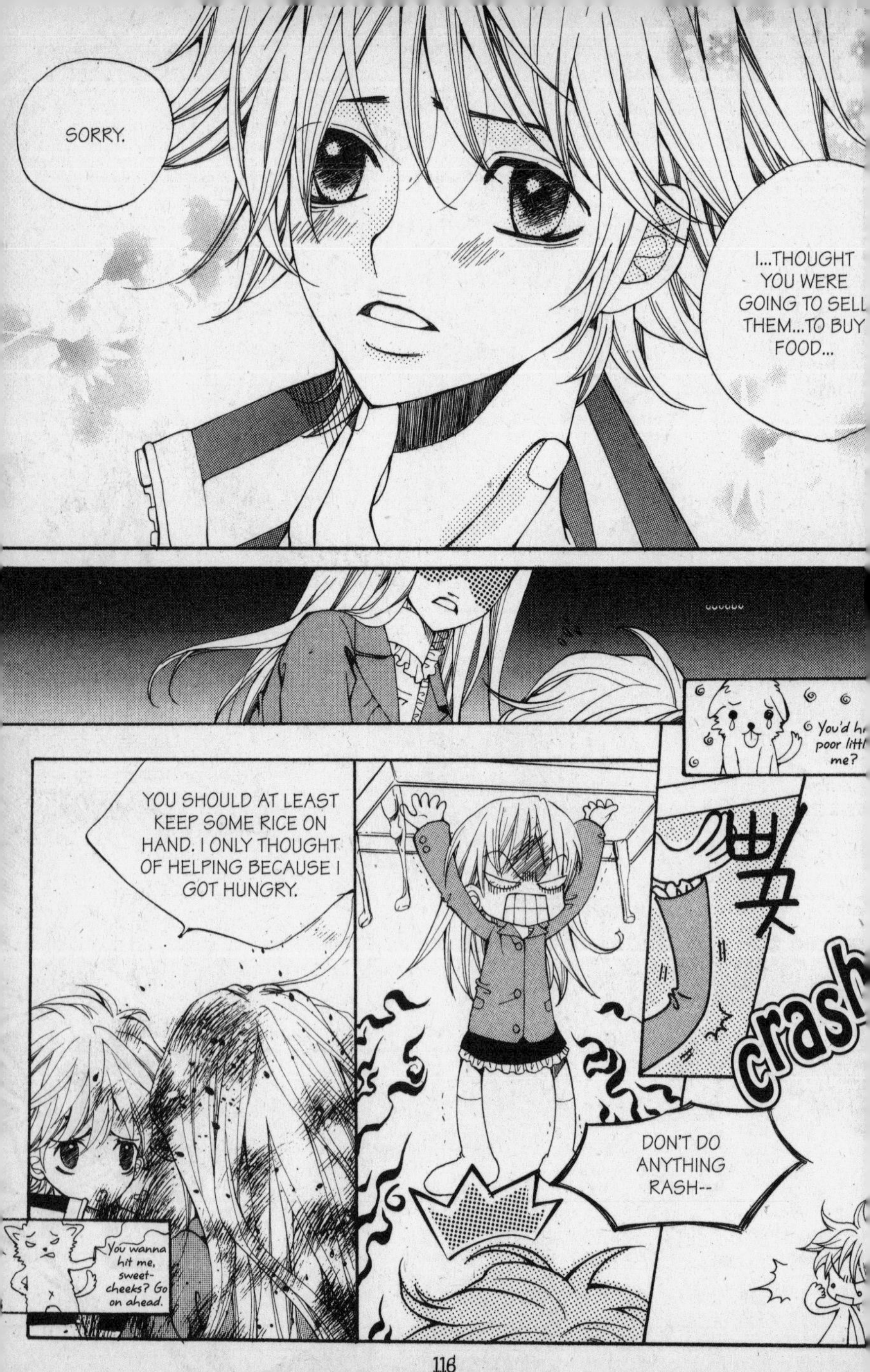
SORRY.
I...THOUGHT YOU WERE GOING TO SELL THEM...TO BUY FOOD...
You'd h poor littl me?
YOU SHOULD AT LEAST KEEP SOME RICE ON HAND. I ONLY THOUGHT OF HELPING BECAUSE I GOT HUNGRY.
You wanna hit me, sweet-cheeks? Go on ahead.
DON'T DO ANYTHING RASH--
crash

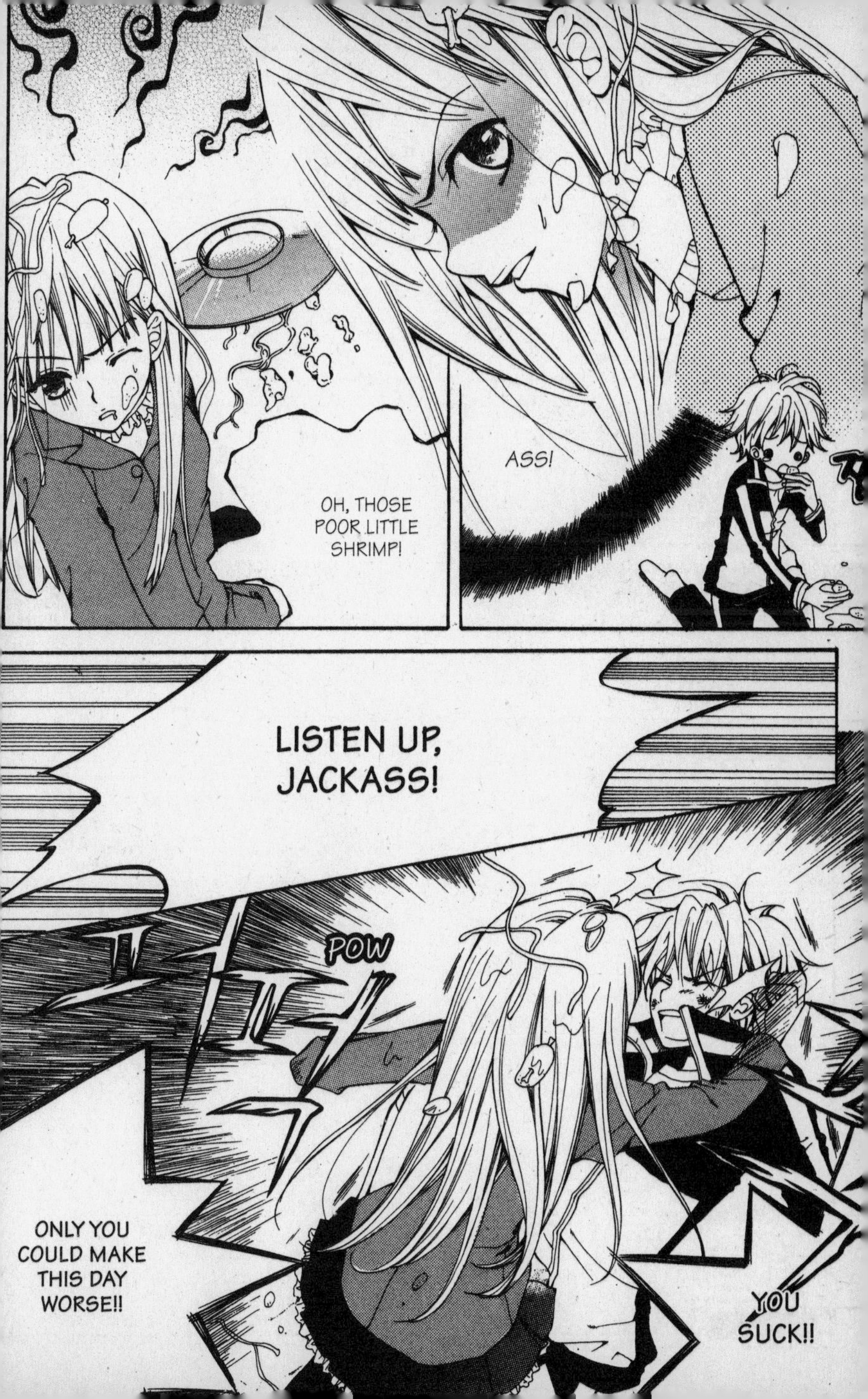
OH, THOSE POOR LITTLE SHRIMP!
ASS!
LISTEN UP, JACKASS!
POW
ONLY YOU COULD MAKE THIS DAY WORSE!!
YOU SUCK!!

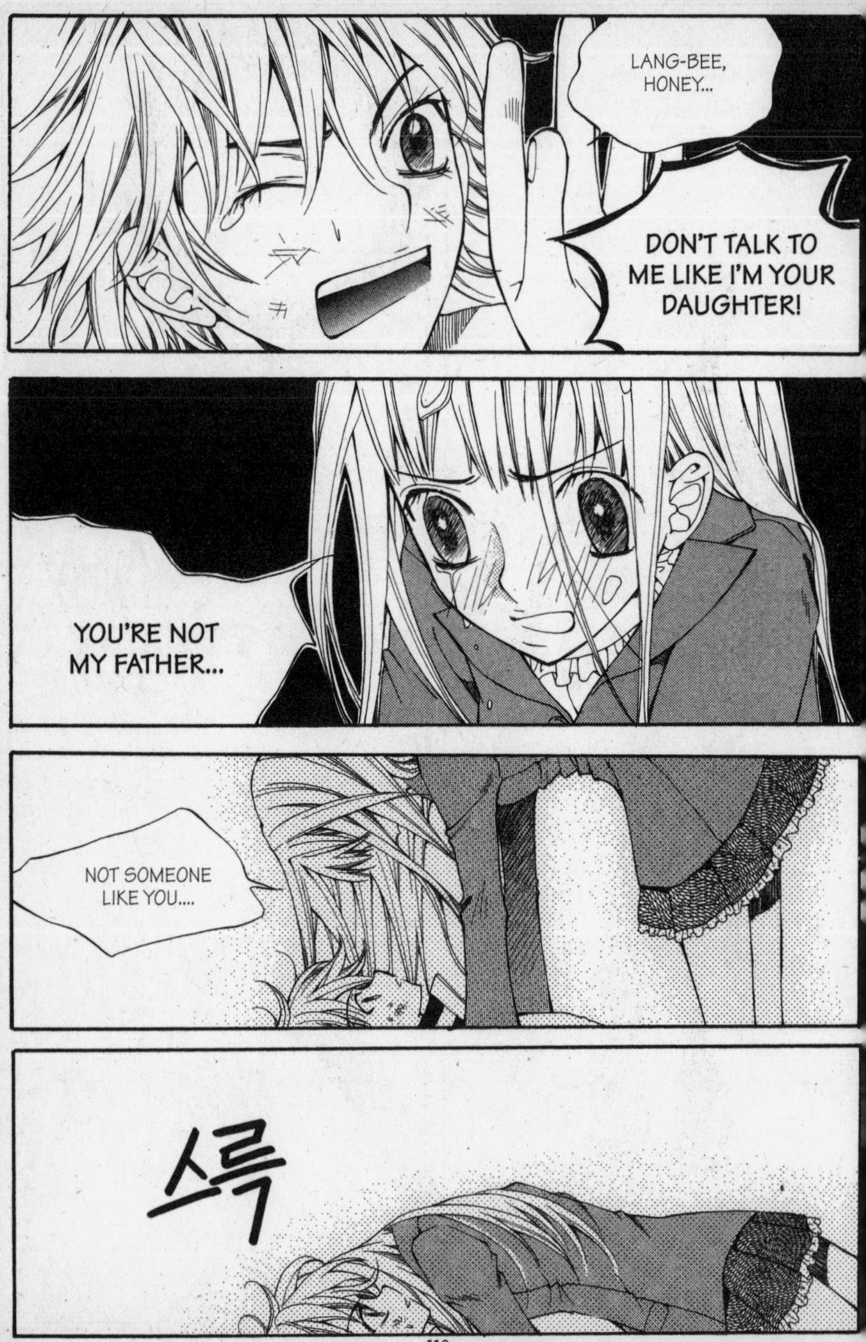
LANG-BEE, HONEY...
DON'T TALK TO ME LIKE I'M YOUR DAUGHTER!
YOU'RE NOT MY FATHER...
NOT SOMEONE LIKE YOU....
스륵

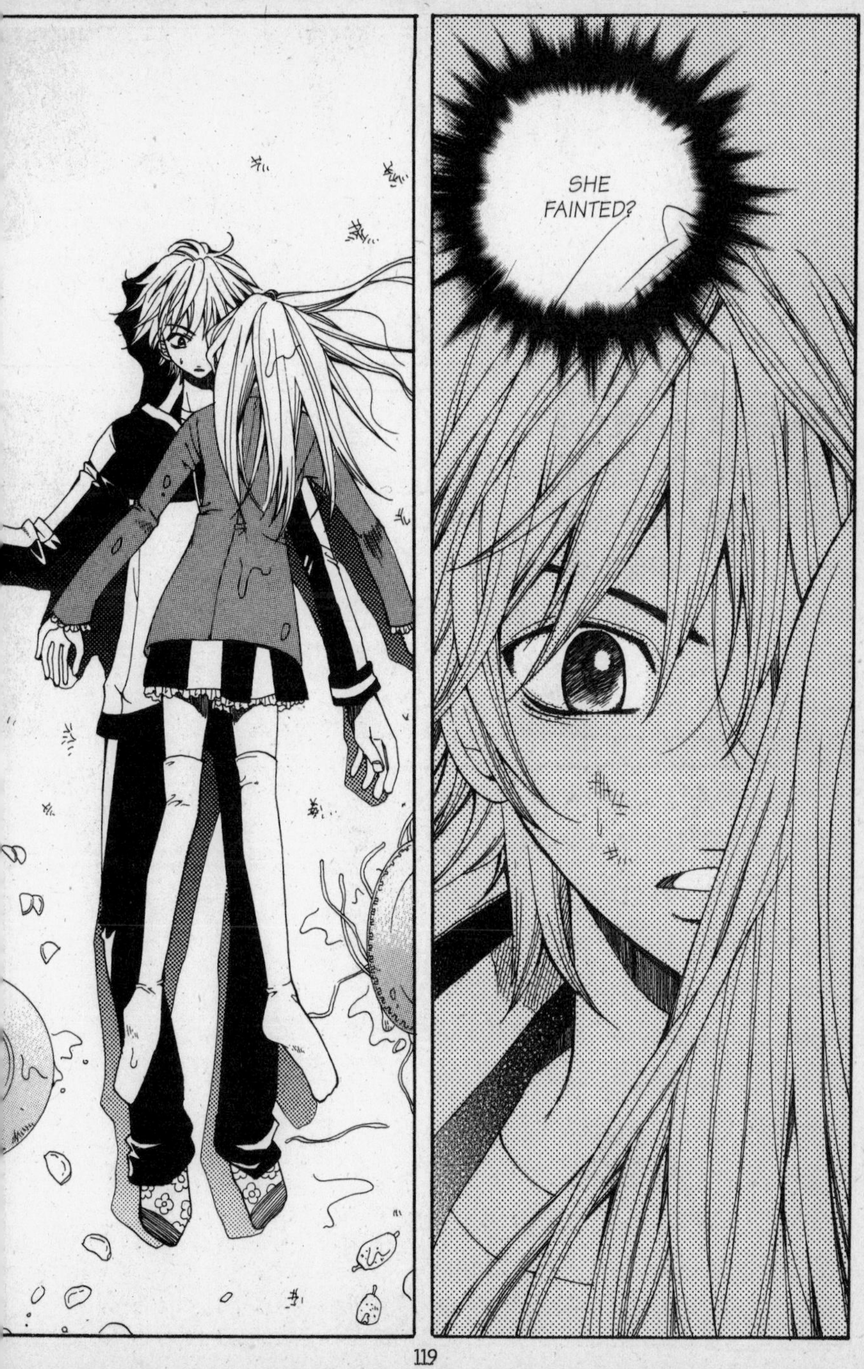
SHE FAINTED?

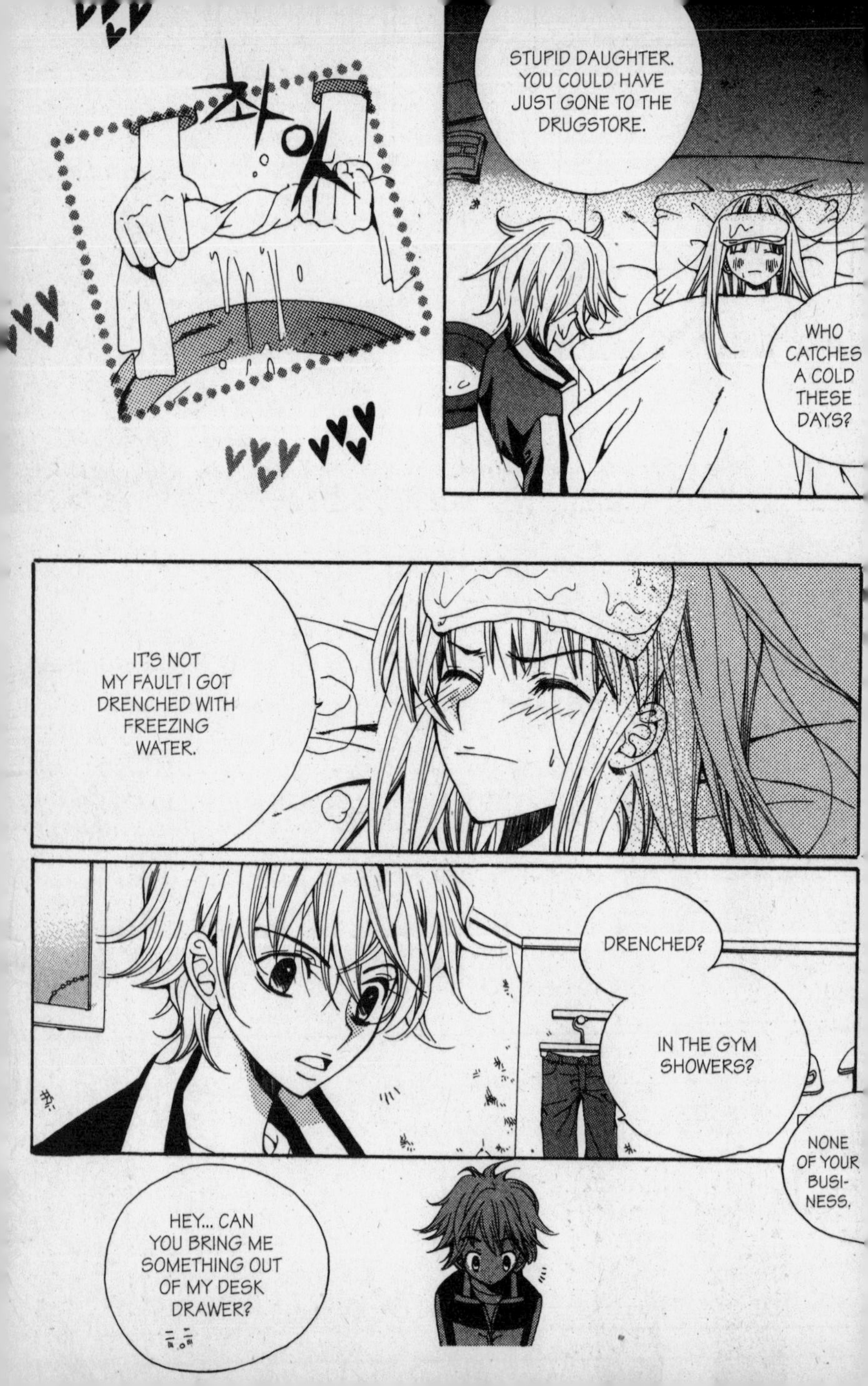
STUPID DAUGHTER. YOU COULD HAVE JUST GONE TO THE DRUGSTORE.
WHO CATCHES A COLD THESE DAYS?
IT'S NOT MY FAULT I GOT DRENCHED WITH FREEZING WATER.
DRENCHED?
IN THE GYM SHOWERS?
NONE OF YOUR BUSI-NESS.
HEY... CAN YOU BRING ME SOMETHING OUT OF MY DESK DRAWER?

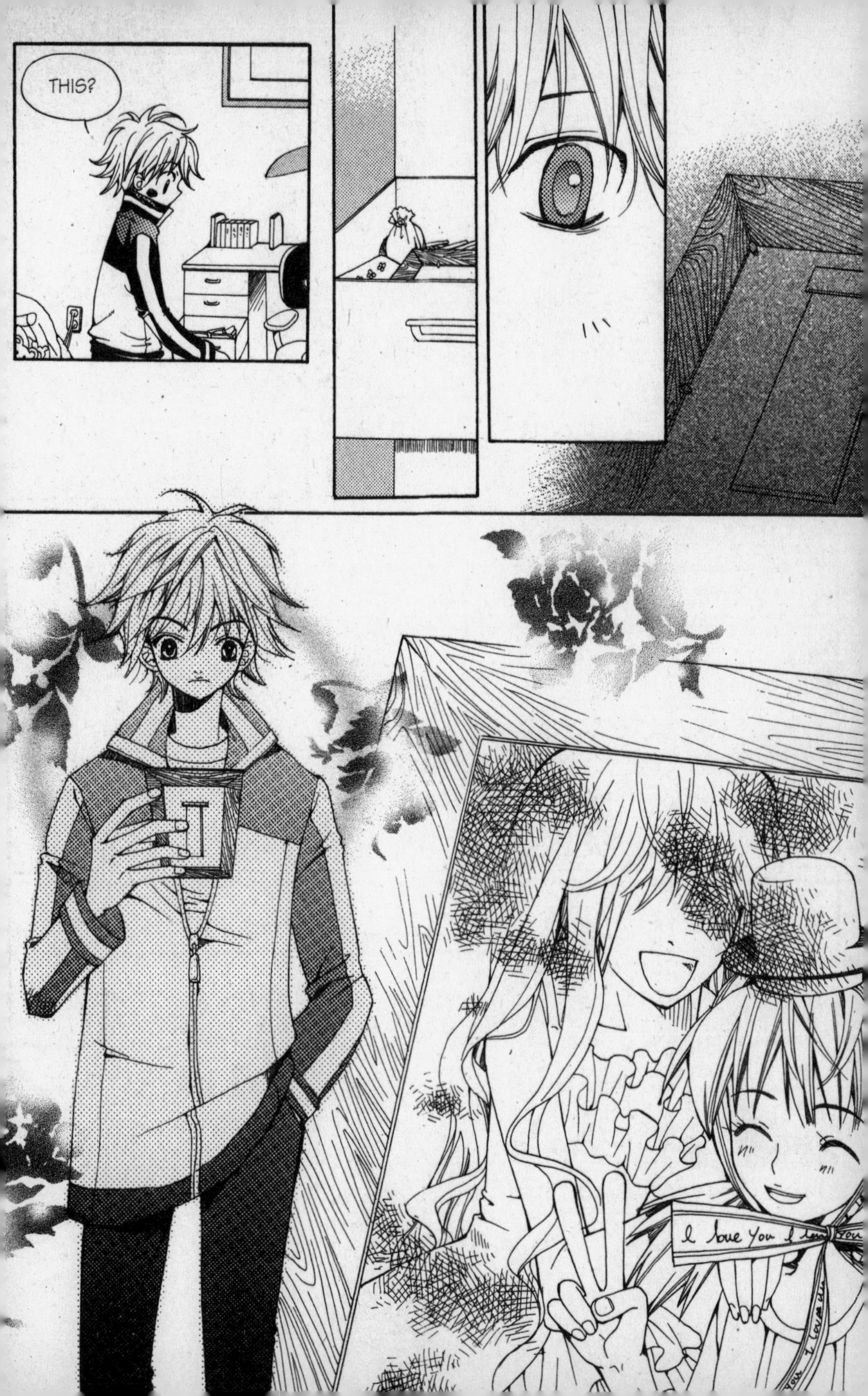
THIS?
I love You

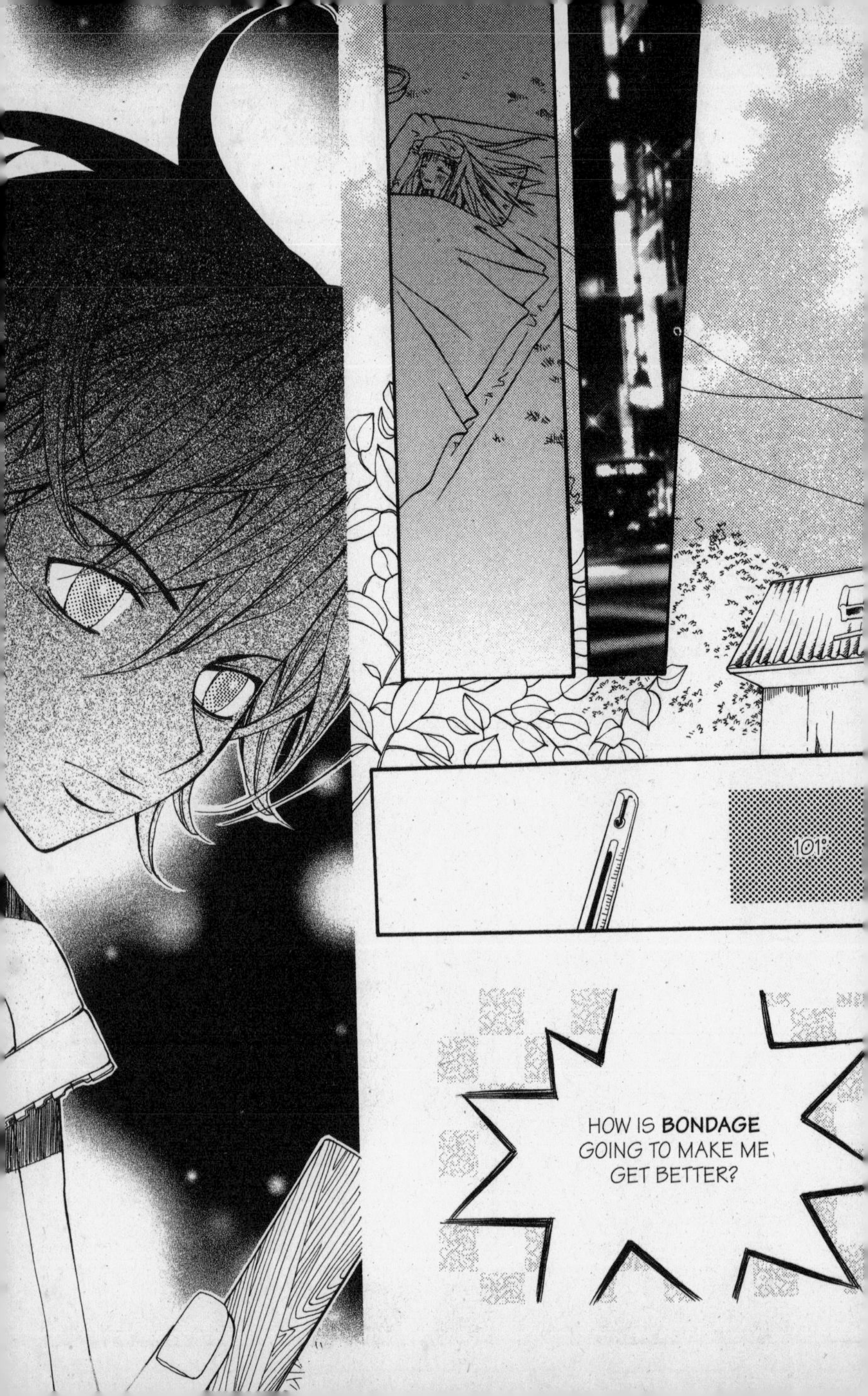
101°
HOW IS BONDAGE GOING TO MAKE ME GET BETTER?

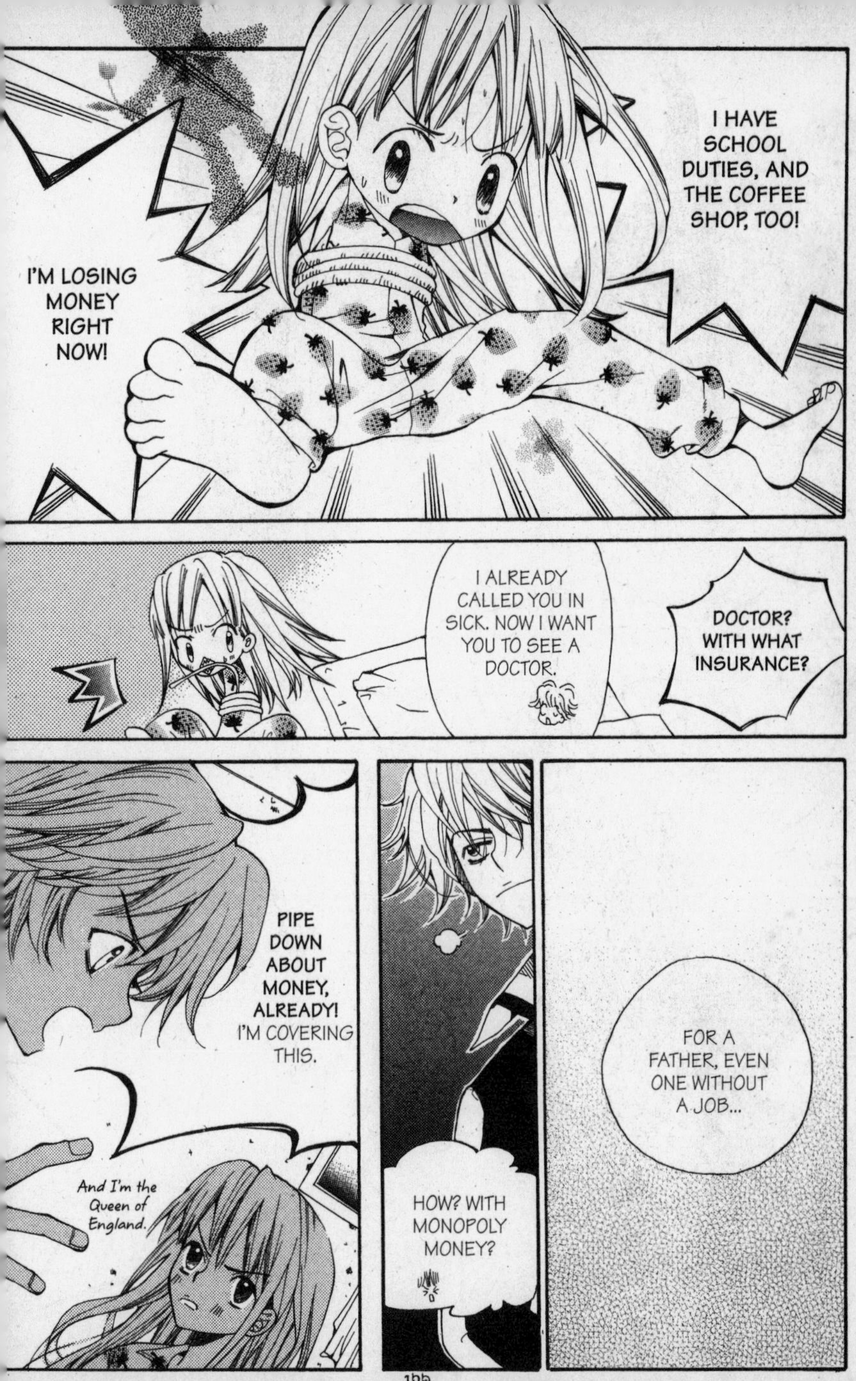
I'M LOSING MONEY RIGHT NOW!
I HAVE SCHOOL DUTIES, AND THE COFFEE SHOP, TOO!
I ALREADY CALLED YOU IN SICK. NOW I WANT YOU TO SEE A DOCTOR.
DOCTOR? WITH WHAT INSURANCE?
PIPE DOWN ABOUT MONEY, ALREADY! I'M COVERING THIS.
And I'm the Queen of England.
HOW? WITH MONOPOLY MONEY?
FOR A FATHER, EVEN ONE WITHOUT A JOB...

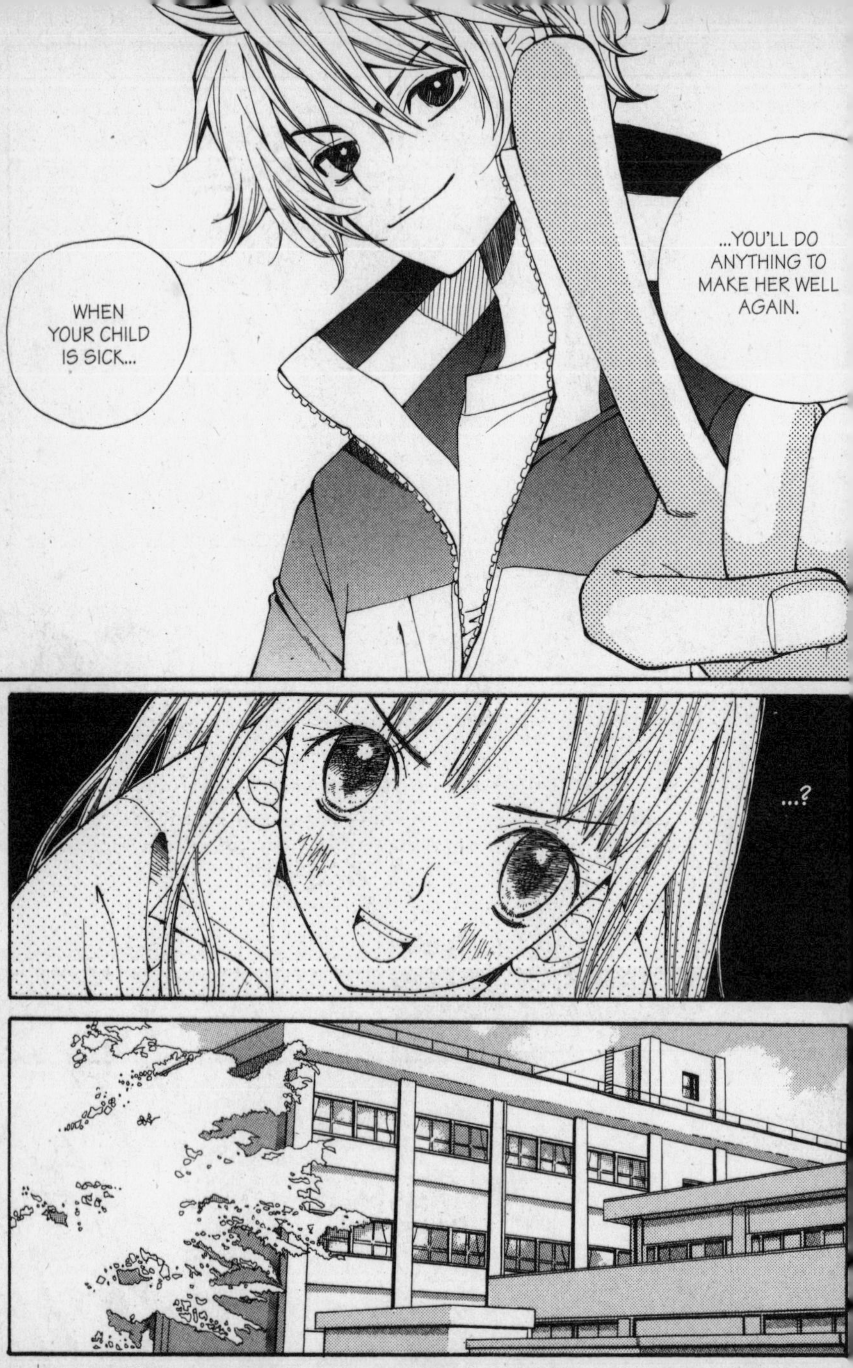
WHEN YOUR CHILD IS SICK...
...YOU'LL DO ANYTHING TO MAKE HER WELL AGAIN.
...?

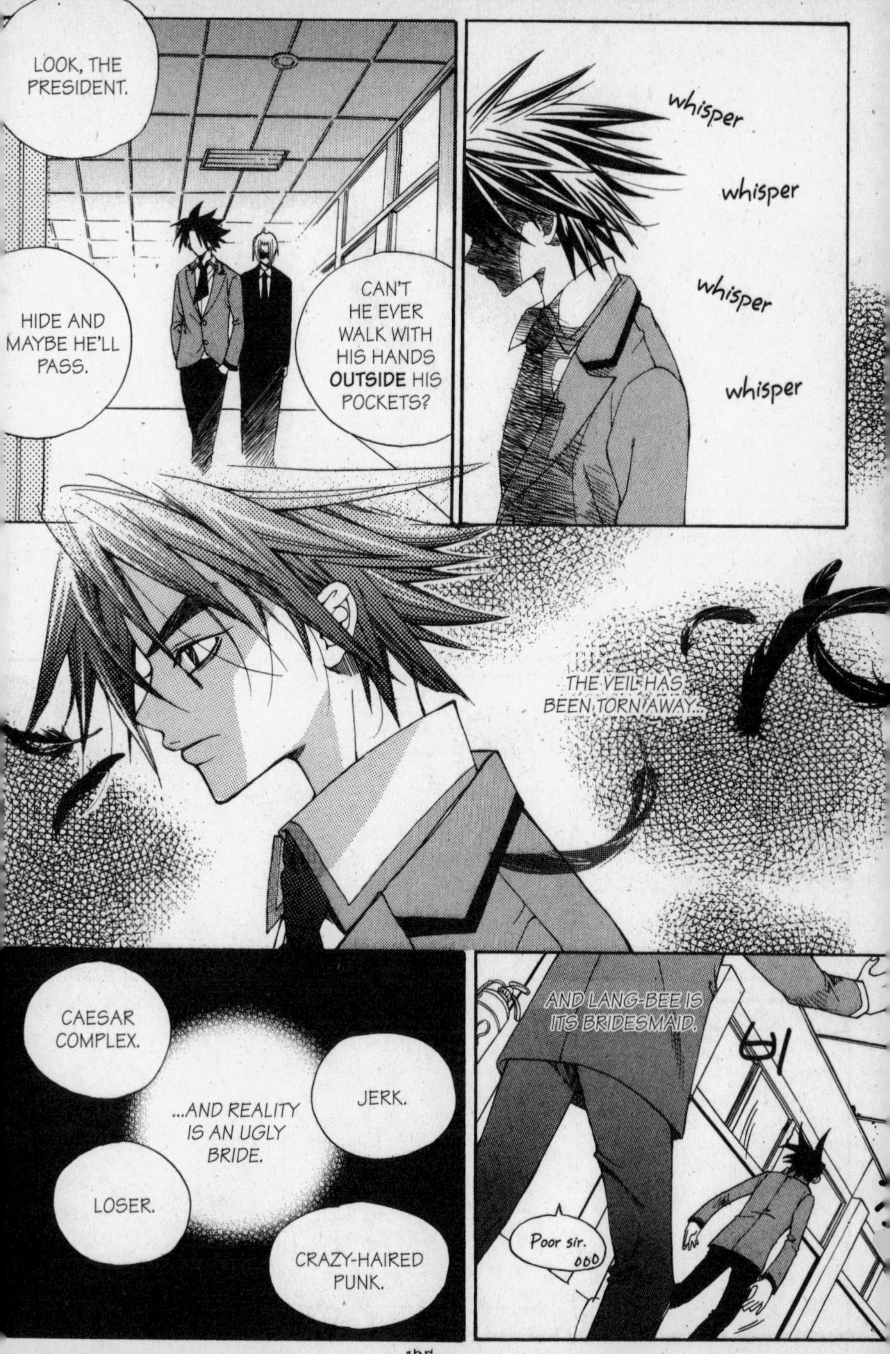

LOOK, THE PRESIDENT.
HIDE AND MAYBE HE'LL PASS.
CAN'T HE EVER WALK WITH HIS HANDS **OUTSIDE** HIS POCKETS?
whisper
whisper
whisper
whisper
THE VEIL HAS BEEN TORN AWAY...
CAESAR COMPLEX.
JERK.
...AND REALITY IS AN UGLY BRIDE.
LOSER.
CRAZY-HAIRED PUNK.
AND LANG-BEE IS ITS BRIDESMAID.
Poor sir.

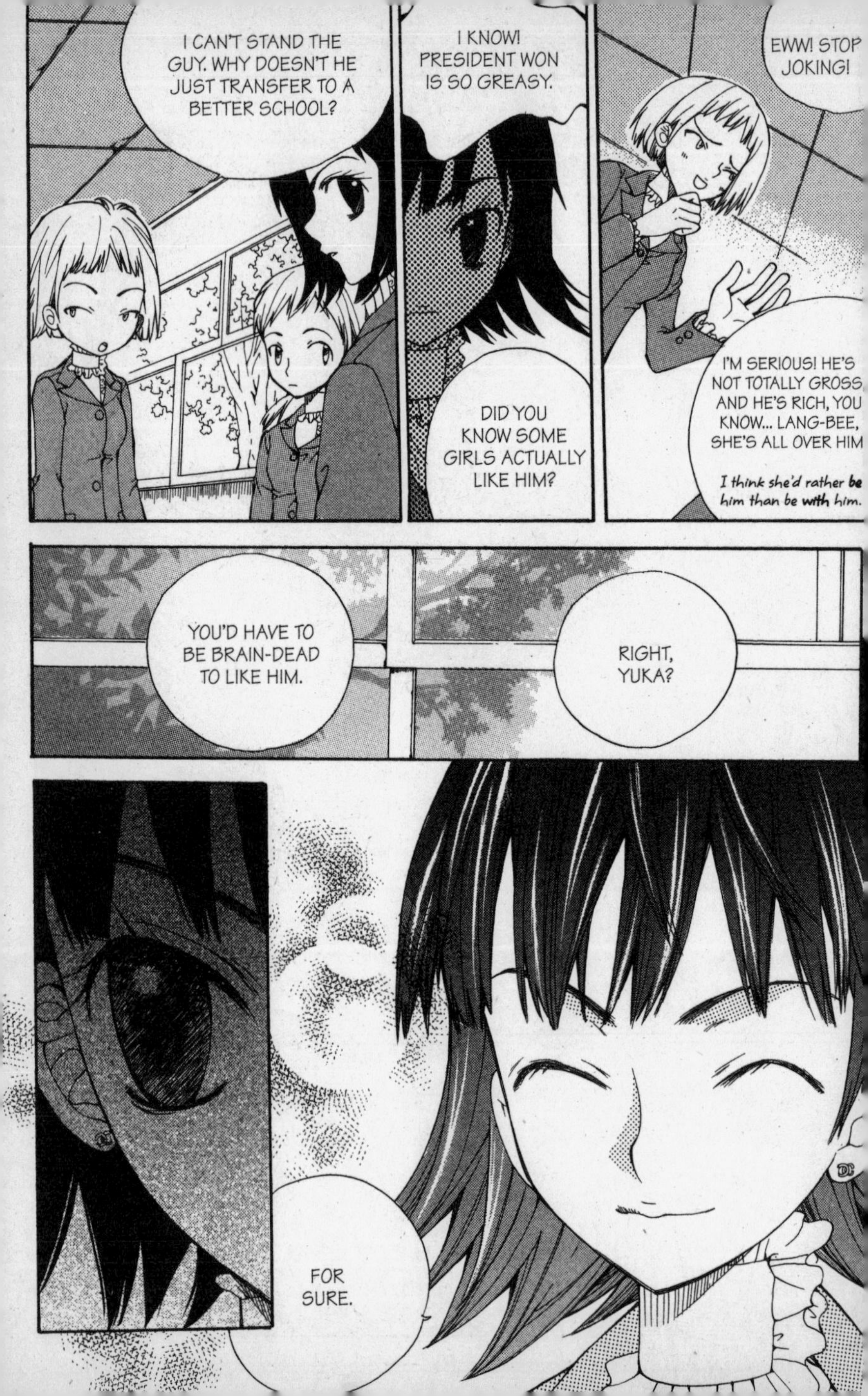

I CAN'T STAND THE GUY. WHY DOESN'T HE JUST TRANSFER TO A BETTER SCHOOL?
I KNOW! PRESIDENT WON IS SO GREASY.
DID YOU KNOW SOME GIRLS ACTUALLY LIKE HIM?
EWW! STOP JOKING!
I'M SERIOUS! HE'S NOT TOTALLY GROSS AND HE'S RICH, YOU KNOW... LANG-BEE, SHE'S ALL OVER HIM
I think she'd rather be him than be with him.
YOU'D HAVE TO BE BRAIN-DEAD TO LIKE HIM.
RIGHT, YUKA?
FOR SURE.

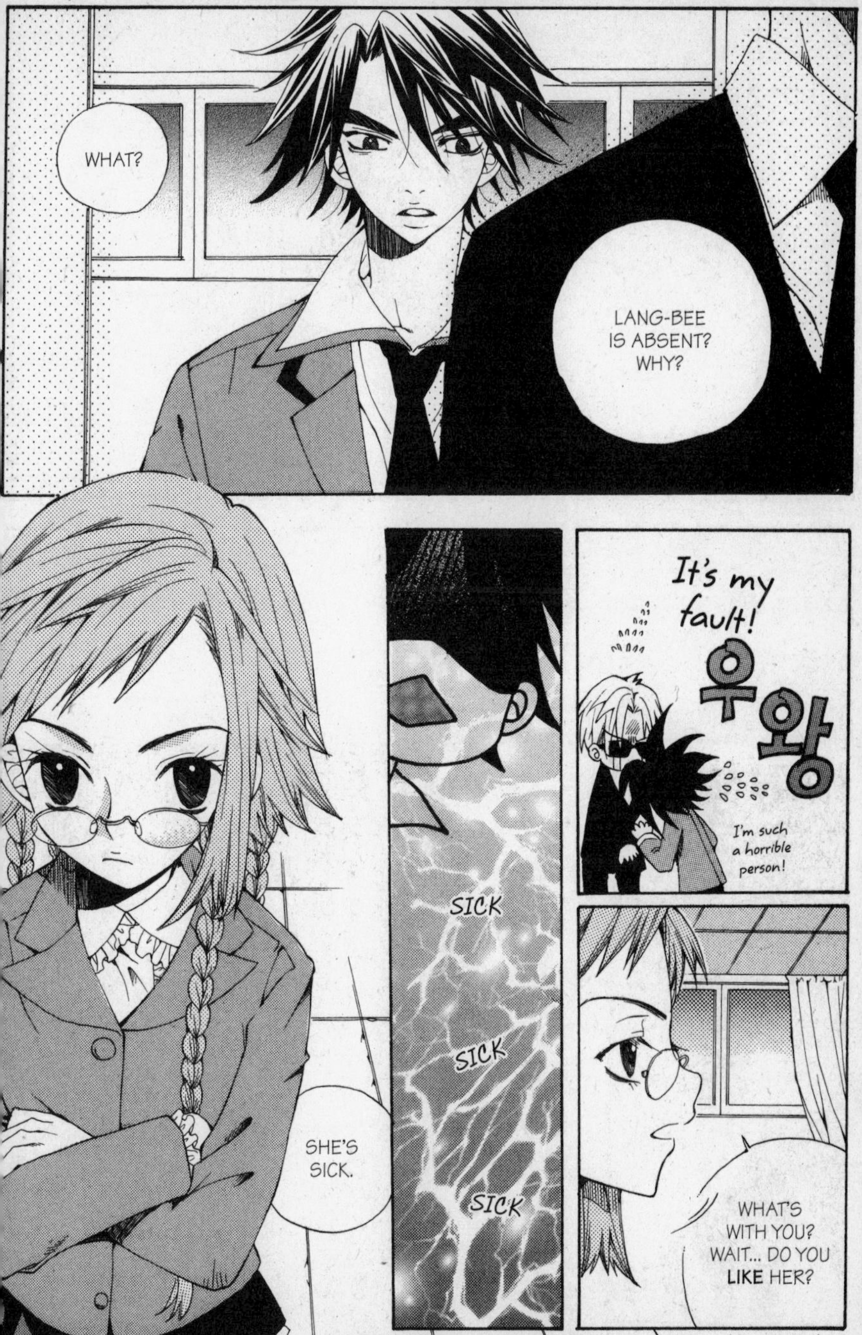
WHAT?
LANG-BEE IS ABSENT? WHY?
SHE'S SICK.
SICK
SICK
SICK
It's my fault!
우왕
I'm such a horrible person!
WHAT'S WITH YOU? WAIT... DO YOU **LIKE** HER?

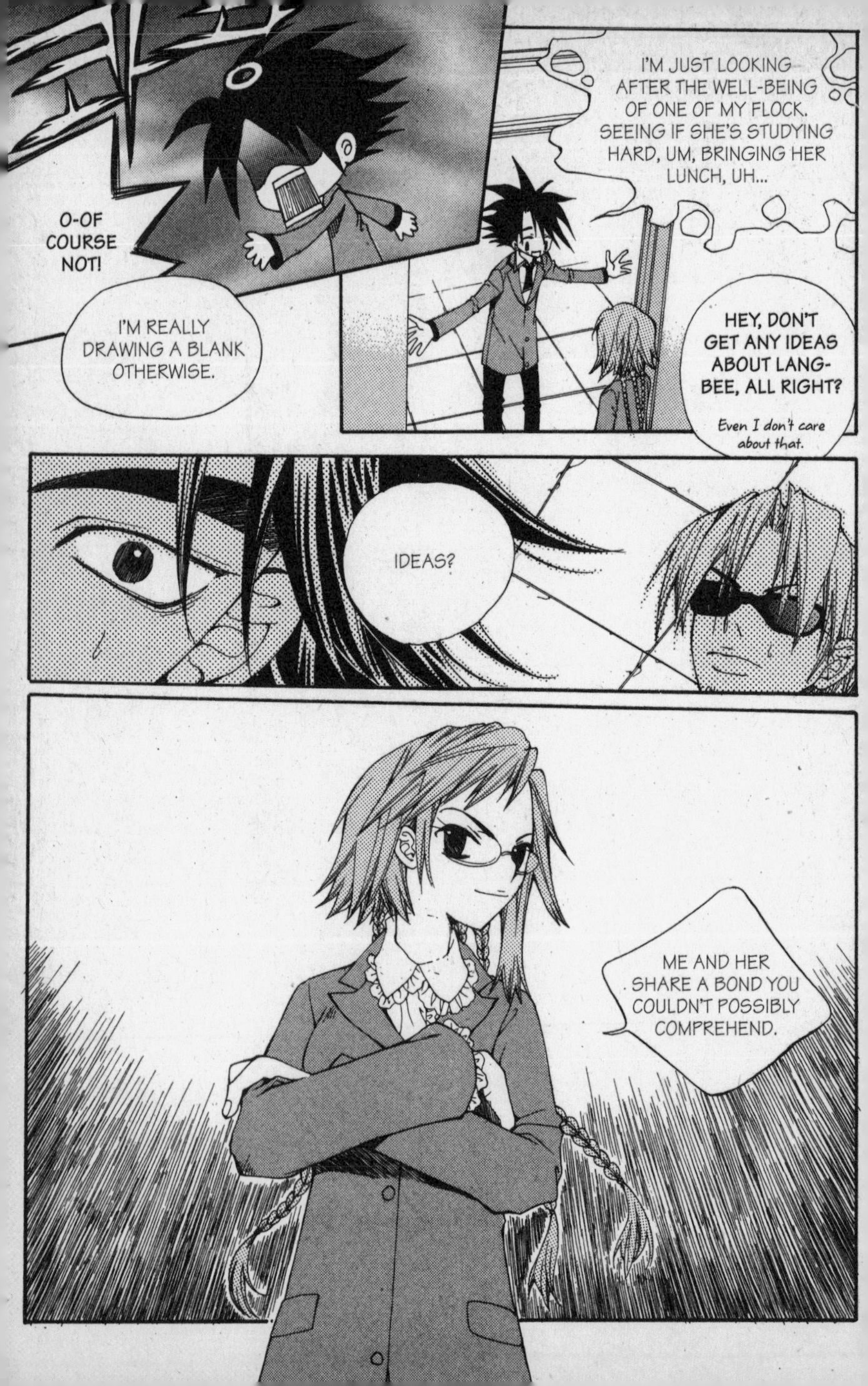
O-OF COURSE NOT!
I'M REALLY DRAWING A BLANK OTHERWISE.
I'M JUST LOOKING AFTER THE WELL-BEING OF ONE OF MY FLOCK. SEEING IF SHE'S STUDYING HARD, UM, BRINGING HER LUNCH, UH...
HEY, DON'T GET ANY IDEAS ABOUT LANG-BEE, ALL RIGHT?
Even I don't care about that.
IDEAS?
ME AND HER SHARE A BOND YOU COULDN'T POSSIBLY COMPREHEND.

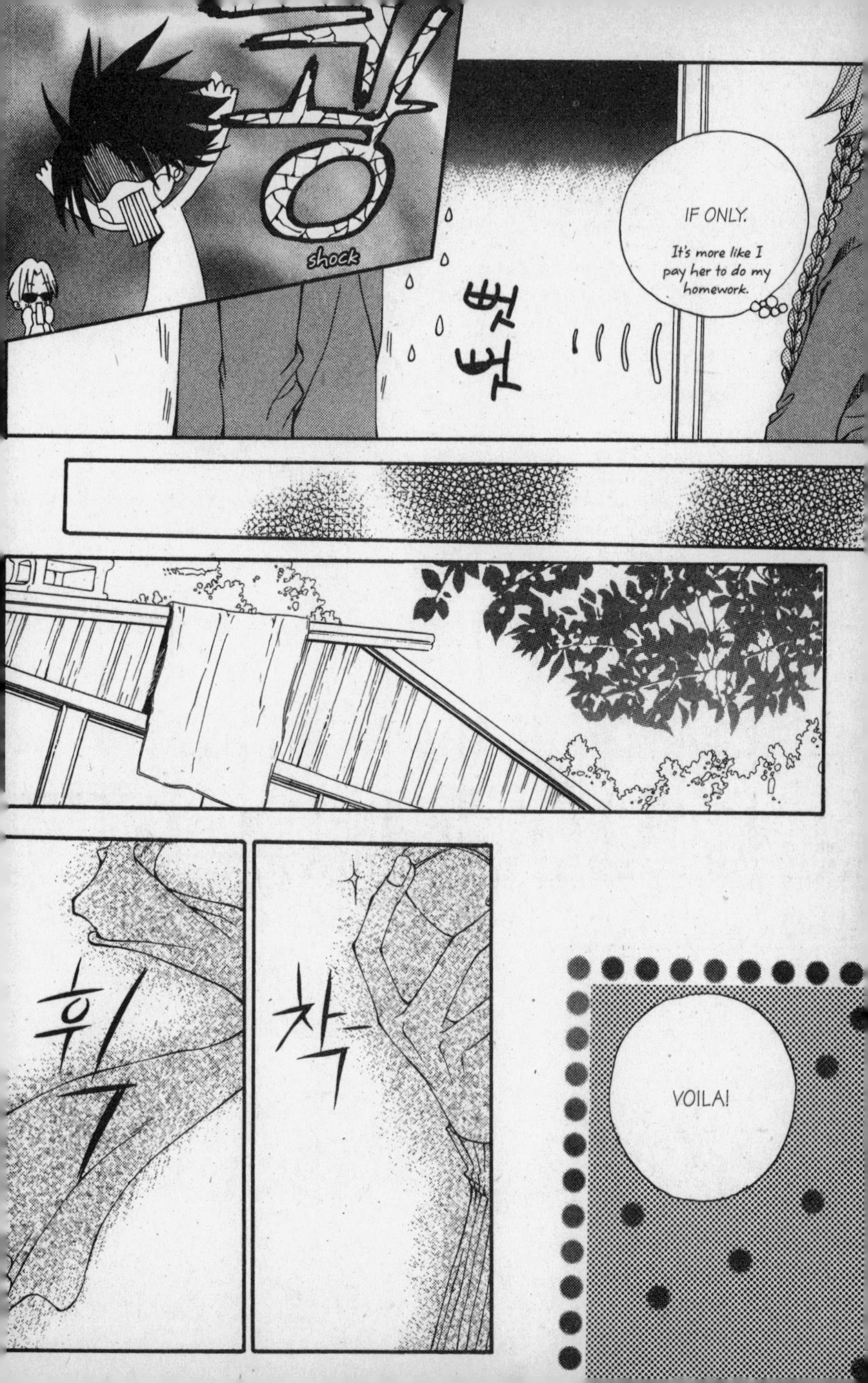
쾅
shock
뻔뻔
IF ONLY.
It's more like I pay her to do my homework.
휙
착
VOILA!

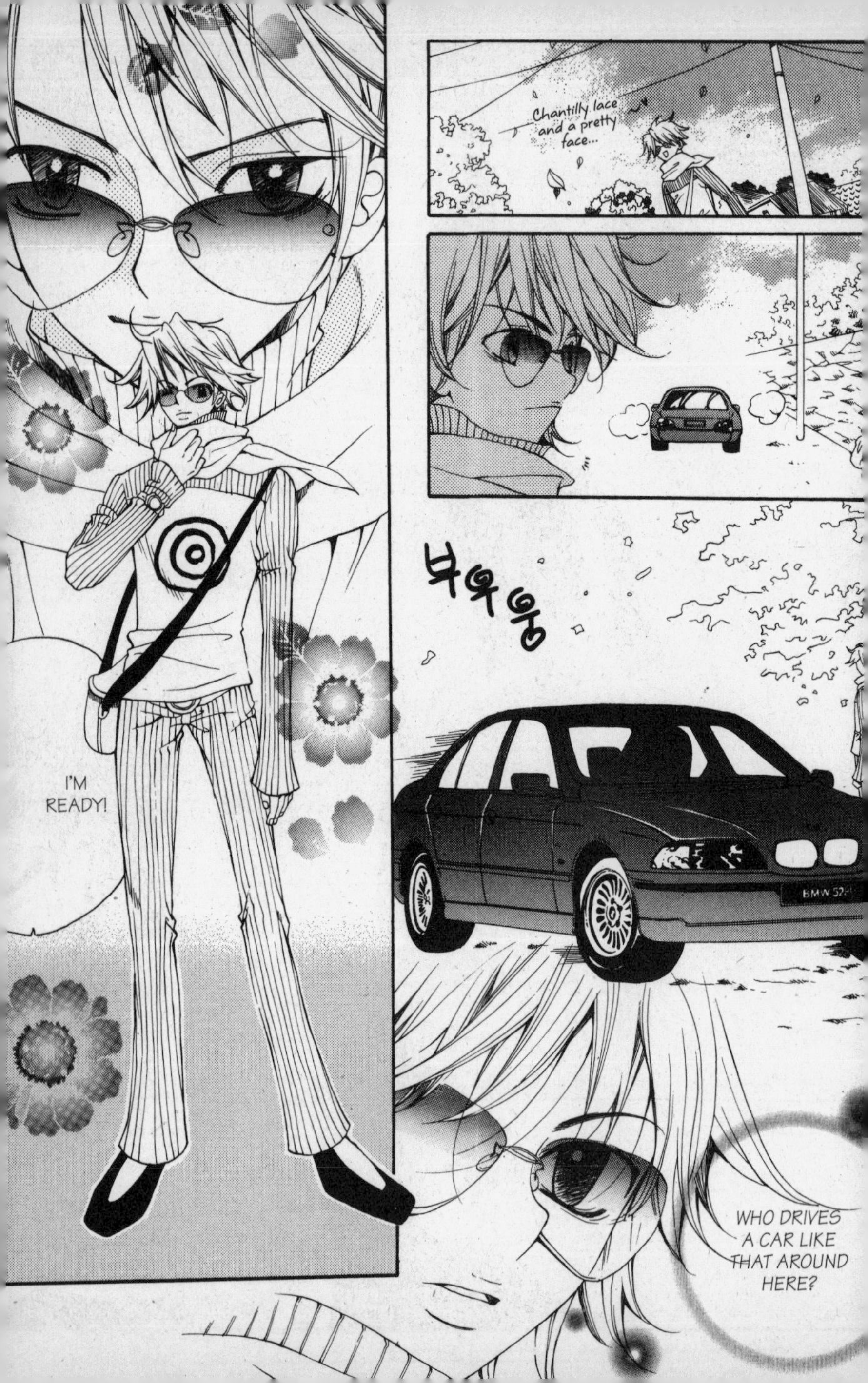
I'M READY!
Chantilly lace and a pretty face...
부우웅
WHO DRIVES A CAR LIKE THAT AROUND HERE?

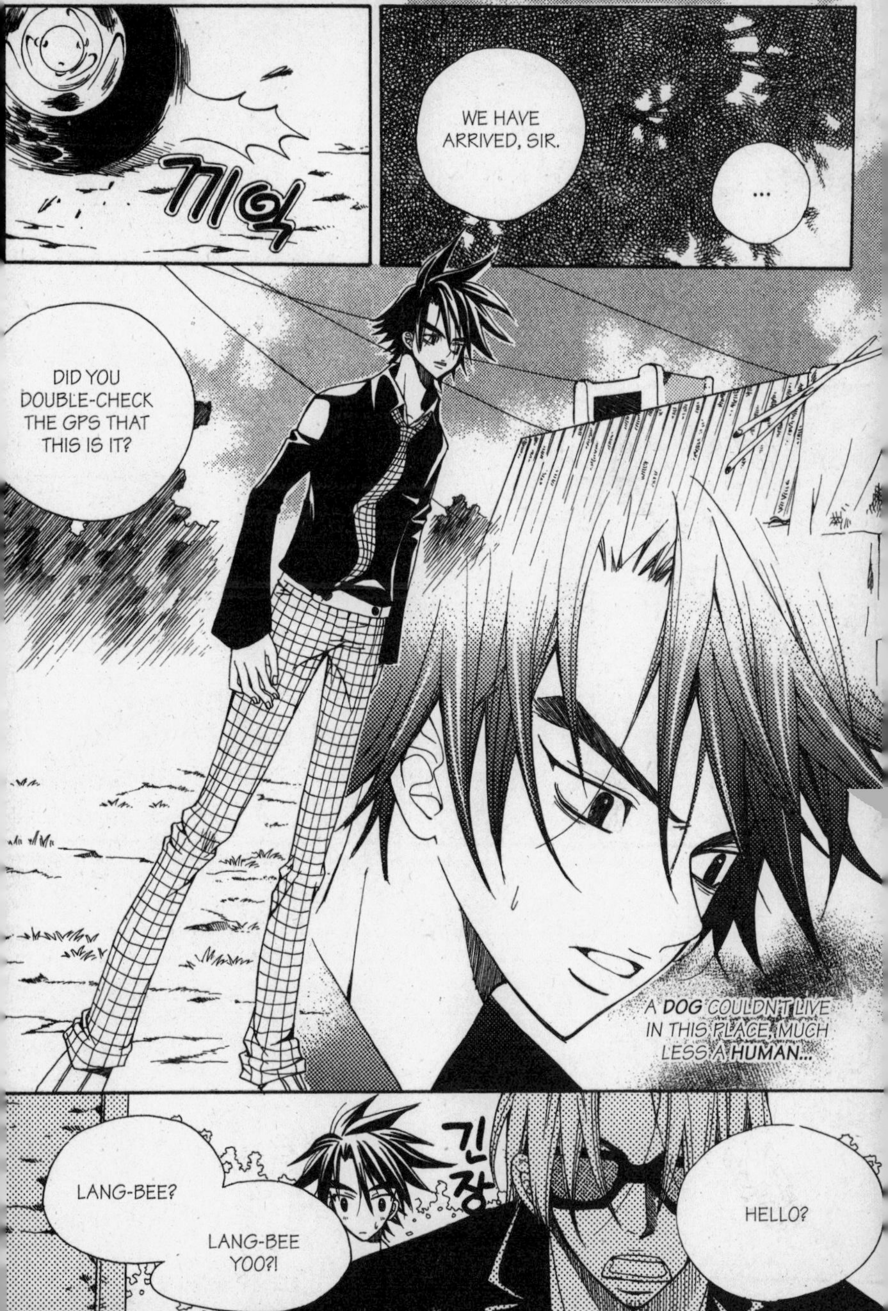
끼억
WE HAVE ARRIVED, SIR.
...
DID YOU DOUBLE-CHECK THE GPS THAT THIS IS IT?
A DOG COULDN'T LIVE IN THIS PLACE, MUCH LESS A HUMAN...
LANG-BEE?
LANG-BEE YOO?!
긴장
HELLO?

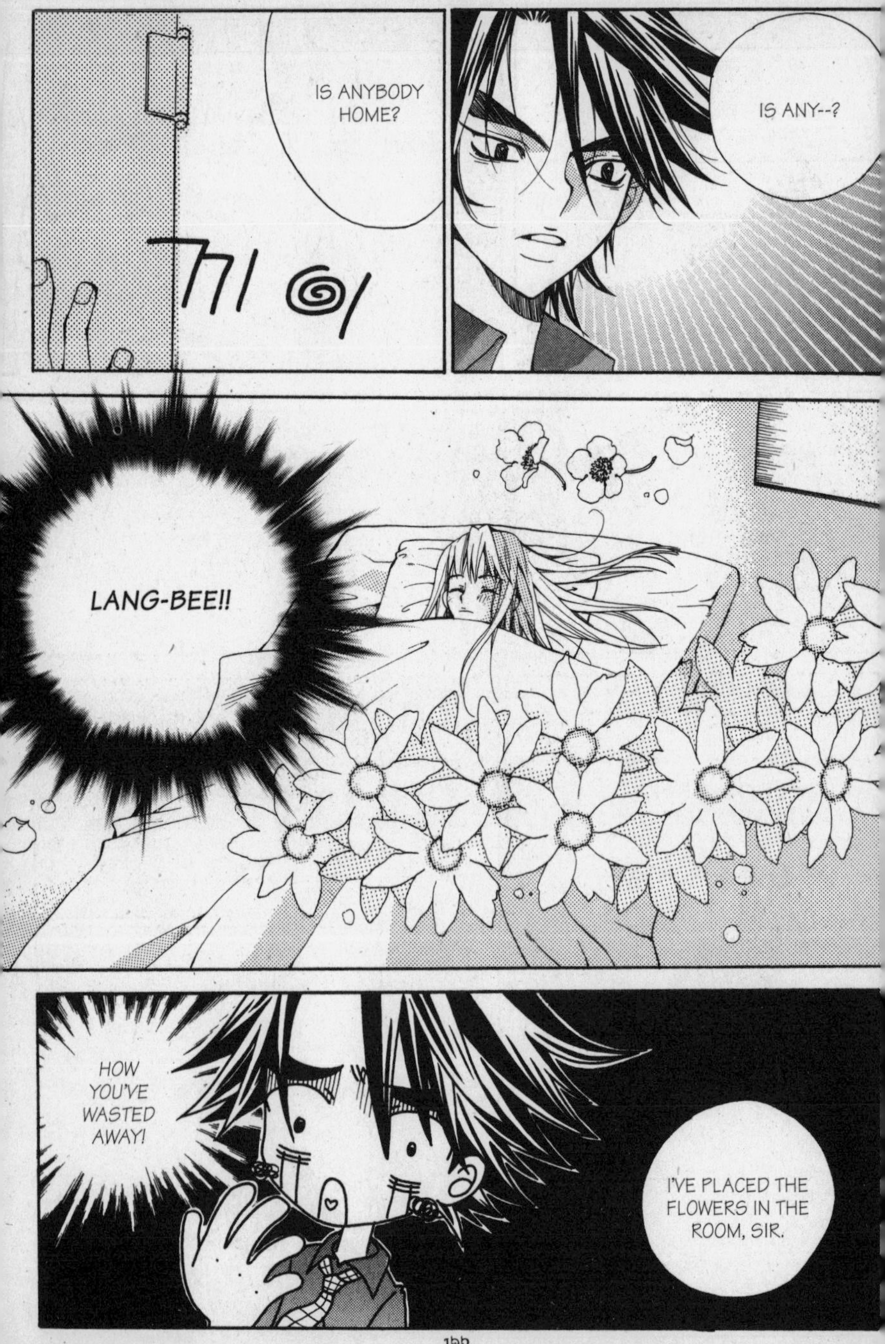
IS ANYBODY HOME?
끼이
IS ANY--?
LANG-BEE!!
HOW YOU'VE WASTED AWAY!
I'VE PLACED THE FLOWERS IN THE ROOM, SIR.

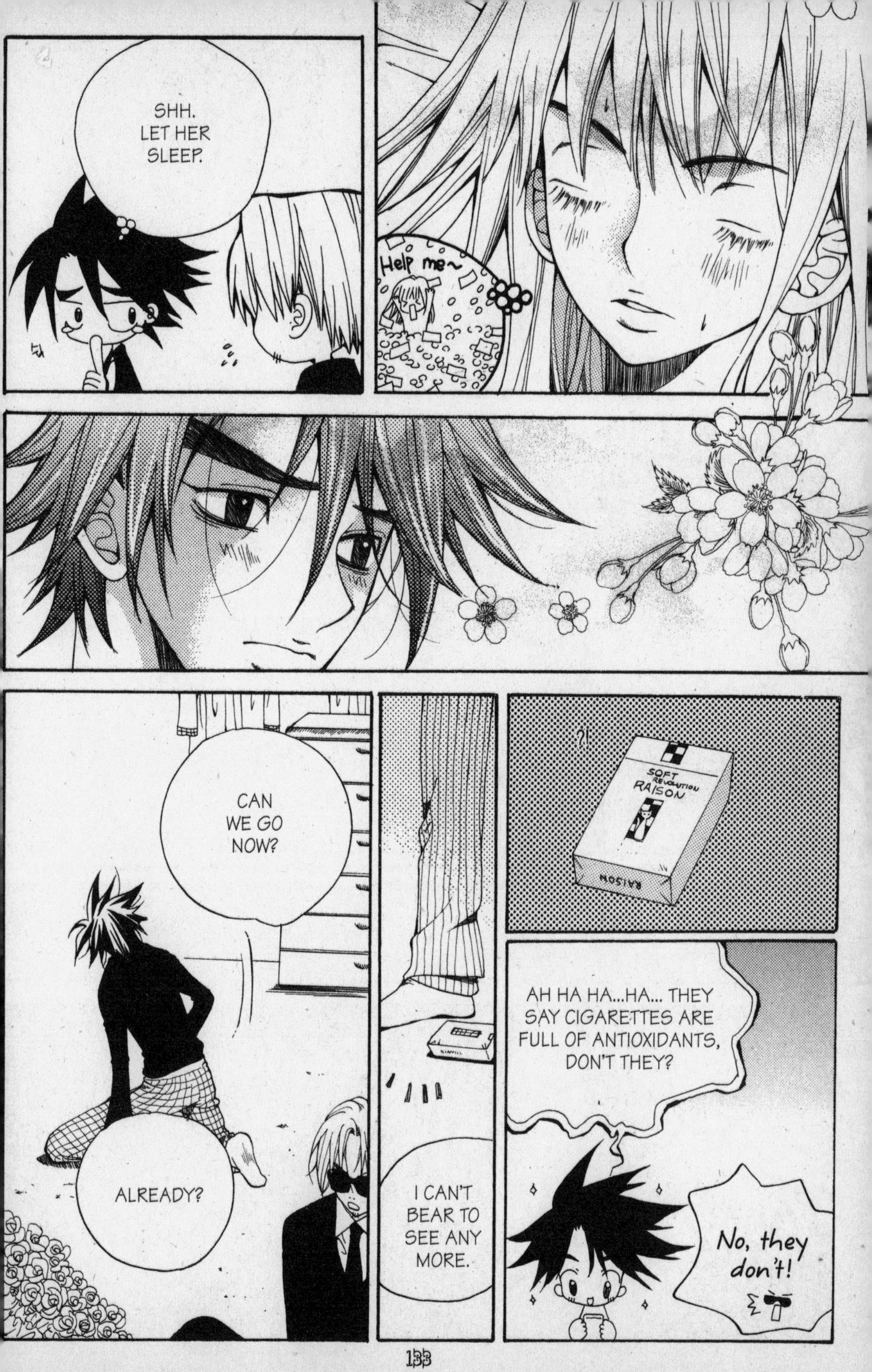
SHH. LET HER SLEEP.
Help me~
CAN WE GO NOW?
ALREADY?
I CAN'T BEAR TO SEE ANY MORE.
?!
SOFT REVOLUTION RAISON
AH HA HA...HA... THEY SAY CIGARETTES ARE FULL OF ANTIOXIDANTS, DON'T THEY?
No, they don't!

Quiet!!

ALL KINDS OF GIRLS SMOKE THESE DAYS, I GUESS. LET'S GO BEFORE SHE WAKES UP.

......

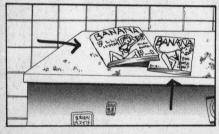

BANANA

BANANA

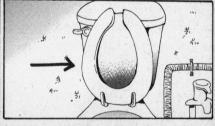

DOESN'T SHE LIVE ALONE?

IS SOMETHING THE MATTER, SIR?

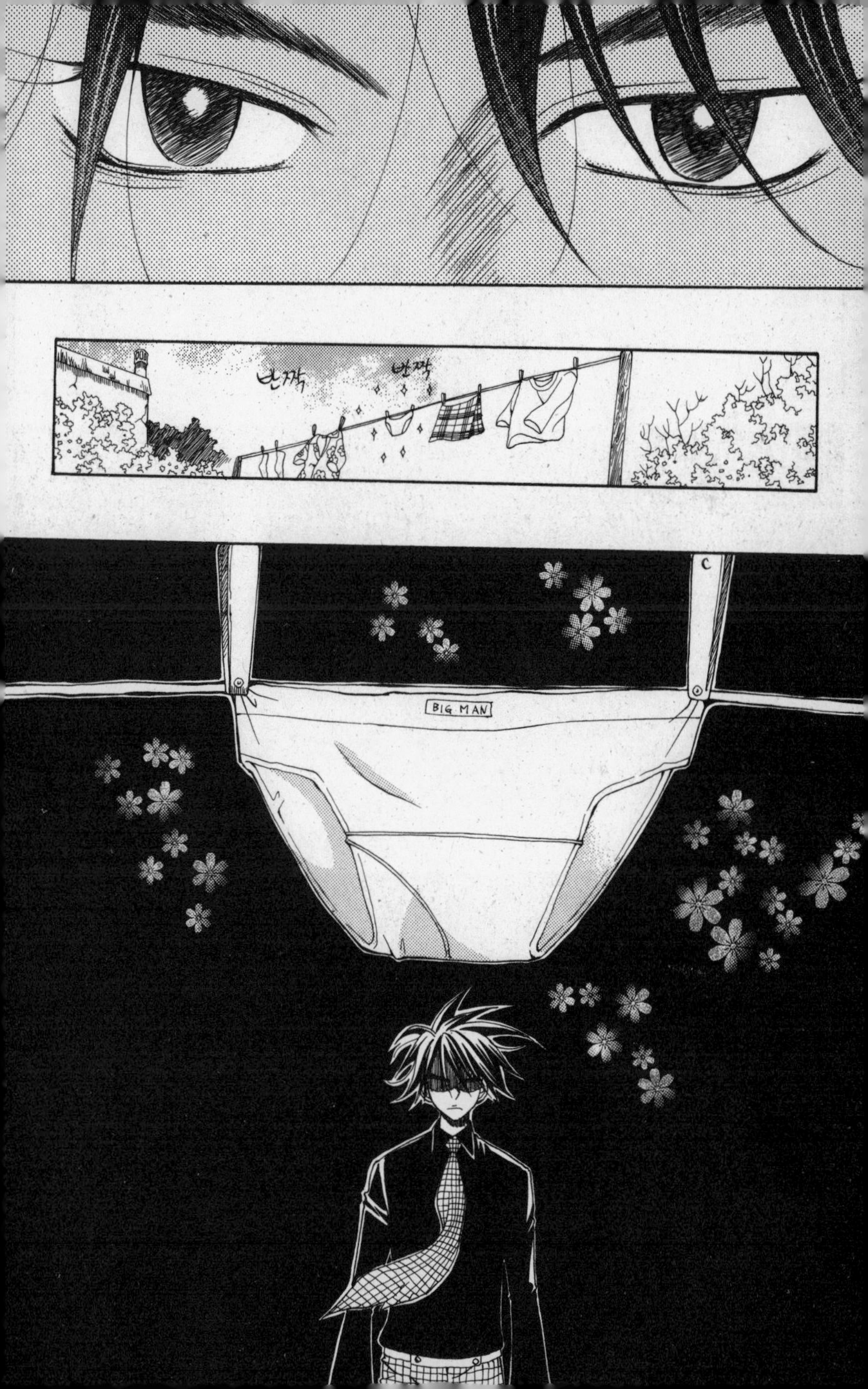
반짝
반짝
BIG MAN

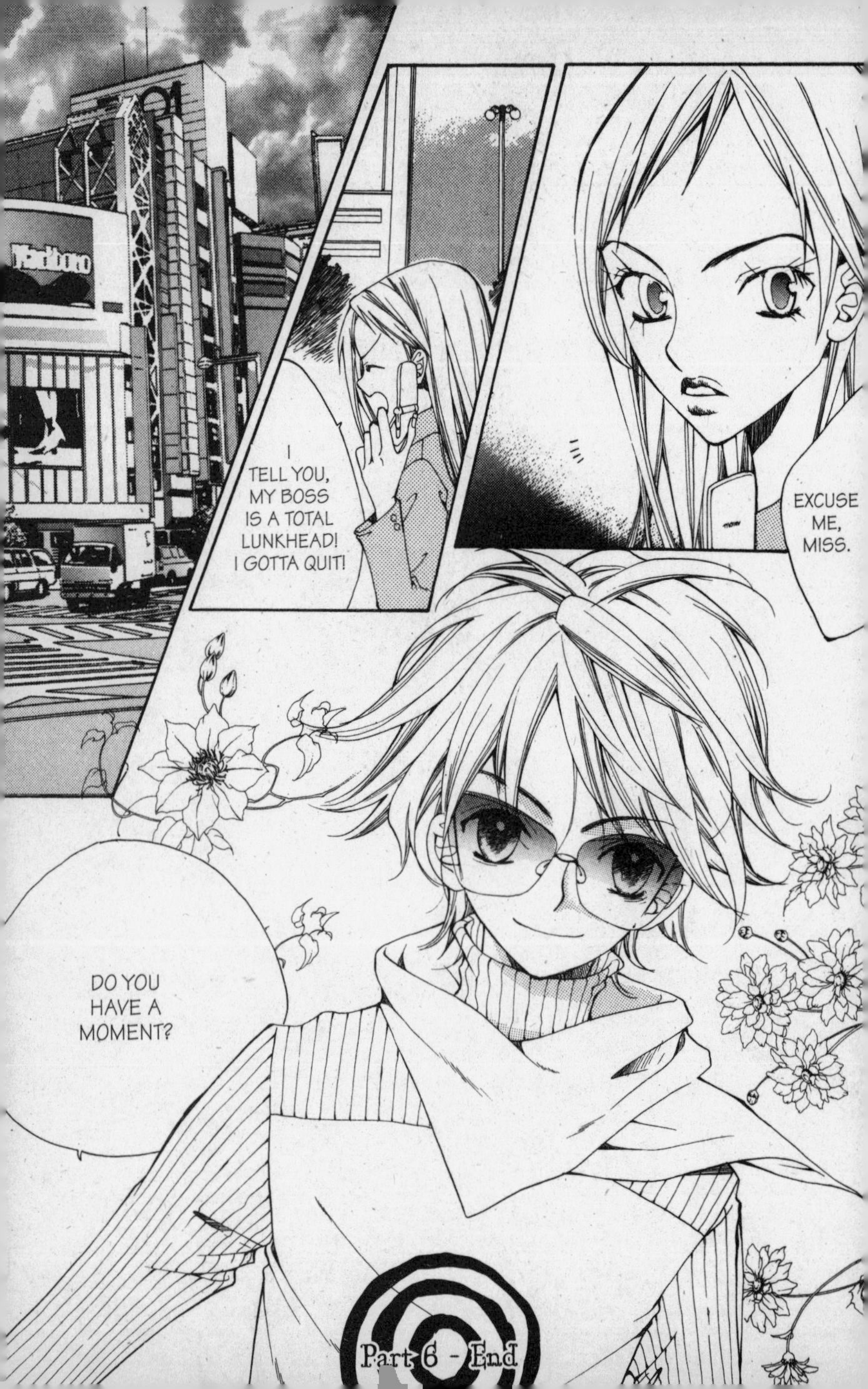
Marlboro
I TELL YOU, MY BOSS IS A TOTAL LUNKHEAD! I GOTTA QUIT!
EXCUSE ME, MISS.
DO YOU HAVE A MOMENT?
Part 6 - End

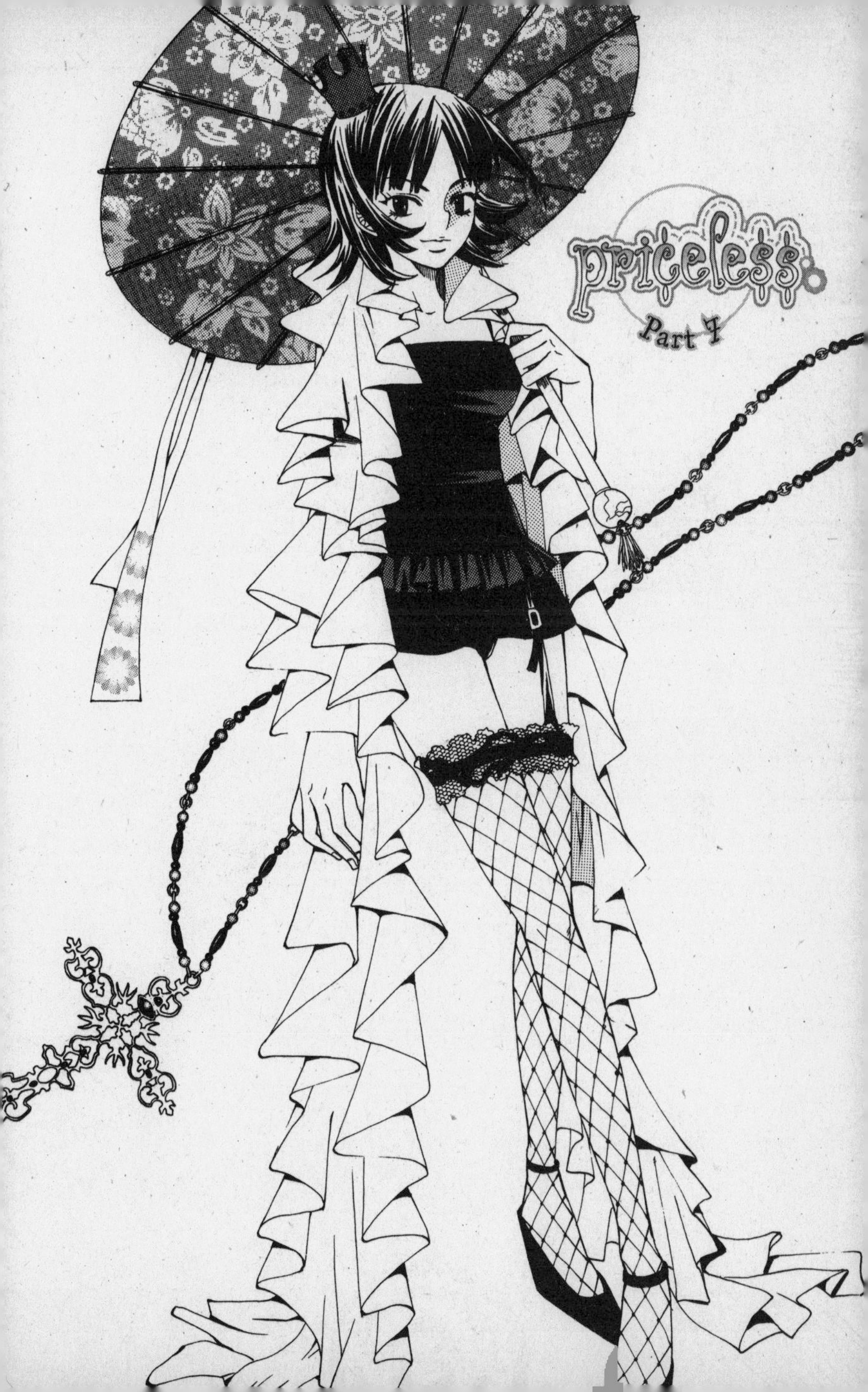
priceless
Part 7

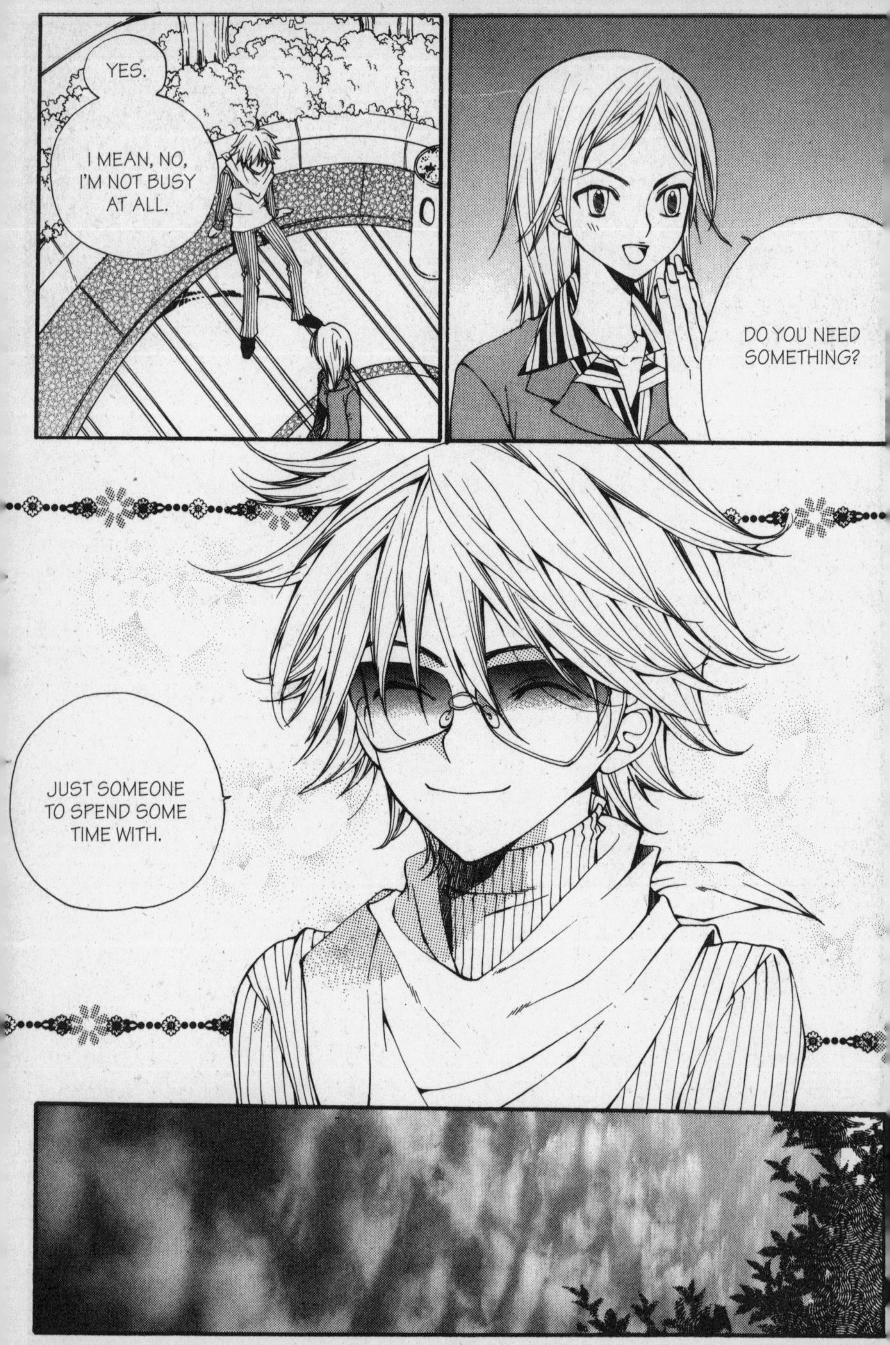
YES.
I MEAN, NO, I'M NOT BUSY AT ALL.
DO YOU NEED SOMETHING?
JUST SOMEONE TO SPEND SOME TIME WITH.

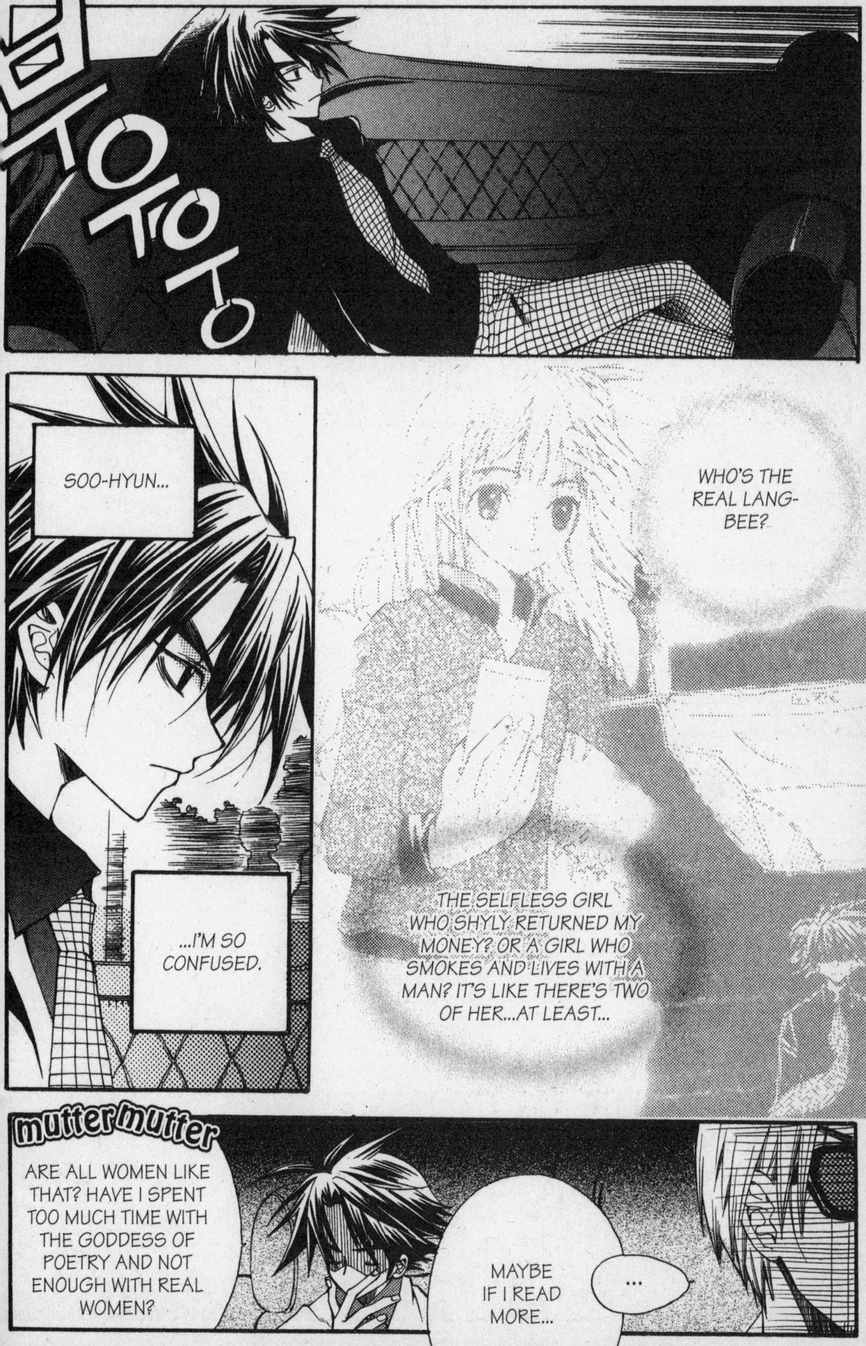
SOO-HYUN...
...I'M SO CONFUSED.
WHO'S THE REAL LANG-BEE?
THE SELFLESS GIRL WHO SHYLY RETURNED MY MONEY? OR A GIRL WHO SMOKES AND LIVES WITH A MAN? IT'S LIKE THERE'S TWO OF HER...AT LEAST...
mutter mutter
ARE ALL WOMEN LIKE THAT? HAVE I SPENT TOO MUCH TIME WITH THE GODDESS OF POETRY AND NOT ENOUGH WITH REAL WOMEN?
MAYBE IF I READ MORE...
...

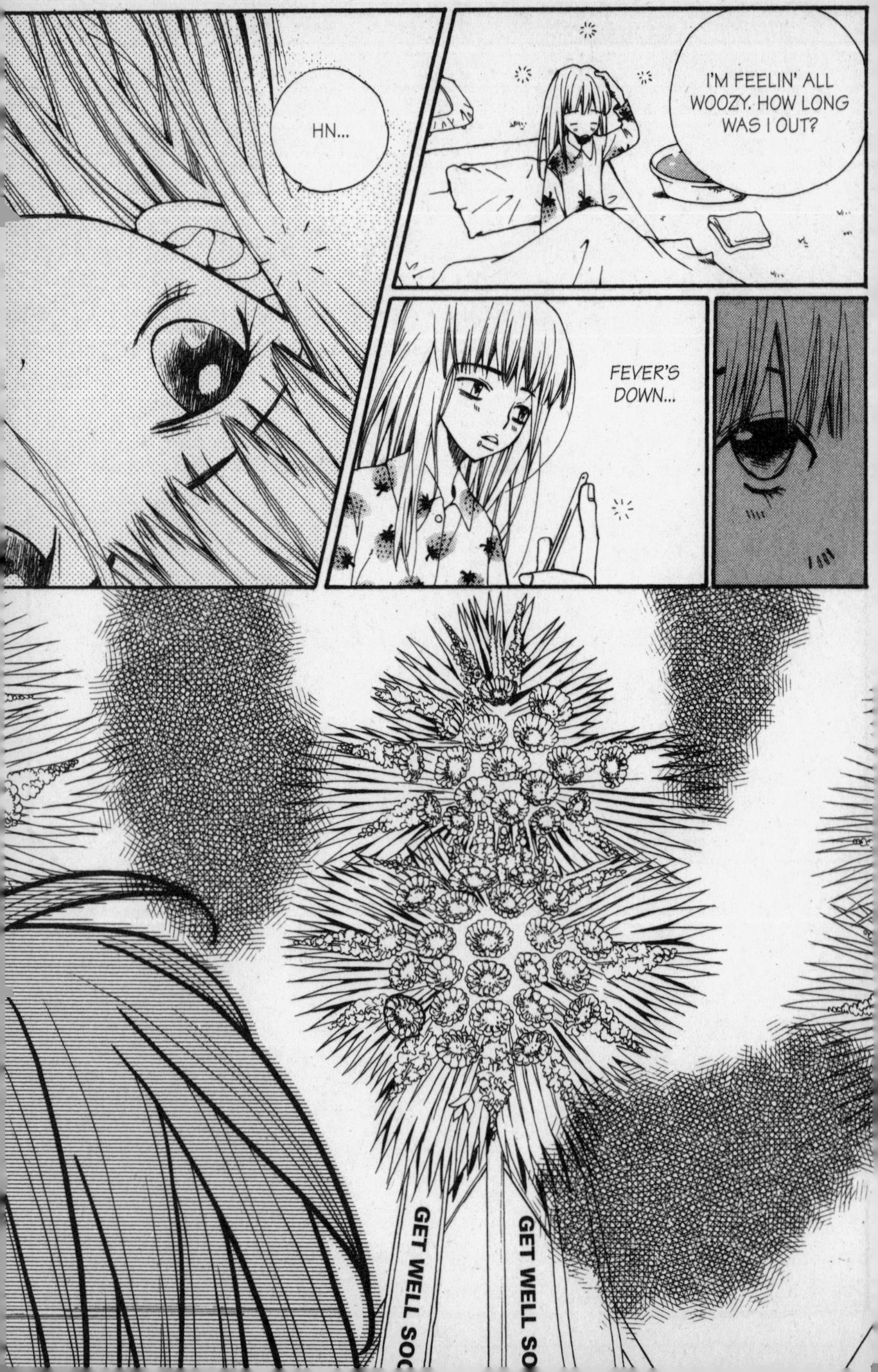
HN...
I'M FEELIN' ALL WOOZY. HOW LONG WAS I OUT?
FEVER'S DOWN...
GET WELL SOO
GET WELL SO

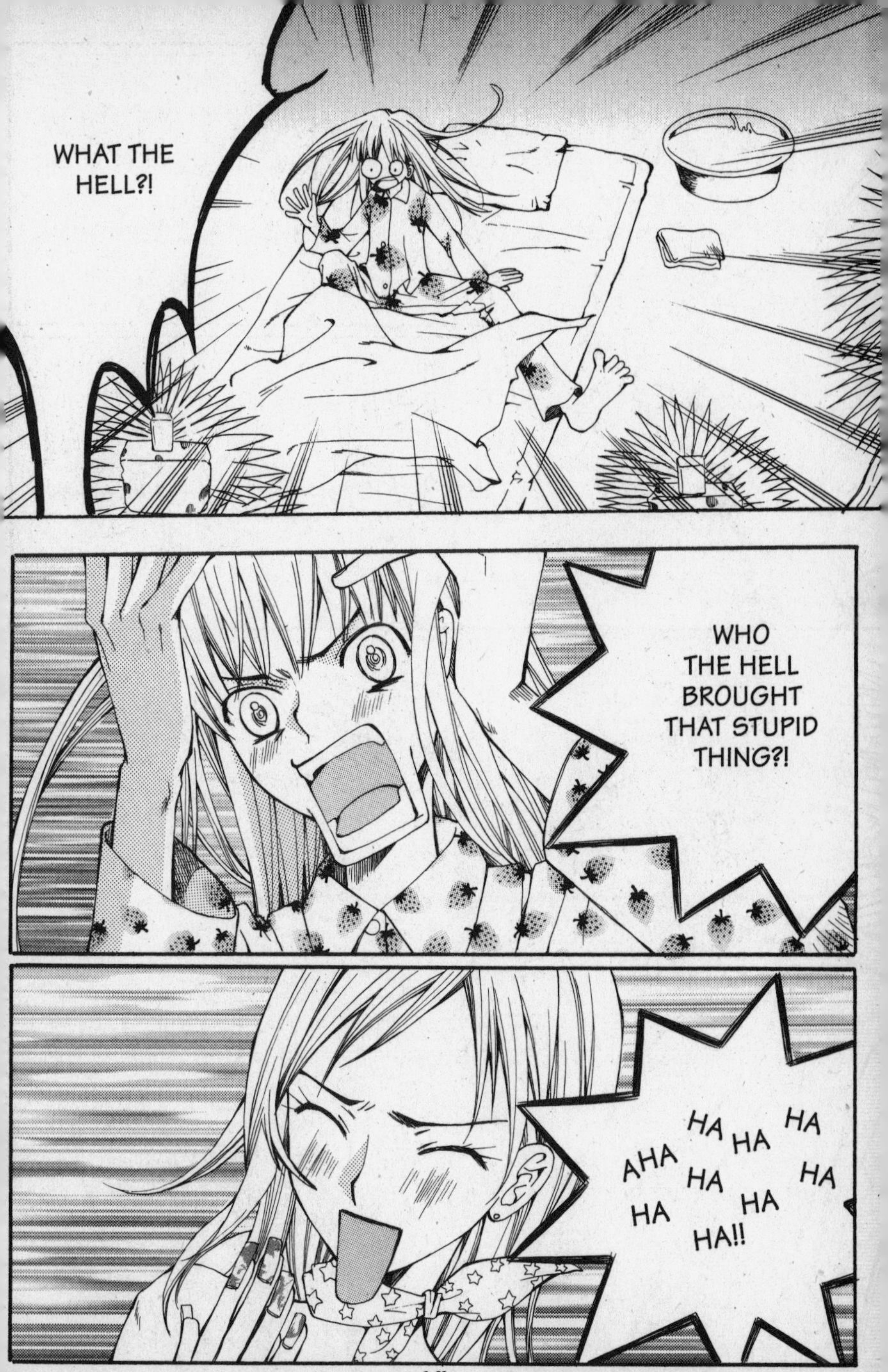
WHAT THE HELL?!
WHO THE HELL BROUGHT THAT STUPID THING?!
AHA HA HA HA HA HA HA HA HA!!

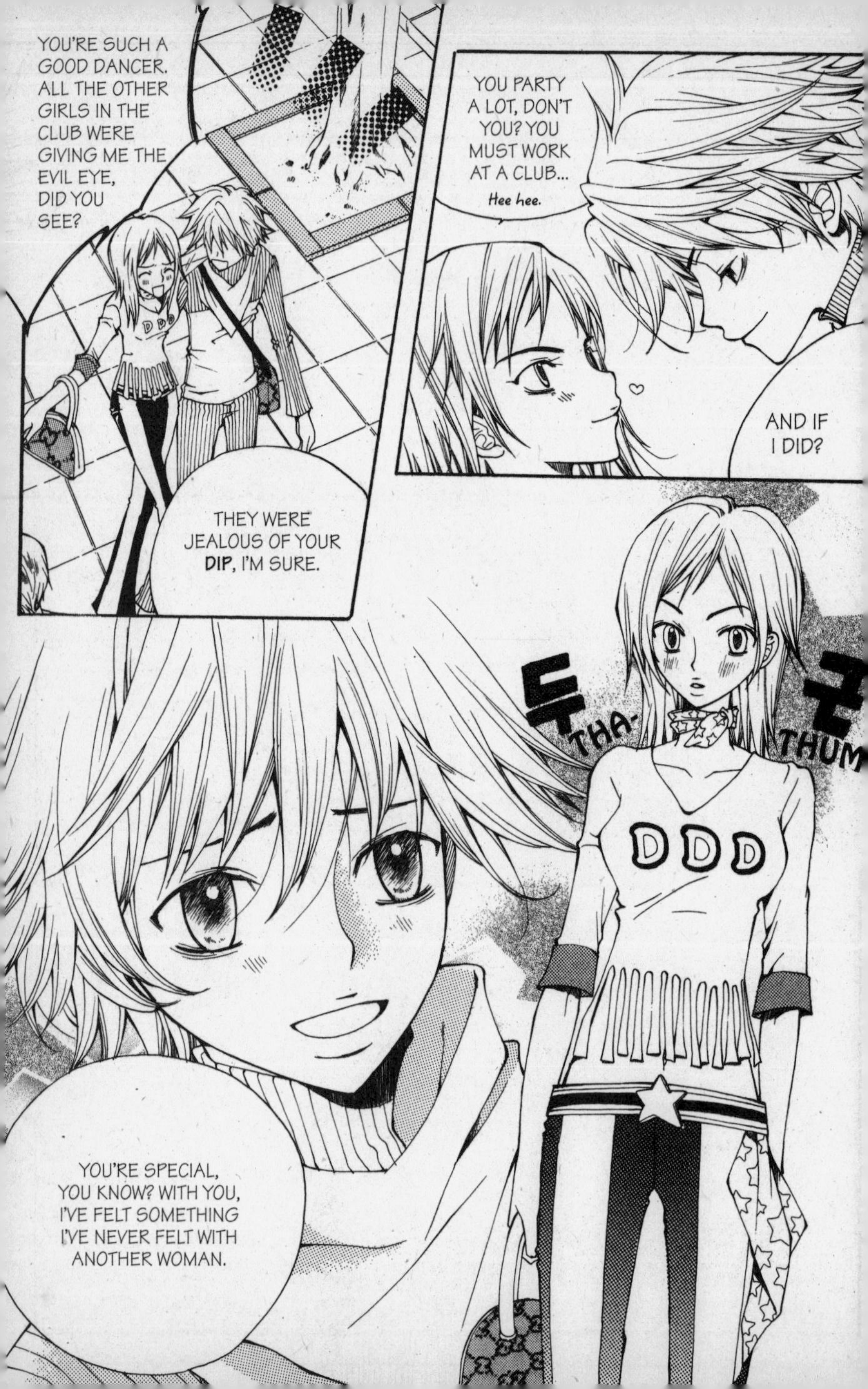
YOU'RE SUCH A GOOD DANCER. ALL THE OTHER GIRLS IN THE CLUB WERE GIVING ME THE EVIL EYE, DID YOU SEE?
THEY WERE JEALOUS OF YOUR **DIP**, I'M SURE.
YOU PARTY A LOT, DON'T YOU? YOU MUST WORK AT A CLUB...
Hee hee.
AND IF I DID?
YOU'RE SPECIAL, YOU KNOW? WITH YOU, I'VE FELT SOMETHING I'VE NEVER FELT WITH ANOTHER WOMAN.
THA-
THUM

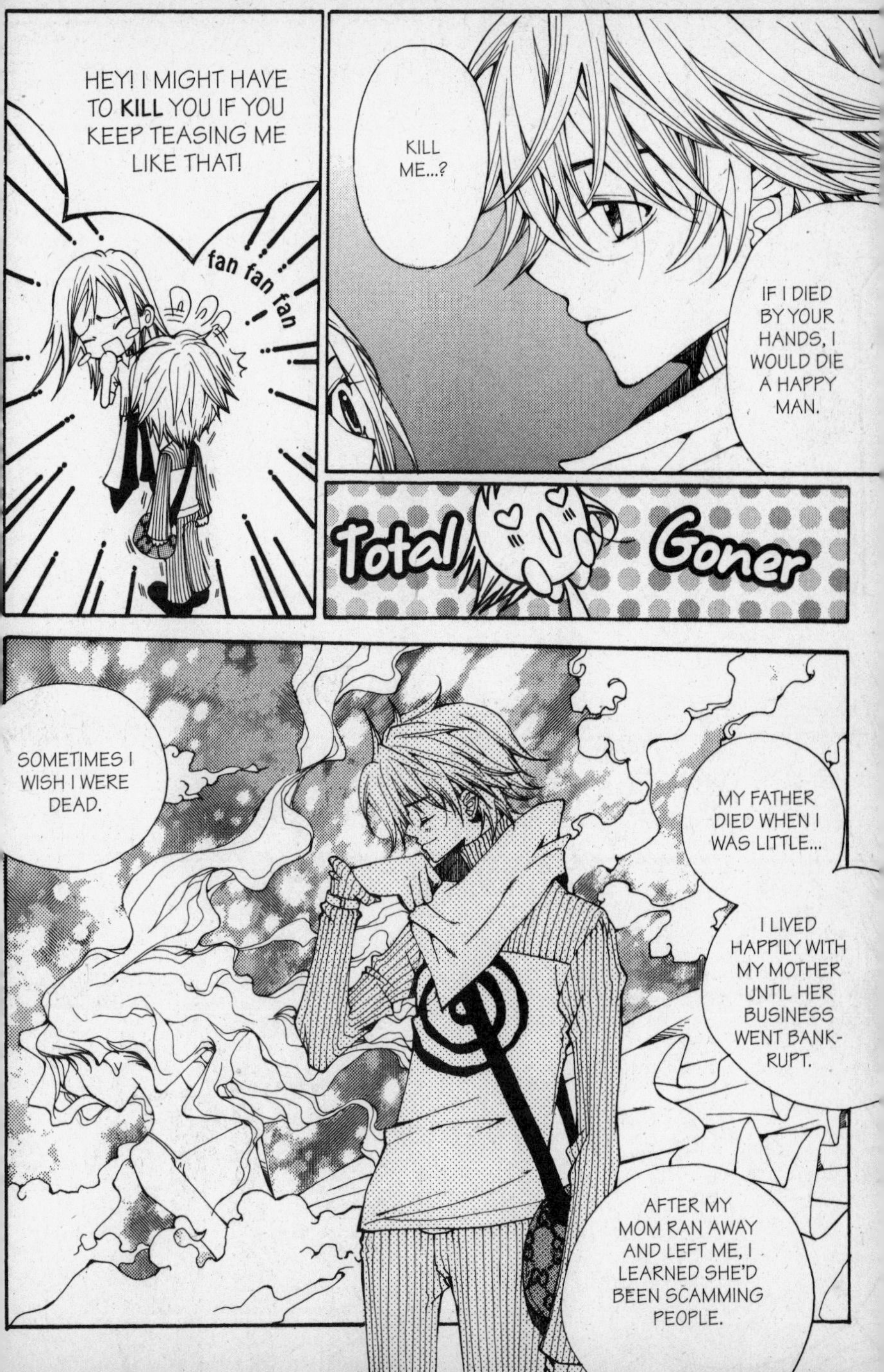
HEY! I MIGHT HAVE TO **KILL** YOU IF YOU KEEP TEASING ME LIKE THAT!
fan fan fan
KILL ME...?
IF I DIED BY YOUR HANDS, I WOULD DIE A HAPPY MAN.
Total Goner
SOMETIMES I WISH I WERE DEAD.
MY FATHER DIED WHEN I WAS LITTLE...
I LIVED HAPPILY WITH MY MOTHER UNTIL HER BUSINESS WENT BANK-RUPT.
AFTER MY MOM RAN AWAY AND LEFT ME, I LEARNED SHE'D BEEN SCAMMING PEOPLE.

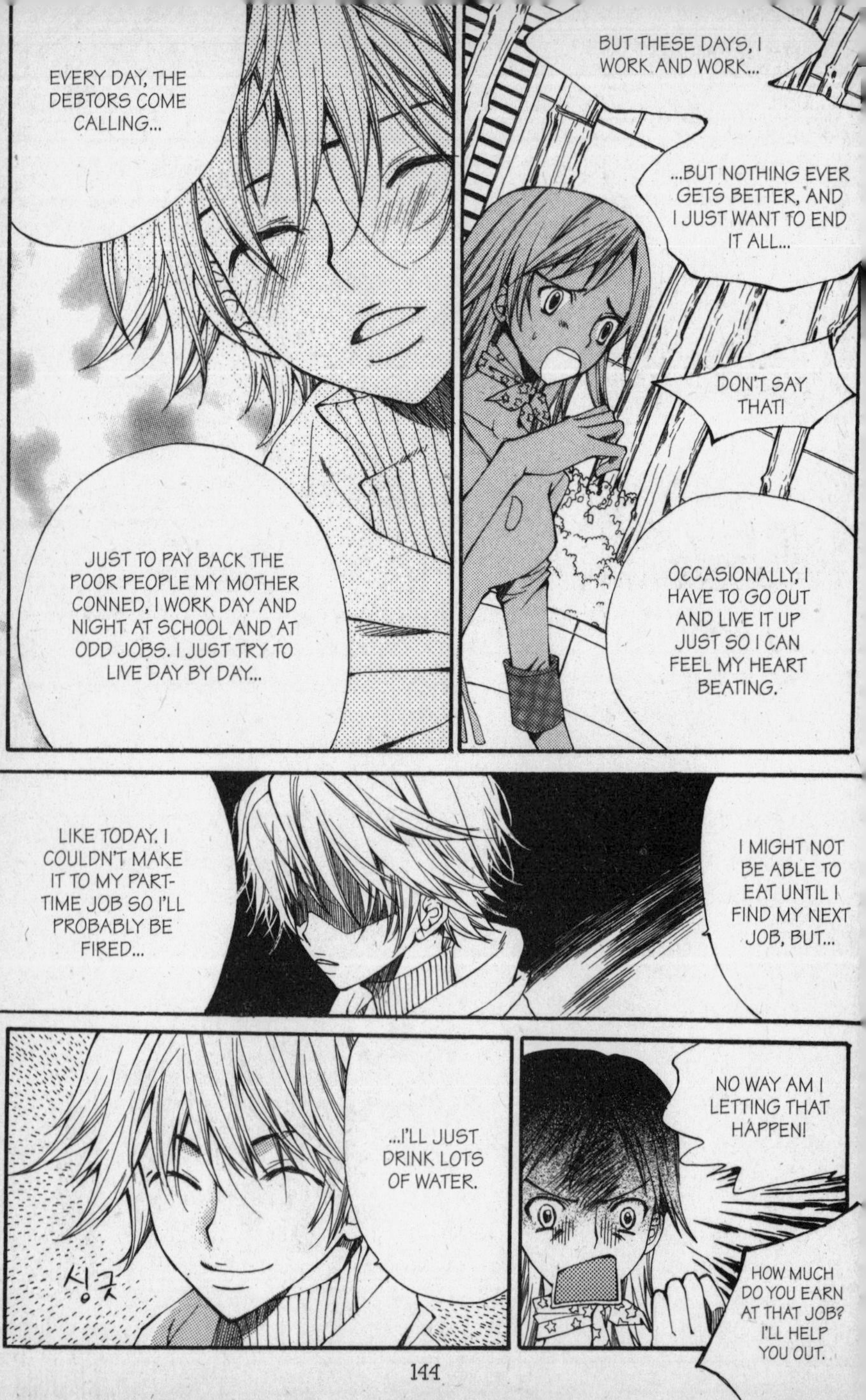
EVERY DAY, THE DEBTORS COME CALLING...
JUST TO PAY BACK THE POOR PEOPLE MY MOTHER CONNED, I WORK DAY AND NIGHT AT SCHOOL AND AT ODD JOBS. I JUST TRY TO LIVE DAY BY DAY...
BUT THESE DAYS, I WORK AND WORK...
...BUT NOTHING EVER GETS BETTER, AND I JUST WANT TO END IT ALL...
DON'T SAY THAT!
OCCASIONALLY, I HAVE TO GO OUT AND LIVE IT UP JUST SO I CAN FEEL MY HEART BEATING.
LIKE TODAY. I COULDN'T MAKE IT TO MY PART-TIME JOB SO I'LL PROBABLY BE FIRED...
I MIGHT NOT BE ABLE TO EAT UNTIL I FIND MY NEXT JOB, BUT...
...I'LL JUST DRINK LOTS OF WATER.
싱긋
NO WAY AM I LETTING THAT HAPPEN!
HOW MUCH DO YOU EARN AT THAT JOB? I'LL HELP YOU OUT.

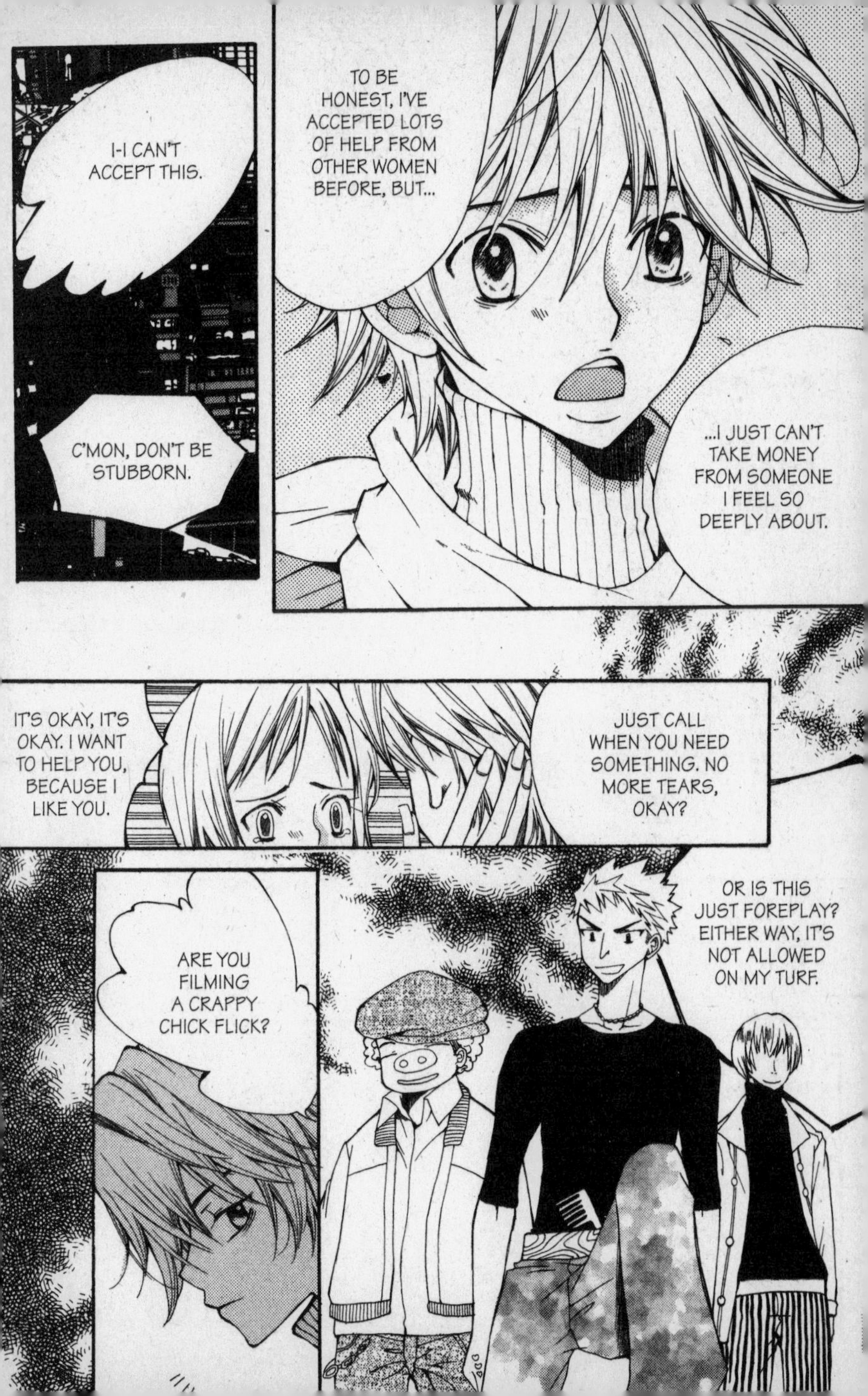
I-I CAN'T ACCEPT THIS.
C'MON, DON'T BE STUBBORN.
TO BE HONEST, I'VE ACCEPTED LOTS OF HELP FROM OTHER WOMEN BEFORE, BUT...
...I JUST CAN'T TAKE MONEY FROM SOMEONE I FEEL SO DEEPLY ABOUT.
IT'S OKAY, IT'S OKAY. I WANT TO HELP YOU, BECAUSE I LIKE YOU.
JUST CALL WHEN YOU NEED SOMETHING. NO MORE TEARS, OKAY?
ARE YOU FILMING A CRAPPY CHICK FLICK?
OR IS THIS JUST FOREPLAY? EITHER WAY, IT'S NOT ALLOWED ON MY TURF.

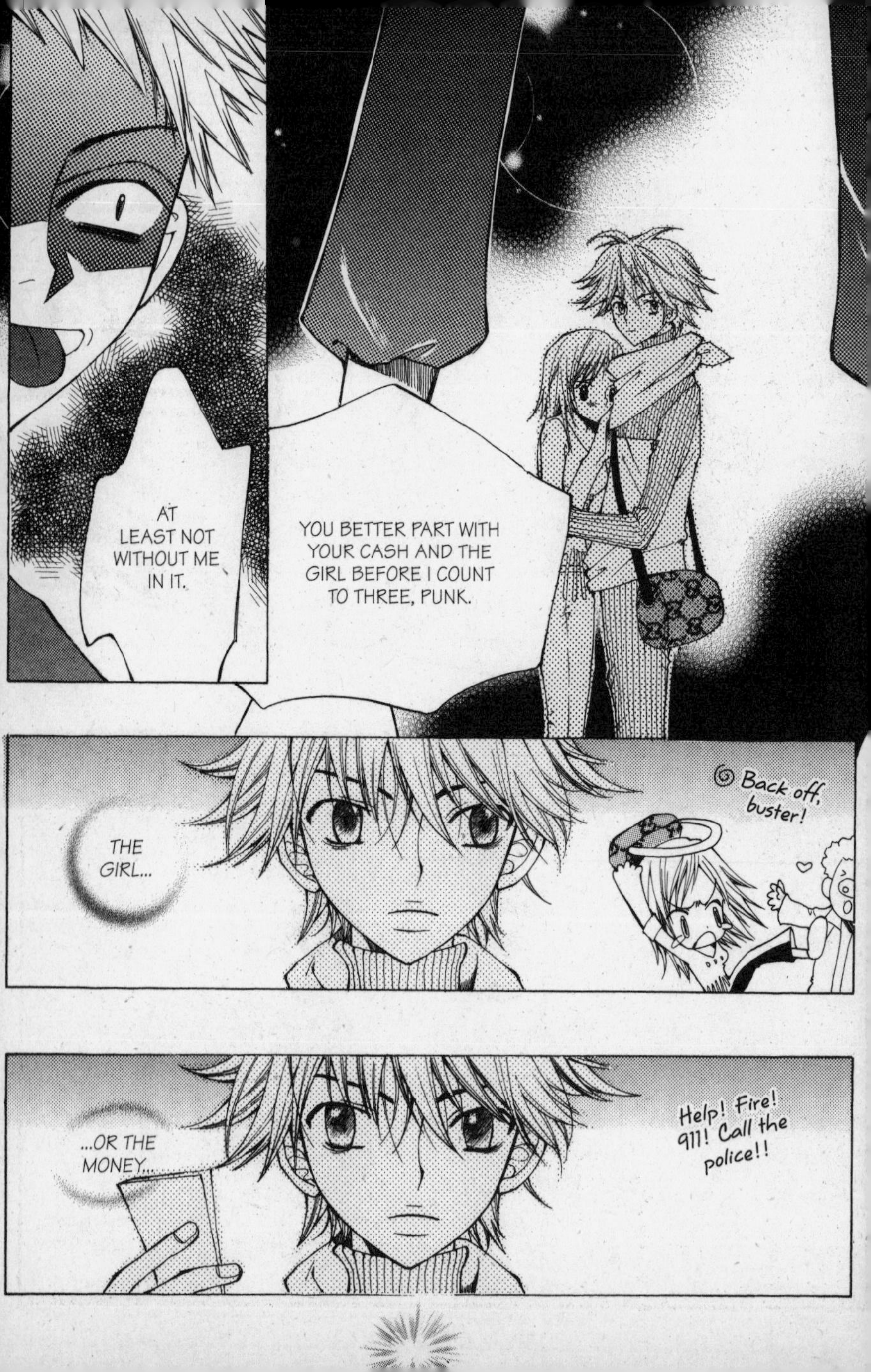
AT LEAST NOT WITHOUT ME IN IT.
YOU BETTER PART WITH YOUR CASH AND THE GIRL BEFORE I COUNT TO THREE, PUNK.
THE GIRL...
Back off, buster!
...OR THE MONEY...
Help! Fire! 911! Call the police!!

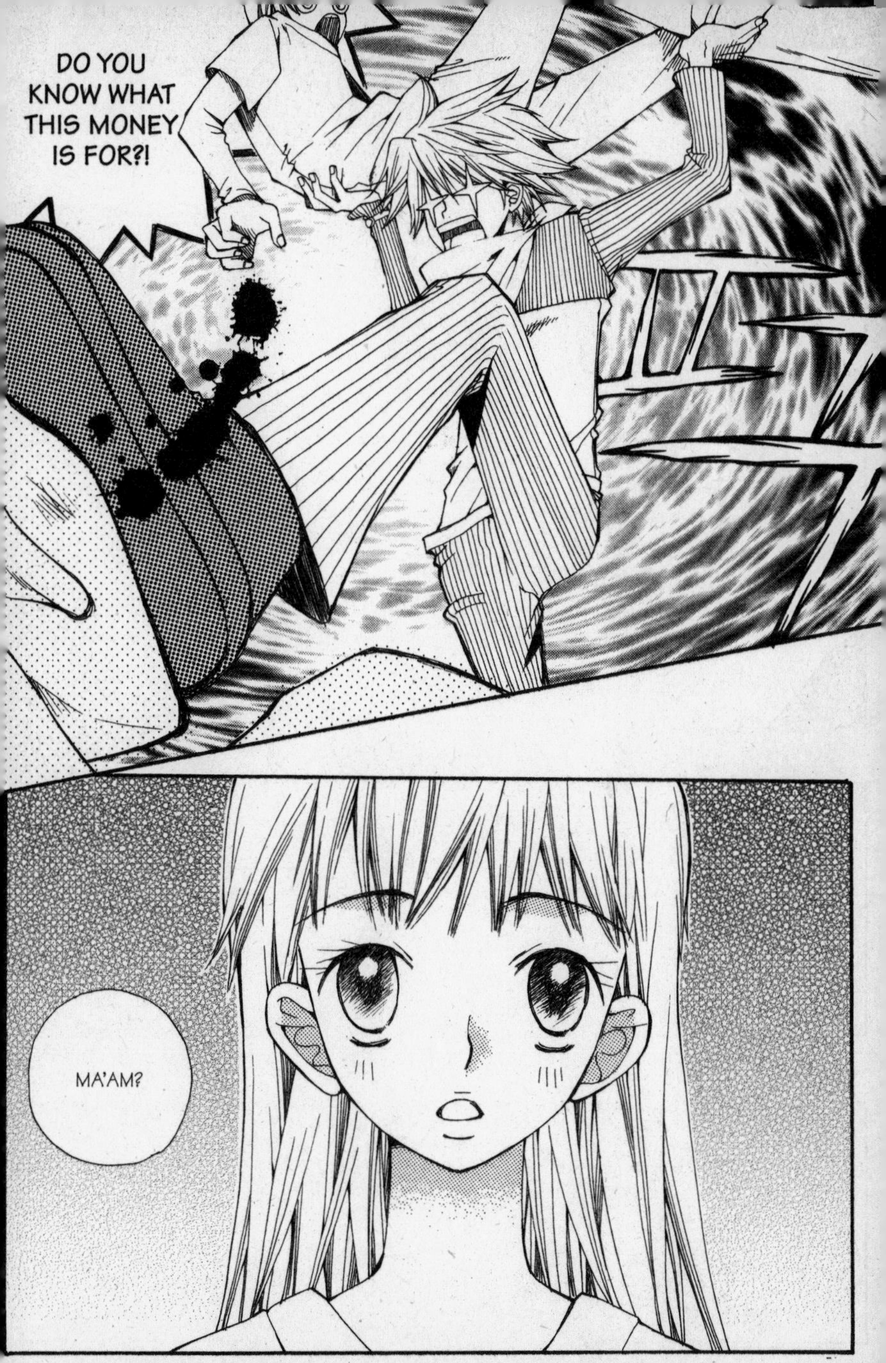
DO YOU KNOW WHAT THIS MONEY IS FOR?!
MA'AM?

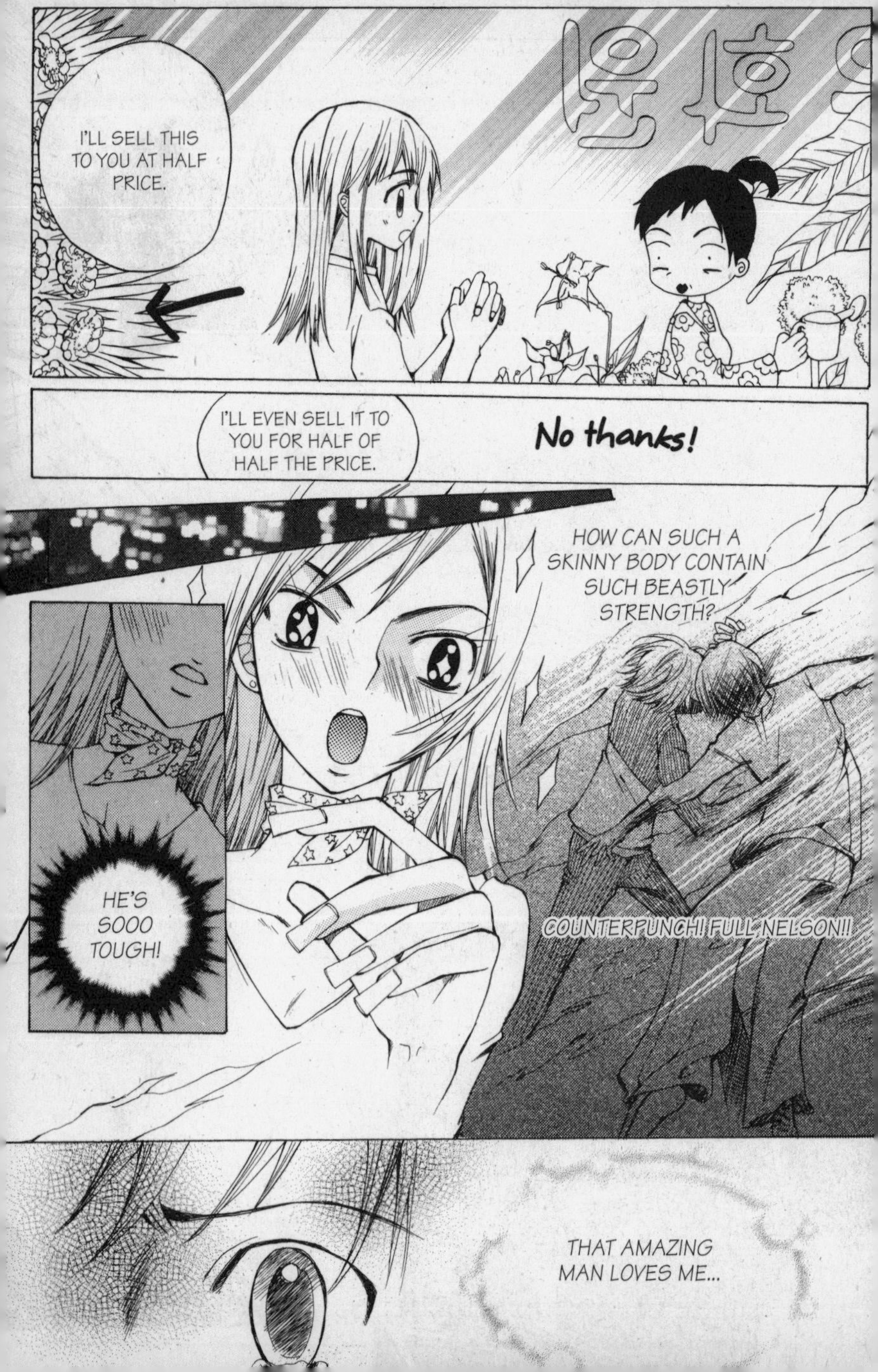
I'LL SELL THIS TO YOU AT HALF PRICE.
I'LL EVEN SELL IT TO YOU FOR HALF OF HALF THE PRICE.
No thanks!
HOW CAN SUCH A SKINNY BODY CONTAIN SUCH BEASTLY STRENGTH?
HE'S SOOO TOUGH!
COUNTERPUNCH! FULL NELSON!!
THAT AMAZING MAN LOVES ME...

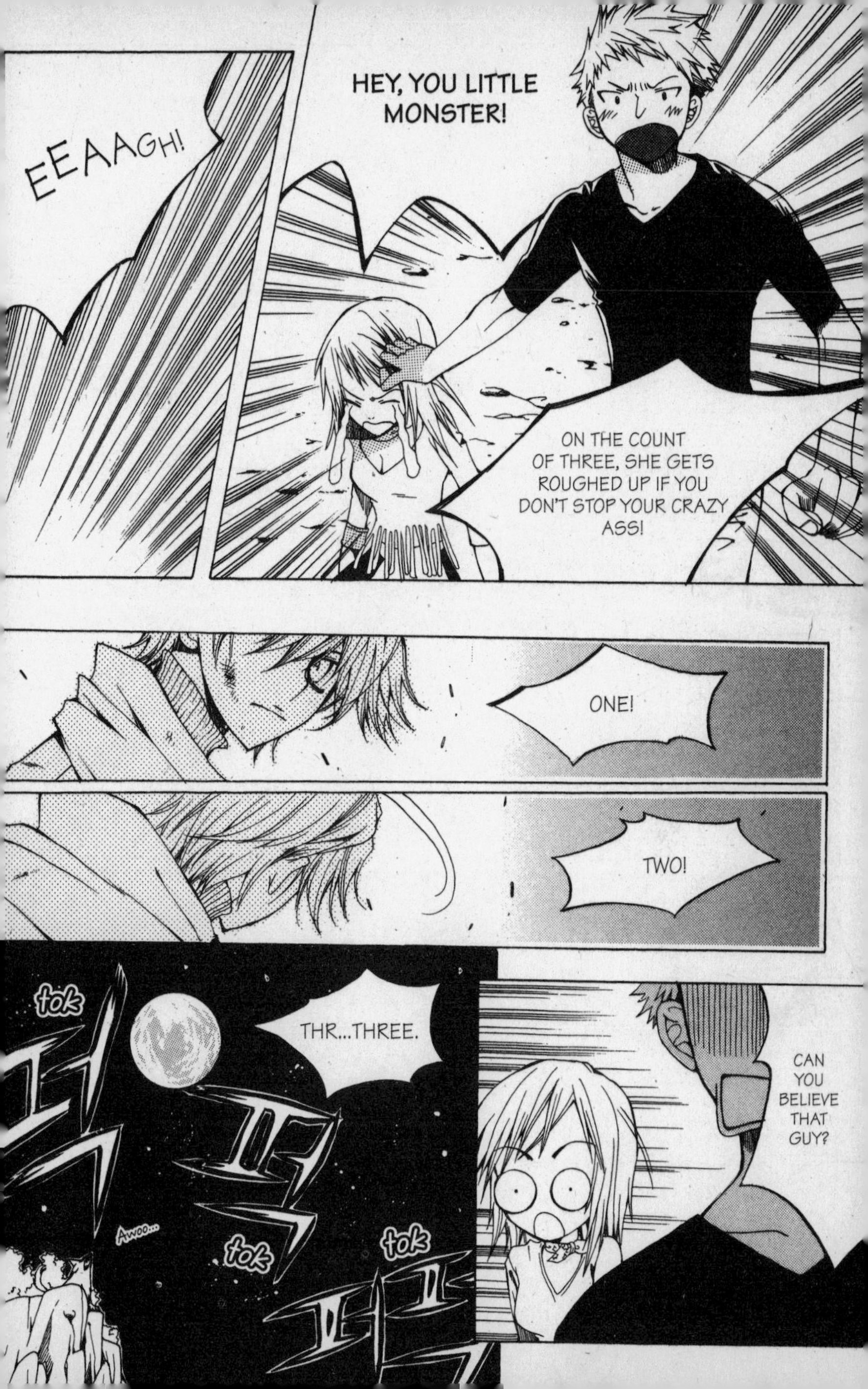
EEAAGH!
HEY, YOU LITTLE MONSTER!
ON THE COUNT OF THREE, SHE GETS ROUGHED UP IF YOU DON'T STOP YOUR CRAZY ASS!
ONE!
TWO!
tok
THR...THREE.
Awoo...
tok
tok
CAN YOU BELIEVE THAT GUY?

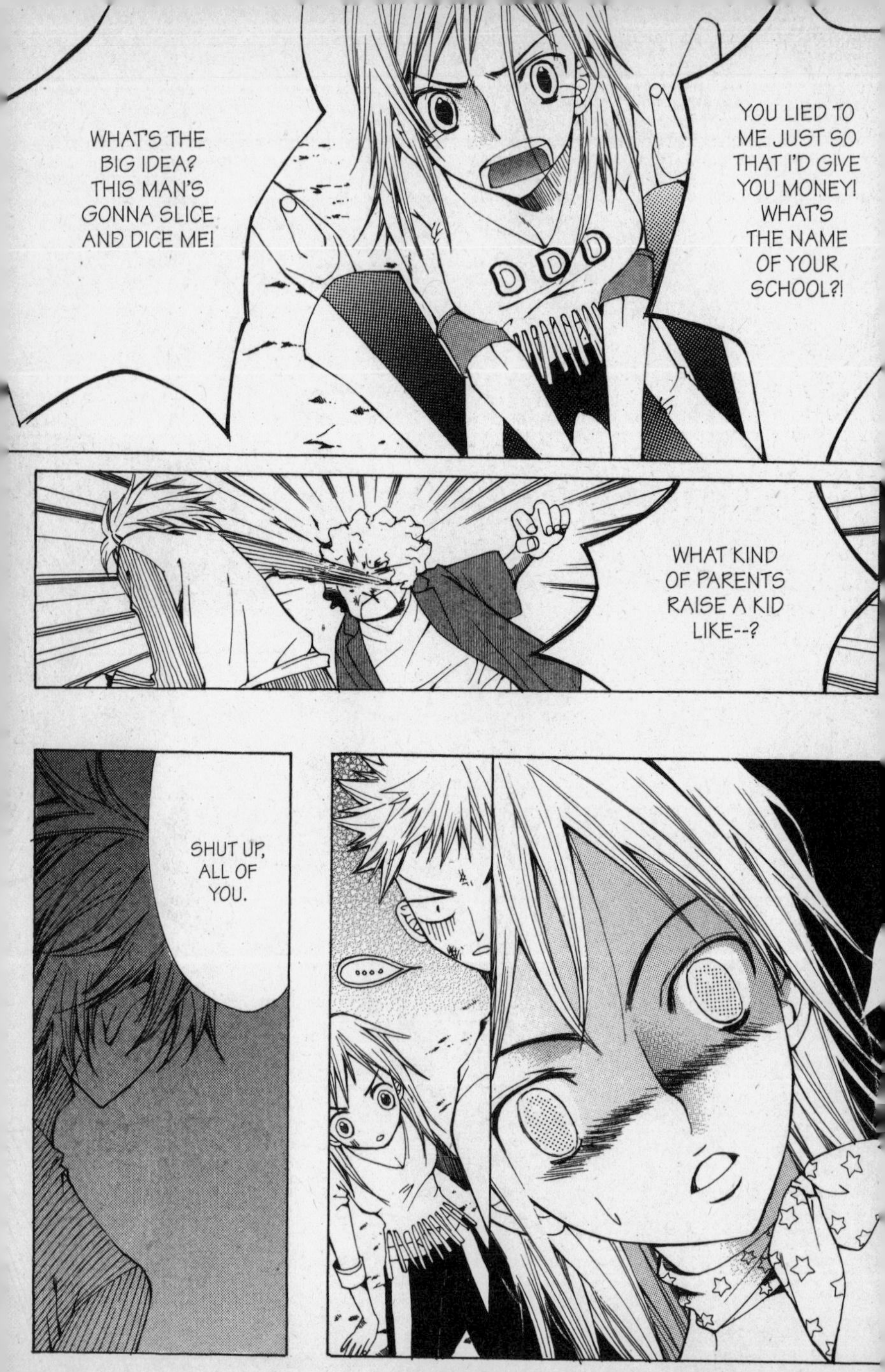
WHAT'S THE BIG IDEA? THIS MAN'S GONNA SLICE AND DICE ME!
YOU LIED TO ME JUST SO THAT I'D GIVE YOU MONEY! WHAT'S THE NAME OF YOUR SCHOOL?!
WHAT KIND OF PARENTS RAISE A KID LIKE--?
SHUT UP, ALL OF YOU.
....

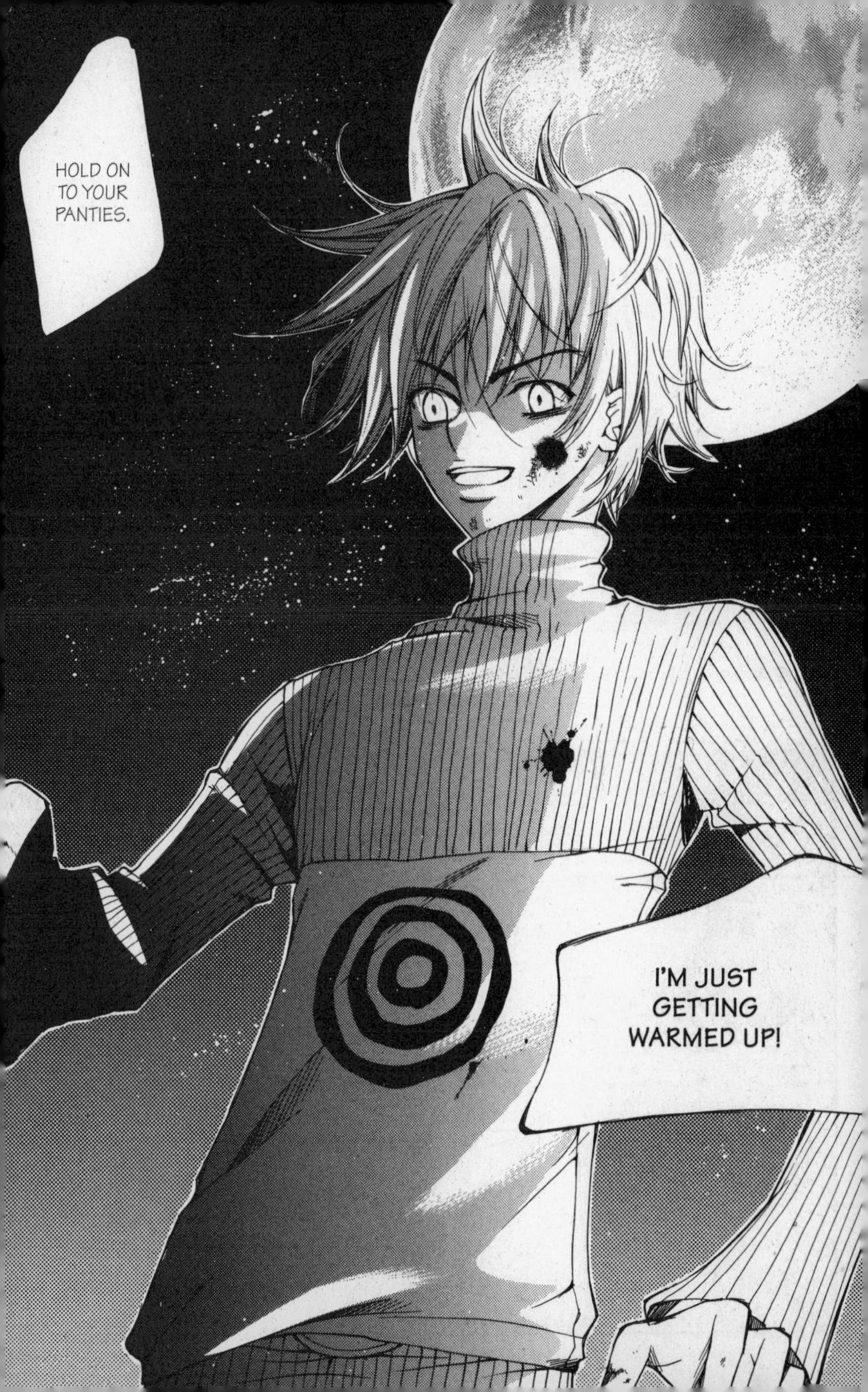
HOLD ON TO YOUR PANTIES.
I'M JUST GETTING WARMED UP!

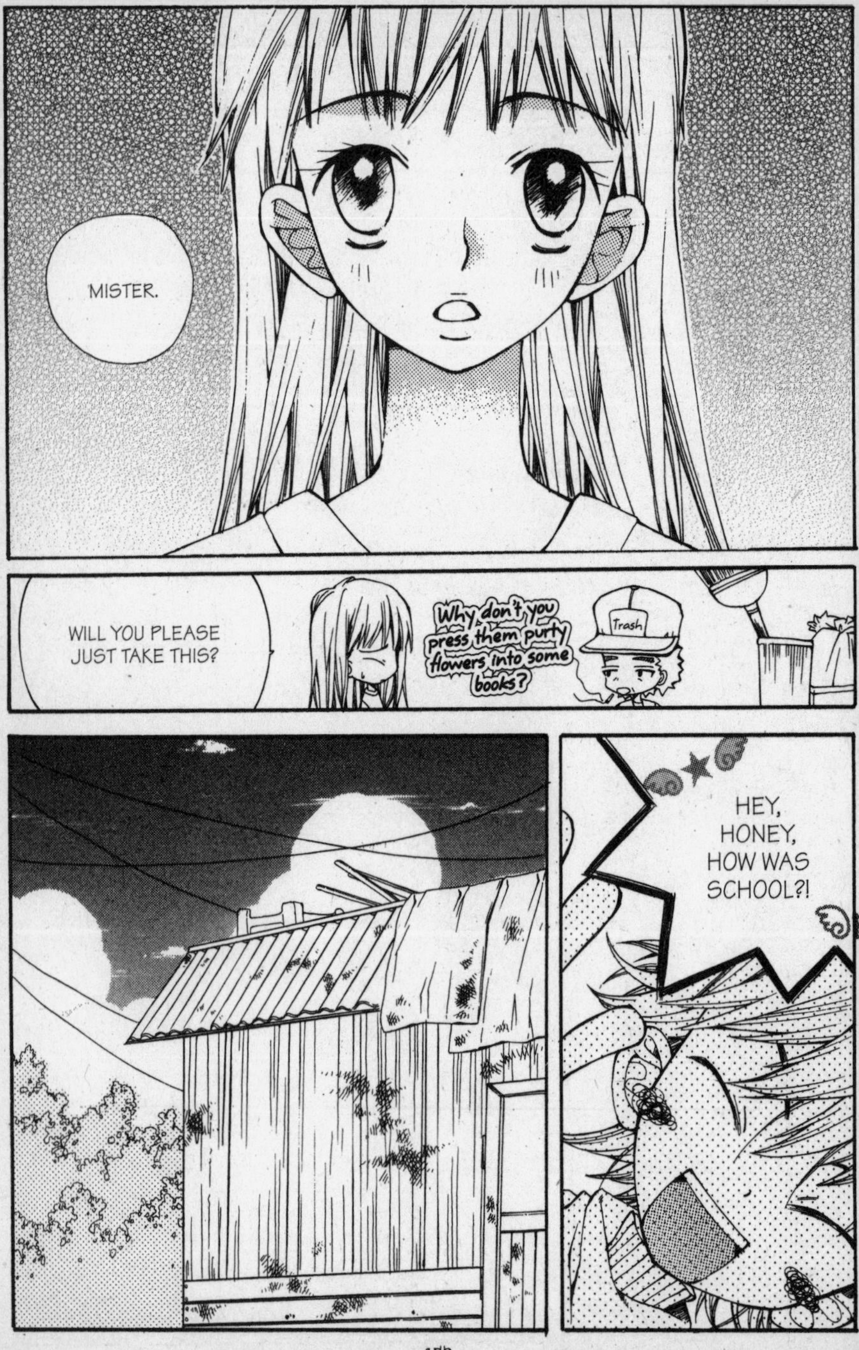
MISTER.
WILL YOU PLEASE JUST TAKE THIS?
Why don't you press them purty flowers into some books?
Trash
HEY, HONEY, HOW WAS SCHOOL?!

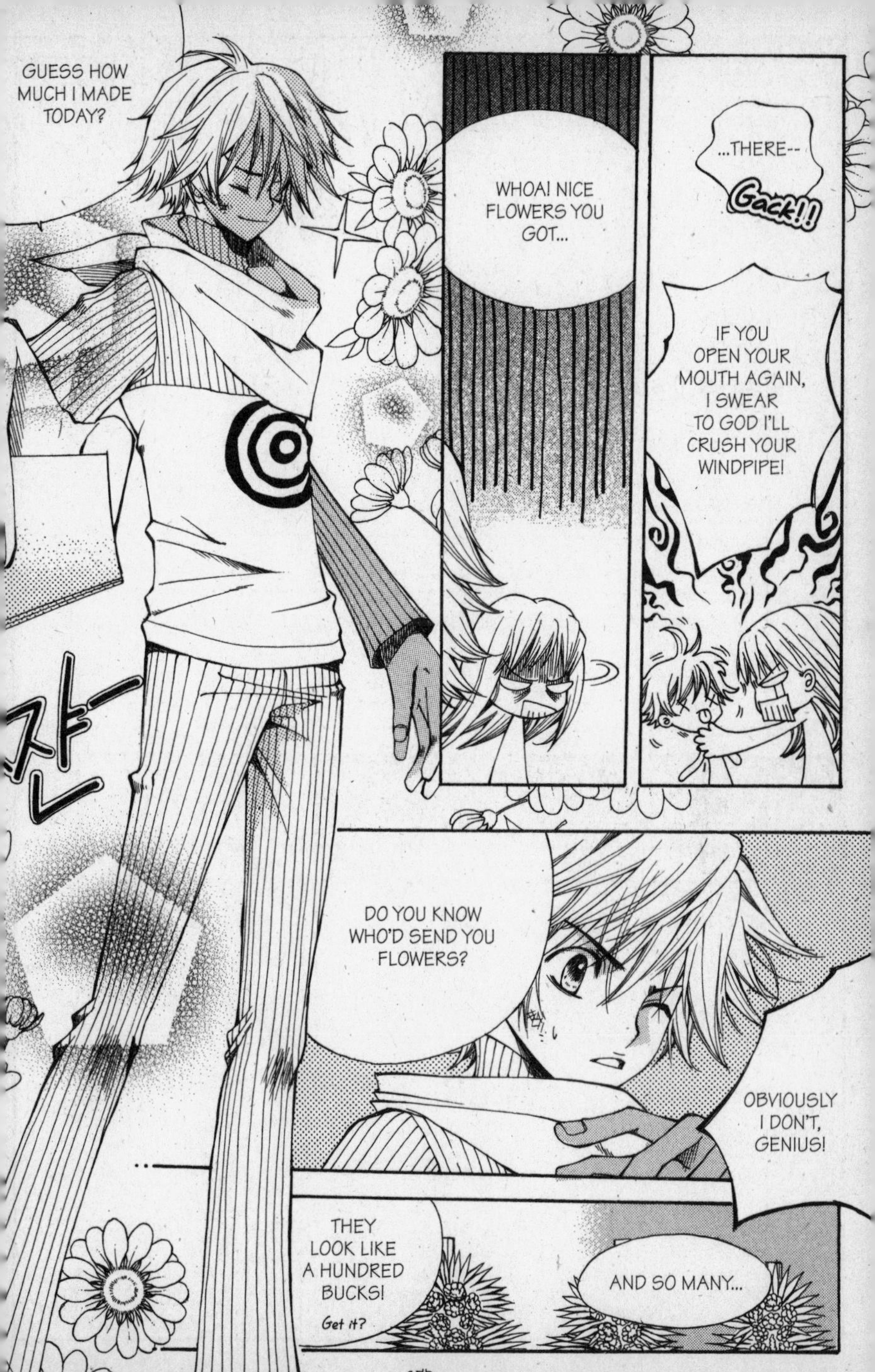
GUESS HOW MUCH I MADE TODAY?
WHOA! NICE FLOWERS YOU GOT...
...THERE--
Gack!!
IF YOU OPEN YOUR MOUTH AGAIN, I SWEAR TO GOD I'LL CRUSH YOUR WINDPIPE!
DO YOU KNOW WHO'D SEND YOU FLOWERS?
OBVIOUSLY I DON'T, GENIUS!
THEY LOOK LIKE A HUNDRED BUCKS!
Get it?
AND SO MANY...

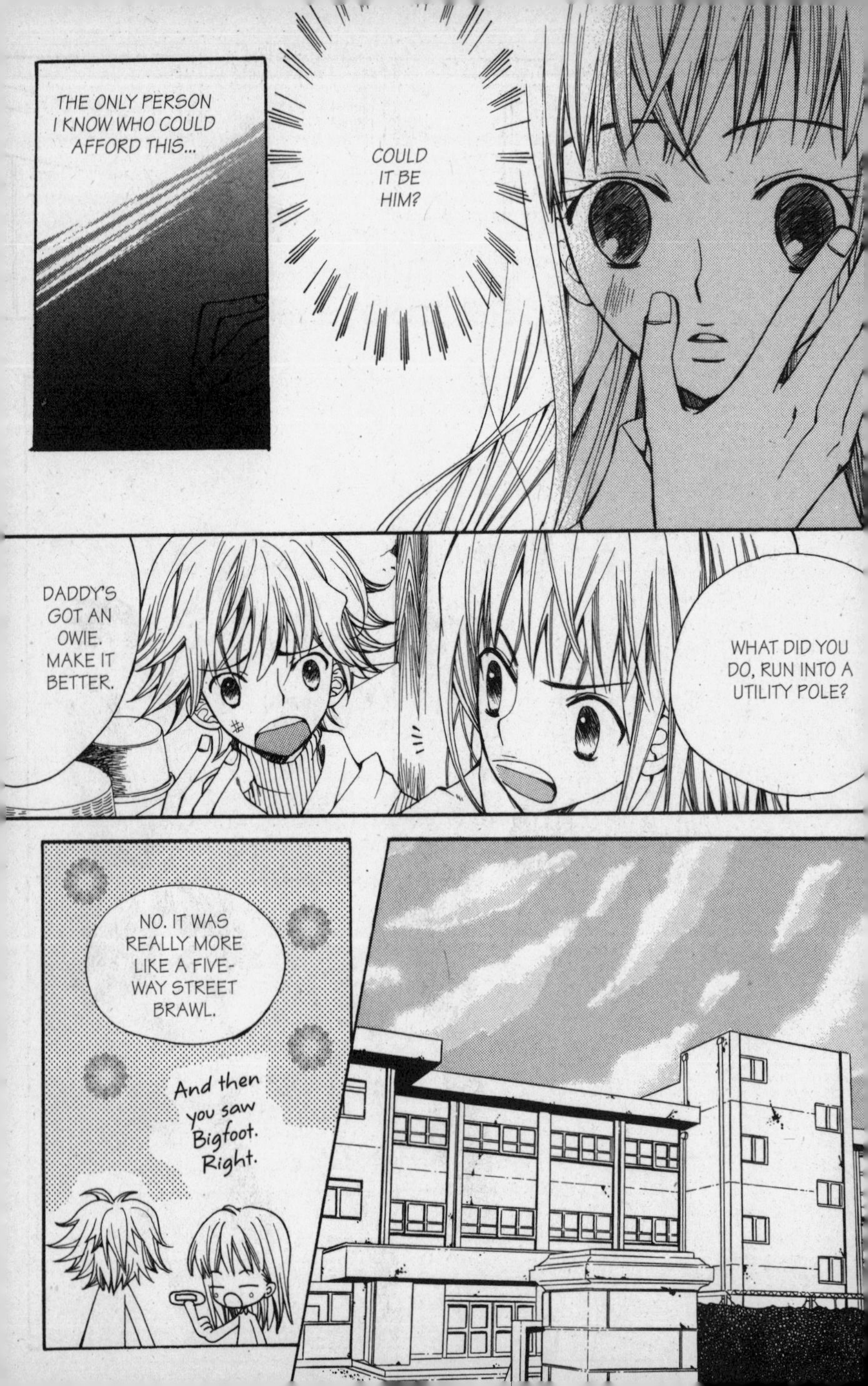
THE ONLY PERSON I KNOW WHO COULD AFFORD THIS...
COULD IT BE HIM?
DADDY'S GOT AN OWIE. MAKE IT BETTER.
WHAT DID YOU DO, RUN INTO A UTILITY POLE?
NO. IT WAS REALLY MORE LIKE A FIVE-WAY STREET BRAWL.
And then you saw Bigfoot. Right.

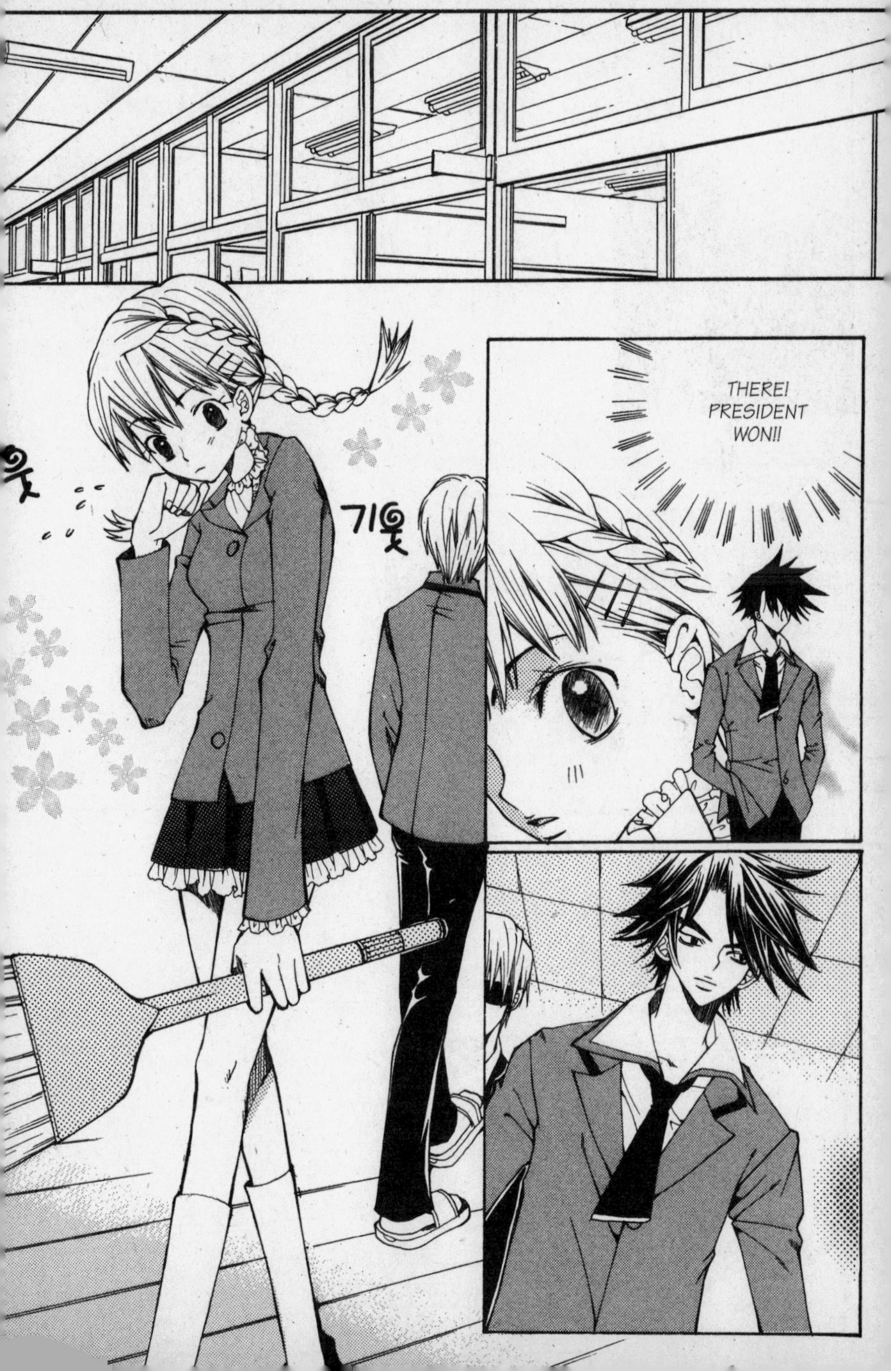
훗
기웃
THERE! PRESIDENT WON!!

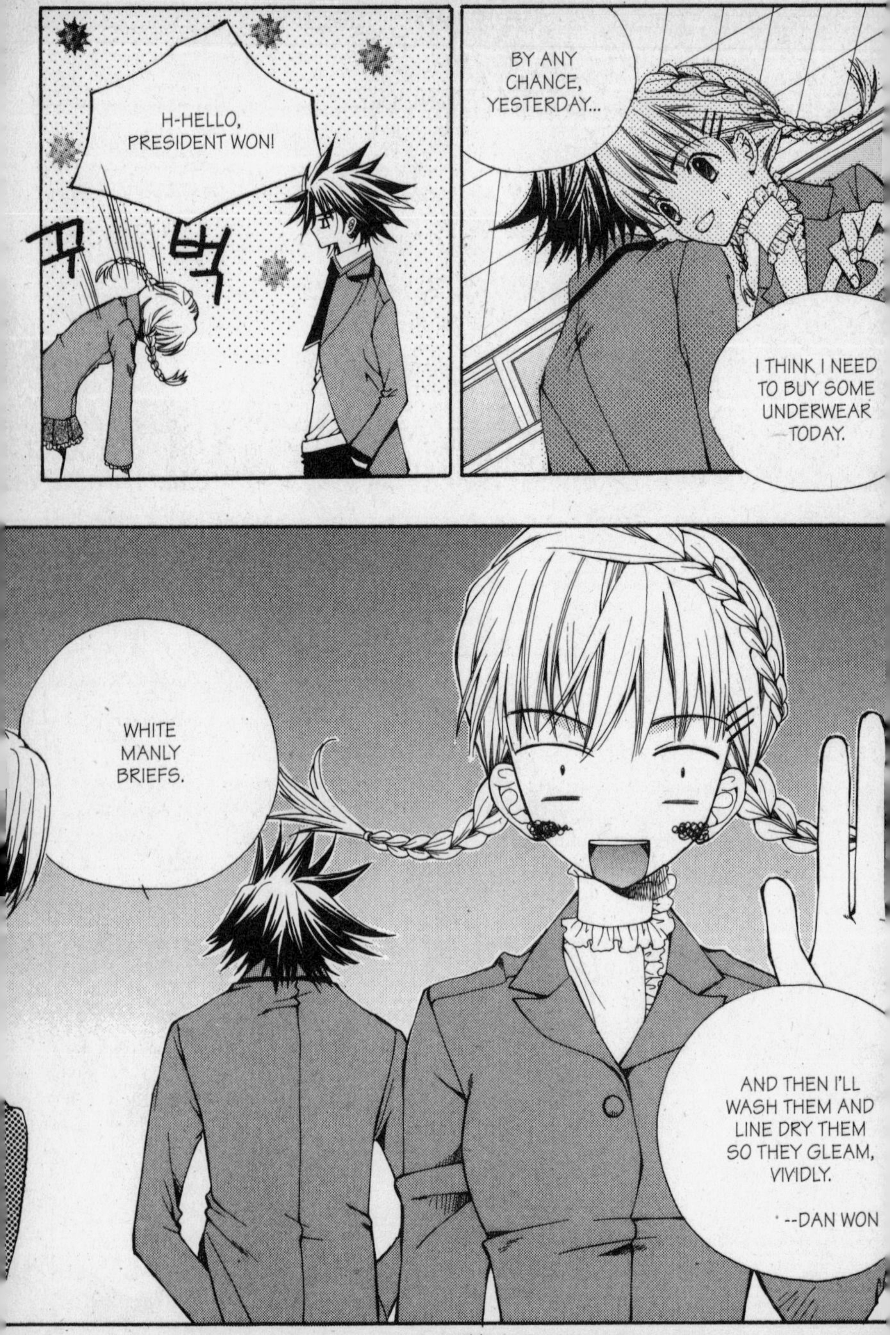
H-HELLO, PRESIDENT WON!
꾸벅
BY ANY CHANCE, YESTERDAY...
I THINK I NEED TO BUY SOME UNDERWEAR TODAY.
WHITE MANLY BRIEFS.
AND THEN I'LL WASH THEM AND LINE DRY THEM SO THEY GLEAM, VIVIDLY.
--DAN WON

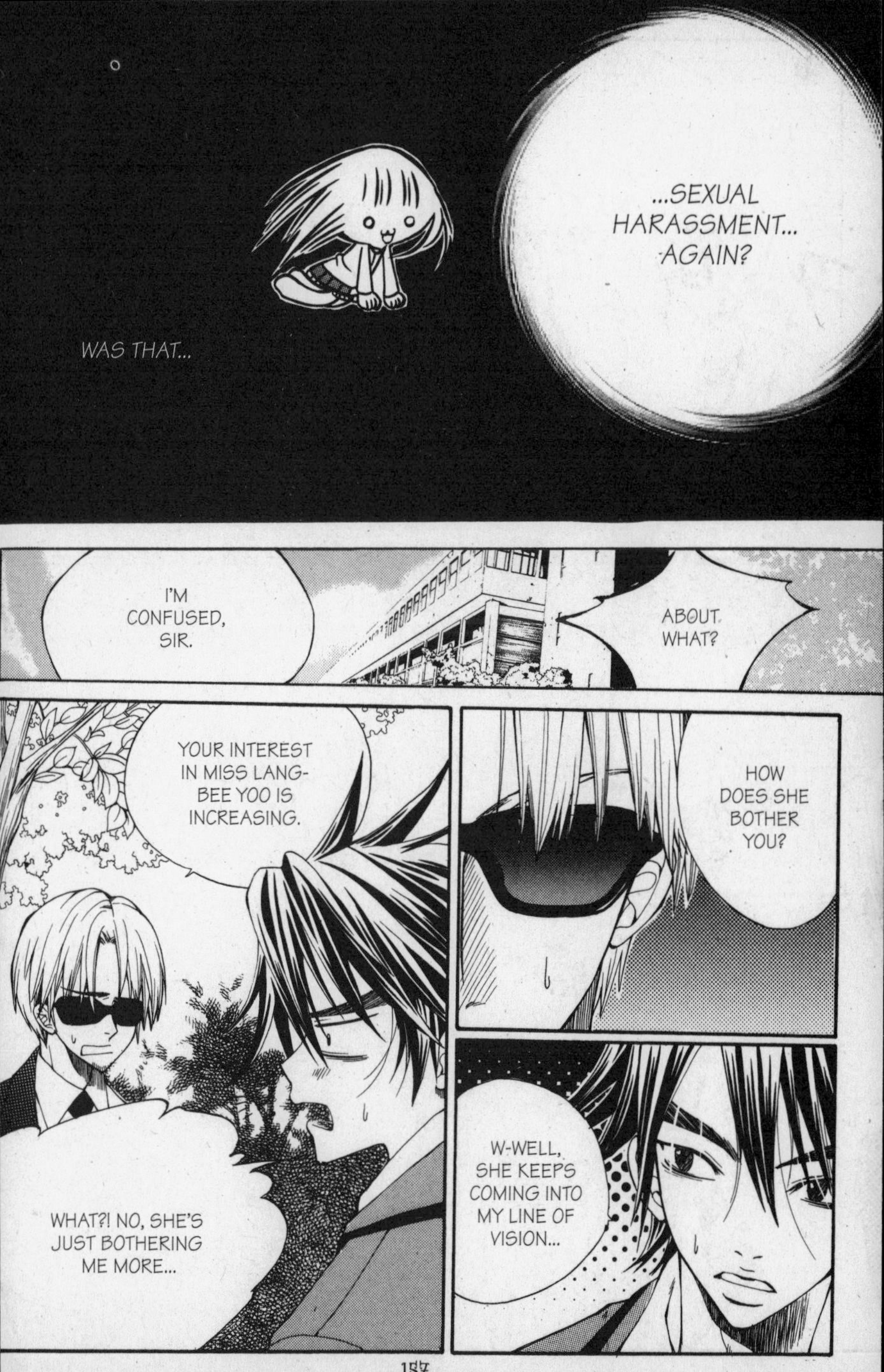
WAS THAT...
...SEXUAL HARASSMENT... AGAIN?
I'M CONFUSED, SIR.
ABOUT WHAT?
YOUR INTEREST IN MISS LANG-BEE YOO IS INCREASING.
WHAT?! NO, SHE'S JUST BOTHERING ME MORE...
HOW DOES SHE BOTHER YOU?
W-WELL, SHE KEEPS COMING INTO MY LINE OF VISION...

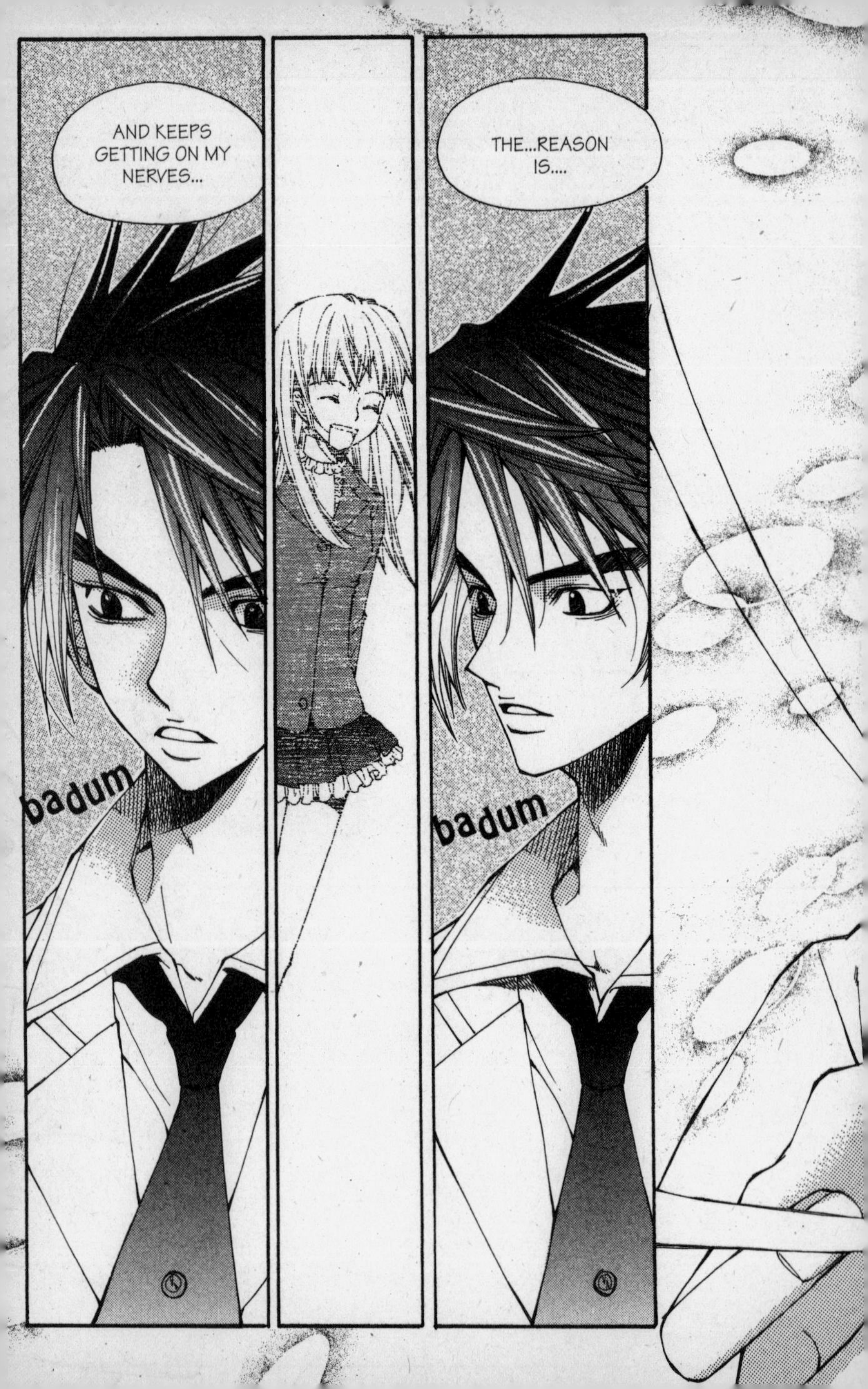
AND KEEPS GETTING ON MY NERVES...
badum
THE...REASON IS....
badum

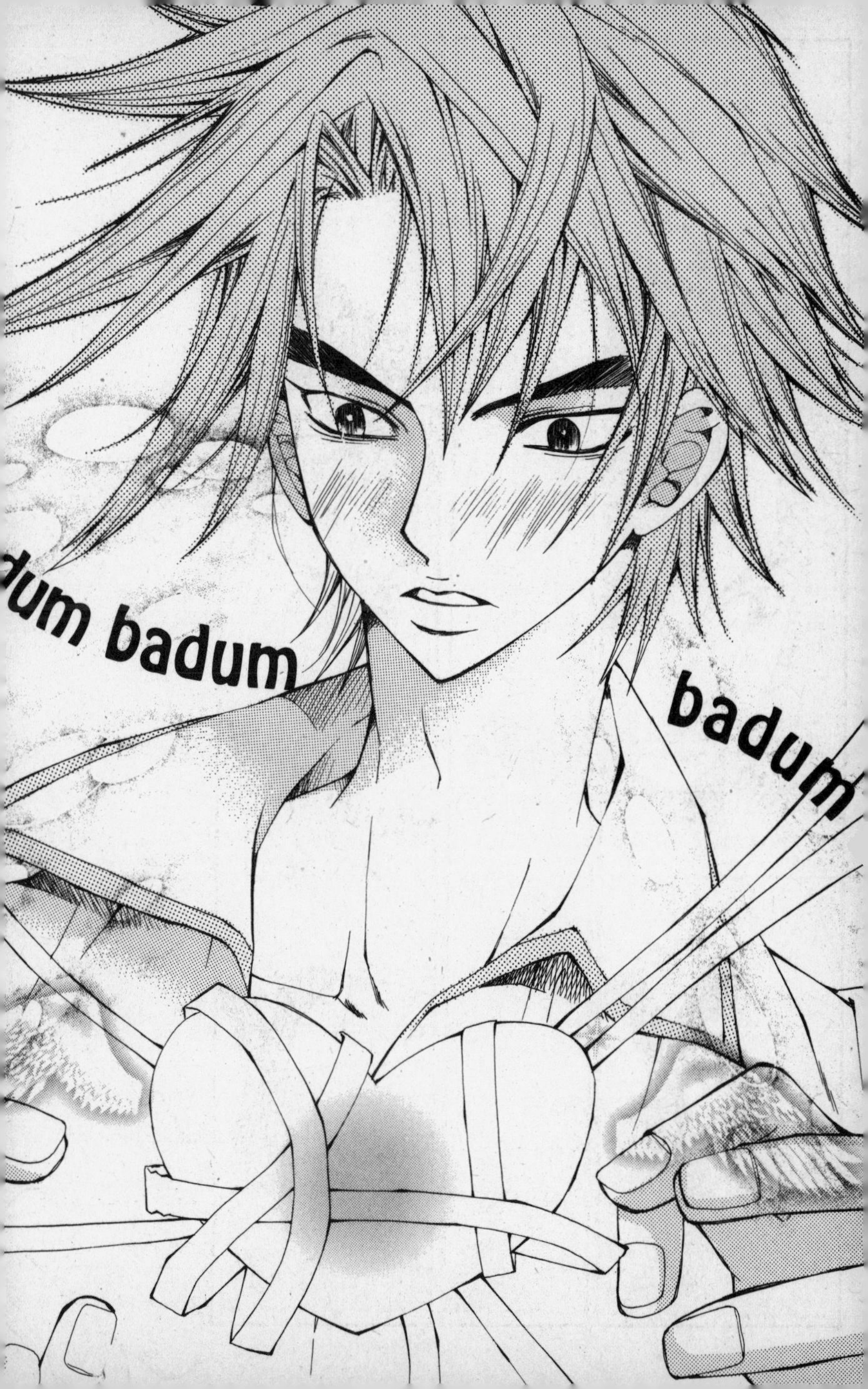
dum badum
badum

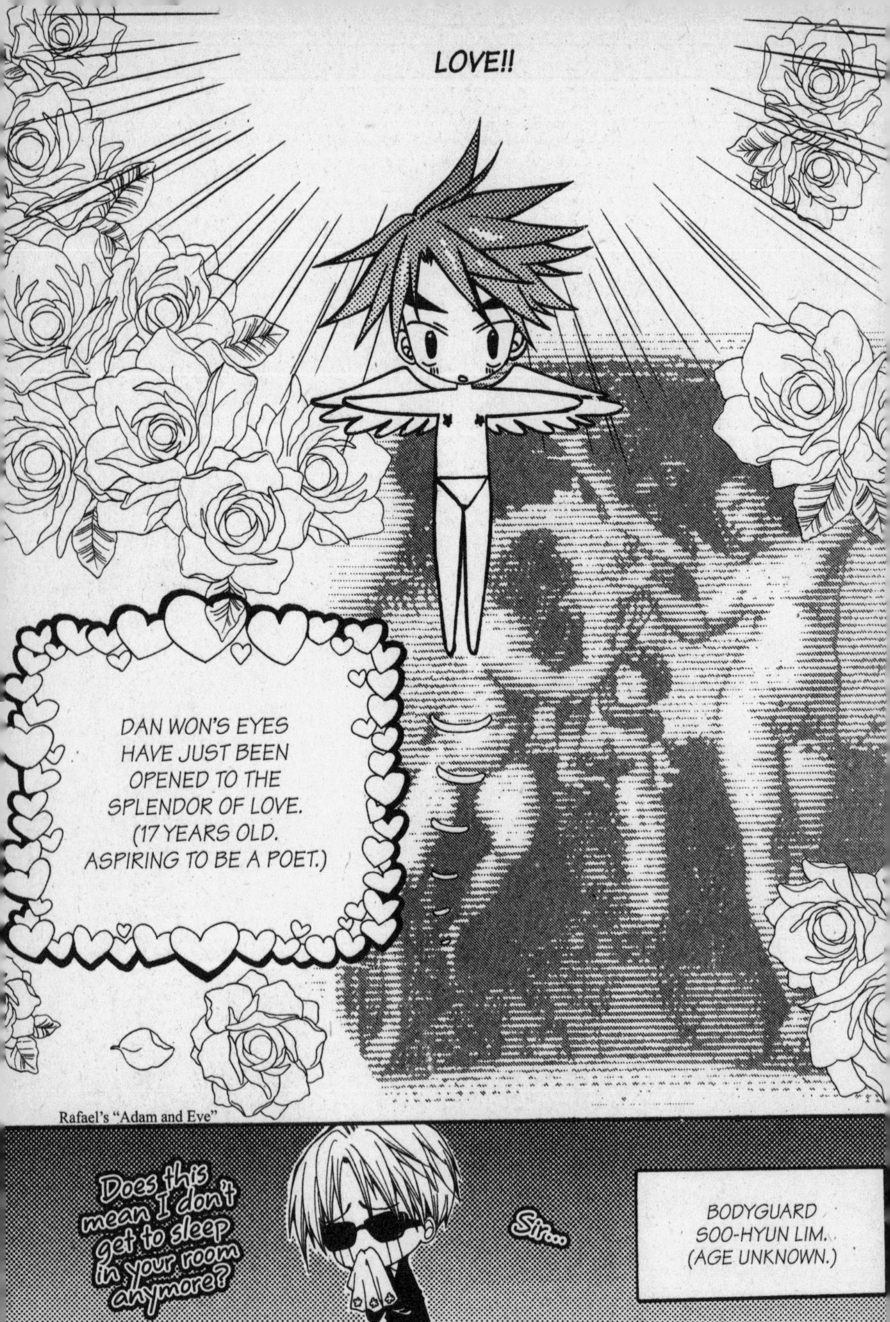
LOVE!!
DAN WON'S EYES HAVE JUST BEEN OPENED TO THE SPLENDOR OF LOVE. (17 YEARS OLD. ASPIRING TO BE A POET.)
Rafael's "Adam and Eve"

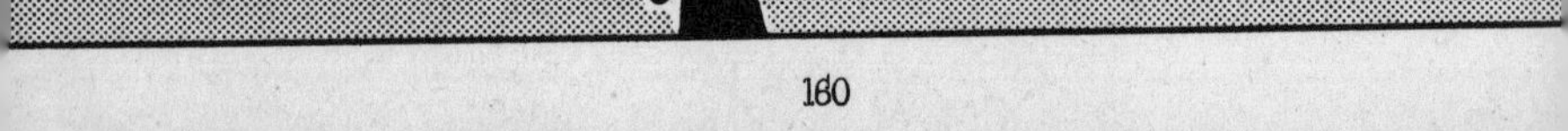
Does this mean I don't get to sleep in your room anymore?
Sir...
BODYGUARD SOO-HYUN LIM. (AGE UNKNOWN.)

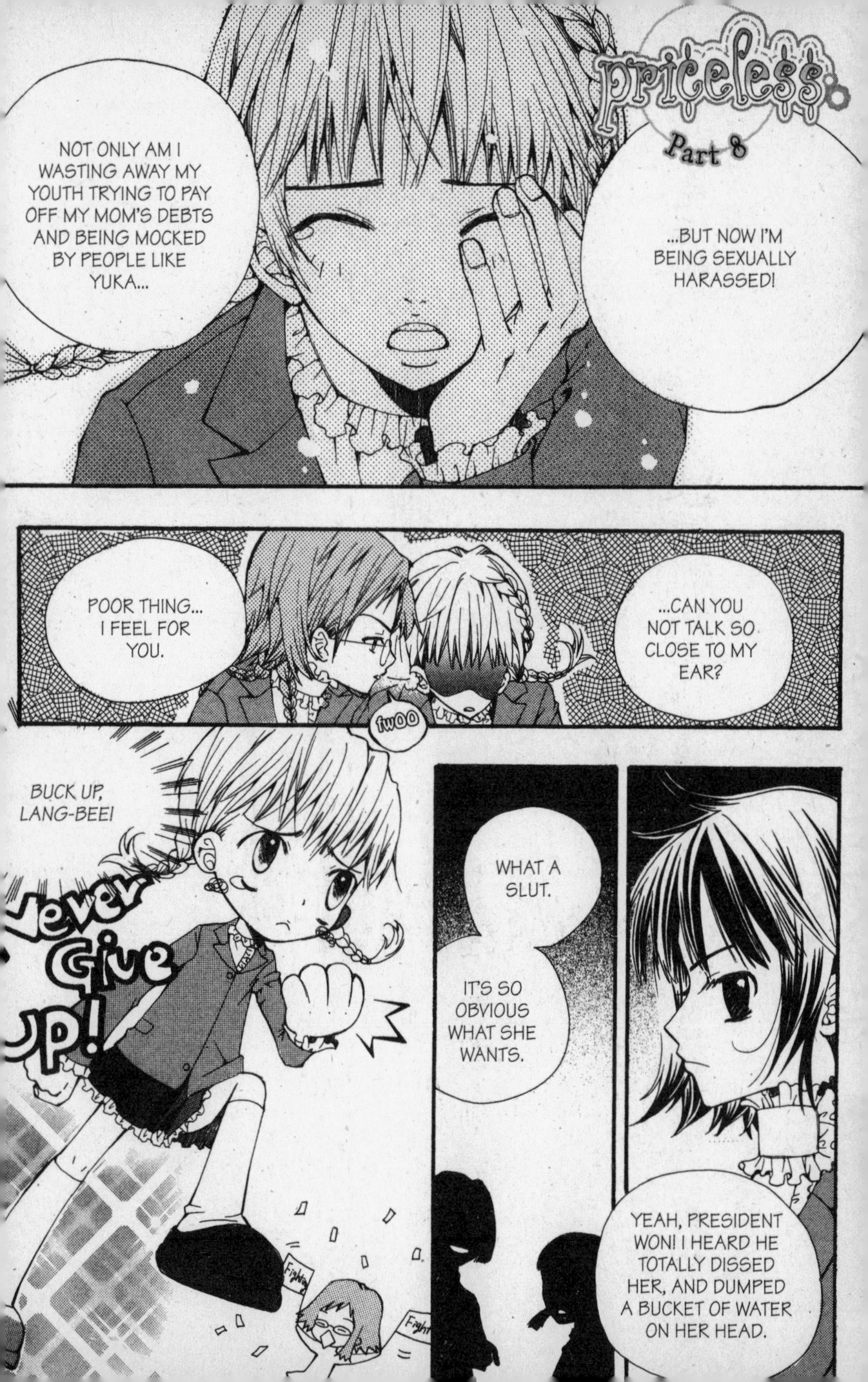
NOT ONLY AM I WASTING AWAY MY YOUTH TRYING TO PAY OFF MY MOM'S DEBTS AND BEING MOCKED BY PEOPLE LIKE YUKA...
priceless
Part 8
...BUT NOW I'M BEING SEXUALLY HARASSED!
POOR THING... I FEEL FOR YOU.
twoo
...CAN YOU NOT TALK SO CLOSE TO MY EAR?
BUCK UP, LANG-BEE!
Never Give Up!
WHAT A SLUT.
IT'S SO OBVIOUS WHAT SHE WANTS.
YEAH, PRESIDENT WON! I HEARD HE TOTALLY DISSED HER, AND DUMPED A BUCKET OF WATER ON HER HEAD.

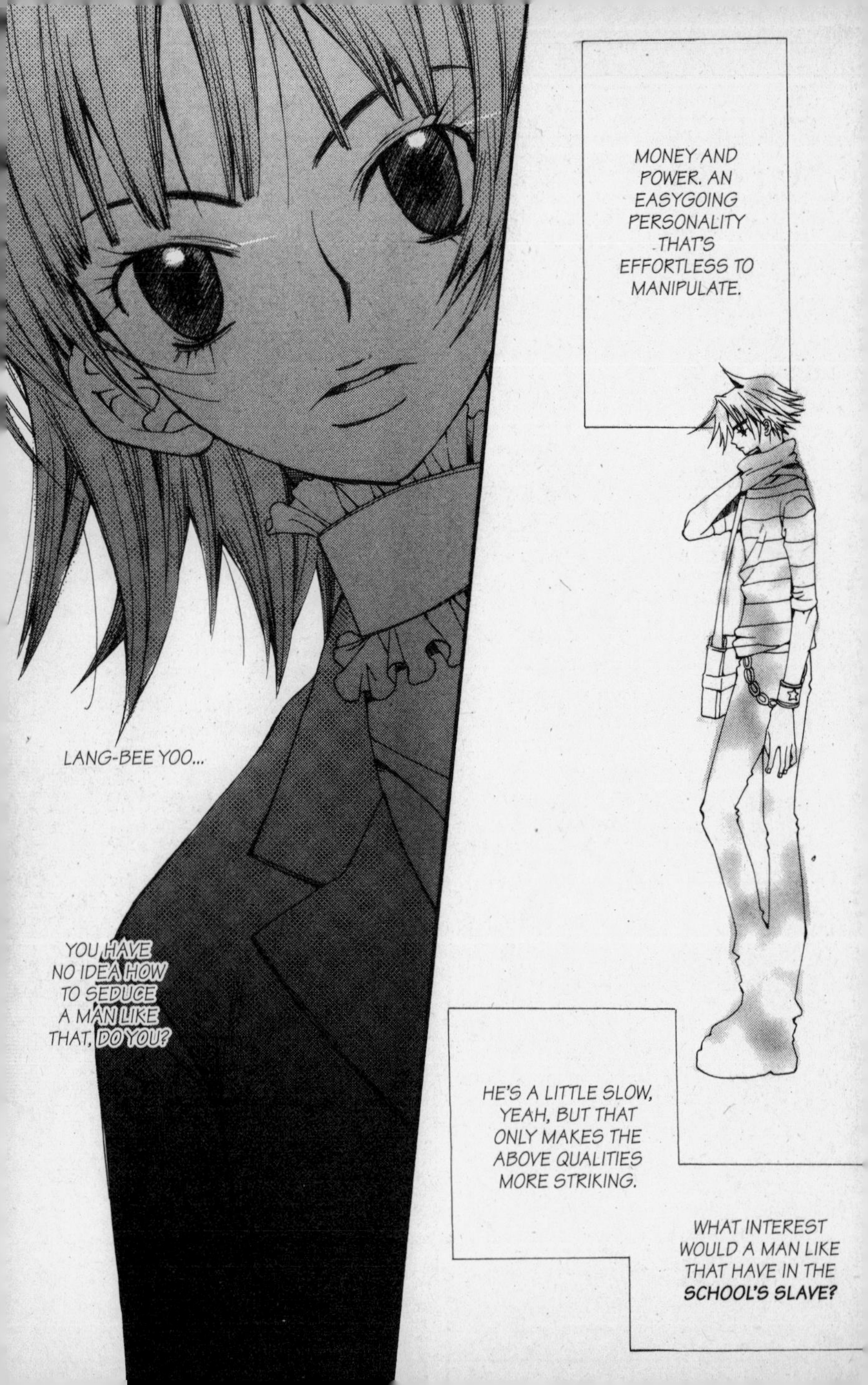
LANG-BEE YOO...
YOU HAVE NO IDEA HOW TO SEDUCE A MAN LIKE THAT, DO YOU?
MONEY AND POWER. AN EASYGOING PERSONALITY THAT'S EFFORTLESS TO MANIPULATE.
HE'S A LITTLE SLOW, YEAH, BUT THAT ONLY MAKES THE ABOVE QUALITIES MORE STRIKING.
WHAT INTEREST WOULD A MAN LIKE THAT HAVE IN THE **SCHOOL'S SLAVE?**

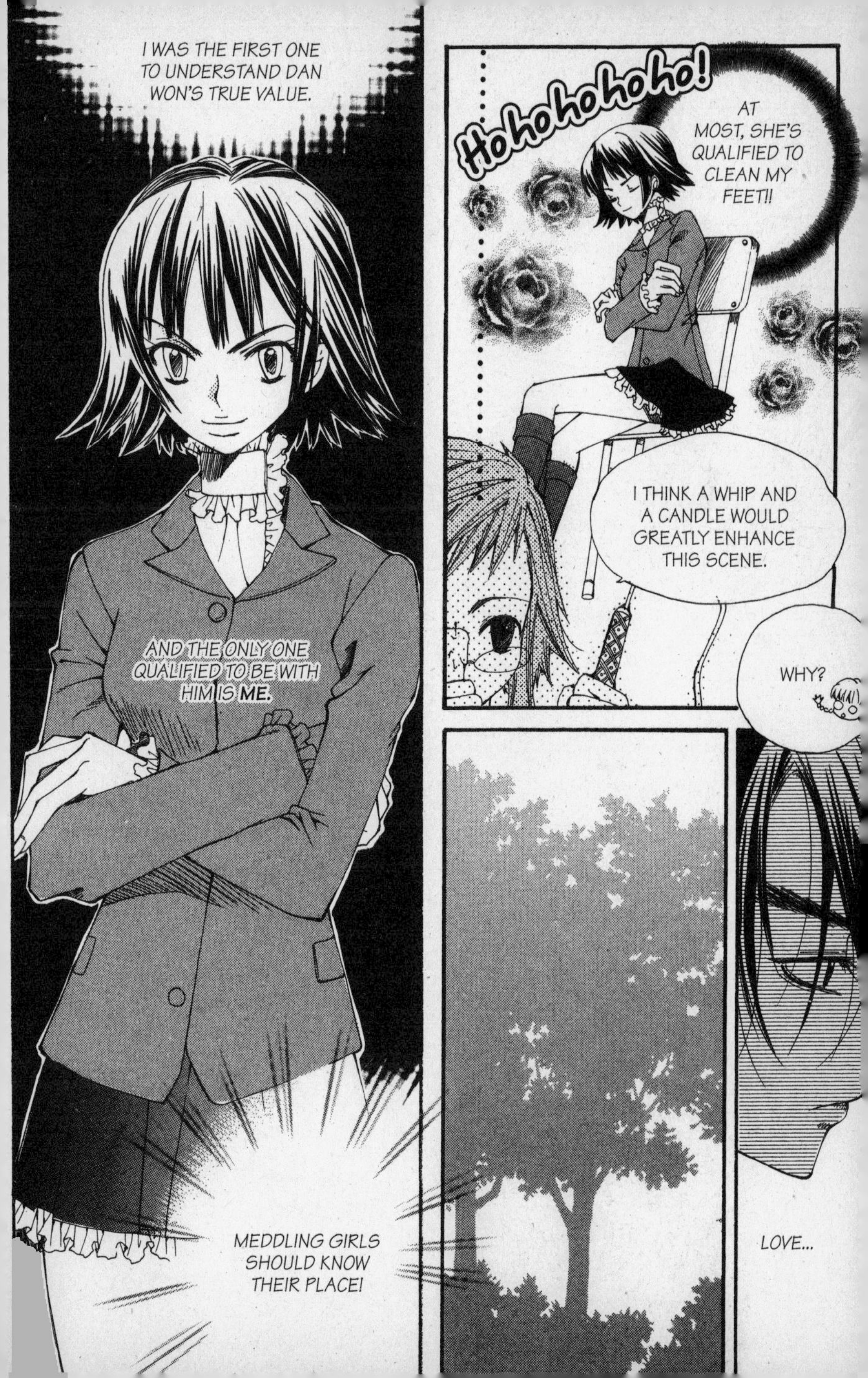
I WAS THE FIRST ONE TO UNDERSTAND DAN WON'S TRUE VALUE.
AND THE ONLY ONE QUALIFIED TO BE WITH HIM IS ME.
MEDDLING GIRLS SHOULD KNOW THEIR PLACE!
Hohohohoho!
AT MOST, SHE'S QUALIFIED TO CLEAN MY FEET!!
I THINK A WHIP AND A CANDLE WOULD GREATLY ENHANCE THIS SCENE.
WHY?
LOVE...

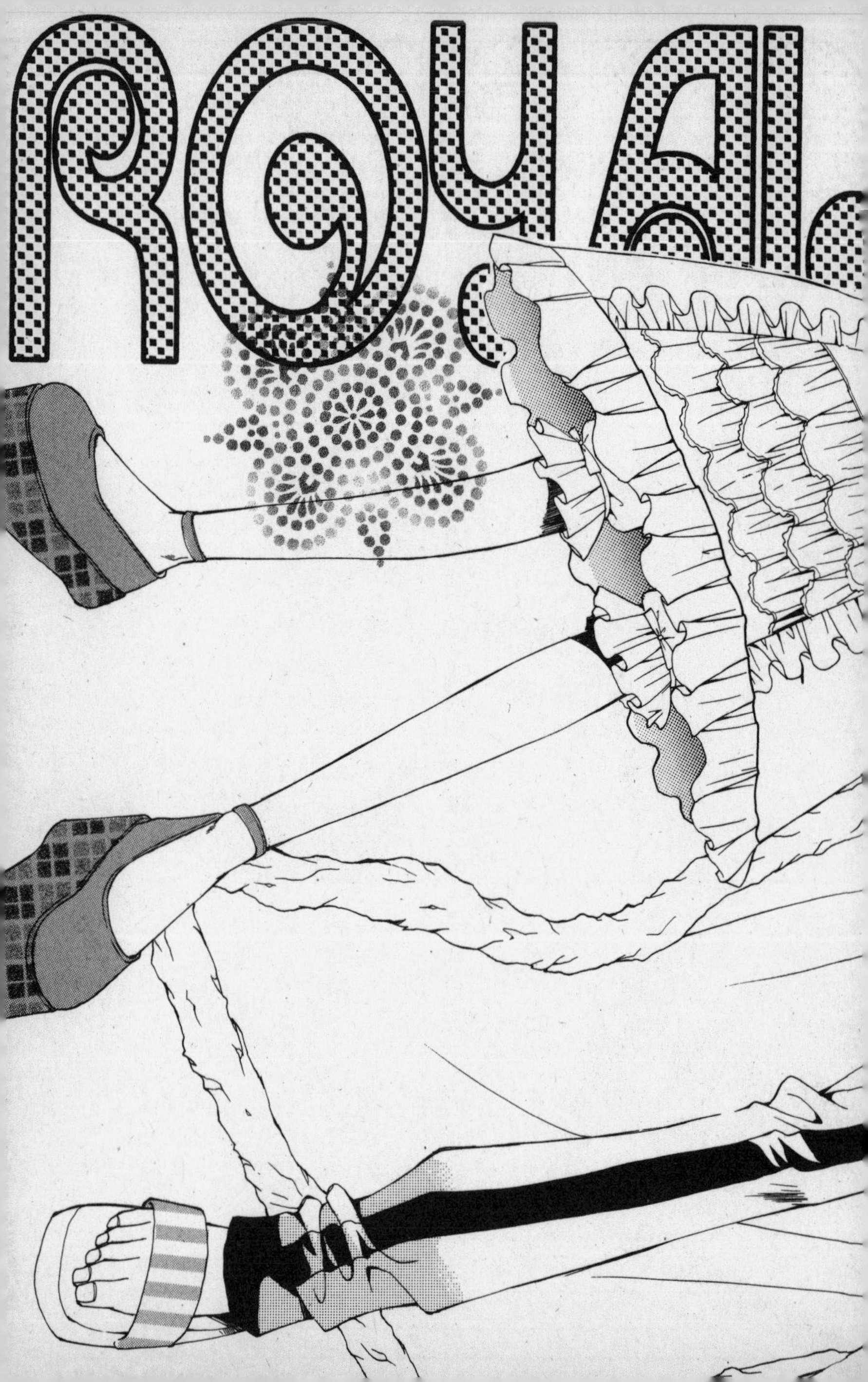
ROYAL

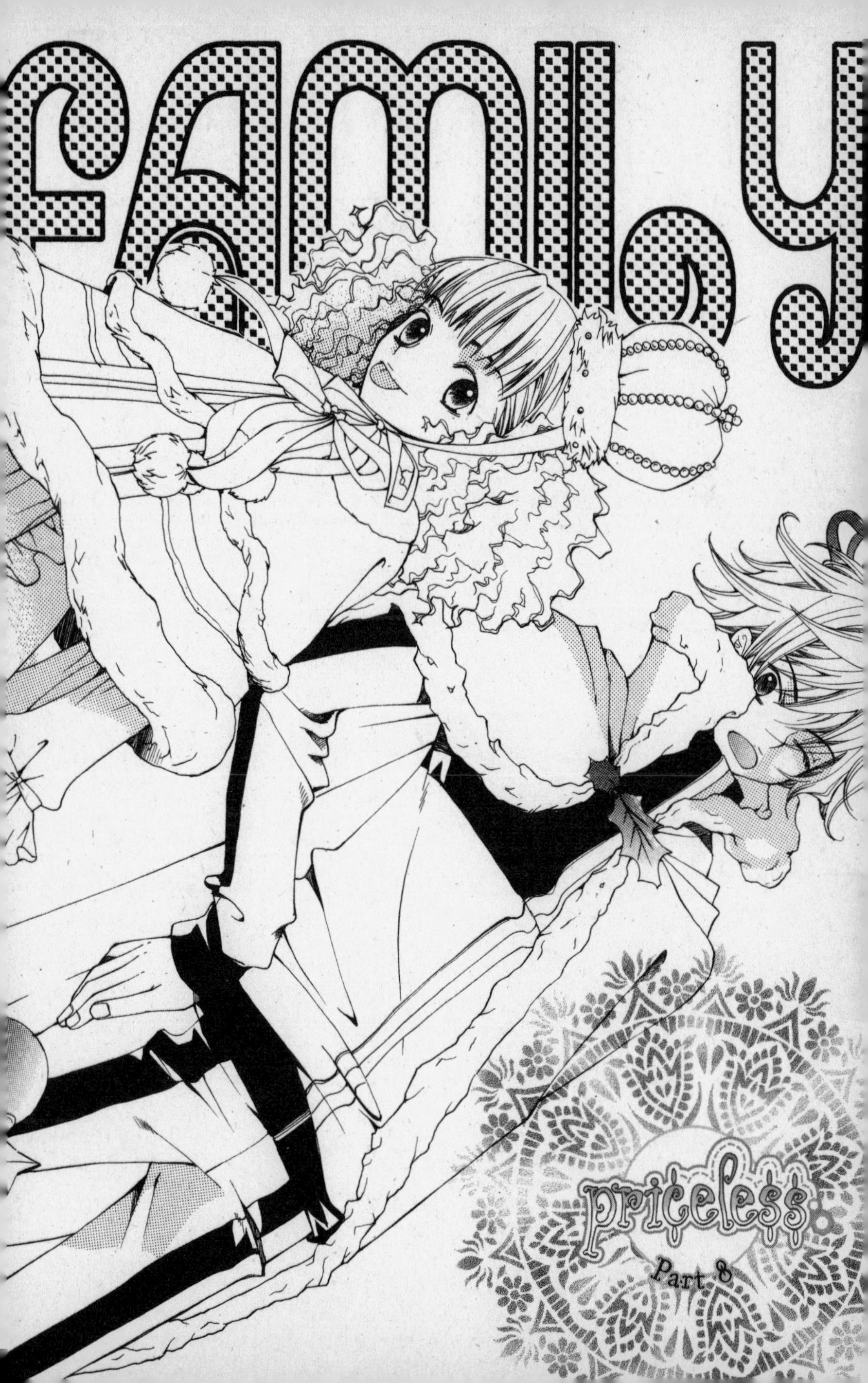
family
priceless
Part 8

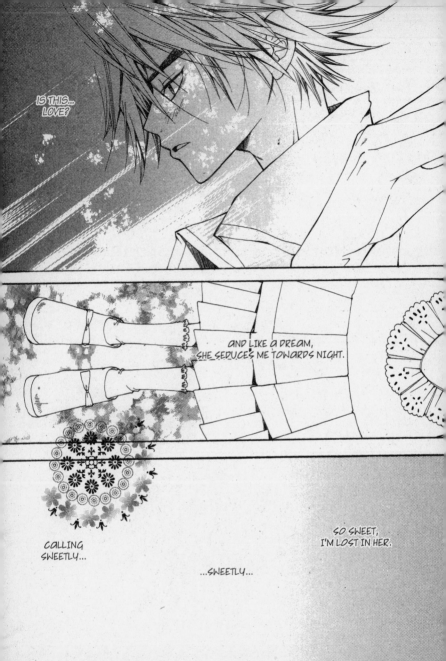

IS THIS... LOVE?

AND LIKE A DREAM, SHE SEDUCES ME TOWARDS NIGHT.

CALLING SWEETLY...

...SWEETLY...

SO SWEET, I'M LOST IN HER.

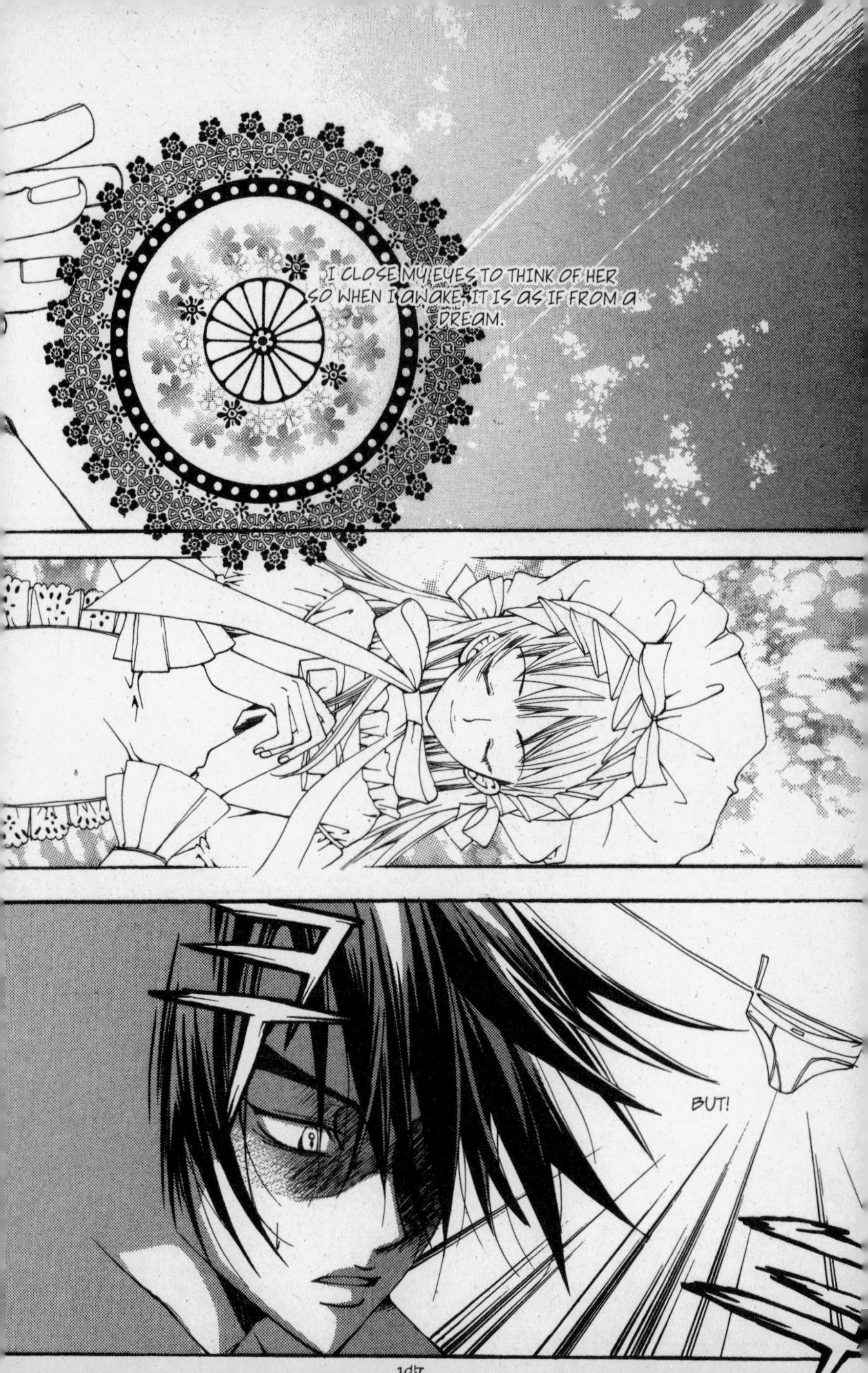
I CLOSE MY EYES TO THINK OF HER SO WHEN I AWAKE, IT IS AS IF FROM A DREAM.
BUT!

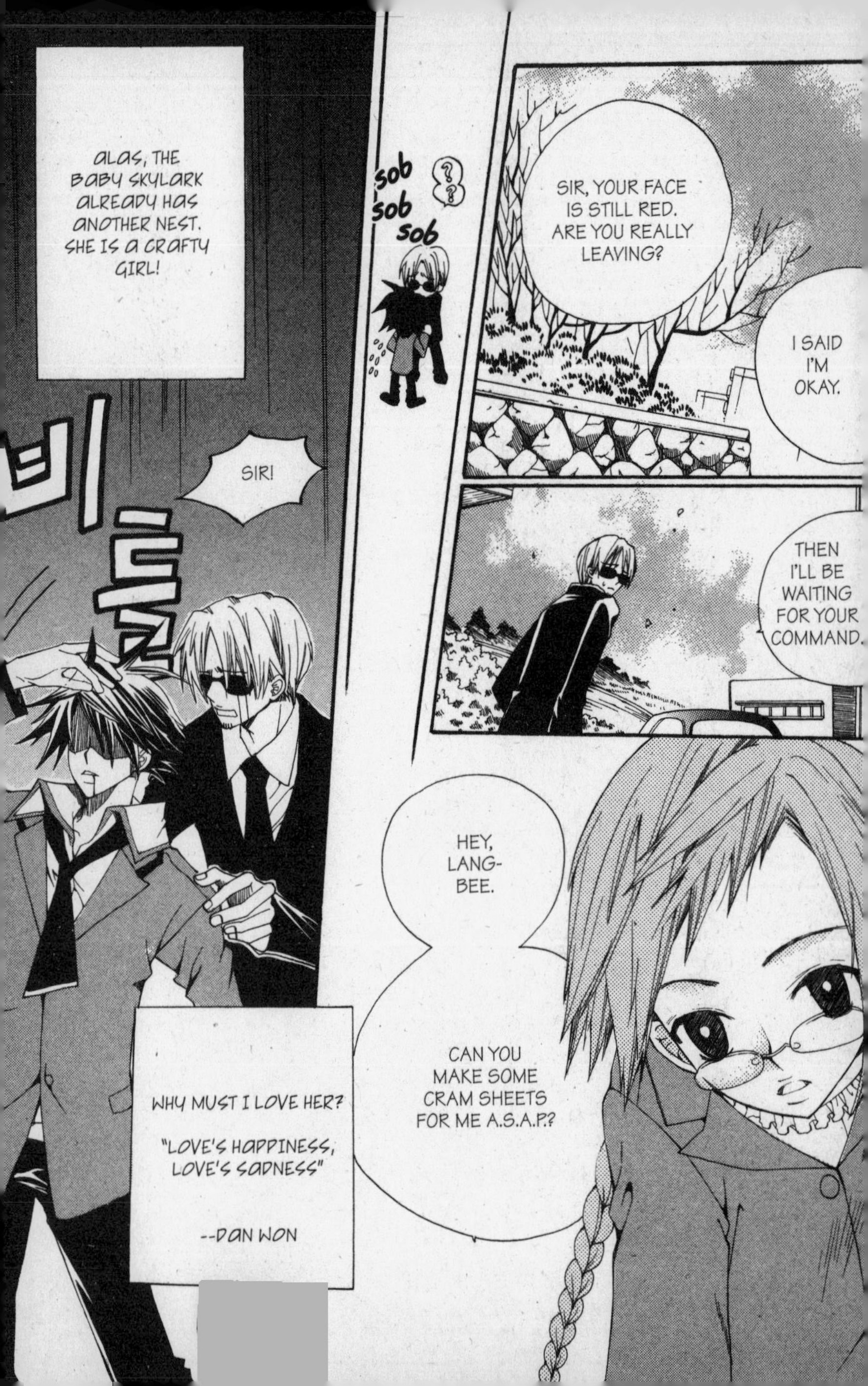
ALAS, THE BABY SKYLARK ALREADY HAS ANOTHER NEST. SHE IS A CRAFTY GIRL!
SIR!
WHY MUST I LOVE HER?
"LOVE'S HAPPINESS, LOVE'S SADNESS"
--DAN WON
SOB SOB SOB
??
SIR, YOUR FACE IS STILL RED. ARE YOU REALLY LEAVING?
I SAID I'M OKAY.
THEN I'LL BE WAITING FOR YOUR COMMAND.
HEY, LANG-BEE.
CAN YOU MAKE SOME CRAM SHEETS FOR ME A.S.A.P.?

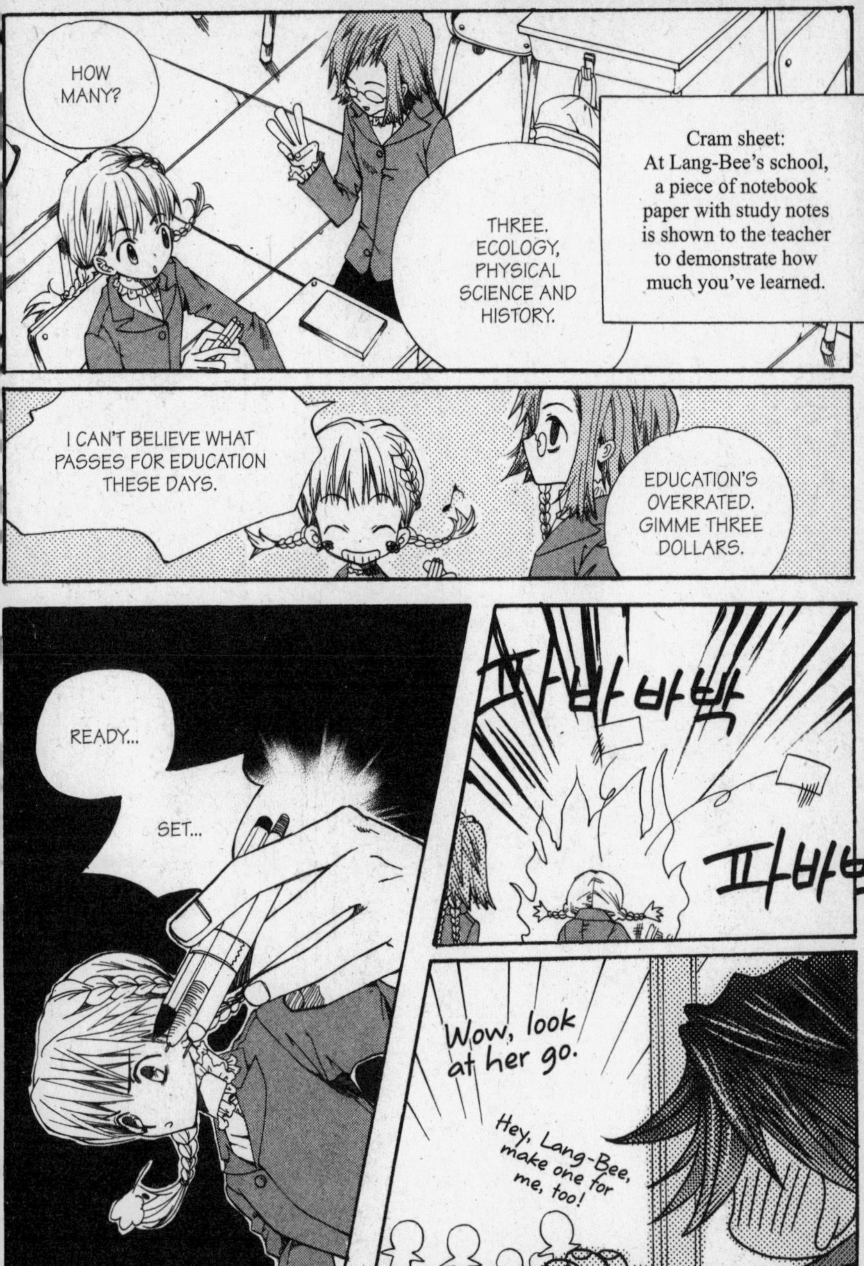
HOW MANY?
THREE. ECOLOGY, PHYSICAL SCIENCE AND HISTORY.
Cram sheet: At Lang-Bee's school, a piece of notebook paper with study notes is shown to the teacher to demonstrate how much you've learned.
I CAN'T BELIEVE WHAT PASSES FOR EDUCATION THESE DAYS.
EDUCATION'S OVERRATED. GIMME THREE DOLLARS.
READY...
SET...
파바바박
파바바
Wow, look at her go.
Hey, Lang-Bee, make one for me, too!

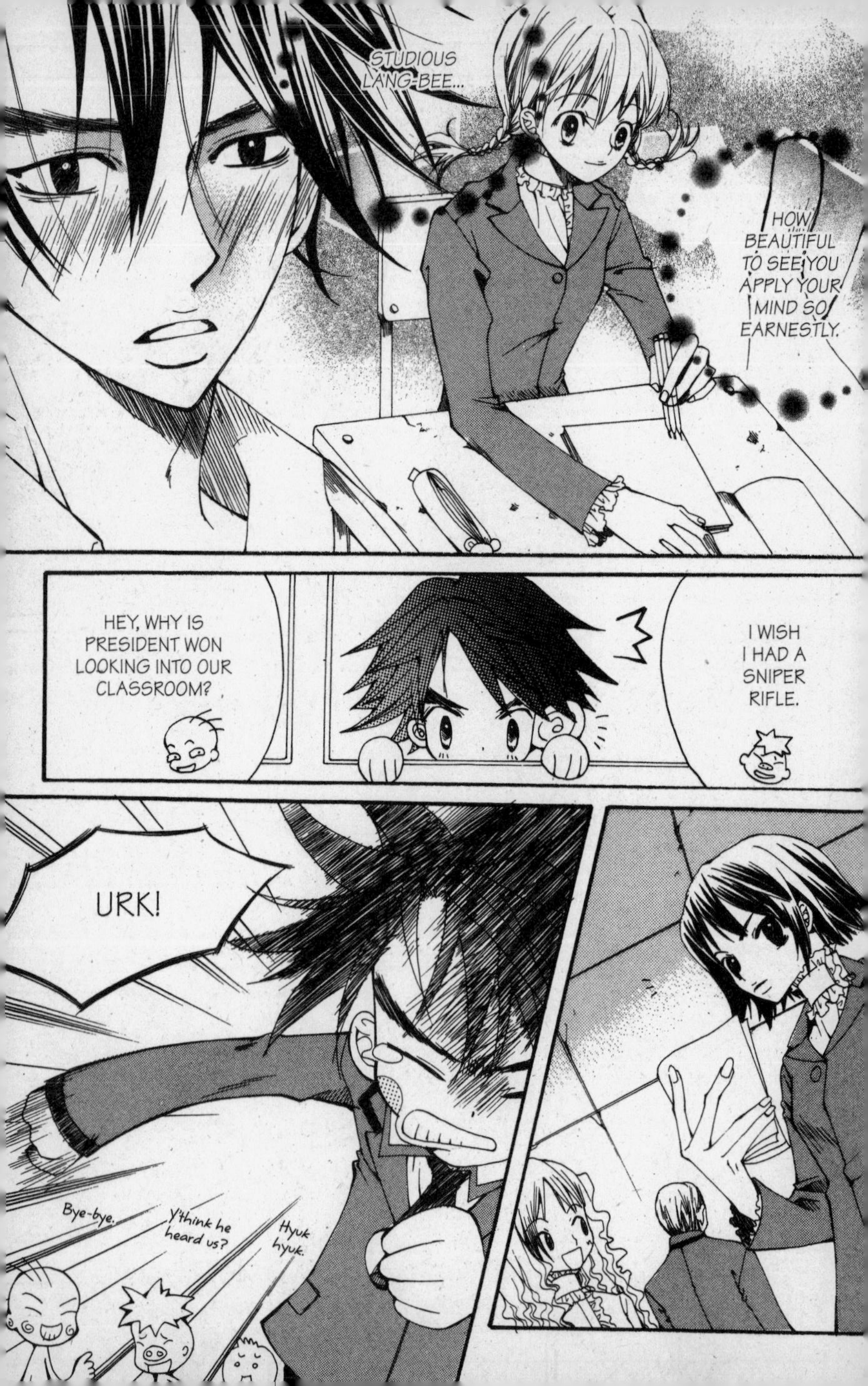
STUDIOUS LANG-BEE...
HOW BEAUTIFUL TO SEE YOU APPLY YOUR MIND SO EARNESTLY.
HEY, WHY IS PRESIDENT WON LOOKING INTO OUR CLASSROOM?
I WISH I HAD A SNIPER RIFLE.
URK!
Bye-bye.
Y'think he heard us?
Hyuk hyuk.

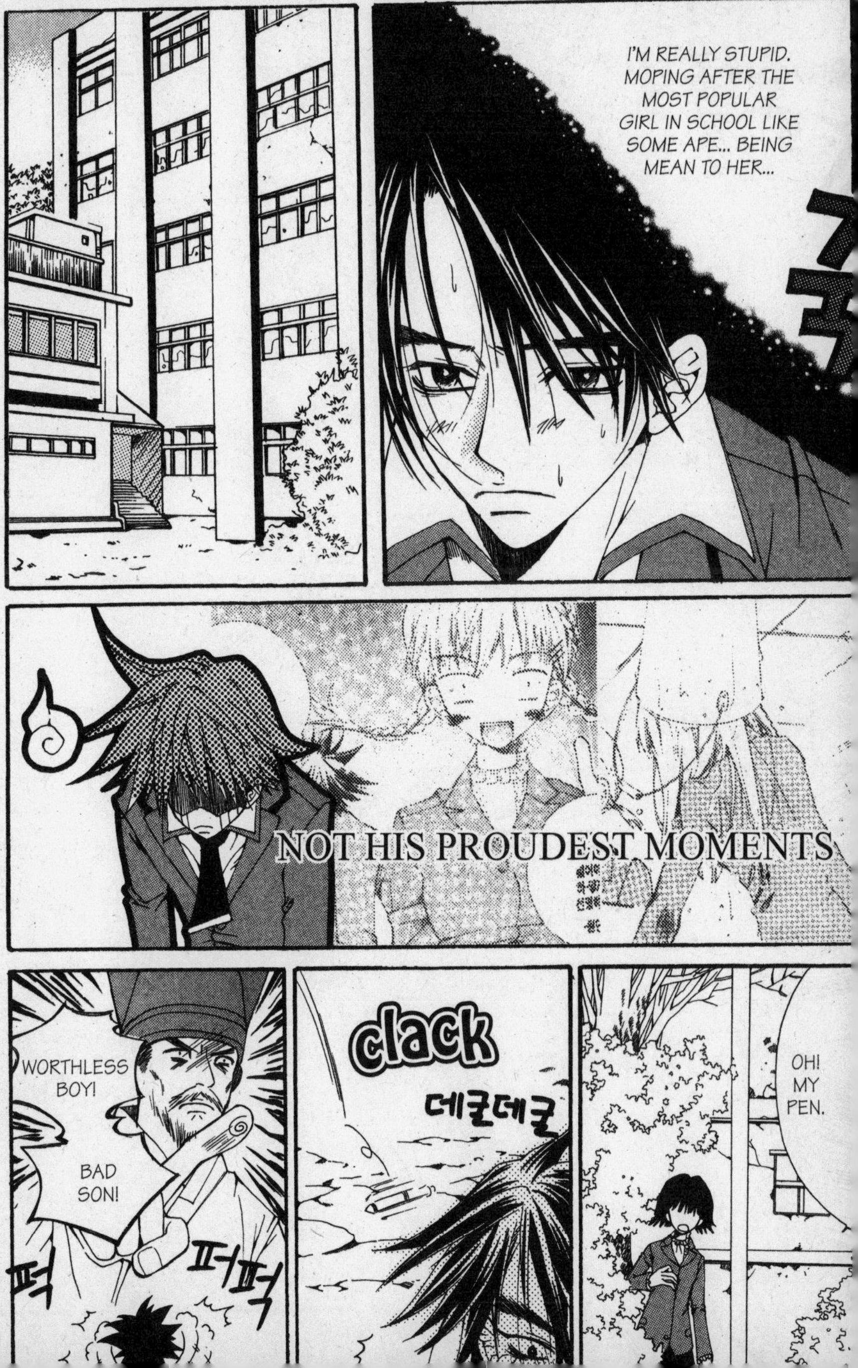
I'M REALLY STUPID. MOPING AFTER THE MOST POPULAR GIRL IN SCHOOL LIKE SOME APE... BEING MEAN TO HER...
NOT HIS PROUDEST MOMENTS
WORTHLESS BOY!
BAD SON!
퍽
퍼퍽
clack
데굴데굴
OH! MY PEN.

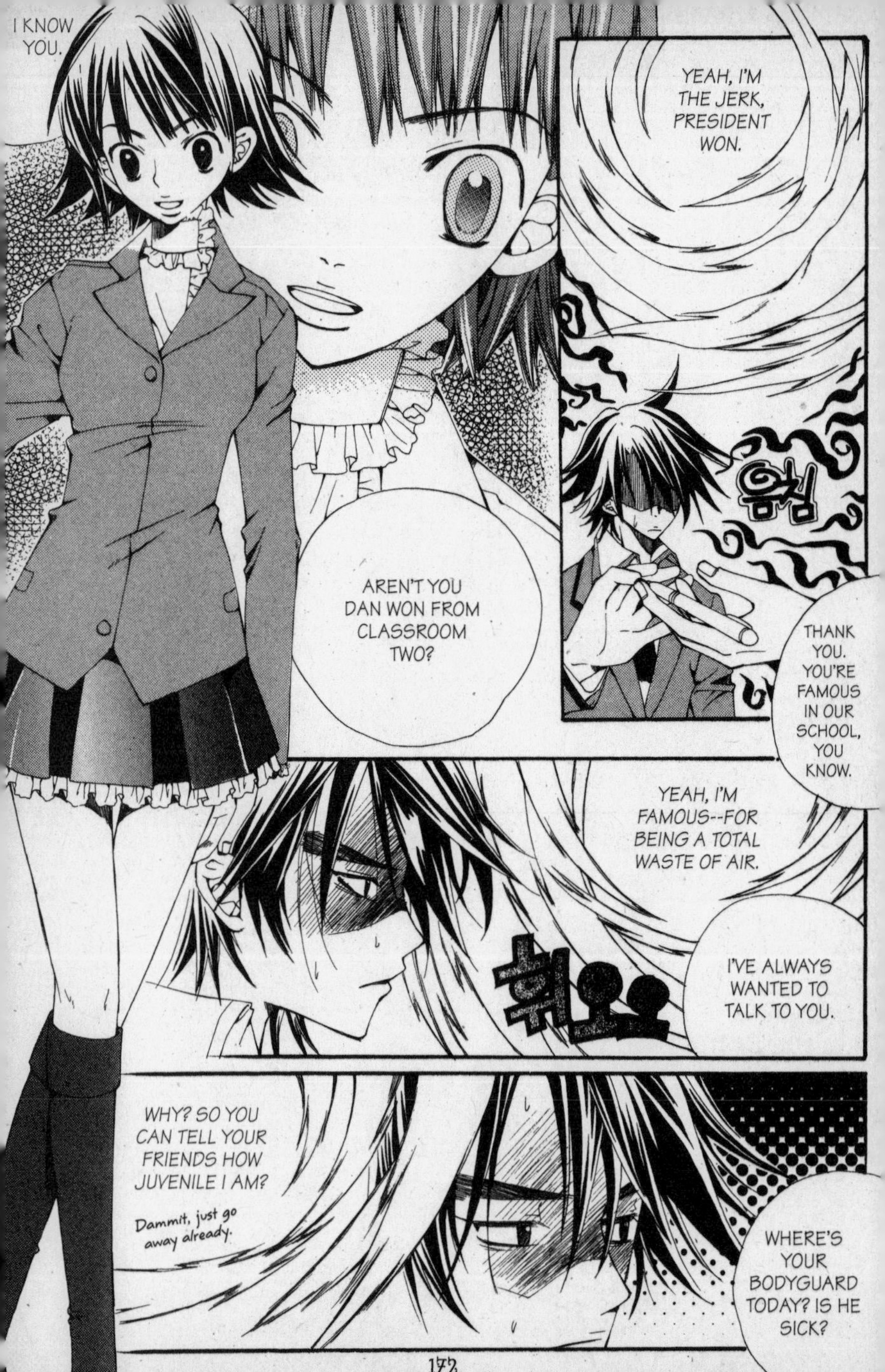
I KNOW YOU.
AREN'T YOU DAN WON FROM CLASSROOM TWO?
YEAH, I'M THE JERK, PRESIDENT WON.
THANK YOU. YOU'RE FAMOUS IN OUR SCHOOL, YOU KNOW.
YEAH, I'M FAMOUS--FOR BEING A TOTAL WASTE OF AIR.
휘오오
I'VE ALWAYS WANTED TO TALK TO YOU.
WHY? SO YOU CAN TELL YOUR FRIENDS HOW JUVENILE I AM?
Dammit, just go away already.
WHERE'S YOUR BODYGUARD TODAY? IS HE SICK?

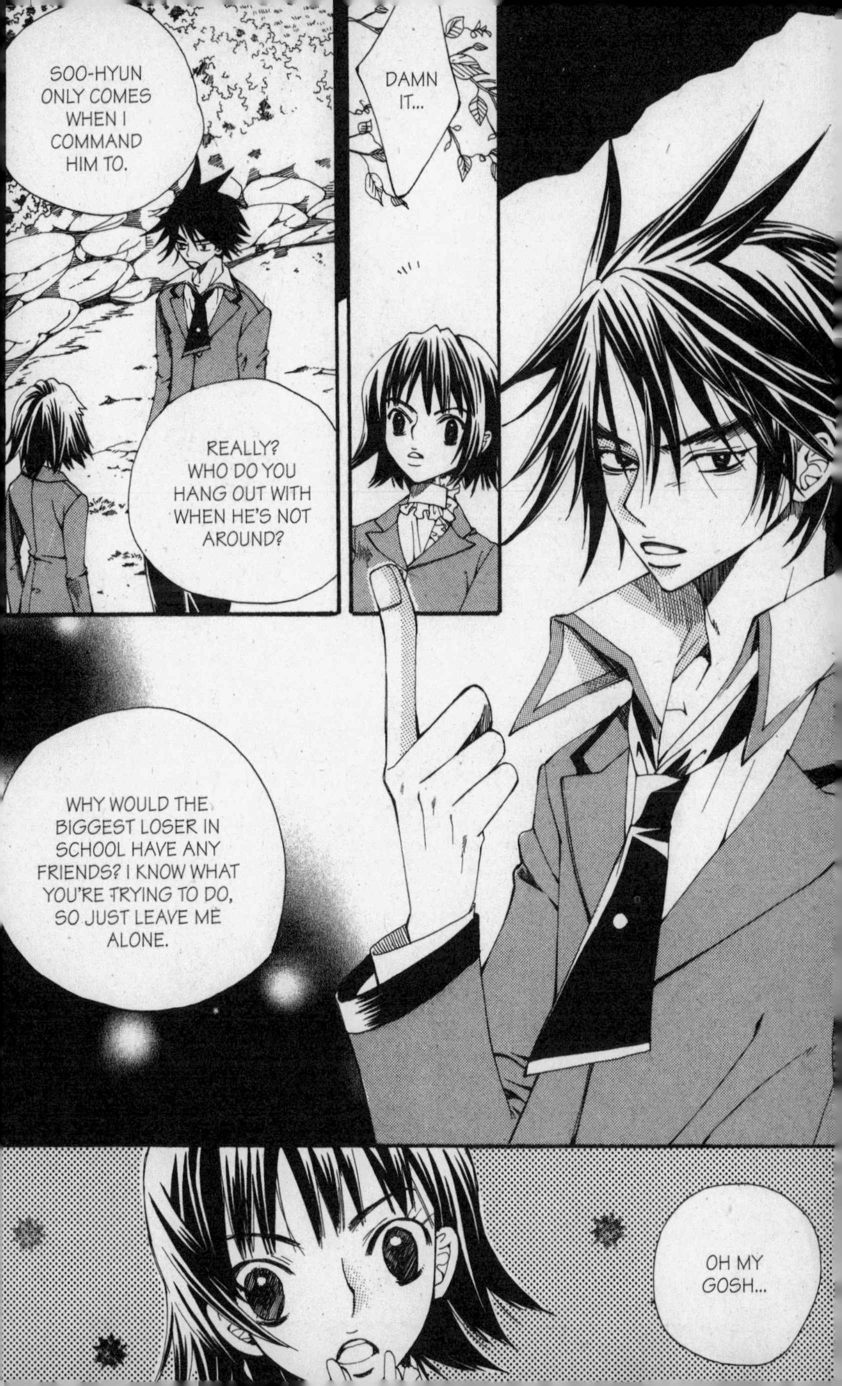
SOO-HYUN ONLY COMES WHEN I COMMAND HIM TO.
REALLY? WHO DO YOU HANG OUT WITH WHEN HE'S NOT AROUND?
DAMN IT...
WHY WOULD THE BIGGEST LOSER IN SCHOOL HAVE ANY FRIENDS? I KNOW WHAT YOU'RE TRYING TO DO, SO JUST LEAVE ME ALONE.
OH MY GOSH...

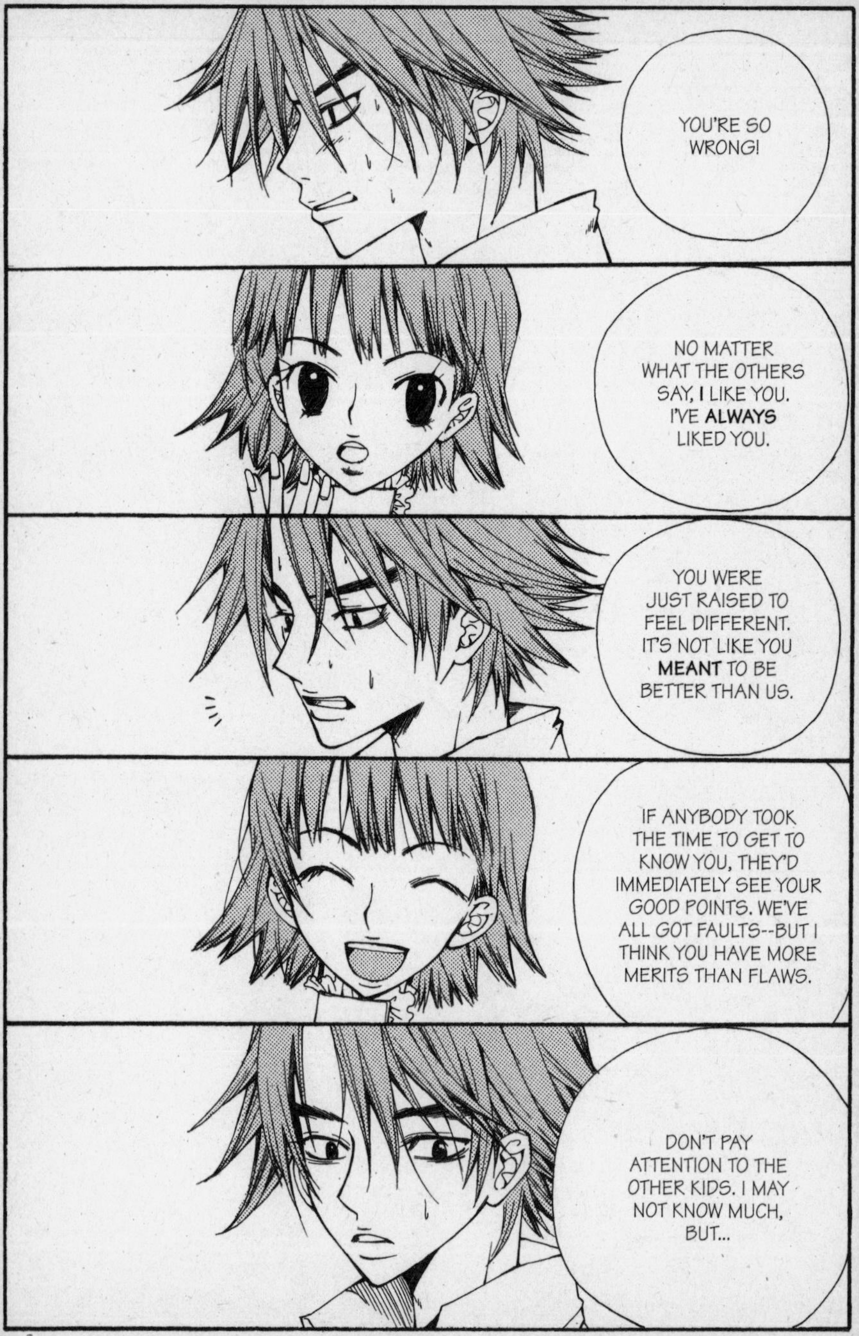
YOU'RE SO WRONG!
NO MATTER WHAT THE OTHERS SAY, I LIKE YOU. I'VE **ALWAYS** LIKED YOU.
YOU WERE JUST RAISED TO FEEL DIFFERENT. IT'S NOT LIKE YOU **MEANT** TO BE BETTER THAN US.
IF ANYBODY TOOK THE TIME TO GET TO KNOW YOU, THEY'D IMMEDIATELY SEE YOUR GOOD POINTS. WE'VE ALL GOT FAULTS--BUT I THINK YOU HAVE MORE MERITS THAN FLAWS.
DON'T PAY ATTENTION TO THE OTHER KIDS. I MAY NOT KNOW MUCH, BUT...

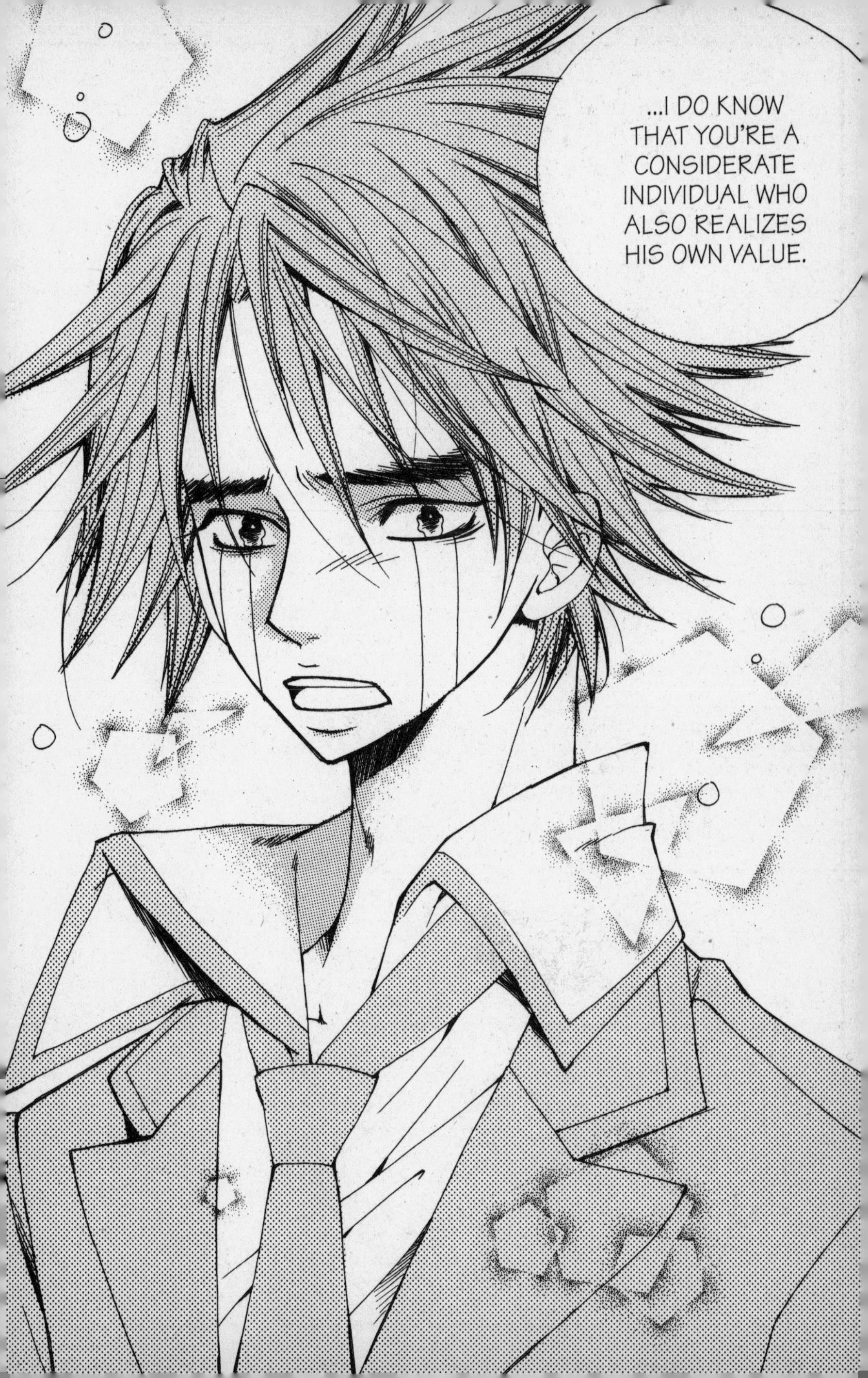
...I DO KNOW THAT YOU'RE A CONSIDERATE INDIVIDUAL WHO ALSO REALIZES HIS OWN VALUE.

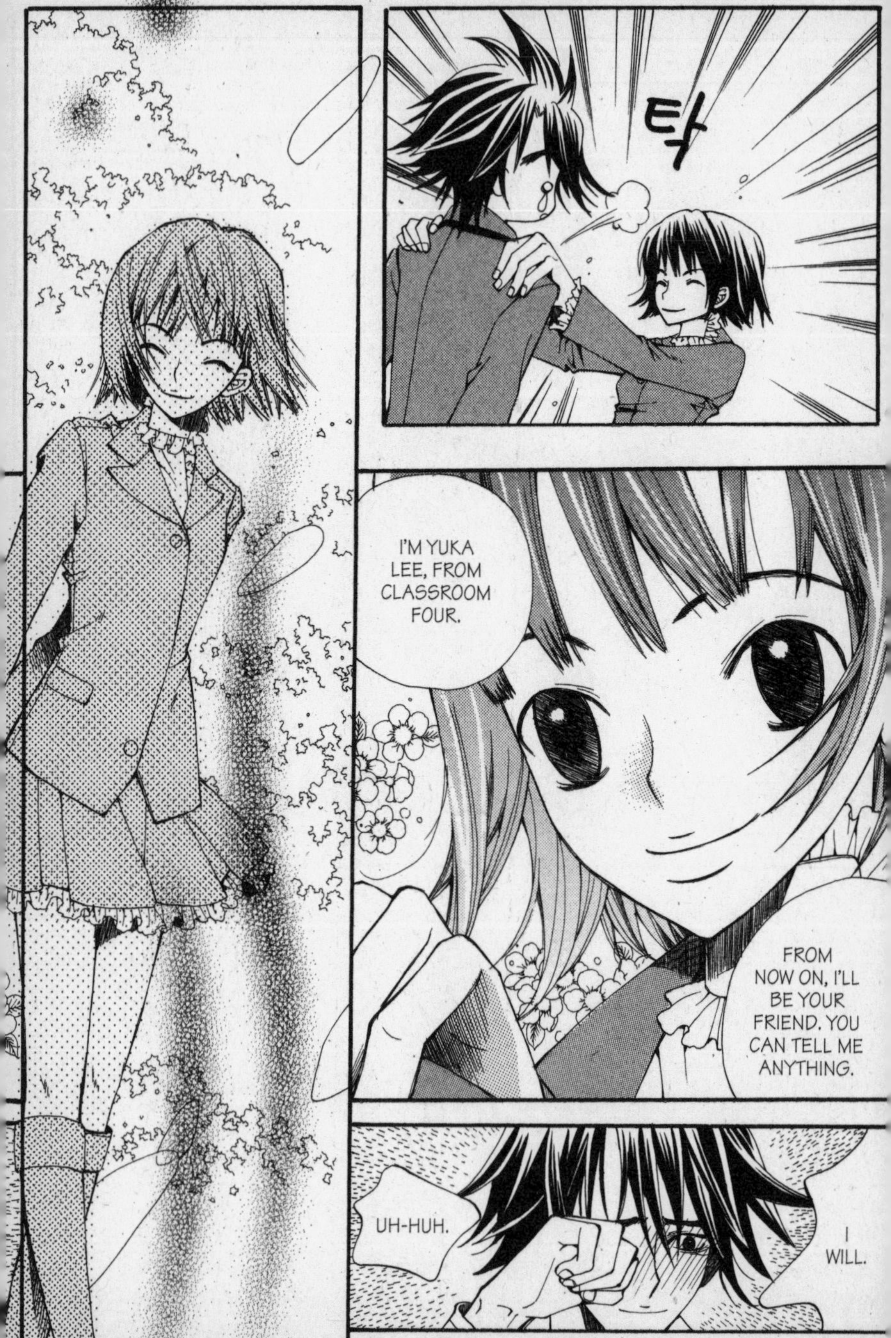
탁
I'M YUKA LEE, FROM CLASSROOM FOUR.
FROM NOW ON, I'LL BE YOUR FRIEND. YOU CAN TELL ME ANYTHING.
UH-HUH.
I WILL.

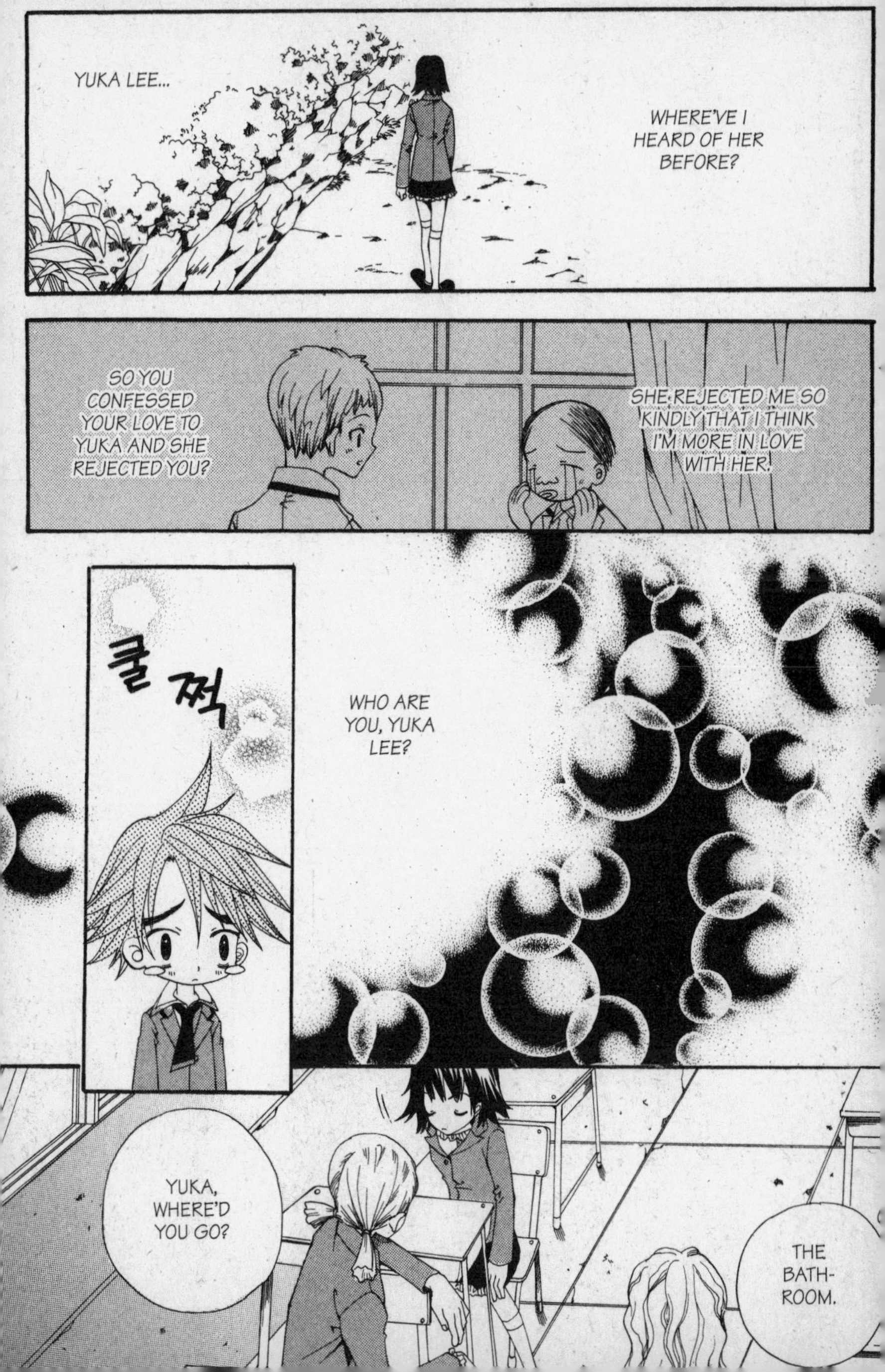
YUKA LEE...
WHERE'VE I HEARD OF HER BEFORE?
SO YOU CONFESSED YOUR LOVE TO YUKA AND SHE REJECTED YOU?
SHE REJECTED ME SO KINDLY THAT I THINK I'M MORE IN LOVE WITH HER.
쿨 쩍
WHO ARE YOU, YUKA LEE?
YUKA, WHERE'D YOU GO?
THE BATH-ROOM.

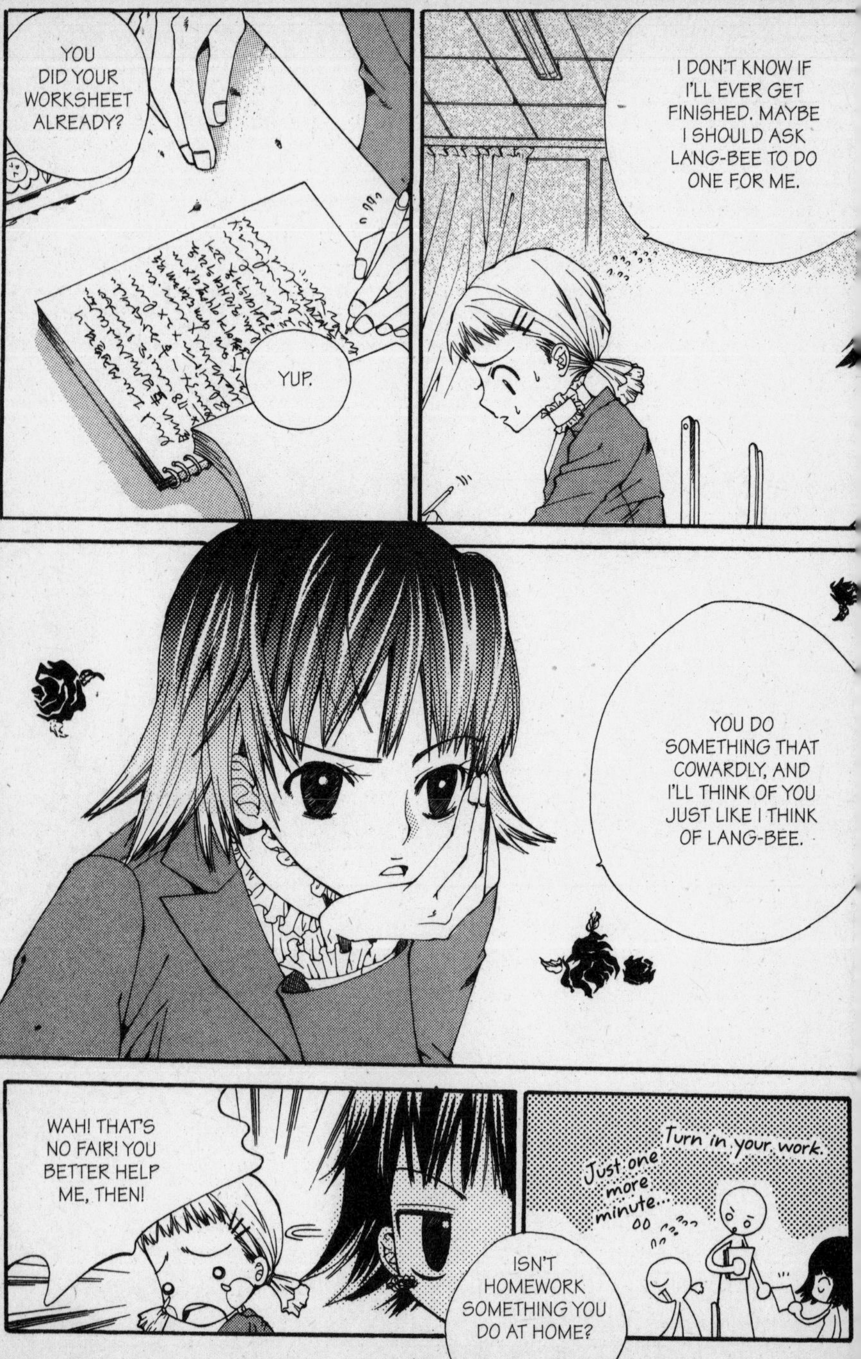
YOU DID YOUR WORKSHEET ALREADY?
YUP.
I DON'T KNOW IF I'LL EVER GET FINISHED. MAYBE I SHOULD ASK LANG-BEE TO DO ONE FOR ME.
YOU DO SOMETHING THAT COWARDLY, AND I'LL THINK OF YOU JUST LIKE I THINK OF LANG-BEE.
WAH! THAT'S NO FAIR! YOU BETTER HELP ME, THEN!
ISN'T HOMEWORK SOMETHING YOU DO AT HOME?
Turn in your work.
Just one more minute...

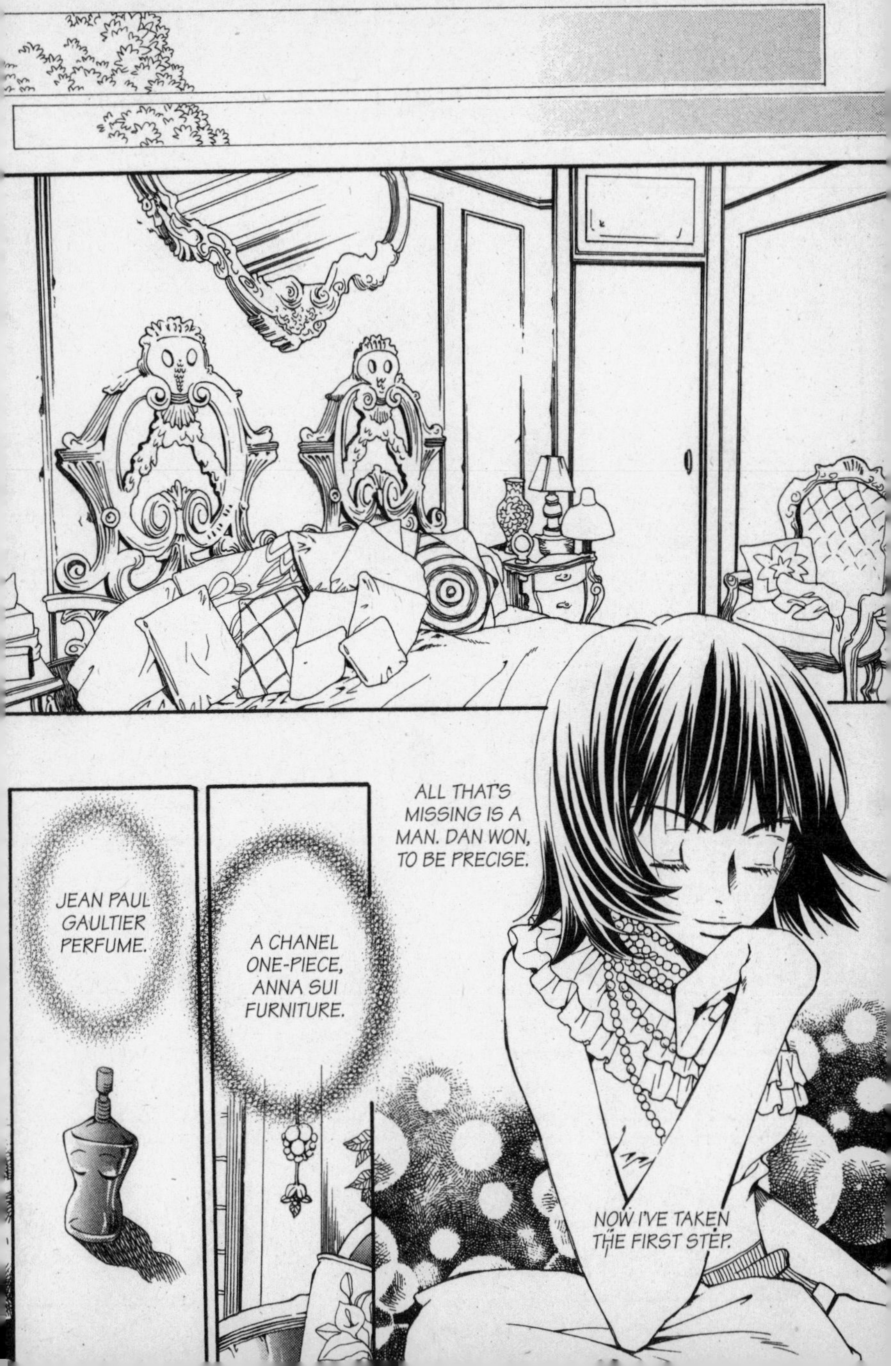
JEAN PAUL GAULTIER PERFUME.
A CHANEL ONE-PIECE, ANNA SUI FURNITURE.
ALL THAT'S MISSING IS A MAN. DAN WON, TO BE PRECISE.
NOW I'VE TAKEN THE FIRST STEP.

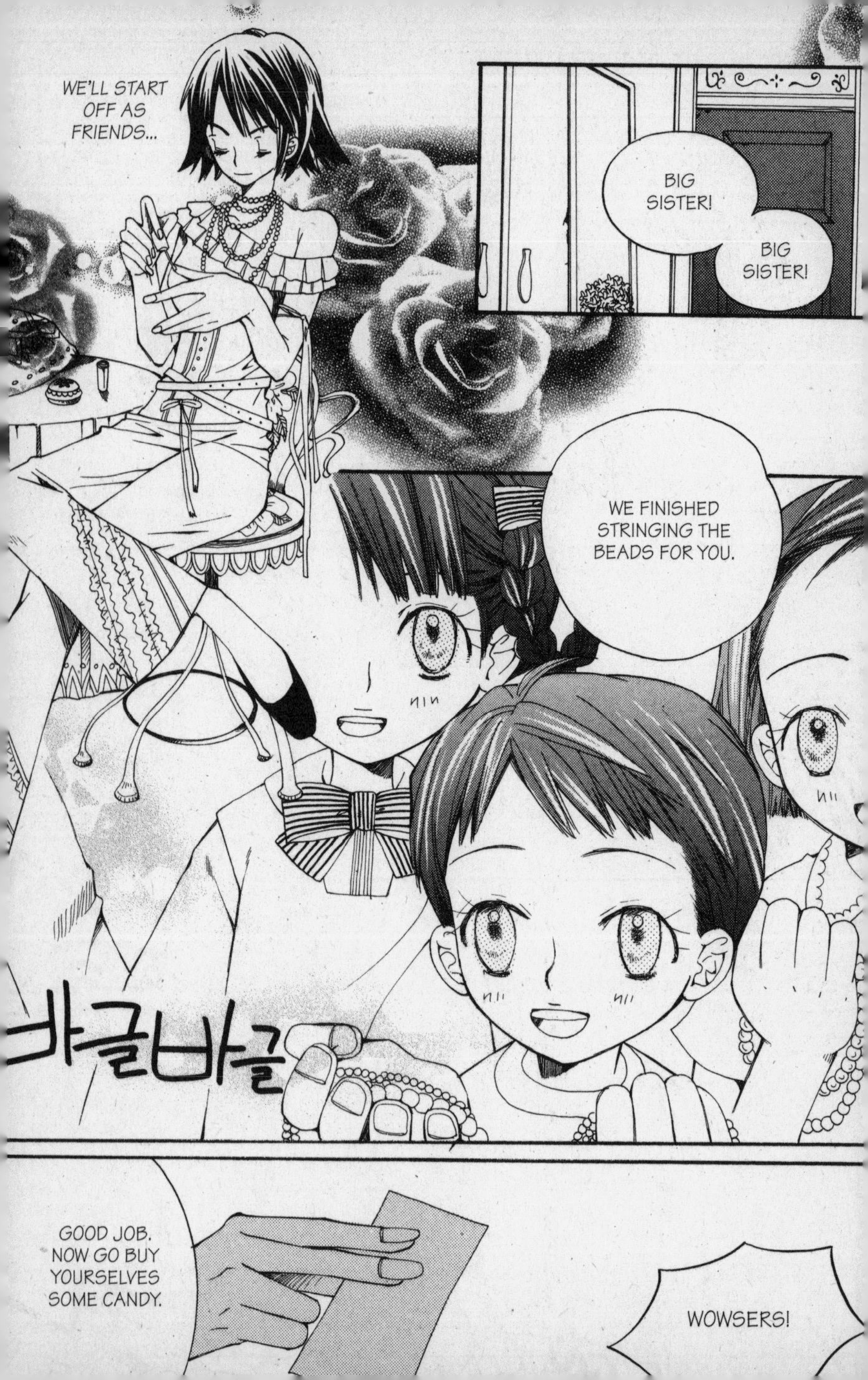
WE'LL START OFF AS FRIENDS...
BIG SISTER!
BIG SISTER!
WE FINISHED STRINGING THE BEADS FOR YOU.
바글바글
GOOD JOB. NOW GO BUY YOURSELVES SOME CANDY.
WOWSERS!

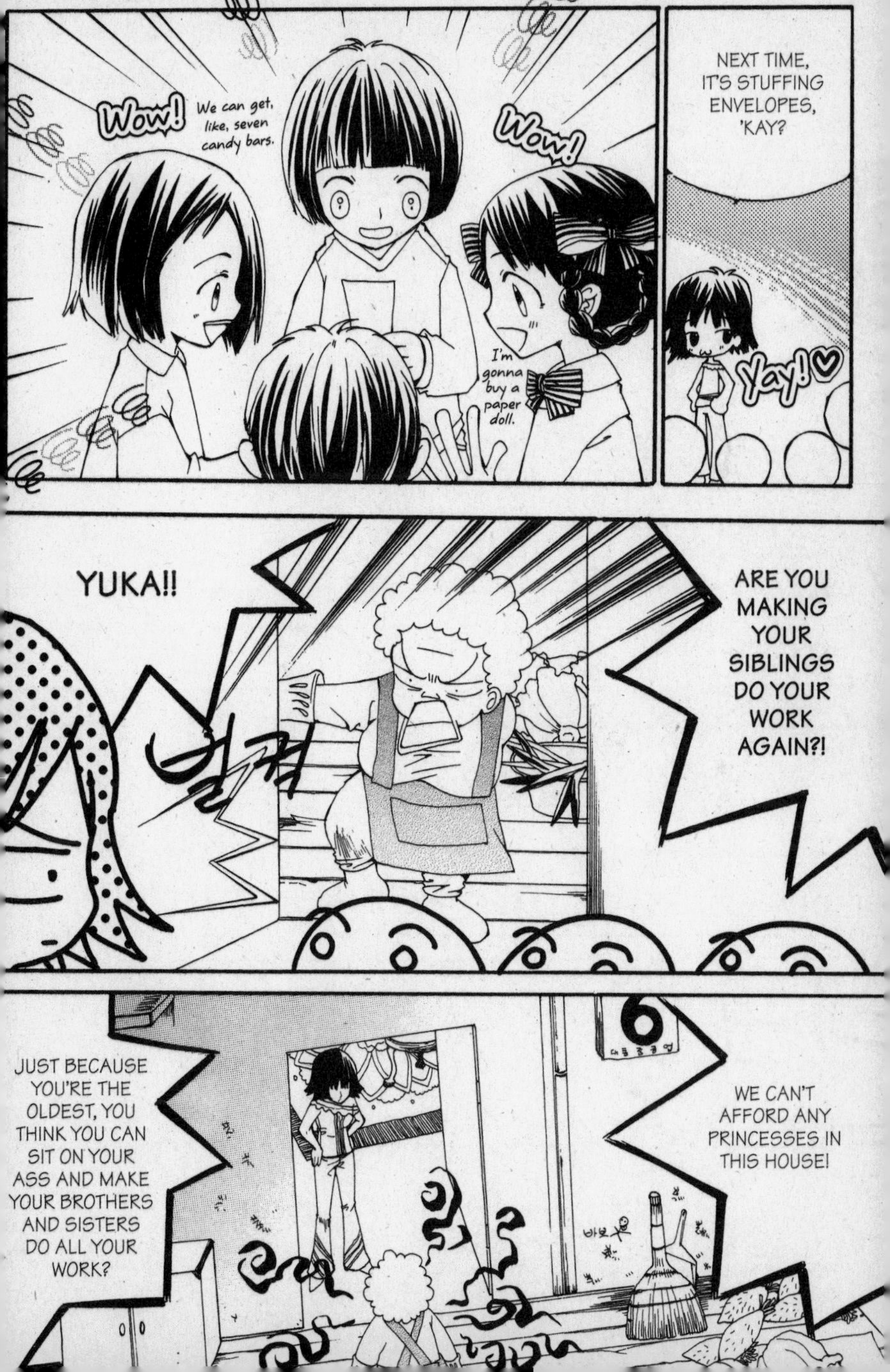
Wow!
We can get, like, seven candy bars.
Wow!
I'm gonna buy a paper doll.
NEXT TIME, IT'S STUFFING ENVELOPES, 'KAY?
Yay!♡
YUKA!!
ARE YOU MAKING YOUR SIBLINGS DO YOUR WORK AGAIN?!
JUST BECAUSE YOU'RE THE OLDEST, YOU THINK YOU CAN SIT ON YOUR ASS AND MAKE YOUR BROTHERS AND SISTERS DO ALL YOUR WORK?
WE CAN'T AFFORD ANY PRINCESSES IN THIS HOUSE!

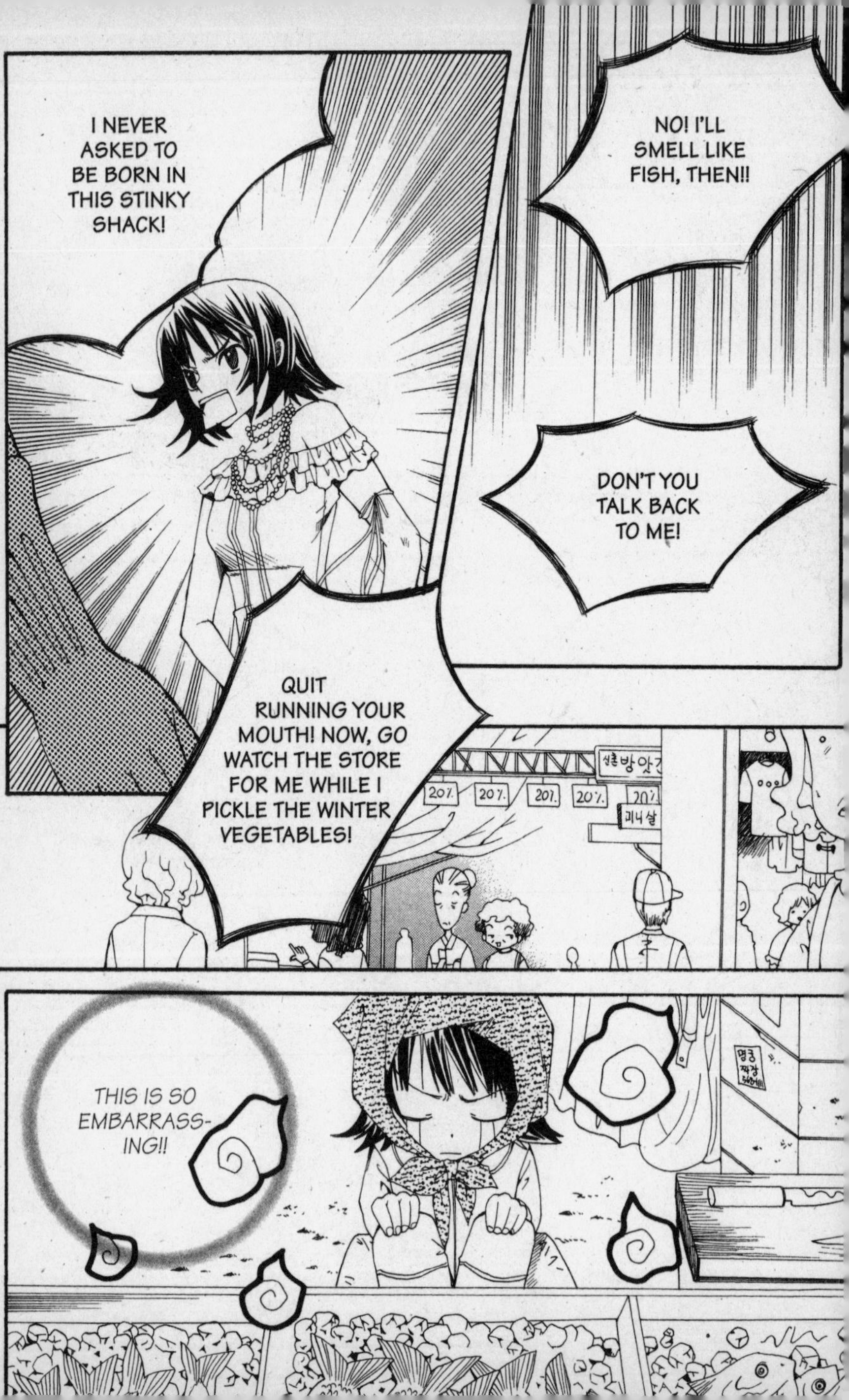
I NEVER ASKED TO BE BORN IN THIS STINKY SHACK!
NO! I'LL SMELL LIKE FISH, THEN!!
DON'T YOU TALK BACK TO ME!
QUIT RUNNING YOUR MOUTH! NOW, GO WATCH THE STORE FOR ME WHILE I PICKLE THE WINTER VEGETABLES!
THIS IS SO EMBARRASS-ING!!

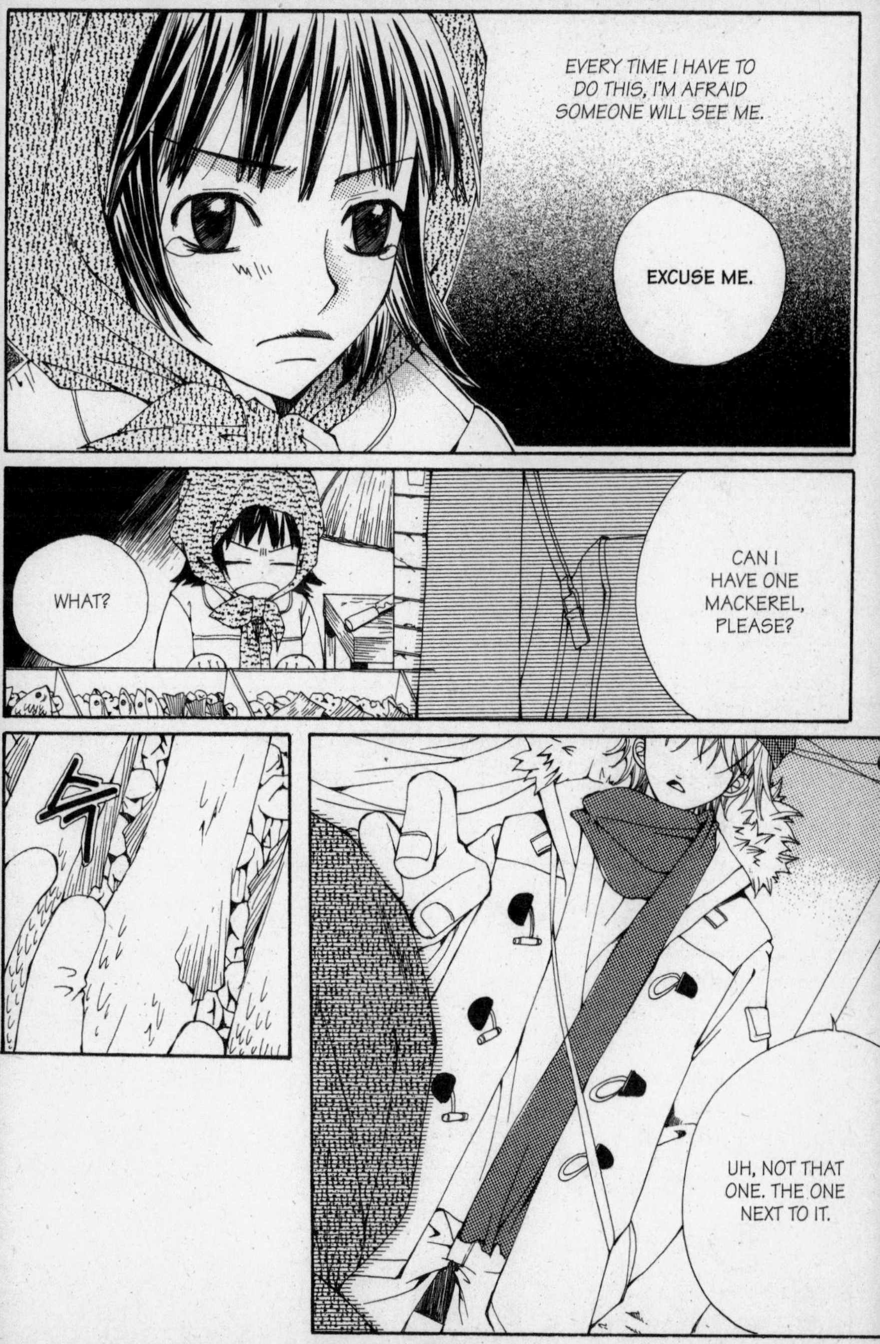
EVERY TIME I HAVE TO DO THIS, I'M AFRAID SOMEONE WILL SEE ME.
EXCUSE ME.
WHAT?
CAN I HAVE ONE MACKEREL, PLEASE?
UH, NOT THAT ONE. THE ONE NEXT TO IT.

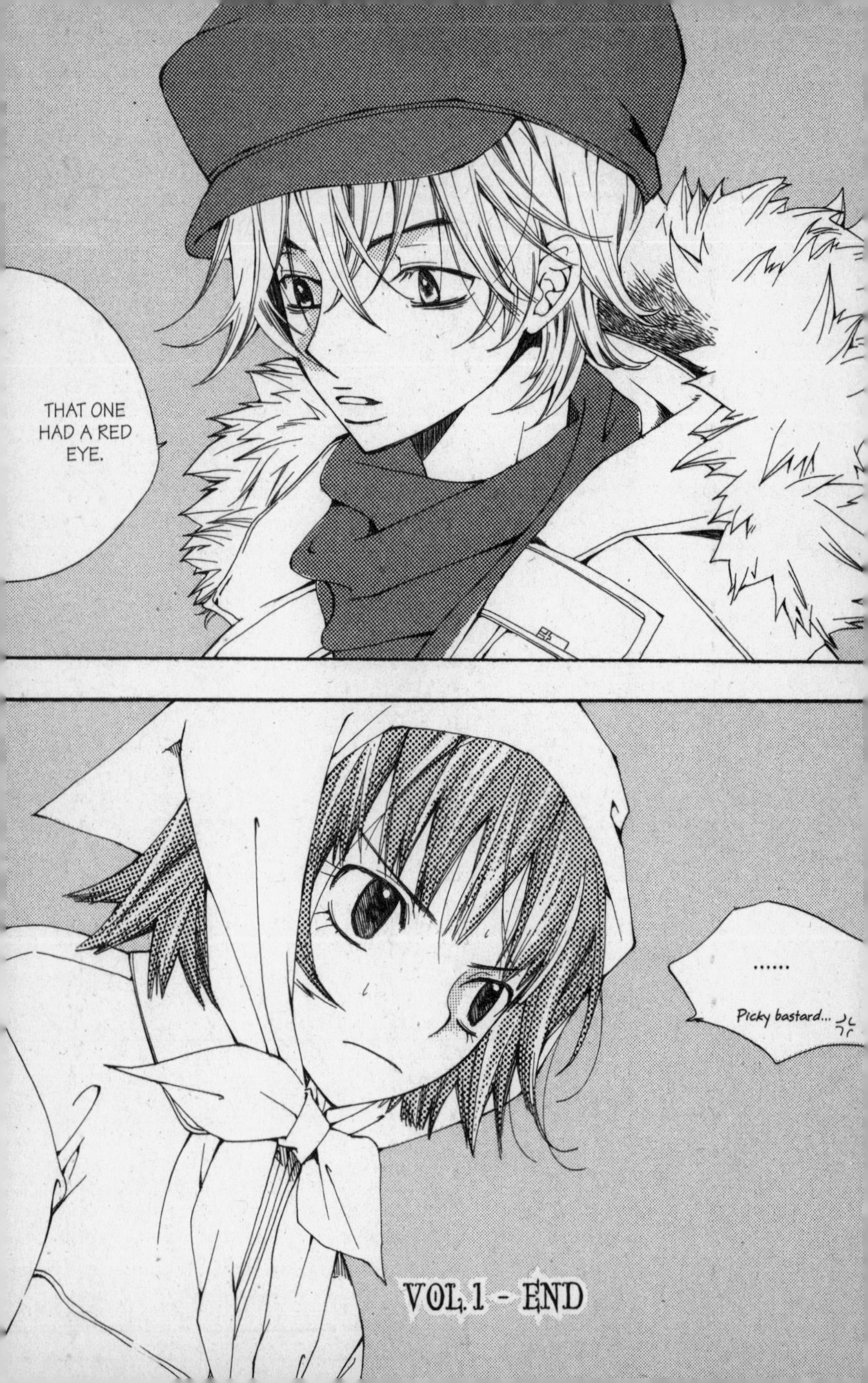
THAT ONE HAD A RED EYE.
......
Picky bastard...
VOL. 1 - END

IN THE NEXT VOLUME OF

THERE ARE DIRTY DEALINGS AND ROMANTIC FEELINGS APLENTY, WHEN LANG-BEE DISCOVERS YUKA'S STINKY LITTLE SECRET! NOW IT'S HER TURN TO HOLD THAT SNOOTY LITTLE GOLD-DIGGER'S FEET OVER THE COALS! AND THAT POOR LITTLE RICH BOY, DAN WON, CONTINUES TO LOSE HIS FRAGILE HEART TO OUR FAIR LANG-BEE. BUT OUR RESIDENT TEEN DAD, JIMMY, ISN'T SO SURE WON'S THE RIGHT GUY FOR HIS "LITTLE GIRL." OH, THAT JIMMY, HE MEANS WELL! AND WHEN JIMMY GOES SO FAR AS TO MAKE AN "EXTENDED APPEARANCE" AT LANG-BEE'S SCHOOL...WELL, LET'S JUST SAY THE REACTION IS **PRICELESS!**

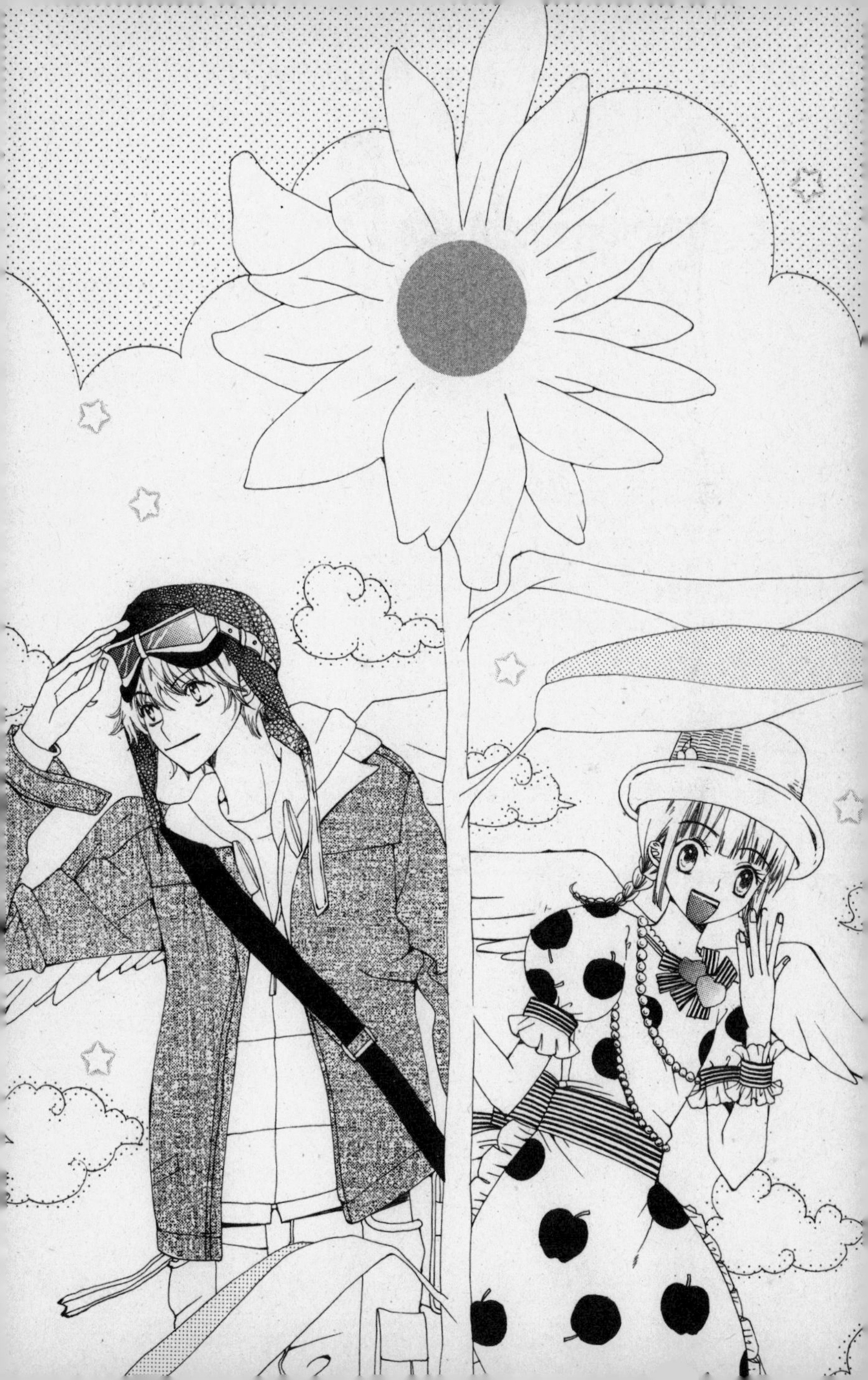

LIFE
BY KEIKO SUENOBU

Ordinary high school teenagers...
Except that they're not.

OT
OLDER TEEN
AGE 16+

© Keiko Suenobu

Ayumu struggles with her studies, and the all-important high school entrance exams are approaching. Fortunately, she has help from her best bud Shii-chan, who is at the top of the class. But when the test results come back, the friends are surprised: Ayumu surpasses Shii-chan's scores and gets into the school of her choice—without Shii-chan! Losing her friend is so painful for Ayumu that she starts cutting herself to ease her sorrow. Finally, Ayumu seeks comfort in a new friend, Manami. But will Manami prove to be the friend that Ayumu truly needs? Or will Ayumu continue down a dark path?

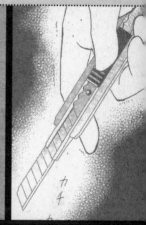

TOKYOPOP
Volume 1
LIFE
Keiko Suenobu

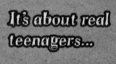

It's about real teenagers...

It's about real high school...

It's about real life.

WWW.TOKYOPOP.COM/LIFE

BIZENGHAST

Dear Diary,
I'm starting to feel

TOKYOPOP SHOP